Business Process Design, Management, and Improvement

Connecting Process and Strategy for Competitive Advantage

Business Process Design, Management, and Improvement

Connecting Process and Strategy for Competitive Advantage

Willbann D. Terpening

Gonzaga University

HERCHER Publishing Incorporated
Naperville, Illinois 60564

Richard T. Hercher Jr., *Publisher*
Elizabeth Hercher, *Editorial Assistant*
Jennifer Murtoff, *Editor*
Carol Rose, *Managing Editor*
Laurie Entringer, *Designer*
Lachina, *Composition*
Tributary Sales Resources, *Marketing*
LSC Communications, *Printing*

Cover Illustration
FENCE POSTS & FINAL WORDS
60 × 77 mixed media on canvas
By Rebecca O'Day
Lamy, New Mexico
ArtistRebeccaO'Day@AltaArtAnex

© 2017 by Hercher Publishing Incorporated

All rights reserved. No part of this book may be reproduced or transmitted in any form or by any means, electronic or mechanical, including photocopying, recording, or any information storage and retrieval system, without permission in writing from the author.

Printed in the United States of America
ISBN: 978-1-939297-03-7
e-book ISBN: 978-1-939297-16-7

Table of Contents

Preface   xiii

1 Introduction to Business Process Management   1

A Brief History of the Process and Systems Views   1
What Is a Process?   3
    Inputs and Outputs   3
    Activities and Buffers   4
    Resources   5
    Information Flows   5
Process Classifications   6
Business Process Management (BPM) Activities   8
    BPM Lifecycle   8
    Organization of the Text   9
BPM and Technology   11

Chapter Glossary   13
Discussion Questions and Problems   13
References   18

PART ONE
Metrics and Tools in Business Process Management

2 Metrics in Business Process Management   23

Classifying Metrics   23
    Observed Versus Subjective Metrics   24
    Financial Versus Nonfinancial Metrics   24
    Leading Versus Lagging Metrics   24
Customer Metrics   25
    Customer Satisfaction   25
    Customer Product or Service Requirements   25
Process Metrics   26
Supplier Metrics   28

Resource Metrics 29
Guidelines for Metrics 29
Pitfalls in Metrics 30
Metrics and BPMS Software 30

Chapter Glossary 31
Discussion Questions and Problems 31
References 31
Appendix 32

3 Benchmarking and the Balanced Scorecard 43

Benchmarking 44
Types of Benchmarking 44
Process Benchmarking: A Step-by-Step Approach 46
Benchmarking Code of Conduct 47
Benchmarking Examples and Best Practices 48
Benchmarking Surveys 49
Balanced Scorecard 49
The Scorecard Components 50
Balanced Scorecard Examples 53

Chapter Glossary 55
Discussion Questions and Problems 56
References 57
Appendix 57

4 Introduction to Queuing and Simulation 60

The General Queuing Phenomenon and Terminology 61
Calling Population 62
Arrival Process 62
Queue Configuration 63
Queue Discipline 65
Activity Times 66
Performance Measures 66
The Economics of Queues 67
The Psychology of Waiting 67
The Economic Costs of Waiting 69
The Need for Queuing Models 69
Analytical Queuing Models 70
Kendall Notation 70
The M/M/1 Model 71
Little's Law 72
The M/M/s Model 73

  The M/M/s/K Model (Finite Queue) 74
  The M/G/1 Model (General Service Times) 76
  The G/G/s Model (Allen-Cunneen Approximation) 77
Queuing Theory and Decision Making 78
  Costs Can Be Estimated 78
  Costs Cannot Be Estimated 79
Introduction to Simulation 80
  Static Versus Dynamic Models 80
  Deterministic Versus Probabilistic Models 80
  Discrete Versus Continuous (Analog) Models 81
  Basics of Discrete Event Simulation 81
  Building a Spreadsheet Simulation 82

Chapter Glossary 84
Discussion Questions and Problems 85
References 87
Appendix 88

5 Using XLSim in Process Simulation 91

Running the Software 92
  Set Macro Security Settings 92
  Use Trusted Locations 94
The XLSim Working Environment 94
  Area 1—The XLSim Ribbon 94
  Area 2—The Simulation Parameters Section 96
  Area 3—The Model Building Blocks 97
  Area 4—The Model Canvas 97
Building a Model 97
  Connecting Blocks 97
  The Link Block 98
  Attributes and Resources 98
  Model Building Blocks 98
Defining Attributes and Resources 106
  Defining Attributes 106
  Defining Resources 107
Setting Up and Running the Simulation 107
  Simulation Setup 107
  Running the Simulation 109
  Output Options 110
A Sample Model 110

Chapter Glossary 112
Discussion Questions and Problems 113

PART TWO
Process Analysis and Design

6 Objectives and Strategy in Business Process Design 117

Strategy and Process Design 118
    Selecting Processes to Redesign 118
    Understanding the Process 120
    Evaluate Enablers of Process Redesign 121
Basic Principles of Process Design 123

Chapter Glossary 125
Chapter Questions and Problems 125
References 126

7 Tools for Process Design 127

Process Mapping 127
Flow-Oriented Diagrams 128
    Relationship Mapping 128
    Process-Flow Diagrams 129
    Flowcharts 131
    Process Activity Charts 131
    Cross-Functional Flowcharts 132
    Service System Mapping and Service Blueprints 133
    Multilevel Flowcharts 135
Data-Oriented Diagrams 137
    Data-Flow Diagrams (DFDs) 137
Creatively Combining Different Methods 138
Interface Mapping 140
Customer Input and Quality Function Deployment 140
Flowcharting with Microsoft Office and Visio 140
    Flowcharting with Excel 140
    Flowcharting with Visio 142
BPMS Software and Process Design 144
    Process Modeling Tools and Repositories 146
    Reference Models 146
    Process Design and Simulation 147
    Developing Software Applications 147

Chapter Glossary 148
Chapter Questions and Problems 148
References 150

8 Simulation and Process Design   151

The Role of Simulation in Process Design   152
Using Time Units in XLSim   153
Run Length and Replications   153
    Terminating Versus Nonterminating Processes   154
    Estimating Performance Versus Evaluating Alternative Designs   154
Model Verification and Validation   155
    Model Verification   155
    Model Validation   156
Analysis of Simulation Inputs   156
    Finding the Appropriate Probability Distribution   156
    Estimating Parameters   159
Analysis of Simulation Outputs   159
    Estimation of Performance   159
    Comparing Alternatives   160

Chapter Glossary   160
Chapter Questions and Problems   160
Cases Projects   161
References   169

PART THREE
Process Management

9 Managing Process Flows   173

The Concept of Process Flow   174
    Flow Rates   174
    Inventory   175
    Flow Times   176
    Little's Law: The Relationship of Throughput, Inventory, and Cycle Time   176
    Process Measures and Financial Measures   177
The Analysis of Flow Times   178
    Measuring Flow Time   178
    Rework   180
    Multiple Paths   181
    Theoretical Cycle Time and Cycle-Time Efficiency   183
    Levers for Managing Flow Times   183
The Analysis of Flow Rates and Capacity   185
    Measuring Flow Rates and Capacity   185
    Resources and Capacity   185

    Levers for Managing Throughput 189
  The Analysis of Inventory 190
    Levers for Managing Inventories 191

  Chapter Glossary 192
  Chapter Questions and Problems 193
  References 197

10 Implementing, Executing, and Monitoring the Process 198

  Implementation 198
    Person to Person 199
    Person to System 199
    System to System 200
  Execution 200
  Monitoring 200
    The Purpose of Process Monitoring 200
    Process-Monitoring Tools 201
    Feedback Control Principle 201
    Types of Data 202
    Tools for Qualitative Data 202
    Tools for Quantitative Data 206
  Using Process Control Charts 211
  Process Capability 212
  Using the SPC Templates 214
  Implementation, Execution, and Monitoring with BPMS 216
    Application Development 217
    Business Process Engine (BPE) 217
    Business Rules Engine (BRE) 218
    Business Activity Monitoring (BAM) 218

  Chapter Glossary 218
  Chapter Questions and Problems 219
  References 223

PART FOUR
Process Improvement

11 Approaches to Process Improvement 227

  Continuous Improvement 228
    Historical Origins of Continuous Improvement 228
    The Case for Continuous Improvement 229

Radical Innovation 229
    Historical Origins of Radical Innovation—Reengineering 229
    The Case for Radical Innovation 230
Comparison of Continuous and Radical Improvement 230
    Similarities and Differences between the Approaches 230
    The Need for Both Types of Change 231
Major Approaches to Process Improvement 234
    Deming's Plan-Do-Check-Act (PDCA) Cycle 234
    Six Sigma 235
    Lean 237
    Theory of Constraints 238
    Business Process Reengineering (BPR) 240
The Improvement Paradox 241
BPMS and Process Improvement 241

Chapter Glossary 242
Chapter Questions and Problems 243
References 243

12 Managing the Change Process 245

The Nature of Change 246
Organizational Change 246
    The Organization as Machine 247
    The Organization as a Political System 247
    The Organization as Biological Organism 247
    The Organization as a Nonlinear System 248
Models of Organizational Change 249
    Lewin's Force Field Analysis 249
    Kotter's Eight-Step Model 250
    Beckhard and Harris Change Equation 250
    Peter Senge 251
Individual Change 251
    The Behavioral Approach 251
    The Cognitive Approach 252
    The Psychodynamic Approach 253
    The Humanistic Psychology Approach 253
Leading Change 254
    Selling the Urgency of Change 254
    The Role of the Leader 255
Resistance to Change 256
The Future of Change Management 257

Chapter Glossary 258
Chapter Questions and Problems 258
References 259

13 Building the Process Enterprise 261

Process Maturity Assessment 262
- *Process and Enterprise Maturity Model (PEMM) 262*
- *Business Process Maturity Model (BPMM) 263*
- *Comparison of the Two Frameworks 264*
- *The QUT-BPMM 265*
- *Summary of the Maturity Models 266*

Process Governance 267
- *Governance Roles 268*
- *BPM Center of Excellence (CoE) 269*
- *Strategic Process Council 272*
- *Building a Governance Structure 272*

Organizational Structure 273

Necessary Organizational Changes 277
- *Building a Process Culture 277*
- *Performance Evaluation and Reward Structures 279*
- *Developing People 279*

The Future of Process Management 280

Chapter Glossary 282
Chapter Questions and Problems 282
References 283

Index 285

Preface

This text is an attempt to gather together and organize the fragmented evidence on the importance of the process view to modern business organizations. After encouraging progress in the 1990s in changing the way we view the business organization, the academic literature has been largely silent on the topic during the first part of this century. This can be seen from the fact that there are still only three text books that are primarily related to processes, and two of these are primarily operations management texts. Without a continued effort to organize business thought around a process view, we are in danger of slipping back into the functional silos of old. Although much of the material in this text originally appeared primarily within the operations management literature, this is not just an operations management text. Indeed processes are important to every functional area of study because (1) processes are involved in every function in the organization from accounting and finance to marketing and human resource management, and (2) because most of the critical processes in the modern enterprise are cross-functional in nature and can no longer be managed in isolation. To this end, I have tried throughout the book to utilize examples and cases from all aspects of business. The cross-disciplinary aspect of process management is further illustrated by the key enabler of process innovation, namely information technology. Modern information technology is what enables the reintegration of processes that heretofore have operated in fragmented ways in separate functional silos.

I have also attempted to provide insight into the most useful tools in process design, management, and improvement. Some of the most important tools are presented in their own section of the text, and others are covered within the context in which they are primarily used. Because all processes inherently involve variability, insights from the study of queuing phenomenon are particularly relevant to the study of processes. The author still remembers an Executive MBA student over 30 years ago, the CEO of a large hospital, who commented that now that she was aware of what they were, she saw queues everywhere in her organization. Also, since the most important processes are somewhat complex, traditional queuing theory must be supplemented with more flexible tools, such as simulation. Simulation analysis has been shown to be especially useful in the design and improvement of processes, and coverage of simulation techniques, along with a description of a simulation tool that accompanies the text, occupies a large portion of the first section of the book.

The software that accompanies this text is an important part of the package. All of the software is contained in Microsoft Excel files and should work on all versions of Excel from Office 2007 on. Some of the software, such as the SPC and goodness of fit routines, do not require macros and can be used as is without regard to security settings within Excel. The more complex software, such as Queue Solver, and the XLSim simulation package, contain macros written in VBA code and require special security settings in Excel. These settings are described in some detail in Chapter 5.

The primary goal of this text is to promote the process view of the business enterprise and to emphasize the importance of processes throughout the organization. Secondarily, it is hoped that the reader will develop an appreciation for the use of simulation and other process-oriented tools in practice.

Although there is only one name on the cover of this book, it is the product of the efforts of many people. I especially want to thank my undergraduate and MBA students at Gonzaga University who have suffered through the first versions of this text and have provided invaluable feedback. A special thanks to Bill Ramshaw who was kind enough to provide many problems and cases for the text, along with invaluable feedback. I am also grateful to Jennifer Murtoff who saved me from my abuses of the English language. Any remaining abuses are solely my responsibility. I am especially indebted to my publisher Dick Hercher who had enough faith in me, and in this project, to make it happen. Last, but certainly not least, I am appreciative, as always, for my long suffering wife who has had to endure my mood swings and frequent absences for the sake of this project. I can only hope that the final result will be worth the efforts of all of these good people.

Willbann D. Terpening
Spokane, WA
October 11, 2016

Chapter 1

Introduction to Business Process Management

"If you can't describe what you are doing as a process you don't know what you are doing"

—W. Edwards Deming

A Brief History of the Process and Systems Views

Over the last 30 years there has been a quiet revolution in the way in which businesses and other organizations in the United States view themselves. Prior to the late 1970s and early 1980s, most organizations viewed themselves as a set of functions such as Marketing, Manufacturing, Finance and Engineering.[1] The bureaucratic organizational structure and a "do what we do and throw it over the wall to the other guys" mentality were widespread. The inherent conflicts between organizational functions induced by this world view created inefficiencies that were increasingly hard to ignore. The conflicting objectives of the various functions in the organization, along with the incompatible decisions they produced, inevitably led to inefficiencies, higher costs, and dissatisfied customers. In the decades following World War II, booming consumer demand for products and limited competition from foreign competitors allowed executives in U.S. firms to ignore these inefficiencies.

However during the 1970s, it was becoming apparent that consumers were deserting American products in droves in favor of cheaper and better quality import products, particularly those from Japan. Entire consumer product industries such as televisions and air conditioners suddenly disappeared from the American industrial landscape. During the late 1970s and into the 1980s, as U.S. firms started to learn more and more about Japanese manufacturing

---

1. Unfortunately, the organization of most academic Schools of Business still reflects these functional silos.

techniques, and in particular the Toyota Production System (Womack et al., 1990), executives started to reconsider how they viewed the organization and structured its work. By the middle of the 1990s, the perceived need for a process orientation had become commonplace with larger U.S. firms. At the same time, other management thinkers were stressing the importance of a systems point of view. Of particular note were Deming (1986) and Goldratt and Cox (1984). These twin notions of process and a systems view, combined, illustrated the importance of viewing the work of a business enterprise as process and warned of the dangers of taking a narrow view of a process rather than considering the system as a whole.

To fully understand the importance of the process view of an organization, it is useful to contrast it with the traditional functional view. Although different authors often cite different starting points to the functional view of the organization, all of them point to the seminal work of Adam Smith (1776) on the division of labor and specialization as an important landmark in this transition to viewing the organization as a collection of functions. The idea that an organization could achieve peak performance by breaking work down into smaller and smaller tasks and then have those tasks performed by specialists is often pointed to as a key aspect in the amazing increases in the standard of living made possible by the Industrial Revolution. Henry Ford perfected this division of labor with the moving assembly line at Ford Motor Company in the early part of the twentieth century. As Ford was perfecting the mass-production process at Ford, Alfred P. Sloan was developing the quintessential organizational structure to control the sprawling production process at General Motors. The functionally organized hierarchical structure pioneered by Sloan became the predominant organizational structure for U.S. businesses in the twentieth century. The principles of division of labor and mass production along with the hierarchical organizational structure served American industry well throughout the first half of the 20th century and helped make the U.S. a world economic power.

However, by the late 1970s it was becoming apparent that not all was well with the American industrial enterprise. Over the next 10 years executive attention was focused on Asia, primarily Japan and Korea, and to a lesser extent on Europe, in a search for answers. The many books written on the Japanese manufacturing miracle and the many executive tours of Japanese manufacturing facilities started to change the way that U.S. executives viewed their organizations.

Early writings about the just-in-time manufacturing philosophy from Japan stressed the process view of manufacturing (Hall, 1983; Schonberger, 1982) as did the influential work of Eliyahu Goldratt (Goldratt and Cox 1984, 1992; Goldratt, 1990; Goldratt, 1994) on the Theory of Constraints (TOC). Goldratt further emphasized the need to consider the system as a whole rather than optimizing a small part of the system. The emphasis on processes has continued in the lean manufacturing movement that was an outgrowth of just-in-time. The lean movement has been promoted most vigorously by the Association for Manufacturing Excellence (AME). These process and system themes were further amplified by the Total Quality Management (TQM) movement of the 1980s, especially in the writings of W. Edwards Deming (for example, Deming 1986). In fact, Business Process Management (BPM) owes much to these early influences. Indeed, much of the material in this text is a result of the early just-in-time and lean thinking along with the resulting TQM and Six Sigma movements in the quality area.

In 1990 two seminal articles were published by Michael Hammer (1990) and Thomas Davenport (Davenport and Short 1990). These articles were soon followed by two widely read books by Hammer and Champy (1993) and Davenport (1993). This started the reengineering movement, which further delineated the limitations of the functional view of organizations and emphasized the fundamental advantages of the process view. By the mid-1990s most large business organizations in the United States had realized the importance of the process view to their organizations. One highly visible sign of this recognition was a roundtable organized at the Harvard Business School by David Garvin. This roundtable involved the CEO's of four major firms and was published by Garvin (1995) in the *Harvard Business Review*. In this interview, the CEOs described how the process view had radically changed their organizations and the way that they managed them. The importance of the process view was perhaps best expressed by Michael Hammer (1996, p. xii) commenting about the definition of reengineering:

> Originally, I felt that the most important word in the definition was radical. .... I have now come to realize that I was wrong, that the radical character of reengineering, however important and exciting, is not its most significant aspect. The key word in the definition of reengineering is "process": a complete end-to-end set of activities that together create value for a customer.

Although most of the evidence that a process view is advantageous to an organization is anecdotal, there has been at least one study that has shown a relationship between the degree of process orientation in a business and increased business performance, reduced inter-functional conflicts, and improved team spirit (McCormick, 2001).

What Is a Process?

Having argued for the importance of a process view of the organization, it is now time to formally define what we mean by a process. For our purposes in this text, we will define a business process as follows:

> A *business process* is an interconnected network of activities and buffers that utilize resources to transform inputs into outputs that have value for a customer.

Figure 1.1 illustrates the essential components of this definition. An important aspect of this diagram is that a process, uses inputs that flow through the process and that are transformed into outputs that have value to a customer. The work of the process is performed in terms of the activities of the process and resources are used to perform this work. Most, if not all, of the activities have buffers, or storage points, where the flow units may be temporarily held before the work is performed. The diagram also indicates that managing the process is dependent on information or communication flows between the manager of the process and the elements of the process, such as suppliers, inputs, outputs, customers, and the process itself. The customer of a process may be an internal customer within the firm or an external customer. Processes that interface with the outside customers of the firm are the most critical processes to design and manage well.

INPUTS AND OUTPUTS

The first important step in modeling a process is to determine the key inputs and outputs of the process and where the process boundaries are located. The outputs go to the customers of the process who may be external customers or internal to the organization. External customers may be the ultimate consumers of products and services or they may be other external entities. For example, most companies publish an annual report where the customers of this process are the various external stakeholders of the firm. As indicated before, the most important processes in the organization are those that interact with the ultimate customers of the firm's products and services. Although not illustrated in Figure 1.1, you should recognize that processes can have multiple input points and multiple output points. For example, some processes have outputs other than customer outputs, such as waste or pollutants. It is also possible to have multiple customer exit points in a service process.

Figure 1.1 Example of a Business Process

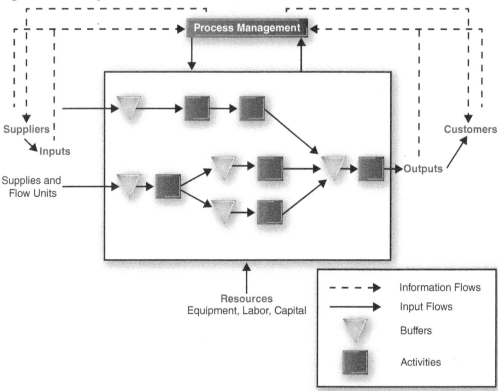

Source: Adapted from Anupindi et al. (2006), Figure 1.2, p. 5.

Supplies and Flow Units

In discussing the inputs to a process, it is important to distinguish between routine supplies as inputs to a process and the flow units of the process. *Flow units* can be defined as the transient elements that flow through the process and that are transformed into the ultimate outputs that the customer desires. Thus, flow units are a central element of the process. The solid arrows in Figure 1.1 indicate the flow of these units through the process. Supplies, on the other hand, are simply input items that are utilized during the transformation of the flow units. The flow of these inputs is not depicted in Figure 1.1, and, although necessary to the process, they are not typically a focus of the process description. An example might help clarify the distinction. Consider the situation of your local dry cleaners where you take your clothes to be dry-cleaned. The flow units are your clothes that you have dropped off to be cleaned. The other inputs are supplies such as marking tags, safety pins, cleaning fluids, and other materials that are used in the process. In describing and understanding this process, the focus will likely be on the flow units and what happens to them rather than on the supplies utilized in the process.

ACTIVITIES AND BUFFERS

A process consists of a network of buffers and activities. *Activities* are things that are done to the flow units as they proceed through the process. *Buffers* are locations where the flow units are stored until an activity is performed. Most activities in the network have implicit buffers or queues as we will call them in Chapter 4.

Distinguishing between *value-adding* and *non-value-adding* activities was a central focus of the early work from a process viewpoint such as lean manufacturing, TQM, and re-engineering. In principle, value-adding activities are those that are important to the customer, i.e., that the customer is willing to pay for. Anything that the customer is not willing to pay for is non-value-adding. Activities such as moving or storing materials, inspection, delays, and rework are regarded as non-value-adding activities. The focus of many process improvement efforts has been on eliminating the non-value-adding activities from the process so that only value-adding activities remain. This is the elimination-of-waste principle so prevalent in the writings about just-in-time and lean thinking. However, it is not always easy to classify activities as value-adding or non-value-adding. For example, how would you classify the activities that are designed to ensure that the organization is in compliance with government regulations? Or activities designed to ensure that the product or service is of high quality? Or how would you classify accounting activities? It is not entirely clear that a customer would be willing to pay for government compliance or accounting activities but they are certainly necessary for the firm. For this reason, some writers add a third category called b*usiness-value-adding* activities that includes those activities that are necessary from a business perspective even if they are not important to the customer. Even here, we realize that although these activities may be necessary from a business point of view, they still are not value-adding activities and should, therefore, be minimized as much as possible.

RESOURCES

Resources are the tangible assets that are necessary to perform the activities of the process. Resources are usually divided into capital assets, such as real estate or equipment, and labor. For example, at a traditional residential university the education process requires many capital assets, such as land and buildings for classrooms, and labor, such as faculty and staff. Although resources are also, in a sense, an input to the process, they differ in one very important respect from the other inputs to the process described earlier. Whereas the other inputs flow through and exit the process or are consumed as part of the process, resources do not exit the process nor are they consumed by it. The resources remain with the process and are an important part of the process description. We often say that resources are utilized during the process to indicate that they are not consumed or used up. For example, in the provision of an airline service, the resources of planes and flight personnel are utilized during a flight from New York to Los Angeles but the fuel for the airliner, as an input, is used or consumed during the process.

INFORMATION FLOWS

Figure 1.1 also illustrates the major part that information flows play in process management. The systems view also encourages the managers to extend their vision beyond the organizational boundaries to consider the interaction of the organization and its environment. Of particular importance are the customers and suppliers of the organization. Information flows to and from the customer are essential to monitoring and managing the customer service interface. Similarly, information flows to and from suppliers are key to managing the supplier relationships. The information flows about the inputs and outputs of the process are even more closely aligned with process management in terms of product and service quality. Lastly, in order to manage and control the process itself, it is vital to receive information about the process status from the process and to transmit corrective information to the process. The importance of feedback is a trademark of the systems view of the organization.

We will discuss information flows whenever they are relevant throughout the text. At this point it is sufficient to say that the flow of timely and accurate information is crucial to process management, and it is through this aspect of the process that information technology has had a major impact in terms of process innovation and improvement.

Process Classifications

There have been many different attempts to systematically classify business processes. Most of these efforts have been associated with benchmarking activities as described in Chapter 3. The simplest means to classify processes is to group them into three basic types:

1. Management processes: These are processes that provide direction and governance of the entire organization. Examples include strategic planning and corporate governance.
2. Operational or mission-oriented processes: These are the critical core processes of the organization that deliver value to the customer. These processes touch the external customer of the firm and are therefore critical to its success.[2]
3. Support processes: These processes provide support for the operational and management processes. Examples might include government compliance reporting, hiring processes, and accounting procedures.

Other classification schemes amplify and elaborate on this basic schema. One such large scale effort is that of the American Productivity and Quality Center (APQC). The general outline of their classification in terms of the 13 primary (level 0) process categories, is shown in Figure 1.2.[3]

This framework was started in 1992 and has been updated and improved for over a decade. This version (Version 7.0.2) was published in 2015. As you can see in the figure, the APQC classification is similar to our three-type classification except that it combines Management and Support processes into one category. The six operating process categories as described in Figure 1.2 are the strategy process, product and service design, marketing and selling, delivery of physical products (sometimes called *order fulfillment*), delivering services, and managing customer service after the sale. Each of these categories can then be broken down into process groups. For example, in the APQC classification, the Develop Vision and Strategy category is broken down further into three process groups:

1.1 Define the business concept and long-term vision
1.2 Develop business strategy
1.3 Execute and measure

Each of these process groups can then be broken down into specific processes. For example, the first process group (Define the business concept and long-term vision) can be broken down further into the following five processes,

1.1.1 Assess the external environment
1.1.2 Survey market and determine customer needs and wants
1.1.3 Assess the internal environment
1.1.4 Establish strategic vision
1.1.5 Conduct organization restructuring opportunities

Each of these processes can, in turn, be broken down into specific activities. It is important to keep in mind that this is a generic classification and therefore the specific process details will not necessarily fit every organization. However, the broad outlines are certainly applicable to most organizations and provide a framework for discussion.

For purposes of comparison, a second process classification scheme was devised by the European Network for Advanced Performance Studies (ENAPS) and is shown in Figure 1.3.

---

2. Anderson (2007) calls these primary processes to emphasize their importance.
3. The classification scheme is available for free at the APQC web site (www.apqc.org) as both a pdf file and an Excel spreadsheet.

Figure 1.2 APQC Classification of Organizational Processes

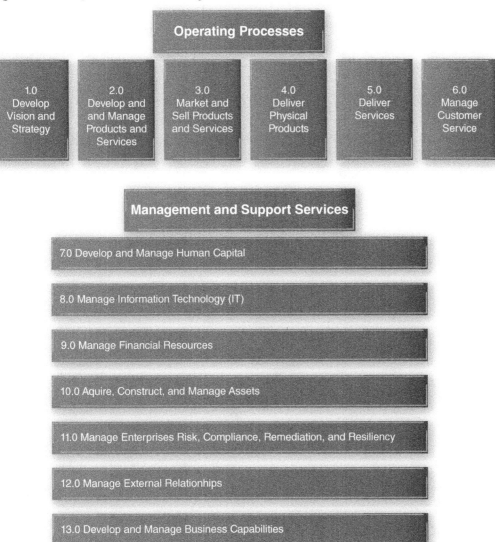

Source: Adapted from APQC Website (www.apqc.org)

As can be seen, there are many similarities in these two figures in terms of the general outlines but many differences in the details. For example, both distinguish between Operating (Business) processes and Management and Support (Secondary) processes. Both include the development of new products and services, marketing and sales, order fulfillment, and customer service as primary business processes although they differ somewhat in their terminology. Also, both include things such as financial, human resource, information, and health and safety management in the support processes. The specific differences are mostly due to different origins (United States for APQC and Europe for ENAPS) or to a different emphasis on type of organization. For example, ENAPS is entirely oriented toward manufacturing, while APQC serves both manufacturing and service organizations. The difference in origins can be noted in such things as the Product Take-back process in the ENAPS classification since this is a legally mandated process throughout most of Europe but not the United States. For all their differences, however, the two frameworks are remarkably similar in their general content. They serve our

Figure 1.3 ENAPS Process Framework

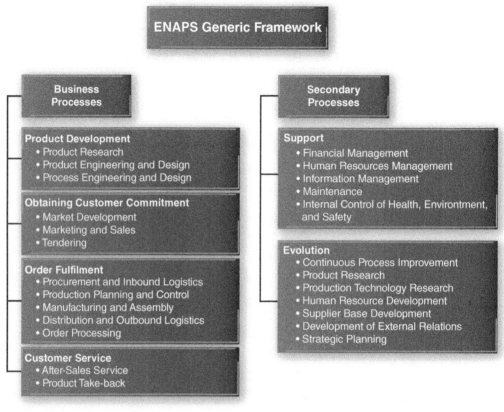

Source: Adapted from Anderson, 2007, page 36

purpose here, which is to indicate the breadth of processes that are present in most organizations, not to develop a detailed classification of processes.

Business Process Management (BPM) Activities

No matter how we classify processes, managing the process, as Figure 1.1 implies, is necessary to ensure that the necessary outputs are delivered to the customer in a timely manner and at a cost that allows the organization to be financially viable. In general, business process management (BPM) involves all of the activities of planning, managing, monitoring, executing, and improving the processes of the organization. These activities are often categorized in terms of the BPM lifecycle.

BPM LIFECYCLE

There are many different versions of the business process management lifecycle in the literature. Figure 1.4 shows a BPM lifecycle roughly patterned after the Association of Business Process Management Professionals (ABPMP) common body of knowledge.[4]

---

4. The Association of Business Process Management Professionals (www.abpmp.org) is an international organization dedicated to the advancement of business process management concepts and practice. The ABPMP publishes a guide to BPM common body of knowledge. This figure is patterned after the lifecycle that appeared in Version 2.0 Second Release.

Figure 1.4 The BPM Lifecycle

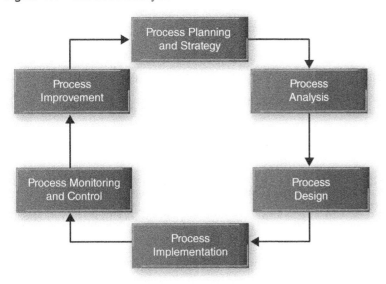

Notice that the cycle is closed, which means it is a continual process. The cycle begins with the planning stage, which is tied to the organizations strategy. All planning related to the processes of the organization must be linked to how the organization provides value to the customer. This is what Franz & Mathias (2012) refer to as value-driven business process management. The organizational processes are then analyzed in the process analysis phase in terms of these strategic objectives. The analysis of the current process may lead to the conclusion that the process should be redesigned to better achieve organizational goals and objectives. This revised process design is then implemented in the process implementation phase. After implementation the process must be monitored and controlled to insure that it is operating as designed and to allow management to allocate appropriate resources to the process so that it can achieve its designated objectives. The process improvement phase closes the loop and indicates that organizations exist in an environment in which they must continually look at how they can improve on the ways they add value to their customers.

ORGANIZATION OF THE TEXT

The BPM lifecycle provides the backdrop for the organization of this text with particular focus on the three principal phases of the lifecycle: analysis and design, management (monitoring and controlling), and improvement. Part I discusses general concepts that are important in all three areas: metrics (Chapter 2), benchmarking and balanced scorecard (Chapter 3), queues (Chapter 4), and a key tool of process modeling and simulation (Chapter 5).

The remainder of the text is divided into four distinct but interrelated sections and is organized around the three principal phases of the BPM lifecycle, namely analysis and design (Part II), process management (Part III), and process improvement (Part IV). Although these topics are discussed in the logical order of the process lifecycle, it should be noted that in practice there is often overlap between the topics. For example, process design is involved in process improvement and some of the questions addressed there are relevant to the design issue as well. Also, many aspects of process improvement are intertwined with process management. Nonetheless, decisions must be made about the order of topics in the presentation and we have done so in hopefully a logical manner.

Part I: Metrics and Tools in BPM

Part I introduces concepts and tools that are used throughout the other three parts of the text. The first concept, which is central to all of the activities in the BPM lifecycle, is metrics. By the term metrics, we mean simply numerical measures of performance. Metrics are central to all three aspects of BPM: design, management and improvement. In the design phase, metrics provide the key goals of design. In order to compare different design alternatives, we have to have a basis of comparison which metrics can provide. In the management phase, metrics provide the feedback information that we need to monitor the performance of the system. We need metrics for key inputs to the process, process performance, and process outputs. The information flows of Figure 1.1 depend on the development of useful metrics. In process improvement, metrics identify the need for change and help guide the evaluation of change alternatives. It is not an overstatement to say that metrics are at the heart of business process management. Metrics should cover all areas of the process and should include at least the following general areas:

- Customers
  - Customer requirements
  - Customer satisfaction
- Process Performance
  - Cycle times
  - Product and service quality
  - Inventories
  - Cost
- Suppliers
  - Supplier performance
- Resources
  - Availability and utilization of key resources
  - Employee satisfaction and well-being
- Finances
  - Profitability
  - Market share
  - Return on investment (ROI) and other standard financial measures

Part I also covers the main tools necessary for understanding processes. Benchmarking and the balanced scorecard are important tools in terms of metrics and in comparing processes, both within the organization and in relation to processes in other organizations. Also, because any nontrivial process involves at least the possibility of queues, or waiting lines, a discussion of the general concepts of queues and some of the tools for managing and improving them is necessary. These tools, especially queuing models and simulation, will be used extensively in the other three sections of the text.

Process Analysis and Design

Part II combines two interrelated activities and focuses on the analysis of existing processes and on process design. Process design can involve designing entirely new processes or more often, redesigning existing processes that are not operating in the most efficient manner. A key component of process design is ensuring that the process is aligned with the organization's strategic goals and objectives and also that it meets the needs of the customers of the process, whether internal or external to the organization. In this section of the text, we will introduce a variety of tools commonly used in process analysis and design and discuss the critical linkages with the strategic goals and objectives of the organization. From a systems perspective, a critical factor in process design is to maintain a broader perspective of the process to avoid *suboptimization*—the act of optimizing one part of the system to the detriment of the performance of the entire system.

Part III: Process Management (Monitoring and Control)

Process management involves monitoring the process to ensure that it is performing properly and correcting it if necessary. In many respects, this is similar to the activities involved in quality management, and many of the tools we will discuss in this topic are borrowed from this area. This is also an important area of intersection with information technology in terms of business process management suites (BPMS), which are large-scale systems for managing the flow of information in a process.

Part IV: Process Improvement

The business press and book authors have long given the most attention to one aspect of business process management—process improvement. The concept of continuous improvement was a hallmark of the just-in-time movement and has continued as a key concept through the total quality management (TQM) and lean manufacturing movements today. The reengineering movement of the 1990s emphasized the idea of radical improvement, or, as Davenport (1993) refers to it, process innovation. In this view, the most important process changes are those that yield quantum improvements in performance. This debate of continuous versus radical change will be taken up in this section. This section will also examine the types of change involved in the process. In general, there are three broad approaches to changing a process as suggested by Rouse and Baba (2006):

- Improve how the work of the process is currently done
- Perform the work differently
- Perform different work

Part IV will also examine the enablers of process improvement, the most important of which is information technology.

BPM and Technology

The acronym BPM means different things to different people and can be used in several ways, depending on the context. In a process context BPM is usually used in the same sense that we use it here—business process management. However, in other contexts the same letters are used to refer to business performance measurement or business performance management. To make things even more confusing, when some authors use the term BPM in the context of business processes, they are referring to software systems. If you Google the letters BPM, one of the links you will likely find is to bpm.com. If you go to that site you will find very little about management but a lot about computer software systems. Technology is often very important in business process management but as an enabler to process improvement, not as a substitute for management. Despite the optimism of Smith & Fingar (2003), you cannot buy successful business process management off the shelf as a software package. Business process management is much more important in terms of a set of methods in managing the key processes of an organization, and even more so as an overall philosophy of how the organization should be managed. In this book we will discuss technology as it relates to the management of business processes when it seems appropriate, but our focus is not on the software aspects of BPM. To distinguish between BPM as both a methodology and a philosophy of business and the software that supports it, we will use the terms BPMS for business process management suites (systems) when referring to the computer technology.

BPMSs differ in terms of the components included in the software. The components included depend primarily on the historical origins of the software and the stage of their evolution into a full scale BPMS. Some BPMS software is an outgrowth of the work-flow technologies of the 1990s, which were primarily designed to aid in the flow of documents used in the execution of the process. Other BPMS software offerings were derived from the so-called enterprise application integration (EAI) market, which focused on system-to-system communication. Still other vendors evolved from the data warehousing market and the so-called extract, transform, and load (ETL) systems. With these diverse origins it is not surprising that different vendors view the components necessary in a BPMS in different ways. Figure 1.5 shows the most common components included in most modern BPMS software.

One way to understand the nature of these components and their role in BPM is in terms of the BPM life cycle from Figure 1.4. If we begin with process analysis and design from the life cycle, the critical components in Figure 1.5 are the process-modeling capability, the repository for storing process designs, and the process simulation capabilities. In terms of this text, we will discuss process simulation in detail in Chapters 4, 5, and 8; process modeling in Chapters 7 and 8. Application development, which involves developing the software applications to support the process execution after it is designed, is beyond the scope of this text. After a process is designed and relevant applications are developed, then process execution becomes important. The Business process engine (BPE) and business rules engine (BRE) form the core of process execution. The BPE is primarily a work-flow application that controls the flow of information and documentation used in the execution of a process. The BRE enforces the policies that support the strategy of the organization. For example, an insurance company will have a number of policies about what types of potential customers are eligible for health or life insurance and elaborate policies and procedures for determining the rate structure for a potential client. These policies and rules would be encoded in the BRE. Besides acting as a workflow director and business rule enforcer, the BPMS tracks the key performance indicators (KPIs) and other performance metrics of the process and provides feedback to managers in the organization via software dashboards. This is done by the business activity monitoring (BAM) component. Process monitoring will be discussed in more detail in Chapter 10. The final component of the BPMS, process analytics, is the most recent addition to BPMS software and relates to the

Figure 1.5 Common Components of a BPMS

use of analytical methods to improve design and execution of processes. These analytical results are important in the process improvement phase of the life cycle, along with the process analysis and design features, especially process simulation.

Chapter Glossary

Activities Actions that are performed on the flow units and supplies by the resources involved in the process.
Buffers Locations where the flow units are stored until the activity is performed
Business process An interconnected network of activities and buffers that utilizes resources to transform inputs into outputs that have value for a customer.
Business-value-adding Activities that are necessary for the business as an organization but are not value-adding from a customer perspective.
Flow units The transient elements that flow through the process and are transformed into the ultimate outputs that the customer wants.
Metrics Numerical measures of performance.
Nonvalue-adding Activities that do not add value to the customer, i.e. waste.
Order Fulfillment The activities involved in transferring the product or service to the customer.
Resources Tangible assets necessary to perform the activities of the process.
Suboptimization Optimizing a part of the system in a way that leads to poorer performance of the system as a whole.
Value-adding Activities that add value for the customer, i.e., that the customer would be willing to pay for.

Discussion Questions and Problems

1. Identify a process that you are familiar with. This may be a process at work or school or something you encounter in your daily activities.
   a. Outline the activities involved in this process.
   b. Where are buffers located in the process?
   c. Classify the activities as value-adding, non-value-adding or business-value-adding.
   d. What resources are involved in performing the activities?
   e. Who is the customer in the process?
2. Search for information on the "process" versus "functional" organization of a business. What arguments can be advanced for the importance of a process orientation? What factors favor a functional organization?
3. Bob Raney is the manager in the accounting department at a large firm. One of the responsibilities of his group is to approve business trips and then to reimburse the employee after the trip is completed. There have been numerous complaints from employees about the length of time it takes to get trips approved and even more so about getting reimbursement after the trip. Bob wants to know why it takes so long to get these things done and who is to blame for the delays. He has asked you to first look at the travel approval process to identify the problem. You talk to various people in the department and discover the following information:

Table 1.1 Process Steps in the Travel Approval Process

Step	Time in Minutes
1. Employee completes and submits a travel approval request form with the required business justification.	15
2. Employee's travel approval request form waits to be processed. Accounting promises that travel approval requests will be reviewed within 72 hours, or three calendar days.	4320
3. The accounting clerk reviews the travel approval request form for completeness and accuracy.	30
a. The form has problems and needs to return to step 1. The employee's travel approval request form is returned to the employee to provide additional information and resubmit for approval.	15
b. The form is complete and accurate. The employee's travel approval request form is forwarded to the accounting manager for approval.	5
4. The accounting manager reviews the employee's travel approval request form and approves or denies the request.	15
a. If denied, accounting notifies the employee and requests that the form be resubmitted with an additional business justification.	15
b. If approved, the employee's travel approval request form is returned to the employee authorizing the trip.	5

    a. Using Table 1.1, sketch out the business process. Who are the suppliers? Who are the customers? What are the inputs, supplies and flow units? What resources are required? (e.g. equipment, labor, capital) What are the outputs?

    b. What business process measures should be put in place? Based on your review of the process, what is a reasonable service expectation timeframe for the customer? Will this meet the customer's needs? If not, why not?

    c. List the value-adding, non-value-adding, and business-value-adding activities and the necessary buffer locations.

    d. Classify the processes as management, operational/mission oriented, or support processes.

    e. How would you redesign the process to improve it? Specifically what can be done to streamline the process?

4. Bob Raney, the manager of the accounting department, was quite impressed with the nice work that you did on figuring out the travel approval process. As a follow-on assignment he has asked you to look more closely at the travel reimbursement process. While talking with the employees about the reimbursement process, you uncovered the following information:

Table 1.2 Process Steps in the Travel Reimbursement Process

Step	Time in Minutes
1. Employee completes the travel reimbursement form.	15
2. Employee attaches travel receipts.	5
3. Employee reviews the travel reimbursement form for completeness and accuracy.	5
4. Employee submits the travel reimbursement form electronically.	1

Step	Time in Minutes
5. The employee's travel reimbursement form waits to be processed. Accounting promises that travel reimbursement requests will be reviewed within 72 hours, or three calendar days.	4320
6. An accounting clerk reviews the employee's travel reimbursement form for accuracy and completeness.	30
a. If there are problems, the employee's travel reimbursement request form is returned to the employee to provide additional information and resubmit for approval.	15
b. If there are no problems, the employee's travel reimbursement request form is forwarded to the accounting manager for approval.	2
7. The travel reimbursement request form is considered by the accounting manager and either approved or denied.	5
a. If denied, accounting notifies the employee. The employee can appeal the denial to their immediate supervisor.	10
i. If the supervisor feels that there are extenuating circumstances that the supervisor will hold a conference with the accounting manager and together they reach a joint decision. The decision should be finalized within 4 working days.	1440–5760
b. If approved, the employee's travel reimbursement form is queued for payment.	5
8. Employee's travel reimbursement waits for payment. Travel reimbursements are paid each week on Friday.	1440–9600
9. Employee travel reimbursement sent to the employee's bank electronically.	1

    a. Using Table 1.2 sketch out the business process. Who are the suppliers? Who are the customers? What are the inputs, supplies and flow units? What resources are required? (e.g., equipment, labor, capital) What are the outputs?
    b. What business process measures should be put in place? Based on your review of the process what is a reasonable service expectation timeframe for the customer? Will this meet the customer's needs? If not, why not?
    c. List the value-adding, non-value adding, and business-value-adding activities and the necessary buffer locations.
    d. Classify the processes as management, operational/mission oriented, or support processes.
    e. How would you redesign the process to improve it? Specifically what can be done to streamline the process?

5. Rod Potski is a loan officer at a small bank. He processes from four to six loan applications per day. However, his customers are calling him nearly every day wondering about the status of their loan applications and when their loan might be approved. These daily customer calls are causing Rod to spend increasingly more and more of his day finding out the status of his customers' loan applications and less and less time actually initiating loan applications for new customers. Because Rod is compensated when a customer's loan is funded, this is beginning to become a big concern for Rod. After a particularly stressful week spent trying to find out what happened to his customers' loan applications Rod decides to figure this out once and for all. After a couple of days of digging Rod discovers the following:

Table 1.3 Process Steps in the Loan Application Process

Step	Time in Minutes
1. Customer contacts the bank via telephone and sets up an initial consultation appointment with a loan officer.	15
2. Normal wait time for a loan officer assignment and appointment setting is three business days (or up to five calendar days if the appointment request is made on a Friday).	4320–7200
3. Customer's initial consultation visit with a Loan Officer.	60
4. The customer fills out a hard copy of the loan application form and submits to it to the loan officer. This process typically takes from 1 to 4 calendar days.	1440–5760
5. The customer's loan application waits for the loan officer's review. The bank's loan officers are required to process a customer's loan application within 24 hours.	1440
6. The loan officer requests the customer's credit score.	5
7. The loan officer performs an initial review of the customer's loan application for completeness and accuracy.	15
8. If required, the loan officer requests additional information from the customer.	15
a. It typically takes from 1 to 5 days for the customer to respond to this information request.	1440–7200
9. The loan officer submits the completed customer loan application to the bank underwriter.	15
10. The wait for the next available underwriter can take up to 72 hours.	4320
11. The underwriter reviews the customer's loan application.	30
12. If required, the underwriter requests additional information from customer. This can take up to 72 hours.	4320
13. The underwriter either approves or denies the customer's loan application.	5
a. If the underwriter denies the customer's loan application, the loan officer is notified and the customer is contacted.	30
b. If the underwriter approves the customer's loan application, the customer's loan is sent to accounting for funding.	5
14. The customer's loan waits to be funded. This normally takes 72 hours or three days.	4320
15. Accounting funds the loan and the customer is notified that the funds have been deposited.	15

    a. Using Table 1.3 sketch out the business process. Who are the suppliers? Who are the customers? What are the inputs, supplies and flow units? What resources are required? (e.g., equipment, labor, capital) What are the outputs?

    b. What business process measures should be put in place? Based on your review of the process what is a reasonable service expectation timeframe for the customer? Will this meet the customer's needs? If not, why not?

    c. List the value-adding, non-value adding, and business-value-adding activities and the necessary buffer locations.

d. Classify the processes as management, operational/mission oriented, or support processes.
e. How would you redesign the process to improve it? Specifically what can be done to streamline the process?

6. Rob Star works for Acme Software, a software firm that specializes in providing manufacturing information system solutions to small- to medium- sized manufacturers. After years of hard work, Rob recently received a well-deserved promotion to district sales manager. However, in his first meeting with his new boss Jim Driver, regional sales manager, Rob is informed that he needs to dramatically improve visibility into his sales pipeline so Acme can more accurately project the company's software sales revenue. While a little surprised by the request, Rob is up to the challenge. He calls a meeting with the six account managers assigned to his district and documents the following Software Sales process:

Table 1.4 Process Steps in the Software Sales Process

Step	Time in Business Days
1. Customer requests that an Acme account executive contact him or her.	1
2. Customer's contact request waits for the assignment of an account executive. Depending on the volume of customer requests this can take between 2 to 5 business days.	2–5
3. The account executive makes initial contact with the customer and completes an initial needs assessment.	1
4. The account executive contacts Acme's software architecture department and requests that a solution architect be assigned to the customer account.	1
5. The account executive waits for the assignment of a solutions architect. Depending on workloads this can take up the 15 business days.	5–15
6. The account executive meets with the assigned solutions architect to review the customer's needs.	1
7. The account executive contacts the customer to schedule a follow-up needs assessment appointment.	1
8. Account executive waits for an appointment with customer.	5–15
9. Account executive and solutions architect meet with the customer.	1
10. Based on this meeting the solution architect develops a customer proposal.	5–15
11. The account executive reviews the solution architect's proposal for completeness and submits the customer proposal for pricing review.	1
12. Customer proposal waits for a pricing review. These reviews are normally held each week on Wednesday.	1–5
13. Account executive submits the solution proposal along with the pricing information to the customer for review.	1
14. Customer reviews Acme's solution proposal. If the customer does not respond to the proposal within 30 days the account executive reinitiates contact with the customer.	1–30

Continued

Step	Time in Business Days
15. Customer contacts Acme's account executive with one of the following decisions:	
a. Customer asks for the solution proposal to be modified and re-priced. Return to Step 9.	1
b. Customer Declines the proposal.	1
c. Customer approves the solution proposal. Approval initiates a separate process to develop a statement of work (SOW). A nominal timeframe to complete and execute a SOW is 45-days.	45

    a. Using Table 1.4 sketch out the business process. Who are the suppliers? Who are the customers? What are the inputs, supplies and flow units? What resources are required? (e.g., equipment, labor, capital) What are the outputs?
    b. What business process measures should be put in place? Based on your review of the process what is a reasonable service expectation timeframe for the customer? Will this meet the customer's needs? If not, why not?
    c. List the value-adding, non-value adding, and business-value-adding activities and the necessary buffer locations.
    d. Classify the processes as management, operational/mission oriented, or support processes.
    e. How would you redesign the process to improve it? Specifically, what can be done to streamline the process?

References

Anderson, B. *Business Process Improvement Toolbox*, 2nd Edition, 2007, Milwaukee: Quality Press.
Anupindi, R., Chopra, S., Deshmukh, S.D., Van Mieghem, J.A. & Semel, E. *Managing Business Process Flows*, 2nd Edition, 2006, Upper Saddle River NJ: Prentice-Hall.
Davenport, T.H. *Process Innovation: Reengineering Work through Information Technology*, 1993, Boston: Harvard Business School Press.
Davenport, T.H. & Short, J.E. The New Industrial Engineering: Information Technology and Business Process Redesign. *Sloan Management Review*, 1990, 31, 3, 11–27.
Deming, W.E. *Out of the Crisis: Quality, Productivity and Competitive Position*, 1986, Cambridge, MA: Cambridge University Press.
Franz, P. & Mathias, K. *Value-Driven Business Process Management: The Value-Switch for Lasting Competitive Advantage.* 2012, New York: McGraw-Hill.
Garvin, D.A. Leveraging Processes for Strategic Advantage: A Roundtable with Xerox's Allaire, USAA's Herres, Smithkline Beecham's Leschly and Pepsi's Weatherup, *Harvard Business Review*, 1995, 73, 5, 76–90.
Goldratt, E. *What is This Thing Called the Theory of Constraints and How Should It be Implemented*, 1990, Great Barrington, MA: North River Press.
Goldratt, E. *It's Not Luck*, 1994, Great Barrington, MA: North River Press.
Goldratt, E. & Cox, J. *The Goal: Excellence in Manufacturing*, 1984, Great Barrington, MA: North River Press.
Goldratt, E. & Cox, J. *The Goal: Excellence in Manufacturing*, 2nd edition, 1992, Great Barrington, MA: North River Press.
Hall, R.W. *Zero Inventories*, 1983, Homewood Illinois: Dow-Jones Irwin.
Hammer, M. Reengineering Work: Don't Automate, Obliterate. *Harvard Business Review*, 1990, 68, 4, 104–114.

Hammer, M. *Beyond Reengineering: How the Process-Centered Organization is Changing Our Work and Our Lives*, 1996, New York: Harper Business.

Hammer, M. & Champy, J. *Reengineering the Corporation*. 1993, New York: Harper Business.

McCormick, K. Business Process Orientation: Do You Have It? ASQ Quality Progress, 2001, 1, 51–57.

Rouse, W.B. & Baba, M.L. Enterprise Transformation, *Communications of the ACM*, 2006, 49, 7, 67–72.

Schonberger, R.J. *Japanese Manufacturing Techniques: Nine Hidden Lessons in Simplicity*, 1982, New York: The Free Press.

Smith, A. *An Inquiry into the Nature and Causes of the Wealth of Nations*, 1776, London: Methuen and Co., Ltd.

Smith, H. & Fingar, P. *Business Process Management: The Third Wave*, 2003, Tampa FL: Meghan-Kiffer.

Womack, J.P., Jones, D.T. & Roos, D. *The Machine That Changed the World*, 1990, New York, NY: Rawson Associates.

Part I
Metrics and Tools in Business Process Management

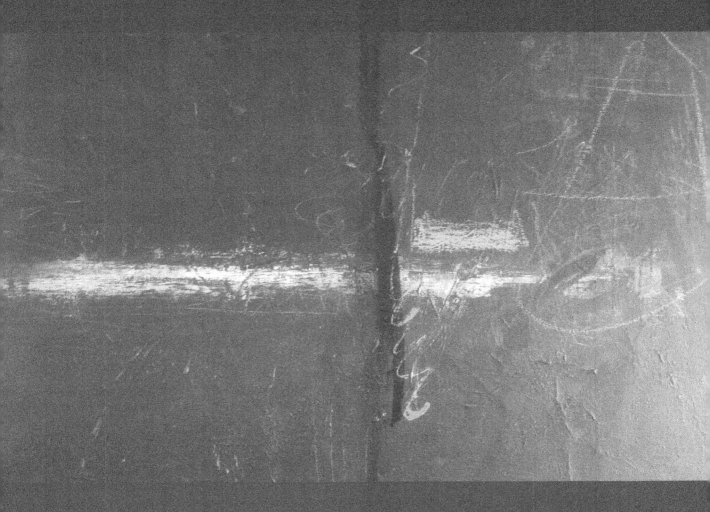

Chapter 2

Metrics in Business Process Management

"I often say that when you can measure what you are speaking about and express it in numbers you know something about it; but when you cannot measure it, when you cannot express it in numbers, your knowledge is of a meager and unsatisfactory kind"

—Lord Kelvin

As the above quote implies, to even begin to understand something, we have to be able to measure it or express it in numbers. If we take the rather obvious position that we need to understand a process and its context before designing, managing, or improving it, then it becomes clear that metrics are important to BPM.[1] Furthermore, the importance of information flows and system feedback described in Chapter 1 require measures of system performance. Therefore, in this chapter we will look at the development and application of metrics in more detail, taking special care to clarify that metrics are situation specific. In other words, metrics must be customized for the situation and purpose at hand. As we will see later in the text, metrics appear in our discussion of all three major types of activities in BPM: design, management, and improvement. In fact, as some companies have found out, better process metrics can, in and of themselves, lead to improved process performance.

Classifying Metrics

Before discussing metrics that are specifically designed to measure process performance, we will first discuss ways in which metrics have traditionally been classified. Each of these

---

1. The letters BPM are also used by consultants and vendors of large information systems to refer to Business Performance Measurement or Business Performance Management. Again, the emphasis is on metrics.

distinctions has important implications for metrics in general and process metrics in particular. These distinctions are important to keep in mind as we discuss different process metrics.

OBSERVED VERSUS SUBJECTIVE METRICS

Metrics can be distinguished on the basis of whether they are measured through direct observation, sometimes also called hard metrics or quantitative measures, or through less-tangible measures that have to be inferred from other behaviors, sometimes called soft metrics or qualitative measures. Observed metrics are used widely by companies and include monetary measures but also include such measures as defect rates or product yields. Subjective metrics are less tangible aspects of performance such as customer satisfaction or employee job satisfaction. Some companies are reluctant to measure the "soft" metrics thinking that they are not objective and are therefore not useful. However, as Deming (1986) observed many times, it is often the most important things that are difficult to attach numbers to but this does not mean that we can ignore them. Because of a distrust of subjective measures, firms sometimes attempt to use surrogate measures that are more objective. For example, rather than measuring customer satisfaction a firm may monitor the number of customer complaints or warranty costs. However, there is at best a tenuous relationship between such measures as the number of customer complaints or warranty claims and overall customer satisfaction. The use of surrogate measures usually leads to problems.

FINANCIAL VERSUS NONFINANCIAL METRICS

Financial metrics use monetary values as the basic unit of measurement and are by far the most widely used business metrics. However, this does not mean that we should ignore nonfinancial measures. Indeed, Kaplan and Norton (1992, 1993, 1996) have argued that a balanced view of a firms performance must include nonfinancial as well as financial measures. We will discuss this balanced scorecard approach in the next chapter.

It should be apparent that financial measures are typically objective measures rather than subjective. However, this does not mean that all nonfinancial metrics are necessarily subjective measures. Indeed measures like yield or number of customer complaints are clearly objective measures but are nonfinancial as well. Of course many common nonfinancial measures like customer satisfaction or employee job satisfaction are also subjective measures.

LEADING VERSUS LAGGING METRICS

Kaplan and Norton (1996) use the term leading and lagging metrics to describe the distinction between measures that record the results of a process after the fact (*lagging metrics*) from those that are more predictive of future results (*leading metrics*). Using only lagging metrics has been described as being analogous to driving a car using only the rear-view mirror. Although this may be an overstatement, it does make the important point that we need to have at least some metrics that provide an early warning system rather than simply recording things after the fact. The results come at the end of the process and by then it is too late to change the outcome. Since most financial measures tend to be lagging metrics, this is further argument for the necessity of nonfinancial measures in assessing process and business performance. According to studies done by APQC, analytical methods used on process measures can serve as leading indicators of process performance and as early-warning devices.[2]

---

2. http://www.apqc.org/knowledge-base/download/224238/a%3A1%3A%7Bi%3A1%3Bi%3A2%3B%7D/inline.pdf

As stated earlier, metrics are situation specific and therefore will vary from organization to organization and from process to process within an organization. However, there are some general guidelines that we can discuss for developing and using metrics, and there are some common metrics that are applicable to almost any process. As we noted in Chapter 1, metrics should cover at least the areas of customers, process performance, suppliers, resources, and finances. We will discuss each of these areas in turn.

Customer Metrics

Perhaps the most important measures are those related to the customer because without the customer there would be no need for a process. There are a variety of metrics that may apply to the customer depending on the process, but certainly customer satisfaction would be a key metric for any process.

CUSTOMER SATISFACTION

The difficulty with customer satisfaction is that it is a subjective concept and not a simple one at that. This makes it very difficult to measure. For example, a customer may be satisfied with some aspects of a process but dissatisfied with others. Customer satisfaction is also notoriously difficult to measure in many service environments such as restaurants. For this reason customer complaints are sometimes used as a surrogate for customer dissatisfaction. The one advantage of customer complaints is that they are an "objective" measure. However, there are many problems with using customer complaints to measure customer dissatisfaction. For one, many customers who are dissatisfied will not complain. Therefore the number of complaints can seriously underestimate customer dissatisfaction. Just because there are no complaints does not necessarily indicate that customers are satisfied. Despite these difficulties, customer-oriented metrics are very important and should be developed for any process. Typically these involve some type of subjective assessment.

Customer satisfaction measures are most often obtained by surveys and typically involve some kind of Likert scale, for example a 5-point scale from highly dissatisfied to highly satisfied. Many organizations routinely assess customer satisfaction with their products or services. Customer satisfaction is obviously an important process metric and it has been shown to be related to financial performance in several studies (Anderson et al. 1994; Anderson et al. 2004; Fornell et al. 2006).[3] However, there is a problem with overall satisfaction measures. They do not tell us anything about the reasons for satisfaction or dissatisfaction with our products or services. In other words, they are too general to be of much use in process management. In process management we need specific measures that are related to the process. There should be some connection between the customer satisfaction measures and process measures such as cycle time, inventory, and the other process measures discussed later.

CUSTOMER PRODUCT OR SERVICE REQUIREMENTS

When developing products or services (the new-product development process) it is important to get customer input in terms of what is important to them. An understanding of key customer requirements is also essential to designing and managing the processes that deliver the products and services.

Often the customer requirements are gathered through market research, customer surveys, or customer comments. A more rigorous way of integrating customer requirements is through

---

3. All of these studies were based on the American Customer Satisfaction Index published by the National Quality Research Center at the University of Michigan http://www.theacsi.org.

quality function deployment (QFD). QFD was originally developed by Shigeru Mizuno and Yoji Akao in the 1960s for use in Japanese manufacturing. The intent of QFD as designed by Mizuno and Akao was to introduce customer requirements (i.e. the voice of the customer) into the design of products *before* they are produced. The first published work on QFD in the United States was by Masao and Akao (1983) and the approach quickly became widely used in the auto industry (Hauser & Clausing, 1988). It was only later that the original Japanese publications were translated into English by Glenn Mazur (Akao, 1990; Mizuno & Akao, 1994).

The Hauser & Clausing (1988) publication popularized the notion that the principles of QFD could be captured in a "house of quality" concept and that notion has remained in the popular literature despite the insistence of Professor Akao that this is only part of quality function deployment and that this term was not even used in the original developments of the concept. Nonetheless, the house of quality does encapsulate the principal ideas of capturing the customer requirements in the design process as illustrated in Figure 2-1. As can be seen there are six sections of the house of quality. The first, and most important segment, is for customer requirements. This is the "voice of the customer" and details what the customers feel is important in the product or service and usually includes an expression of their relative priorities. The second section is for the technical requirements that relate to the customer requirements. These may be engineering requirements in a manufactured product or service process requirements in a service environment. The third section shows the interrelationships of customer and technical requirements. The fourth section of the house of quality shows the competitive position of the firm's products or services in relation to their competitors in terms of these customer requirements. The fifth section shows the interrelationships of the technical requirements. As is often the case in designing processes, the key requirements are not independent of one another. This means that in designing the product or service and the associated process, we may have to make trade-offs. In other words, if we want more of one thing we may need to take less of something else. The sixth and final segment of the house of quality is for the target design specifications which take into account all of the other sections to produce a final design of the product or service. A completed example of a house of quality is shown in Figure 2.2.

Process Metrics

At the heart of process management are the measures related to the operation of the process itself. Although some of these measures will be specific to the organization and the process, the following general measures are often utilized in any process:

- **Cycle Time:** *Cycle time* is the time between when a flow unit[4] enters a process and when it leaves the process. Cycle time will be used extensively in this text as a primary metric of a process. The principal difficulty in defining cycle time is in defining the boundaries of the process in order to identify when the flow unit enters and leaves the process.
- **Inventory:** The term *inventory* is used in this text to represent the number of flow units in the process or within a specific portion of the process. Thus, the term can refer to inventory in the traditional sense of material used in producing a product or service or it can refer to customers within a process or documents setting on a desk.
- **Throughput:** *Throughput* refers to the rate at which the flow units exit the process. Throughput is a rate and thus is always measured as the number of units per time period. For example, "5 claim documents per hour" or "10 audit reports per month."

---

4. In this text the term *flow unit* will be used for the items that flow through the process. The term is very general and can represent, for example, material in a manufacturing process, customers in a service environment, documents in an insurance process, or information in an information network.

Figure 2.1 The Key Elements of the House of Quality

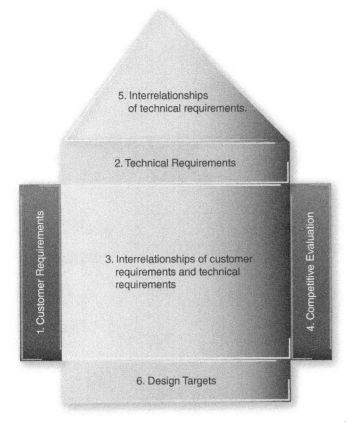

- **Productivity:** The concept of productivity relates to the efficiency with which the flow units are output from the process. It is usually expressed as a ratio of the units of output to the amount of resources required to produce that output.
- **Quality:** Here, *quality* measures refer to the output of the process as it relates to the design specifications for that output (i.e., are the outputs of acceptable quality compared to the specifications designed into the product or service).
- **Costs:** The *costs* involved in the process are widely used metrics. The process costs primarily relate to the inputs used in the process and the resources required to perform the activities involved in the process.
- **Utilization:** *Utilization* is a commonly used metric related to the use of resources. It is commonly stated in terms of the percentage of time the resources are engaged in performing the activities of the process.
- **Key Performance Indicators (KPI):** *Key performance indicators* are specific to a process and refer to crucial performance measures that are critical to monitoring the behavior of a process. For example, a retail store might use sales per square foot of retail space as a KPI.

This is not meant to be an exhaustive list of process metrics but an introduction to some of the most commonly used measures. Other metrics will be introduced where appropriate in the text. In addition, APQC has published a list of performance measures that accompany their classification of processes introduced in Chapter 1. The list is too long to publish in its entirety here, but a partial list of these metrics is contained in the appendix to this chapter.

Figure 2.2 An Example of the House of Quality

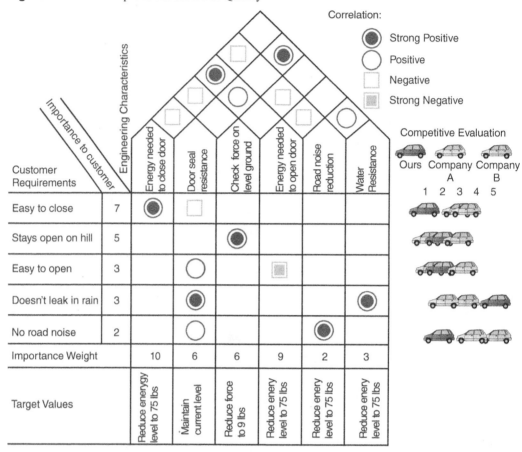

Source: Adapted from Houser and Clausing (1988), Exhibit X, p. 72

Although process metrics are important in terms of monitoring the efficiency of a process, we have noted before that a key aspect of defining process metrics is the ability to link them to customer requirements on the output side and to supplier requirements on the input side of the process. It is also critical to be able to link the process metrics to the strategic goals and objectives of the organization. It is important to keep these points in mind when devising process metrics.

Supplier Metrics

Suppliers provide important inputs that are utilized in the process. In a manufacturing context suppliers may provide the material inputs that become the flow units in the process. In nonmanufacturing settings, suppliers are more likely to provide items that are used in the performance of the process but that are not the flow units themselves. In both cases, having the necessary supplies at the proper time is important to the performance of any process, and supplier metrics are important inputs to the design and management of a process. Like other measures, supplier metrics are often situation specific but we can specify certain broad categories of supplier metrics:

- **Cost Measures:** There are a variety of cost measures that can be used with suppliers. Among them are initial price, availability of discounts, and process costs which involve the costs associated with managing the interactions with a supplier.

- **Availability:** Availability measures are related to the suppliers delivery of materials and can include measures such as on-time delivery, delivery lead time, and vendor responsiveness.
- **Quality:** These metrics relate to the quality of the supplies received from this supplier such as product defects, existence of quality assurance systems, or responsiveness to quality problems.
- **Relationship Quality:** These metrics relate more to the quality of the relationship we have with a supplier. These measures could include such things as the level of trust that exists, problem-solving and conflict-resolution quality, and level of mutual commitment.

As is the case with customer metrics, it is important that there be connections between supplier metrics and the process metrics used to manage the process. For example, the availability measures developed should be measures that have a critical impact on the process in some way.

Resource Metrics

Resource metrics relate to the usage of the resources used in the process. Resources consist primarily of labor, equipment, and capital. Some common resource-related metrics are

- **Utilization:** The percentage of time that the resource is engaged in the activities of the process. Although the traditional view has been that 100% utilization is best, we will see throughout the text that 100% utilization is not always optimal, or even necessarily desirable. Nevertheless, utilization is an important metric to monitor in a process.
- **Costs:** The costs associated with the resources. This is most often the costs associated with human resources, or labor costs.
- **Resource Well-Being:** These measures relate to the relative health of the resources. For example, employee satisfaction has been shown to be very important to financial success in many service industries. Therefore, monitoring employee satisfaction may be an important resource metric.

Guidelines for Metrics

No matter what type of metric we are developing, there are certain guidelines that are helpful in developing useful measures. These guidelines are often stated under the rubric of SMART:[5]

- **Specific:** The measures targeted specifically to what you are trying to measure. For example, customer satisfaction might be measured by the number of customer complaints. However, complaints are only an indirect measure of customer satisfaction, and are, in reality, a measure of dissatisfaction only. A better measure would more specifically target customer satisfaction.
- **Measurable:** The metrics should be such that we can easily collect data that is accurate and complete. For example, establishing a metric for length of time before a support call is answered will not meet this criterion if we cannot accurately and reliably measure the time it takes to answer the call.
- **Actionable:** The metrics should be actionable in the sense that they should be apparent whether performance is improving or deteriorating in which case we have to take action.

---

5. The SMART acronym is also sometimes used in the context of setting goals and objectives. There the letters commonly refer to Specific, Measurable (or Meaningful), Achievable, Relevant, and Time-Bound.

- **Relevant:** The metrics should be important for some purpose. Unfortunately, sometimes there is a tendency to measure things just because we can measure them easily without regard to whether or not they are relevant to process performance.
- **Timely:** This simply means that you can get the data when you need it. Information that comes too late to take action is of little value.

In general, metrics should be simple and easy to understand and targeted to what we are trying to measure.

PITFALLS IN METRICS

There are also some common problems or pitfalls in developing metrics, most of which involve principles of human behavior. We will briefly describe some of them here.

1. **Developing too many measures:** A common problem in developing metrics is to have too many of them. If there are too many metrics people have trouble keeping track of them and become confused. The end result is that to simplify things individuals will decide for themselves which metrics are important and then attend to those measures. This may well not be the result that is best for the organization. Pick only the most important metrics to track.
2. **Developing metrics that no one understands:** If a metric is overly complex and people do not understand it, they will quickly ignore it. A metric that is widely ignored will be of little value in managing the process.
3. **Developing metrics for which you cannot get accurate data:** Metrics that sound great, but which don't have any data to back them up are less than useless; they are downright dangerous. Measures such as customer service often fall into this category.
4. **Developing metrics that cause counterproductive behavior:** There is an old saying that you should be careful what you measure because you will get what you measure. In other words, behaviors in the organization will adapt to what is being measured. This is a common flaw in the functional organization where important processes span organizational boundaries. Metrics that make sense from a functional point of view may actually encourage behaviors that have a negative impact from a process point of view. For example, historically manufacturing was evaluated primarily on the basis of costs and marketing and sales on the basis of units sold and revenue generated. This encouraged marketing to promise the customer anything to get a sale and often caused severe headaches in manufacturing. Similarly, since manufacturing was evaluated on cost there was incentive to minimize inventories and to produce only easy-to-produce products. This is often not very conducive to sales. Although each metric makes sense in its functional context, the resulting behaviors are very detrimental to getting the right products and services to the customer in a timely manner.

Metrics and BPMS Software

Metrics and KPIs are crucial in most all activities involved in BPM and are used extensively in a BPMS. As we will discuss in later chapters, metrics are an important element in the documentation of the process designs in a BPMS. These metrics are used in the simulations involved in the design of processes and are also used by the software to monitor processes and provide feedback to managers related to process performance. Although the BPMS software does not help in the design of appropriate metrics, the system cannot operate effectively without them.

Chapter Glossary

Cycle time The total time between when a flow unit enters a process until it exits the process.
Inventory The number of flow units within a process or within a part of the process
Lagging metrics Measures that record the results of a process after it is finished
Leading metrics Measures that are predictive of future process results.
Productivity The efficiency with which inputs are converted into outputs. Typically measured as the ratio of outputs to inputs.
Quality function deployment (QFD) A tool for incorporating customer requirements and preferences into the design of a product before it is produced. Uses the House of Quality.
Throughput The rate at which flow units exit the process as completed units.
Utilization The percentage of time that a resource is busy performing the activities of the process.

Discussion Questions and Problems

1. You are planning on opening a new high-end restaurant. In order to "get it right" you plan on performing a survey of potential customers concerning what they think is important in such a restaurant. You then plan on building a "house of quality" that incorporates these customer requirements along with the technical service design of the restaurant. For this scenario, develop some realistic customer requirements and then develop parts 1, 2 and 3 of the house of quality.

2. Identify a process that you are familiar with. This may be a process at work, something you encounter in your daily activities, or a process at school.
   a. Develop some specific metrics that might be useful in managing this process.
   b. Specify at least one leading metric for the process.
   c. Identify a key performance indicator for this process.

3. For problem 1, identify some specific customer satisfaction metrics you might want to develop based on the customer requirements that you identified. What process metrics might be linked to these satisfaction measures?

4. Access the KPI Library at www.kpilibrary.com and pick a category within either the industry or process classification. Select the five metrics that you think would be important across all organizations either in this industry or across all industries. Justify your inclusion of each metric chosen. (Note: The site requires you to register but registration is free).

5. The point was emphasized in this chapter that metrics are situation specific. Consider a utility company that provides electricity to its customers versus a health care organization such as a hospital. Using either the list of performance metrics in the appendix and at the APQC website at http://www.apqc.org or those in the KPI Library at www.kpilibrary.com, find at least five metrics that would be useful in one type of organization but not in the other. (Note: The KPI Library site requires you to register but registration is free).

References

Akao, Y. (Ed) *Quality Function Deployment: Integrating Customer Requirements into Product Design*, 1990, Cambridge, MA: Productivity Press (Translated by Glen H. Mazur).
Anderson, E.W., Fornell, C.G. & Lehmann, D.R. Customer Satisfaction, Market Share, and Profitability: Findings from Sweden. *Journal of Marketing*, 1994, 58, 3, 53-66.

Anderson, E.W., Fornell, C.G. & Mazvancheryl, S.K. Customer Satisfaction and Shareholder Values. *Journal of Marketing*, 2004, 68, 4, 172-185.

Deming, W.E. *Out of the Crisis: Quality, Productivity and Competitive Position*, 1986, Cambridge, MA: Cambridge University Press.

Fornell, C.G., Mithas, S., Morgeson, F. & Krishnan, MS. Customer Satisfaction and Stock Price: High Returns, Low Risk, *Journal of Marketing*, 2006, 70, 1, 3-14.

Hauser, J. R. & Clausing, D. The House of Quality, *Harvard Business Review*, 1988, 66, 3, 63-73

Kaplan R. S. & Norton D. P. The Balanced Scorecard: Measures That Drive Performance, *Harvard Business Review*, 1992, 70, 1, 71-80.

Kaplan R. S. & Norton D. P., Putting the Balanced Scorecard to Work, *Harvard Business Review*, 1993, 71, 5, 2-16.

Kaplan, R.S. & Norton, D.P. *The Balanced Scorecard: Translating Strategy into Action*, 1996, Boston: Harvard Business School Press.

Masao, M. & Akao, Y. Quality Function Deployment and CWQC in Japan, *Quality Progress*, 1983, 16, 10, 25-29.

Mizuno, S. & Akao, Y. *QFD: The Customer-Driven Approach to Quality Planning & Deployment*, 1994, Productivity Press. (Translated by Glen H. Mazur)

Appendix

This appendix contains a partial list of possible performance measures (metrics) placed within the process classification introduced by APQC. Many of these metrics come from previous lists that were available on the APQC website for earlier versions, but are no longer available. Others are from the KPI library at www.kpilibrary.com. This is not meant to be an exhaustive list of metrics but only a sample to give the reader an idea of what some real-world metrics might be and to provide a more detailed look at the APQC process classification.

1.0 Develop Vision and Strategy Process Measures

Personnel cost to perform this process per $1,000 revenue
Number of full-time corporate planners per <$1 billion> revenue
Number of iterations of strategic plan per year
Percentage error in planning estimates
Percentage of goals accomplished from most recent strategic plan
Strategic planning operating budget per <$1,000> revenue
Percentage of strategic objectives achieved

2.0 Develop and Manage Products and Services

GOVERN AND MANAGE PRODUCT/SERVICE DEVELOPMENT PROGRAMS

Personnel cost to perform this process per $1,000 revenue
Percentage of client/customer facing employees

GENERATE AND DEFINE NEW PRODUCT/SERVICE IDEAS

Total cost of new product development per <$1,000> revenue
Ratio of R&D to capital equipment
Percentage of sales due to product/services launched in the past year
Number of product/service improvements generated annually
Percentage of existing product/service improvements launched on time
Incremental profit from new products
New product success rate
Time to market in days for existing product/service improvement projects

Percentage of sales from products launched the previous year
Percentage of new product/service developments launched on budget
Amount spent on research and development activities as a percentage of revenue
Average development costs per new product

3.0 Market and Sell Products and Services Process Measures

UNDERSTAND MARKETS, CUSTOMERS, AND CAPABILITIES

Percentage of customers using your website for information gathering on your products/services
Percentage of customers using social media for information gathering on your products/services
Percentage of customers using mobile applications for information gathering on your products/services
Inquiries per $10,000 of advertisement

DEVELOP MARKETING STRATEGY

Customer wallet share
Market share
Key customer growth
Key customer profitability
Key customer retention rate
Relative change in brand performance over the past three years
Percentage of customers who can name brand in unaided recall test
Percentage of customers who would recommend product/service to family/friends
Percentage of revenue attributed to customers who made first purchase of the brand
Percentage of customers claiming to be satisfied
Customer retention rate

DEVELOP AND MANAGE MARKETING PLANS

Marketing expenses to sales
Total marketing cost as a percentage of revenue
Marketing budget per marketing FTE
Total annual cost incurred to execute direct marketing campaigns as a percentage of revenue generated
Percentage of business entity's growth in revenues from the top twenty percent of customers
Conversion rate of marketing/sales campaigns

DEVELOP SALES STRATEGY

Budget for sales as a percentage of revenue
Sales budget per sales FTE
Average monthly forecast error measured by the mean absolute percentage error (MAPE)
Percentage error in market forecasts

DEVELOP AND MANAGE SALES PLANS

Average monthly sales forecast error within a product family
Sales FTEs as a percentage of total business entity FTEs
Average sales cycle time from the time the lead/opportunity is identified and the sale is closed
Percentage of order inquiry contacts received through new (such as digital/electric) channels
Percentage of qualified leads where the sale is closed
Number of active customers per sales FTE

Percentage of active customers who are profitable
Percentage of annual net sales revenue attributable to repeat customers
Percentage of active customers who are repeat customers
Average cost per sales order for orders received through new channels
Average cost per sales order for orders received
Total revenue per sales order
Number of FTEs that perform the customer order management function per $1 billion revenue
Percentage of sales order line items delivered on time
Personnel cost of the process "Manage sales orders" as a percentage of total process cost
Sales revenue per employee

4.0 Deliver Physical Products

PLAN FOR AND ALIGN SUPPLY CHAIN RESOURCES
Total annual cost of quality per <1,000> revenue
Number of FTEs for the supply chain planning function per <$1billion> revenue
Annual total inventory turn rate
Production schedule attainment rate for a planning period
Cash to Cash cycle time

PROCURE MATERIALS AND SERVICES
Total cost of the procurement cycle per <$1,000> purchases
Percentage of supplier orders delivered on time
Cycle time in hours to place purchase order
Average purchased materials cost compared to budgeted cost
Percentage of purchase orders issued past due
Percentage of target dates missed
Procurement cost as a percentage of goods and services purchased

PRODUCE/MANUFACTURE/DELIVER PRODUCT
Warranty costs (repair & replacement) as a percent of sales
Scrap & rework costs as a percent of sales
Value of plant shipments per employee
Standard customer lead time (order entry to shipment) in days
Finished goods inventory turn rate
Annual Work-in-Process (WIP) inventory turn rate
Percentage of sales orders delivered on time
Manufacturing cycle time in hours
Defective units (ppm) as a percentage of all units
Percentage of processes with yields at six sigma
Rework and repair hours as a percentage of direct manufacturing hours
Scrap and rework percentage reduction
Warranty cost reduction percentage
Yield improvement
Manufacturing cycle time

MANAGE LOGISTICS AND WAREHOUSING
Total cost to perform the this process as a percentage of costs of goods sold
Total transportation cost per $1,000 revenue
Percentage of the total cost of the supply chain function allocated to transportation
Total cost of the this process per $1 billion revenue

Cycle time in hours from receiving a customer's order to completing the order's preparation
Expedited costs as a percentage of total cost of the logistics process group
Turnover rate of logistics personnel
Cost of damaged product as a percentage of sales
Value of inventory shrinkage as a percentage of cost of goods sold (COGS)
Direct labor as a percentage of total labor used in this process
Percentage of orders expedited
Percentage of sales orders filled completely from the primary sourcing location
Percentage of orders shipped complete and on time
Inventory accuracy
Picking error rate
Warehouse inventory (dollar value) as a percentage of sales dollars
Stock turns per year

5.0 Deliver Services

ESTABLISH SERVICE DELIVERY GOVERNANCE AND STRATEGY
Total cost to perform this process per $1,000 revenue
Personnel cost to perform this process per $1,000 revenue
Percentage of client/customer facing employees

MANAGE SERVICE DELIVERY RESOURCES
Personnel cost to perform this process per $1,000 revenue
Percentage of client/customer facing employees

DELIVERY SERVICE TO CUSTOMERS
Personnel cost to perform this process per $1,000 revenue
Percentage of client/customer facing employees
Number of complaints
First-call resolution rate
Percentage of incidents reported more than once by customer
Percentage of customers who are satisfied
Percent of overdue service requests
Percentage of on-time deliveries
Average response time to resolve complaint

6.0 Manage Customer Service

DEVELOP CUSTOMER CARE/CUSTOMER SERVICE STRATEGY
Total cost to perform this process per $1,000 revenue
Number of FTEs that perform this process per $1 billion revenue
Number of languages supported at the business entity

PLAN AND MANAGE CUSTOMER SERVICE CONTACTS
Personnel cost to perform these processes per active customer
Average call handling time in seconds
Average seat utilization
Call agent availability rate
First call resolution rate
Average number of calls customer service representatives handle per week
Average time to resolve a customer inquiry
Number of FTEs who perform the customer service function per $1 billion revenue

Customer call waiting time
Duration of typical customer service phone call
Percentage of calls that are abandoned, delayed, or answered by recording

SERVICE PRODUCTS AFTER SALES
Total warranty costs as a percentage of sales
Average cycle time from detection-to-correction of issues
Warranty claims rate
Average annual product return rate
Returned product repair time

EVALUATE CUSTOMER SERVICE OPERATIONS AND CUSTOMER SATISFACTION
Customer attrition (or churn) rate
Amount of time between initial purchase and customer survey
Cost per survey
Current customer satisfaction level
Frequency of surveys
Improvement in customer satisfaction
Survey return rate

7.0 Develop and Manage Human Capital

DEVELOP AND MANAGE HUMAN RESOURCES PLANNING, POLICIES, AND STRATEGIES
Total cost to perform this function per function FTE
Total cost to perform this process per $1,000 revenue
Number of employees served per function employee

RECRUIT, SOURCE, AND SELECT EMPLOYEES
Total cost to perform this function per function FTE
Total cost to perform this process per $1,000 revenue
Number of employees served per function employee
Permanent full-time new hires as a percentage of total new hires
Percentage of new hire retention after 12 months
Average time to recruit
Average open time of job positions
Average cost to recruit per job position
Cycle time in days from identification of need to hire to approval of job requisition
Cycle time in days from transfer request to transfer completion
Ratio of qualified applicants to total applicants
Number of days to respond to applicant

DEVELOP AND COUNSEL EMPLOYEES
Total cost to perform this function per function FTE
Total cost to perform this process per $1,000 revenue
Number of employees served per function employee
Training penetration rate
Percent of new hire retention after 12 months
Percentage of employees receiving regular performance and career development reviews
Average training days per employee
Ratio of promotions to total employees

Ratio of openings filled internally vs. externally
Average number of years or months between promotions
Percentage of employees with development plans

MANAGE EMPLOYEE RELATIONS
Total cost to perform this process per $1,000 revenue
Total cost to perform this function per function FTE
Number of employees served per function employee
Cycle time transfer request to transfer completion

REWARD AND RETAIN EMPLOYEES
Total cost to perform this function per function FTE
Total cost to perform this process per $1,000 revenue
Number of employees served per function employee
Management compensation as a percentage of total compensation
Percentage of total compensation tied to performance
Retirement plan utilization percentage

REDEPLOY AND RETIRE EMPLOYEES
Total cost to perform this function per function FTE
Total cost to perform this process per $1,000 revenue
Number of employees served per function employee
Retirement plan utilization percentage
Average staff turnover costs
Total cost incurred by employee turnover

MANAGE EMPLOYEE INFORMATION AND ANALYTICS
Total cost to perform this function per function FTE
Total cost to perform this process per $1,000 revenue
Percentage of employees with access to Employee Self Service (ESS) system
Cycle time from employee survey/feedback to action plan
Response time from HR specialists on written/e-mail queries

MANAGE EMPLOYEE COMMUNICATION
Total costs of communication with employees processes per <$1,000> revenue
Total costs of communication with employees processes per employee

8.0 Manage Information Technology summary of process measures

MANAGE THE BUSINESS OF INFORMATION TECHNOLOGY
Total cost of IT operations, including depreciation/amortization, per $1,000 revenue
Average build-to-launch time in months for major new or enhanced IT services
Overhead cost of this process per $100,000 revenue
Average IT spending per FTE

DEVELOP AND MANAGE IT CUSTOMER RELATIONSHIPS
Total cost of this process per $1,000 revenue
Percentage of business entity IT FTEs who perform this process of managing customer relationships
Percentage of IT budget allocated to this process

DEVELOP AND IMPLEMENT SECURITY, PRIVACY, AND DATA PROTECTION CONTROLS
Total cost of this process per $1,000 revenue
Percentage of systems (workstations, laptops, servers) with latest antivirus/antispyware signatures
Percentage of virus incidents requiring manual cleanup relative to all virus incidents within a period
Percentage of email spam messages stopped within measurement period
Percentage of downtime due to security incidents
Number of detected (successful and unsuccessful) network attacks

MANAGE ENTERPRISE INFORMATION
Total cost of this process per $1,000 revenue
Average time in weeks to create the enterprise information management strategic plan
Percentage of information elements with assigned and active data custodians
Percentage of availability Service Level Agreements (SLAs) met

DEVELOP AND MAINTAIN INFORMATION TECHNOLOGY SOLUTIONS
Total cost of this process per $1,000 revenue
Average IT budget variance for application development and maintenance projects
Average schedule variance for application development and maintenance projects
Number of applications in the enterprise portfolio per $1 billion in revenue
Average time in minutes to resolve highest priority problems (current year)
Time in months to fulfill a business need with relevant IT solutions for major new/enhanced IT services
Number of service oriented architecture services implemented
Average backlog for the current year
Percentage of projects completed on time

DEPLOY INFORMATION TECHNOLOGY SOLUTIONS
Total cost of this process per $1,000 revenue
Average time in days to deploy new computing capacity
Average time in weeks to deploy a new release into the production environment
Percentage of unscheduled outages from release introductions

DELIVER AND SUPPORT INFORMATION TECHNOLOGY SERVICES
Total cost of this process per $1,000 revenue
Average time in hours to resolve a service commitment disruption
Level of FTE experience in years for this process group
Number of IT FTEs for this process group
Percent of tickets and transactions meeting agreed turn-around time
Average duration of unscheduled outages
Average resolution time of incident reports received

9.0 Manage Financial Resources Process Measures

PERFORM PLANNING AND MANAGEMENT ACCOUNTING
Total cost of this process per <$1,000> in revenue
Personnel cost to perform these processes per process FTE
Cycle time in days to complete the annual budget
Cycle time in days to prepare the financial forecast
Number of budget versions produced before final approval
Percentage error for the inventory cost forecast
Percentage error for the personnel cost forecast

Total revenue per active customer
Cycle time in days to perform financial evaluation of new customers
Revenue per employee for the current reporting period
EBITDA margin (current reporting period)

PERFORM REVENUE ACCOUNTING
Total cost of this process per <$1,000> in revenue
Number of receipts processed per "accounts receivable" FTE
Personnel cost to perform the process "process customer credit" per $1,000 revenue
Total cost to perform the order to invoice processes per $1,000 revenue
Percentage of total receipts that are processed error free the first time
Average days sales outstanding
Cycle time in days from transmission of invoice to receipt of payment
Accounts receivable turnover
Cycle time in days for credit approval

PERFORM GENERAL ACCOUNTING AND REPORTING
Total cost of this process per <$1,000> in revenue
Personnel cost to perform these processes per process FTE
Cycle time in days to complete the monthly financial close
Cycle time in days to produce period-end management reports
Percentage of journal entries that are first time error free
Average age of general ledger systems
Number of errors in financial reports
Cycle time in days to complete the monthly consolidated financial statements

MANAGE FIXED-ASSET PROJECT ACCOUNTING
Total cost of this process per <$1,000> in revenue
Personnel cost to perform these processes per process FTE
Actual capital expenditure as a percentage of budgeted capital expenditures for one year prior
Cycle time in days to approve a capital project
Return on fixed assets
Fixed asset turnover

PROCESS PAYROLL
Total cost of the payroll process per payroll FTE
Total cost of the payroll processes per employee paid
Cycle time in business days to process time, record data, and enter into payroll system
Cycle time in days to process the payroll
Cycle time in days to resolve a payroll error
Span of control: payroll staff to management ratio
Time card/data preparation error rate

PROCESS ACCOUNTS PAYABLE AND EXPENSE REIMBURSEMENTS
Total cost of this process per <$1,000> in revenue
Personnel cost to perform these processes per process FTE
Payables outstanding per $1,000 revenue
Cycle time in days from receipt of invoice until payment is transmitted
Cycle time in days to resolve an invoice error
Percentage of invoices paid on time
Percentage of invoice line items paid on time

MANAGE TREASURY OPERATIONS
- Total cost of this process per <$1,000> in revenue
- Personnel cost to perform these processes per process FTE
- Cycle time in hours to initiate, approve, and dispatch a wire transfer
- Cycle time in hours to reconcile a single bank account
- Cycle time in days to refresh the cash flow forecast

MANAGE INTERNAL CONTROLS
- Total cost of this process per <$1,000> in revenue
- Personnel cost to perform these processes per process FTE
- Percentage of other non-independent members on the compensation committee
- Cycle time in days from the identification of a control violation until the violation is reported
- Number of control violations per 1,000 business entity employees
- Percentage of primary controls that are automated
- Percentage of primary controls that are detective in nature

MANAGE TAXES
- Total cost of this process per <$1,000> in revenue
- Personnel cost to perform these processes per process FTE

10.0 Acquire, Construct, and Manage Property

PLAN AND ACQUIRE ASSETS
- Total cost of this process per <$1,000> in revenue
- Personnel cost to perform these processes per process FTE
- Cash and equivalents as a percentage of assets
- Accuracy of recorded fixed assets
- Long term assets as a percentage of assets

DESIGN AND CONSTRUCT PRODUCTIVE ASSETS
- Total cost of this process per <$1,000> in revenue
- Personnel cost to perform these processes per process FTE
- Construction cost per square foot
- Projects completed on time as a % of total projects

MAINTAIN PRODUCTIVE ASSETS
- Total cost of this process per <$1,000> in revenue
- Personnel cost to perform these processes per process FTE
- Facility maintenance response time
- Facility coefficient
- Annual maintenance expenditures
- Normalized Annual Maintenance Expenditure (NAME)

DISPOSE OF ASSETS
- Total cost of this process per <$1,000> in revenue
- Personnel cost to perform these processes per process FTE
- Percentage of recorded fixed asset disposals that represent actual disposals
- Percentage of fixed asset disposals that are recorded

11.0 Manage Enterprise Risk, Compliance, Remediation, and Resiliency

MANAGE ENTERPRISE RISK
- Total cost of this process per <$1,000> in revenue
- Personnel cost to perform these processes per process FTE

Percentage of staff trained in risk management techniques
Percent of business services not covered by risk analysis
Percent of risk mitigation plans executed on time.
Percentage of risk incident response plans with one or more open issues

MANAGE COMPLIANCE
Total cost of this process per <$1,000> in revenue
Personnel cost to perform these processes per process FTE

MANAGE REMEDIATION EFFORTS
Total cost of this process per <$1,000> in revenue
Personnel cost to perform these processes per process FTE

MANAGE BUSINESS RESILIENCY
Total cost of this process per <$1,000> in revenue
Personnel cost to perform these processes per process FTE
Time in weeks to complete projects that address a business exposure or opportunity

12.0 Manage External Relationships

BUILD INVESTOR RELATIONSHIPS
Total cost of this process per <$1,000> in revenue
Personnel cost to perform these processes per process FTE

MANAGE GOVERNMENT AND INDUSTRY RELATIONSHIPS
Total cost of this process per <$1,000> in revenue
Personnel cost to perform these processes per process FTE
Percent regulations met by required date
Frequency (in days) of compliance reviews
Percentage of compliance issues handled first time correctly
Backlog of compliance issues

MANAGE RELATIONS WITH BOARD OF DIRECTORS
Total cost of this process per <$1,000> in revenue
Personnel cost to perform this processes per process FTE

MANAGE LEGAL AND ETHICAL ISSUES
Total cost of this process per <$1,000> in revenue
Personnel cost to perform these processes per process FTE
Law-related expense as a percent of revenue
Outside legal expense as a percent of total legal expense
Average time to resolve each type of lawsuit

MANAGE PUBLIC RELATIONS PROGRAM
Total cost of this process per <$1,000> in revenue
Personnel cost to perform these processes per process FTE

13.0 Develop and Manage Business Capabilities

MANAGE BUSINESS PROCESSES
Total cost of this process per <$1,000> in revenue
Personnel cost to perform these processes per process FTE
Dollars saved per employee due to new ideas and/or methods
Number of job improvement ideas per employee

Percentage of employees active in improvement teams
Percentage of time of employees available for improvement activities

MANAGE PORTFOLIO, PROGRAM, AND PROJECT
Total cost of this process per <$1,000> in revenue
Personnel cost to perform these processes per process FTE

MANAGE ENTERPRISE QUALITY
Total cost of this process per <$1,000> in revenue
Personnel cost to perform these processes per process FTE
Percentage of quality audits performed on schedule
Percentage of errors detected during design and process reviews
Percentage of lots going directly to stock
Percentage of quality assurance personnel to total personnel
Receiving inspection cycle time
Average time to answer customer complaints

MANAGE CHANGE
Total cost of this process per <$1,000> in revenue
Personnel cost to perform these processes per process FTE
Percent of change projects successfully completed
Number of improvement opportunities documented per project

DEVELOP AND MANAGE ENTERPRISE-WIDE KNOWLEDGE MANAGEMENT (KM) CAPABILITY
Total cost of this process per <$1,000> in revenue
Personnel cost to perform these processes per process FTE
Percentage of enterprise documents accessible to the search engine
Average age of knowledge assets
Ratio of paper to electronic documents
Frequency of use of knowledge assets in hours

MEASURE AND BENCHMARK
Total cost of this process per <$1,000> in revenue
Personnel cost to perform these processes per process FTE
Number of benchmarking projects conducted
ROI on benchmarking projects
Percentage of benchmarking activities that result in implementation of process enhancements
Average time to complete benchmarking study
Average cost of benchmarking study
Number of new metrics developed

MANAGE ENVIRONMENTAL HEALTH AND SAFETY (EHS)
Total cost of this process per <$1,000> in revenue
Personnel cost to perform these processes per process FTE
Hazardous waste generated
Number of environmental audit-non- compliance and risk issues documented
Number of notice of violations (NOVs) from regulatory agencies
OSHA total recordable incident rate (MR) injuries and illnesses
Packaging waste in pounds
Solid waste in tons

Chapter 3

Benchmarking and the Balanced Scorecard

"If winning isn't everything, why do they keep score?"

—Vince Lombardi

"Money was never a big motivation for me, except as a way to keep score. The real excitement is playing the game."

—Donald Trump

The metrics that we discussed in the last chapter have many uses in an organization. As the above quotes imply, one of the primary reasons for keeping score is to be able to tell how well we are doing relative to our competition. In this chapter we will discuss the two recent developments in metrics that are particularly important from a process point of view, the notion of benchmarking and the innovation of the balanced scorecard.

The basic idea of benchmarking is comparing our processes, products, or services with those of another organization. One use of benchmarking is to "keep score" with our direct competitors to see how we are competing. However, benchmarking has many other uses that are just as important, if not more so, not the least of which is learning how to do things better.

We will also discuss the concept of a balanced scorecard. The balanced scorecard was developed by Kaplan and Norton (1992, 1993) as a counterview to the purely financial measures commonly used to measure organizational performance. The balanced scorecard suggests that we view the organization from four perspectives and that we need to develop metrics and gather data with respect to all four perspectives: the customer perspective, the financial perspective, the business process perspective, and the learning and growth perspective.

We have dedicated this chapter to these two concepts for several reasons. First, they both illustrate the necessity for and use of metrics. Second, they both represent approaches to process improvement which forms a major part of this book. Finally, both methods have been very influential in the process management literature and are part of the common body of knowledge in this area.

Benchmarking

The core concept of benchmarking is relatively simple. It is the comparison of our organizational processes with other processes, either within our own organization or within other organizations. Formally defining benchmarking is not as simple, however, and there are many different definitions in the literature. The difficulty is that benchmarking can be used for different purposes which lead to different definitions. One purpose is to see how we are doing in relation to competing or reference organizations. This is known as *competitive benchmarking*. In other words, competitive benchmarking is a way of keeping score in the "game." What we might call *improvement benchmarking* is a comparison of processes and performance with other organizations for the purposes of organizational learning and process improvement. Here the issue is not "keeping score" but trying to improve our organizational processes. No matter what the purpose, comparison is at the heart of the benchmarking process.

Anderson (2007, p. 222) presents a very workable definition of benchmarking most directly aimed at the goal of process improvement:

> "*Benchmarking* is the process of continuously measuring and comparing one's business processes against comparable processes in leading organizations to obtain information that will help the organization identify and implement improvements."

The key words in this definition are (1) *measurement:* benchmarking involves the use of metrics, (2) *comparison:* benchmarking always inherently involves comparisons, (3) *learning:* even with competitive benchmarking, learning is a key benefit of benchmarking, and (4) *improvement:* the end goal of benchmarking is always process improvement. This last point would seem to imply that benchmarking should appear in Part IV of this text which deals with process improvement. Indeed, benchmarking will be part of our discussion in that section. Our purpose in discussing it here is to emphasize the metrics aspect of benchmarking and the importance of process measures.

TYPES OF BENCHMARKING

By its very definition, benchmarking involves two parties, a *client* organization doing the benchmarking and a *target* organization that provides the comparable process. Benchmarking efforts can be classified along two dimensions. The first dimension is defined by the nature of the target organization (which is being compared). There are three different categories based on this dimension:

- Internal benchmarking: The target organization is within the same firm as the client organization.
- Competitor benchmarking: The target organization is a direct competitor of the client organization.
- Global benchmarking: The target organization is the best at what is being benchmarked regardless of location or industry.

These different types of benchmarking differ in terms of purpose and in the difficulty involved in the benchmarking effort. Internal benchmarking tends to be used most often for inter-organizational learning. In other words, it is primarily for use in transferring best practices within the organization. Competitor benchmarking is usually used for monitoring and evaluating an organization's performance relative to its competitors. Finally, global benchmarking, the type most discussed in the literature, is primarily oriented to process improvement by learning from the "best" at that particular process. Also, the further away the target is from the client organization, the more creativity and effort involved in the benchmarking process, as we will discuss in Part IV of the text.

The second method of classifying benchmarking efforts is by the characteristics being benchmarked (what is being compared). There are four categories based on this dimension:

- Performance benchmarking: The comparison of performance metrics between the client and target organizations.
- Process benchmarking: A comparison of how a process is performed. This type of benchmarking goes beyond the metrics to the details of how the process is done.
- Product benchmarking: A direct comparison of products or services provided. One use of this type of benchmarking is in terms of new product design, such as reverse engineering a competing product to get ideas for designing your own product or service.
- Strategic benchmarking: A comparison of how organizations compete at a strategic level.

In theory, a given benchmarking effort can involve any combination of these two dimensions, as shown in Figure 3.1. In practice, some combinations of these are more useful than others. Figure 3.1 rates each combination with regard to the difficulty of performing the benchmarking and the value of the results. The difficulty of performing a benchmarking activity relates primarily to two factors: the degree of cooperation required from the target organization and the availability of the relevant data, i.e. the existence of good metrics. Although the value of a benchmarking effort is a highly subjective evaluation and the results of benchmarking efforts depend on a variety of factors, the values entered into Figure 3.1 are meant to represent the usual results. We do not mean to imply that even in those cells where the value ranking is low that benchmarking will never produce positive results. Thus, these labels are meant to be general guidelines—nothing more, nothing less.

Although all of these benchmarking efforts involve metrics, at least at some level, some of them are more directly tied to good metrics than others. It should be apparent that performance benchmarking, if it is to be objective, requires high-quality metrics. Otherwise the comparison will fall prey to bias and the goals and objectives of those doing the benchmarking. Thus the difficulty rating here depends heavily on the ease of gathering the data. Internal data should be much easier to obtain than external data and certainly easier to obtain than data from a competitor. However, sometimes performance data from competitors may be available through industry groups and trade associations. The value dimension in Figure 3.1 is, first, a combination of estimates of how much the benchmarking will help the improvement efforts of the client organization and secondly, how valuable the improvements will be to the client firm. As we will explore in later

Figure 3.1 Benchmarking Classified by Nature of the Target Firm and Type of Benchmark

	Internal	Competitor	Global
Performance	D: Easy V: Low	D: Moderate to Hard V: Medium to High	D: Moderate to Hard V: Low
Process	D: Easy V: Low to Medium	D: Moderate to Hard V: Medium	D: Moderate to Hard V: High
Product	D: Easy V: Low	D: Moderate to Hard V: Medium to High	D: Hard V: Low
Strategic	D: Easy V: Low	D: Moderate to Hard V: Medium to High	D: Hard V: Low to Medium
Ratings	Difficulty (D) Value (V)	Easy Low	Moderate Medium	Hard High

sections, not all improvements are equal in scope or in terms of value. In general, internal benchmarking is usually of low value to the organization. The one exception is the internal comparisons of processes. Internal benchmarking can be a big part of organizational learning as envisioned by Peter Senge (1990). For example, benchmarking can be a valuable tool for sharing information learned through competitor or global benchmarking with other parts of the organization.

In summarizing Figure 3.1 we can state that some benchmarking efforts are done very frequently but are of dubious value. For example, comparisons of internal performance measures across departments within a company, or companies within a corporation, are a staple in business. Maybe part of the reason is that they are usually very easy to do. On the other hand, they are often of little value in that they do not provide any suggestions for performance improvements. Some cells in the matrix are likely to be of little value, such as generic performance benchmarking, even if it could be done easily. Comparing our performance with an entirely different organization in an entirely different industry is not likely to contribute much insight.

Three cells in the matrix deserve special mention because of their importance. The first is competitor benchmarking of performance. It is always a good idea to have an idea of how well our performance stacks up in comparison with our competitors. The data often published by industry groups and trade associations are an effort to facilitate this type of comparison. A second type of comparison process that is often discussed in the strategic management literature is competitor benchmarking of strategic processes. Data about competitors' strategies may not always be easy to obtain but can be invaluable in planning strategic responses in a highly competitive environment. The last important type of comparison, and the one that is especially important for our purposes, is the generic benchmarking of processes. This is the most useful form of benchmarking for purposes of improvement and it will be the focus in Part IV when we discuss process improvement. Indeed, when publications use the term benchmarking, they are usually referring to this type of comparison.

PROCESS BENCHMARKING: A STEP-BY-STEP APPROACH

If there is one thing that benchmarking experts seem to agree on it is that the benchmarking should be systematic and well organized. Camp (1989) identifies a 10-step approach to good benchmarking practice. These steps are as follows:

1. **Decide what to benchmark:** This is often not as simple as it sounds. You first need to identify the processes that are important to your organization. You also need to determine what metrics are available both internally and externally. External sources may be from industry or trade associations, business publications, governmental sources, and library material.
2. **Identify whom to benchmark:** You next need to identify targets that have superior business processes. Again sources can be the same as above, with special attention paid to organizations receiving awards from professional groups for process improvements.
3. **Plan and conduct investigation:** Spend time looking at statistics and metrics for your firm and others. Try to understand which measures are relevant, timely and accessible. Refine the questions to be asked. Contact other firms that are willing to serve as benchmark partners. Perform site visits. These are not plant tours; rather they are focused on specific practices.
4. **Determine the performance gap:** Identify the areas where internal performance lags industry or a specific firm's performance.
5. **Project future performance levels:** If changes are to be made, where will these measures of performance be in one year? Two years? Ten years?
6. **Communicate benchmarking findings and gain acceptance:** Discuss with management the gaps that have been determined and what increases in performance are possible.

7. **Revise performance goals:** Based upon discussions with management a fine tuning of goals may be needed.
8. **Develop action plan:** In detail identify the changes that will be made to a specific process. This should include technology changes, work-flow revisions, reduction of non-value-added steps, and similar actions. Define measurement criteria for these changes.
9. **Implement specific actions and monitor performance:** Make the changes and see if performance improves or not.
10. **Recalibrate benchmarks:** Review the benchmarks that have been established to determine if targets remain relevant and achievable. Identify new measurements that may become relevant.

This 10-step process emphasizes that benchmarking is not a onetime activity. If implemented fully it is part of the organizations ongoing continuous improvement activities and begins anew with reviewing the performance of the organizations processes and determining which would be good candidates for benchmarking and improvement. Armstrong (2007) provides a good benchmarking example in the context of university housing that illustrates many of these steps in the process.

BENCHMARKING CODE OF CONDUCT

Benchmarking by its very nature involves working closely with another organization. We have also emphasized that benchmarking is not a one-time activity but is an ongoing process. These two facts make it clear that it is in the organization's best interest to maintain good relationships with its benchmarking partners. Ethical conduct in benchmarking is therefore very important. The American Productivity and Quality Center (APQC) has published a code of conduct for benchmarking that is widely used in industry. In fact, many companies such as Kodak will look for explicit reference to the code of conduct in the benchmarking invitation in deciding whether or not to participate. The code of conduct revolves around eight principles:

1. **Principle of Legality:** Ensure that all actions involved in the benchmarking activity are legal, especially with respect to such issues as restraint of trade or price fixing.
2. **Principle of Exchange:** Benchmarking is a two-way street and you should be honest and complete in your information exchange and be willing to provide the same information that you request from the target firm.
3. **Principle of Confidentiality:** Benchmarking information must be treated as confidential and even a firm's participation in a benchmarking study should not be released without their permission.
4. **Principle of Use:** Use the information gained from benchmarking only for the purposes stated to your benchmarking partner.
5. **Principle of Contact:** Respect the corporate culture of the target organization and work with only the representatives designated by the firm.
6. **Principle of Preparation:** Demonstrate commitment to the process by being well prepared in advance of the benchmarking contact. Make the most of your partner's time by being prepared.
7. **Principle of Completion:** Follow through on your commitments to your benchmarking partner and honor all commitments.
8. **Principle of Understanding and Action:** Understand how your benchmarking partner would like to be treated and treat them that way.

By following these guidelines, an organization can help insure that organizations that they deal with in benchmarking efforts will be willing to work with them in future efforts. News travels fast if firms do not follow these guidelines, and noncompliant firms will be hard pressed to find benchmarking partners in the future.

BENCHMARKING EXAMPLES AND BEST PRACTICES

There is certainly no shortage of benchmarking studies in the literature. A few examples are reports of benchmarking in public utilities (Conner, 2007), retail banking (Remink, 2007), financial planning (Powell, 2007), hospitality (Battersby, 2007), hospitals (Sower, 2007), insurance (Boone, 2007), and universities (Armstrong, 2007). More and more trade and industry groups are publishing benchmarking information so that companies can compare their performance with their competition. However, much of this benchmarking activity is oriented toward the competitor-performance cell of Figure 3.1. Although there is nothing wrong with this, we need to keep in mind that the best chance of improving the overall competitive position of the organization is through global-process benchmarking (Sower 2007). In this section, we set forth some reminders and caveats about benchmarking to reset the focus on the primary purpose of benchmarking—learning from others in order to improve our own performance.

Benchmarking Is Not Just Keeping Score

As Sower (2007, p. 58) reminds us, "True benchmarking is not simply comparing outcome measures with industry averages." In fact, simply comparing numbers can often be deceiving. For example, one organization's benchmarking data showed what appeared to be significant performance differences between two company sites. Each site was handling very similar work—in fact, they both were servicing the same client—but figures associated with cost and profitability were dramatically different. The company eventually discovered that one location had operated for over 20 years and the other for only 3 years. The older facility had many employees at the top of their pay scale while the new facility had virtually none, which certainly accounted for the differences in performance and cost. This illustrates that often we need to go beyond the *what* of the numbers to the *why* of the numbers.

Analyze the Hows as Well as the Whats

It is not enough to note that there is a performance gap between your organization and a "best-in-class" firm. The gap tells you nothing about the why. To be useful for process improvement, benchmarking must go beyond the simple performance measurements to understand how the target company does it differently. What about its process and how it does things enable it to produce superior performance? Although it takes a lot more work to dig below the superficial reasons to find the underlying causes, this is where the true value in benchmarking lies. As Bowerman, Ball, and Francis (2001) point out with regard to the public sector, it is very difficult to keep this in mind when the tensions of dealing with performance gaps are so prominent.

Benchmark What Is Needed, Not What Is Easy

The temptation in benchmarking is to use the old familiar metrics like products shipped for a computer manufacturer, or percentage seats filled per flight for an airline. However, these metrics usually will not produce the information that you need to improve your processes. Benchmarking efforts need to be innovative in terms of the metrics that they examine to find those that will help them improve their processes. Target organizations for the benchmarking efforts should be the best at performing the relevant processes, no matter what industry they are in. For example, Rank Xerox, widely credited with the development of the benchmarking practice, targeted the processes and organizations shown in Figure 3.2. As can be seen in the figure, virtually none of these organizations are within Rank Xerox's industry.

Figure 3.2 Rank Xerox Benchmarking Processes and Target Firms

Function/Process	Company Benchmarked
Warehousing and inventory management	L.L. Bean
Billing and collection	American Express
Factory floor layout	Cummins Engines and Ford
Quality improvement	Florida Power and Light
Supplier development	Honda
Research and product development	Hewlett Packard
Manufacturing safety	DuPont

Iacobucci and Nordhielm (2000) recommend using the customer's point of view to determine which metrics to use and which potential target organizations might be the best in class to benchmark. The idea is to review your customers' purchase experience from beginning to end listing all of the steps in the process, and identify factors that influence the customer's perception of value at each step. Then identify measures and potential target organizations that excel at these factors, no matter what industry they are in.

BENCHMARKING SURVEYS

There are a variety of surveys conducted by different organizations that provide benchmarking information across many different processes. Some of these are specific to a particular industry, such as the American Medical Group Association (AMGA). Others are designed to be more general and applicable to a wide variety of industries. Perhaps the best known and most extensive of these is from the American Productivity and Quality Center (APQC). APQC has built a large database of benchmarking data based around their process classification framework described in Chapter 1. The database contains information across a variety of industries for companies all around the world and is available to its members on their website (www.APQC.org). In addition, they provide tools, including survey questions, that can be used for gathering benchmarking information for specific processes. Their website and publications contain a wealth of information about benchmarking.

Balanced Scorecard

Historically, organizations have primarily utilized financial metrics such as ROI, profit, return on equity, and budget compliance to monitor organizational performance and the performance of subunits of the organization. In the 1990s it became increasingly apparent that there were serious weaknesses in a purely financial view of the organization. It was becoming increasingly difficult to connect financial measures with strategic initiatives of the firm and next to impossible to connect them to specific processes and subunits of the firm. For example, although profitability is obviously of prime importance to a for-profit firm, how can we evaluate a function like manufacturing in terms of profitability when so much of what it takes to be profitable, such as sales and revenue generation, is outside the direct control of manufacturing? In addition, although an organization's strategic initiatives should ultimately have implications for financial performance, it is often difficult if not impossible to make a simple direct connection between the two. Kaplan and Norton (1992, 1993) developed an alternative measure of organizational performance, called the balanced scorecard, which was designed to complement traditional financial performance metrics.

THE SCORECARD COMPONENTS

The scorecard is "balanced" by measuring aspects of organizational performance in addition to financial performance. In particular, the balanced scorecard added metrics related to three other areas: internal processes and how well they are performed, external customers and our ability to satisfy them, and the organizations' ability to learn and adapt to its changing environment. All of these measures should be connected to the strategic vision of the organization as illustrated in Figure 3.3. Vision and strategy is at the center because for Kaplan and Norton (1996a, 1996b) the balanced scorecard is very much a tool for strategic planning and execution.

Although Kaplan and Norton's original objective was to balance financial with nonfinancial perspectives, Figure 3.3 also makes it clear that the balanced scorecard also provides additional balance points. For example, it also balances the internal viewpoint with the external (e.g., internal processes and external customers). In addition, it balances past performance (e.g., financial and other backward looking or lagging metrics) with future-oriented measures (e.g., learning and growth).

Figure 3.3   The Four Performance Areas of the Balanced Scorecard

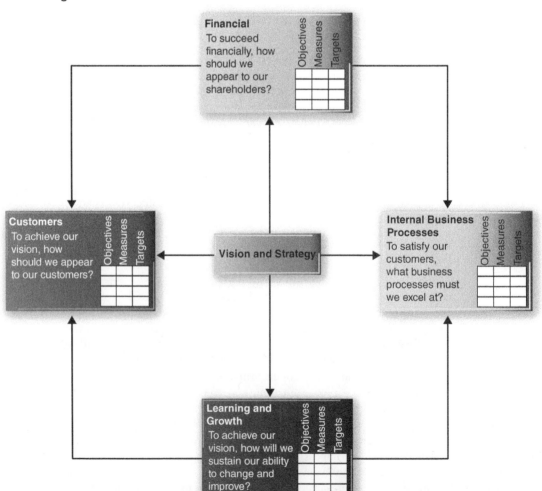

It is important to remember that the balanced scorecard as depicted in Figure 3.3 is a framework, not a detailed performance scorecard. An organization must decide on the specific metrics that are appropriate in each category. In other words, the four categories are generic placeholders for organization-specific metrics. Thus, in many respects, the balanced scorecard forms a framework for organizing the metrics discussed in Chapter 2 and for tying them to organizational strategy.

- **Financial**: The balanced scorecard approach does not suggest that we disregard traditional financial measures; rather, it simply suggests that they be balanced by the other three perspectives and that they link to the vision and strategy of the organization. This involves associating key financial metrics with our strategic objectives. We will explore these linkages more in the next section.
- **Internal Business Processes**: In order to achieve our strategic objectives and fulfill the financial objectives, what internal process do we need to improve and by how much? In other words, what do we need to be good at and how good do we need to be to achieve our objectives?
- **Customer**: From a customer perspective, what do we need to do to achieve our strategic objectives? What kind of measures do we need to track and what factors are important to our customers?
- **Learning and Growth**: This area focuses on the intangible assets of the organization. To achieve our strategic objectives what kinds of employee development are necessary? What kinds of skills do we need to develop to achieve our objectives? The objectives in this area often relate most directly to our objectives in the Internal Business Process component.

Strategy and the Balanced Scorecard

It is important to remember that the balanced scorecard is meant to be a strategic planning tool, and, in fact, the building of the balanced scorecard should be driven by a prior strategic planning process. The strategic objectives should link to objectives in each of the four categories. These objectives in the four components will then lead to the relevant metrics in the four areas.

Example 3.1

A small manufacturer has adopted a strategic objective for the organization of increasing shareholder value. The strategic objective might then link to financial objectives of increasing revenues and decreasing costs. With regard to the customer component, this may translate to an objective of increasing the number of customers. The company will also need to consider what drivers might lead to more customers. For example, it may need to become a price leader in the industry to attract more customers. With regard to the internal business process component, given the objectives already established, it becomes apparent that the company needs to make its core service delivery processes more cost effective. Then in the learning and growth category the company may need to train employees in best practices of cost management or may need to explore technology options to reduce costs. The following diagram shows the linkages discussed above.

Once the strategic objectives are linked to the four components of the scorecard the company can develop metrics and targets for those metrics in each component area. These metrics then become the organization's "dashboard" for performance. It is important to include both outcome metrics (lagged metrics) and driver metrics (leading metrics) in each area. In other words, the outcome metrics show how the company is doing and driver metrics ensure that performance will continue to improve. Some potential metrics and targets for our example situation are shown in Figure 3.5.

Figure 3.4 Strategic Objectives Linked to the Four Components

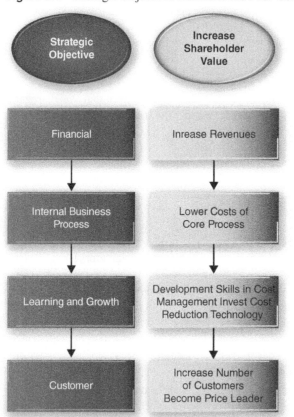

Figure 3.5 Some Example Metrics for Example 3.1

Component	Objective	Metrics	Targets	
			2015	2016
Financial	Revenue Growth	Percent change in Revenue	+10%	+10%
	Utilization of Assets	Utilization Rates	8%	9%
Customer	Customer Retention	Retention Percent	75%	80%
	New Customers	Percent of New Customers	35%	40%
Internal Processes	Manufacturing Costs	Percent of Sales	67%	65%
	Fast Delivery	Delivery Cycle Time	2 hrs	1.5 hrs
	Resource Utilization	Percent of Time Busy	79%	83%
Learning and Growth	Higher Skill Levels	Skill-Set Scores	73%	77%
	Employee Satisfaction	Survey Index	83%	87%

BALANCED SCORECARD EXAMPLES

Perhaps the best way to get a feel for the balanced scorecard approach is to look at some examples. Most of these examples come from the Balanced Scorecard Institute website, which has a variety of materials on the topic (www.balancedscorecard.com). In the interest of space, the examples have been simplified here somewhat. Our purpose in presenting these examples is to illustrate that the balanced scorecard is a framework or approach to linking performance metrics with strategy. As such, the metrics and even the components of the scorecard will vary by application as can be seen from some of the examples. The appendix to this chapter also gives a shortened list of adopters of the balanced scorecard according to the Balanced Scorecard Institute.

University of Virginia Library

The first example comes from the library at the University of Virginia. You may note the slight twist of designating the user perspective rather than the customer perspective in the analysis.

Component	Objective	Metrics	Targets
Financial	Increase the financial base	Library expenditures as a proportion of university expenditures	The library will account for at least 2.50% of the total expenditures
		Amount of development receipts that are unrestricted or minimally restricted	Increase unrestricted (or minimally restricted) giving by 10% each year.
	Maintain sufficient levels of investment to remain a top-flight academic library	ARL index ranking	Rank in the top 20 libraries included in the ARL index.
User	Provide excellent service to users	Overall rating in student and faculty surveys	At least 4.25 out of 5.0 from each of the major user groups
	Provide convenient and timely access to the library's collections	Turn-around time for searches, LEO, and instructional scanning (local resources)	Satisfy the turnaround targets 90% of the time.
Internal Process	Acquire, create, organize, preserve and deliver information resources in a timely, efficient, and accurate manner	Processing time for routine acquisitions	Process 90% of in-print books from North America within one month
	Provide facilities that promote staff productivity, encourage library use, and ensure top quality services	Reliability of servers	Key production servers will be up at least 99.9% of the time
Learning and Growth	Foster learning among its employees to encourage creativity, cooperation, and innovation	Value of library-provided training	An overall rating of at least 4.0 out of 5.0 on training evaluations
	Recruit, develop, and retain productive, highly qualified staff	Retention rate of employees	Retain 95% of employees

Federal Aviation Administration Logistics Center

This example comes from a government application at the Federal Aviation Administration (FAA).

Component	Objective	Metrics	Targets
Financial	Increase revenue and margin	Revenue and cost entries in DAFIS/Delphi general ledger account	Achieve $250M in revenue and obtain 4% margin from operations annually by year 2007. Increase Margin from Operations to a minimum of 2.5% by FY03
	Maintain cost-effective service fee structure for results vehicle	Fee schedule	Fee schedule at or below competition
Customer	Increase customer satisfaction	Customer satisfaction rating	Establish the customer satisfaction baseline by year 2003 and improve rating by 10% by FY07
	Increase customer support to enhance system availability	Response time, back-orders, and issue effectiveness	Establish the baseline by FY03 and improve 25% by FY07 for each measure.
Internal Process	Reduce average repair time for LRU repair and establish an improved methodology for standard repair	Average repair time	Reduce average repair time for LRU in repair facilities by 10% over FY01 baseline
	Reduce the number of reds and yellows in the supportability report and the number of bad actor Line Replaceable Units (LRUs) in the R&M report	Current number of systems reported in the supportability report	Decrease the number of nonsupportable, unreliable and non-maintainable LRUs
Learning and Growth	Increase number of annual technology or tool innovations	Number of innovations; scale of innovations	Minimum of one major innovation per year and (2) minor innovations to achieve $50M in additional acquisition volume per year
	Increase project management and consulting capability.	Number of certified project managers and engineers	85% of project management and consulting workforce certified by end of FY07

Regional Airlines

The last example, shown in Figure 3.5, is a fictional example from the Balanced Scorecard Institute. This example illustrates two additional aspects of the balanced scorecard. First, the example includes a strategy map that shows the strategic linkages for each component. Second, the example also contains initiatives or programs of action to achieve the desired results. This is also a common component of the balance scorecard.

Finally, for an excellent demonstration of the benefits of the balanced scorecard approach in a hospital setting, see Meliones (2000).

Theme: Operating Efficiency	Objectives	Measures	Targets	Initiatives
Financial — Profitability, Lower Costs, Increase Revenue	• Profitability • Increased revenue • Fewer Planes	• Market Value • Seat Revenue • Plane Lease Cost	• 25% per year • 20% per year • 5% per year	• Optimize routes • Standardize planes
Customer — On-time flights, More Customers, Lowest Prices	• On-time Flights • Lowest prices • More Customers	• FAA on time arrival rating • Customer ranking • Number of customers	• First in industry • 98% satisfaction • % change	• Quality management • Customer loyalty program
Business Processes — Improve Turnaround Time	• Fast ground turnaround	• On Ground Time • On-time departure	• Less than 20 Minutes • 92%	• Cycle time optimization program
Learning and Growth — Lowest Prices	• Ground crew alignment	• % Ground crew stockholders • % Ground crew Trained	• yr. 1 70% • yr. 2 90% • yr. 3 100%	• Stock ownership plan • Ground crew training

Source: Adapted from an older file downloaded from the Balanced Scorecard Institute. A newer revised file is available at http://balancedscorecard.org/Portals/0/PDF/REgional_Airline.pdf.

Chapter Glossary

Balanced scorecard A performance measurement approach designed to enhance the strategic planning process and to balance the financial perspective with the other perspectives: the customer, internal business processes, and learning and growth.

Benchmarking The process of continuously measuring and comparing one's business processes against comparable processes in leading organizations to obtain information that will help the organization identify and implement improvements.

Client The organization performing the benchmarking.

Competitive benchmarking Benchmarking in which the target is a competitor and the purpose is to assess the organization's competitive position.

Improvement benchmarking Benchmarking in which the purpose is to improve a process within the organization by comparing it with a superior process of another organization.

Organizational learning The cooperative process by which members of an organization learn to make sense of and respond to changes in the environment as a group.

Target The organization being benchmarked.

Discussion Questions and Problems

1. Discuss how benchmarking might be used in process design and in process improvement. What types of benchmarking would be most useful in the design and improvement activities?

2. Search the Internet to find a case study of an actual benchmarking study. Answer the following questions and make sure to provide the source for your information:
   a. What were the goals of the benchmarking study?
   b. What type of benchmarking was conducted?
   c. What were the outcomes of the benchmarking effort?

3. Vinfen is a private, non-profit human services organization located in Cambridge, Massachusetts that provides a comprehensive array of services to adults and children with mental illness, mental retardation, and behavioral health disabilities. Their mission statement underscores that they are in the business of "transforming lives":

   Vinfen transforms lives by building the capacity of individuals, families, organizations, and communities to learn, thrive, and achieve their goals. As a human services leader, we strive to be the provider, employer, and partner of choice.

   Vinfin works as closely as possible to the people they serve—near their families and in their communities. That's why Vinfen supports more than 300 sites with 2,000 employees in Massachusetts, from the New Hampshire border to Greater Boston to Cape Cod, as well as in Connecticut. Most of their locations are kept intentionally small, enabling them to interact with individuals, families, and communities in a highly personalized manner. Vinfin's primary strategic objective is to remain financially sustainable as an organization. In order to do this, they know that they have to deliver consistent services to their clients. However, increased management and staff turnover has been a problem lately. They also know that they will have to increase public awareness of their organization. They also know that they have to control costs at their facilities, especially the use of overtime. Their executive director has also developed a strategic goal of becoming a learning organization. Part of this emphasis is on recruiting and retaining a highly skilled work force. Develop an outline of a balanced scorecard for Vinfin with appropriate metrics and reasonable targets for each perspective.

4. Stephen Walls College (SWC) is a small private school located in a rural setting with 50 full-time faculty members and another 25 part-time and adjunct faculty. The student body of approximately 1,500 students is overwhelmingly Caucasian and middle class and come primarily from the surrounding region. SWC has a very good academic reputation and is known for its small class sizes and dedicated faculty. The curriculum is primarily liberal arts but SWC does have a School of Business which accounts for about 25% of the student enrollment.

   Like many private colleges SWC is primarily tuition driven with a limited endowment of approximately $25 million and has struggled financially in recent years. The administration at SWC knows that in order to survive the university must do two things: (1) increase financial stability by becoming less tuition dependent by increasing its endowment and (2) increase the diversity of its students, faculty and staff in order to broaden the enrollment base of the university. The president of SWC knows that the school needs to enhance its academic reputation in order to attract more students and to broaden the donor base. Develop an outline of a balanced scorecard for SWC with appropriate goals and related metrics. All four perspectives should be represented in your score card.

References

Anderson, B. *Business Process Improvement Toolbox*, 2nd Edition, 2007, Milwaukee, WI: Quality Press.
Armstrong, M.J. Benchmarking Goes to School, *Quality Progress*, 2007, 40, 5, 54–58.
Battersby, D. Do you measure up on productivity?, *Caterer & Hotelkeeper*, 2007, 197, 2, 40–41.
Boone, E. From Better to Best: The Power of Benchmarking, *Rough Notes*, 2007, 150, 5, 34–38.
Bowerman, M. A. Ball, & Francis, G. Benchmarking as a Tool for the Modernization of Local Government, *Financial Accountability & Management*, 2001, 17, 4, 321–329.
Camp, R.C. Benchmarking: *The Search for Industry Best Practices That Lead to Superior Performance*, 1989, Milwaukee, WI: ASQC Quality Press
Conner, P. Benchmark Your Key Customer Service Processes, *American Gas*, 2007, 89, 3, 36.
Iacobucci, D. & Nordhielm, C. Creative Benchmarking, *Harvard Business Review*, 2000, 78, 6, 24–25.
Kaplan R. S. & Norton D. P., The Balanced Scorecard: Measures That Drive Performance, *Harvard Business Review*, 1992, 70, 1, 71–80.
Kaplan R. S. & Norton D. P., Putting the Balanced Scorecard to Work, *Harvard Business Review*, 1993, 71, 5, 2–16.
Kaplan, R.S. & Norton, D.P., Using the Balanced Scorecard as a Strategic Management System, *Harvard Business Review*, 1996a, 74, 1, 75–85
Kaplan, R.S. & Norton, D.P. *The Balanced Scorecard: Translating Strategy into Action*, 1996b, Boston, MA: Harvard Business School Press.
Meliones, J. Saving Money, Saving Lives, *Harvard Business Review*, 2000, 78, 6, 57–67.
Powell, R. The Boom in Benchmarking Studies, *Journal of Financial Planning*, 2007, 20, 7 Supplement, 5–23.
Remink, T. Benchmarking Your Branches, *Community Banker*, 2007, 15, 3, 36–38.
Senge, P. M. *The Fifth Discipline: The Art and Practice of the Learning Organization*, 1990, London: Random House.
Sower, V.E. Benchmarking in Hospitals: More Than a Scorecard, *Quality Progress*, 2007, 40, 8, 58–60.

Appendix

This is a partial list of adopters of the balanced scorecard from the Balanced Scorecard Institute (www.balancedscrorecard.org). This is not intended to be a comprehensive list of adopters and is not even the full list at the institute. It is intended only to give the reader an impression of what types of organizations are adopting the approach.

Organization	Sector	Country
Allfirst Bank	Banking	USA
Ann Taylor Stores	Retail	USA
AT&T Canada Long Distance	Telecommunications	Canada
Bank of Tokyo-Mitsubishi	Banking	Japan
Blue Cross Blue Shield of Minnesota	Health Care	USA
BMW Financial Services	Financial Services	Germany
Bonneville Power Administration	Utilities	USA
Boston Lyric Opera	Entertainment	USA
British Telecommunications Worldwide	Telecommunications	UK
California State University system	Higher Education	USA

Continued

Organization	Sector	Country
Carleton University	Higher Education	Canada
Caterpillar, Inc.	Manufacturing	USA
Chemical Bank	Banking	USA
Cigna Property & Casualty	Insurance	USA
City of Charlotte	Local Government	USA
Crown Castle International Corp.	Telecommunications	USA
DaimlerChrysler	Manufacturing	Germany
Defense Logistics Agency	Government	USA
Devereux Foundation	Health Care	USA
Duke University Hospital	Health Care	USA
DuPont	Manufacturing	USA
Equifax, Inc.	Financial Services	USA
ExxonMobil Corp.	Energy	USA
Fannie Mae	Banking	USA
Finnforest, UK	Natural Resources	UK
Ford Motor Company	Manufacturing	USA
Foster Farms	Agriculture	USA
General Electric Company	Manufacturing	USA
Hilton Hotels Corp.	Hospitality	USA
Honeywell	Manufacturing	USA
IBM	Information Technology	USA
Indiana University	Higher Education	USA
KeyCorp	Financial Services	USA
Lloyds TSB Bank	Banking	UK
McCord Travel Mgmt (WorldTravel BTI)	Leisure and Travel	USA
Media General	Media	USA
Mercury Computer Systems, Inc.	Information Technology	USA
Mobil North American Marketing & Refining	Energy	USA
NCR Corp.	Information Technology	USA
Northwestern Mutual	Insurance	USA
Nova Scotia Power, Inc.	Utilities	Canada
Ohio State University	Higher Education	USA
Ontario Hospitals	Health Care	Canada
Pfizer Inc.	Pharmaceuticals	USA
Philips Electronics	Manufacturing	Netherlands
Prison Fellowship Ministries	Humanitarian	USA
Reuters America, Inc.	Financial Services	USA
Ricoh Corp.	Manufacturing	Japan
Royal Canadian Mounted Police	Government	Canada
Saatchi & Saatchi Worldwide	Marketing	USA

Organization	Sector	Country
Scudder Kemper Investments Inc.	Financial Services	USA
Sears Roebuck & Company	Retail	USA
Siemens AG	Manufacturing	Germany
Southern Gardens Citrus Processing Corp.	Food Processing	USA
St. Michael's Hospital	Health Care	Canada
T. Rowe Price Investment Technologies, Inc.	Financial Services	USA
The Handleman Company	Wholesale distribution	USA
UK Ministry of Defence	Government	UK
Unicco Service Co.	Industrial Services	USA
United Way of Southeastern New England	Humanitarian	USA
University of Arizona	Higher Education	USA
University of Virginia Library	Higher Education	USA
University of Washington	Higher Education	USA
UPS	Shipping	USA
US Army Medical Command	Health Care	USA
US West	Telecommunications	USA
Verizon Communications, Inc.	Telecommunications	USA
Walt Disney World Company	Entertainment	USA
Wells Fargo Bank	Banking	USA

Chapter 4

Introduction to Queuing and Simulation

"For a nation which has an almost evil reputation for bustle, bustle, bustle, and rush, rush, rush, we spend an enormous amount of time standing around in line in front of windows, just waiting."

—Robert Benchley

"Teach us, O Lord, the disciplines of patience, for to wait is often harder than to work."

—Peter Marshall

"When in a queue, the other line always moves faster and the person in front of you will always have the most complex of transactions."

—Anonymous

Queue is the British term for "waiting line." As the quote from Benchley indicates, Americans are also all too familiar with the concept of waiting lines. In fact, queues are simply part of our existence, and often we do not give them much thought except to be annoyed when the wait is especially long in a particular situation. We wait in line to check out at the grocery store, wait in line to cash our check at the bank, wait in line to mail a package at the post office, and wait in line to buy tickets to a movie. Even when we are not physically standing in line, we are often in a queue. For example, when we are on hold for customer support for a particular computer problem, we are in a queue, even if the line is not visible to us.

In Figure 1.1 in Chapter 1, we represented a process as an interconnected network of activities and buffers. At that time we mentioned that the buffers were temporary holding points for flow units, i.e., they represent queues. Therefore, queues are particularly relevant to process management and the careful study of queues can tell us much about process behavior.

In this chapter we will introduce some basic terminology of queuing and then explore some simple queuing models that are mathematical representations of the queuing situation. We will also introduce Excel spreadsheet programs that we will use to solve queuing problems. Following our discussion of queuing theory we will then introduce the basic ideas of *simulation*, a tool that is capable of handling more complex situations that cannot be easily handled with mathematical queuing models. Please keep in mind when studying this chapter that our goal is not to learn everything there is to know about queuing theory but to build a foundation that we can apply to learning about processes in later sections of the text. Some of the terminology in this chapter may seem different from that discussed in previous chapters of the text, but often the concepts are the same or at least similar. Because queuing theory has a long history, it has developed its own terminology. It is important to understand the connection between the concepts here and in earlier chapters in order to apply this material in later sections of the text.

The General Queuing Phenomenon and Terminology

The basic queuing situation is depicted in Figure 4.1. The queuing system consists of a queue, or waiting line, along with a service mechanism that performs the appropriate activity. The process begins when an arrival (flow unit) arrives from a *calling population* and attempts to enter the queue[1]. Arrivals are governed by an arrival process, typically a probabilistic process. After arrival, the flow unit may refuse to enter the queue because the line is too long (*balking*) or it may be refused entry because the area for the queue is too small to admit any more flow units (*blocking*). If neither of these takes place, the flow unit enters the queue and if the service mechanism is occupied with another flow unit, waits until the service mechanism is available. The arrangement of the queue, the *queue configuration*, is an important design decision as we will discuss later. A flow unit may leave the queue and depart the system (*reneging*) if it decides that it has been waiting too long and does not want to wait any longer. Otherwise, when the service mechanism is available, a flow unit is selected from the queue according to some rule (*queue discipline*), the activity is performed, and the flow unit departs the system. It is important to keep in mind that this is a generalized schema of the queuing phenomenon and that not all of

Figure 4.1 The Basic Queuing System

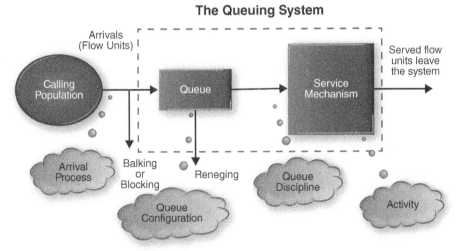

---

1. Arrival is the traditional term used in the queuing literature. Keep in mind that these "arrivals" are flow units in process terminology. We will use both terms in this chapter depending on the context.

these elements will apply to every queuing situation. For example, it is difficult to imagine jobs in a manufacturing facility balking or reneging, although they could be blocked.

CALLING POPULATION

The first element in Figure 4.1 is the calling population. This is the population of all potential arrivals (flow units) that might need the activity performed by the service mechanism. There are several distinctions about the calling population that are important in our discussions of queuing situations.

Homogeneous or Heterogeneous Flow Units

In some situations, the flow units may all be the same (homogeneous) at least with respect to the service being provided. An example might be customers arriving at a grocery store. With respect to providing the basic service, all of these individual customers are largely the same and can be regarded as homogeneous. On the other hand, at a medical clinic there may be distinctly different groups of patients that arrive. For example we might classify patients as walk-ins, appointments, and emergencies. These subgroups often differ in terms of the required services that need to be performed and in terms of their perceptions of waiting. For example, consider the differences in perceptions about waiting for a walk-in patient and an emergency patient. The key point here is that when the calling population is heterogeneous, we may need to treat different flow units differently and take this into account in designing our system.

Finite or Infinite Population Size

A second distinction is whether the calling population is infinite (very large) or finite (very small). Infinity is a mathematical concept that does not often apply in the real world of business, so it is best to think of this in terms of a continuum from a very small population of a few objects or individuals to a population so large that we could not even count all of them. In reality, if a population is quite large we will treat it as being infinite in size and only worry about this distinction if the population is very small. For example, if we are analyzing the customers arriving at a local Walmart or Safeway store, the calling population is quite large, and we can usually safely treat it as infinite in size. On the other hand, if we are analyzing a small four-person real estate office where employees line up to use a copy machine, then the calling population is quite small and we cannot assume an infinite population size. This distinction is very important in developing mathematical models of the queuing situation.

ARRIVAL PROCESS

To adequately describe a queuing system we need to be able to specify the pattern of arrivals to the system. This is usually discussed in terms of what we know about the arrival patterns (i.e., are they deterministic or probabilistic?) and the numerical parameters that we can use to describe the arrivals.

Probabilistic or Deterministic Arrivals

A crucial distinction is whether or not we know the exact pattern of arrivals or if they are essentially random. This usually comes down to a matter of control. If we control or schedule arrivals, such as jobs in a manufacturing facility or appointments for a dentist, then the arrivals can be considered deterministic. If the arrivals are outside of our control, then we usually regard them as probabilistic. If arrivals are probabilistic, then we must specify a probability distribution that describes the pattern of arrivals. Most queuing models assume that arrivals follow what is called a Poisson process so that arrivals have a Poisson probability distribution and the time between arrivals follows an exponential distribution. We will see later in this chapter that it is the randomness of arrivals that make the management of processes with queues so difficult.

Arrival Rates and Times

In addition to knowing the general pattern of arrivals, we also need to know the specific parameters of the arrival distributions. In particular, we need to know at least the mean and standard deviation of the arrivals. The mean arrival parameter can be defined in terms of either a rate or a time. For example, we can state the average arrival rate as 6 per hour. We can also state the arrival parameter as the average time between arrivals, for example the average time between arrivals is 10 minutes. Which method we use to describe the average arrivals is really arbitrary because we can always derive one measure from the other. The relationship between the two measures can be expressed as follows:

$$\text{Rate} = \frac{1}{\text{Time}} \qquad \text{Time} = \frac{1}{\text{Rate}}$$

For example if the average arrival rate is 6 per hour, then the average time between arrivals is

$$\text{Time} = \frac{1}{6} \text{ hours} = 10 \text{ minutes}$$

Conversely, if the average time between arrivals is 10 minutes then the arrival rate is

$$\text{Rate} = \frac{1}{10} \text{ per minute} = 6 \text{ per hour}$$

A common assumption is queuing models is that the arrivals follow a Poisson process. In a Poisson process the following relationship holds between the mean and the standard deviation:

$$\text{Standard Deviation} = \sqrt{\text{Mean}}$$

In other words, in a Poisson process the mean and the variance are the same and the standard deviation is the square root of both values. So if the average arrival rate is 16 per hour, then the standard deviation of arrivals will be 4.

QUEUE CONFIGURATION

The physical arrangement of the queue, where flow units wait, is often an important decision in designing a process. The most interesting configuration issues arise when there is more than one server or resource performing the activity. There are three distinctly different logical queue configurations: (1) an individual queue for each server, (2) a single queue for all servers, or (3) a variation on the take-a-number system which is a single queue with a twist. The three design alternatives are shown in Figure 4.2.

The first configuration with a separate queue for each server is common in grocery and discount stores. There are several disadvantages to such an arrangement. First, as the anonymous quote at the beginning of this chapter (and likely your personal experience) indicates, such an arrangement does not guarantee that just because you are first in line that you will be the first one served. Lines will vary in terms of their speed and it is quite likely that someone who joined another line after you joined your line may be finished before you. This strikes many people as unfair and can also lead to a phenomenon known as *jockeying* where people change lines hoping to find one that moves faster (a strategy that rarely works). Such arrangements are also usually less efficient in the sense of increasing the overall average wait time. The major advantage of such an arrangement is that the servers can be specialized to deal with different types of flow units. Some customers may also have a "favorite" server that they can select in this arrangement. A variant on this arrangement is very familiar to shoppers and is called the express lane. The purpose of an express lane is to reduce the overall average wait of flow units by handling those that can be handled quickly in a separate queue.

Figure 4.2 Possible Queue Configurations

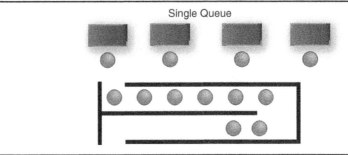

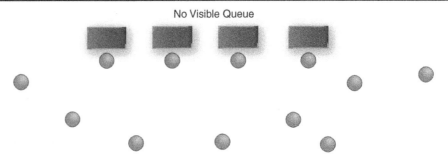

The single queue arrangement is also now familiar to anyone who goes to a bank or a U.S. post office. There are several advantages to this type of arrangement. First, it insures that the system is "fair" in the sense that customers will be served in order of their arrival at the queue, first-come-first-served. Second, it is more efficient than multiple queues in the sense that the overall average wait time tends to be less than it is in multiple queues. It also eliminates the line jockeying behavior that can occur with multiple queues. Lastly, in most of the implementations roped areas are utilized that lead to a "snake" line for the queue (Figure 4.2). This had two additional advantages. It makes the line "appear" to be shorter and therefore tends to reduce balking behavior. The ropes also tend to inhibit reneging behavior since leaving the line is somewhat awkward. On the negative side, this arrangement eliminates freedom of choice of servers for customers and also does not easily allow for differentiation of servers.

The last arrangement in Figure 4.2 is really just a variant on the single queue arrangement where the queue does not physically exist but is contained in the numbering system. The primary benefit of such a system is that balking is reduced because it is difficult to determine how long the queue really is. Many stores that use this type of arrangement have also discovered that it stimulates impulse buying as customers mill around the store waiting for their number to be called. The primary downfall of this system is when the numbering system it is not strictly adhered to. Customers observing others being served without taking a number can cause a great deal of resentment and can cost the organization customers.

QUEUE DISCIPLINE

Flow units are selected from the queue according to a queue discipline rule. This is one area where there is a very clear distinction between manufacturing and service environments. The queue discipline rule used in most service environments, where the flow units are customers, is the first-come-first-served (FCFS) rule. In this rule customers are served in their order of arrival at the queue. However, as we saw earlier, if there are multiple queues, this does not guarantee an overall FCFS over all queues. The problem with the FCFS queue discipline rule is that it ignores all characteristics of the flow units except for their time of arrival at the queue. There are many other characteristics of the flow units whose use may make for more efficient queues. In fact, if flow units arrive at the queue randomly, it can be shown that using the FCFS rule is equivalent to randomly selecting the flow unit to be served next (a decidedly nonrational rule). In a manufacturing context, on the other hand, we can use other characteristics of the flow units because in most cases the flow units are not people. For example we could schedule the flow units in terms of their due dates with the earliest due dates being serviced first (EDD rule) or in terms of how long the activity takes to perform with those having the shortest activity time being performed first (SAT rule). In fact, there is a large body of literature in the operations management area on the use of priority or job shop scheduling rules examining the relative efficiency of different discipline rules in different situations. Our purpose here is simply to illustrate that the queue discipline selected can have an impact on process performance. To illustrate, consider the situation of SameDay dry cleaners.

Example 4.1

SameDay dry cleaning promises same-day service to its customers and in fact, quotes a time that the work will be finished when the customers drop off their dry cleaning. They currently have 6 jobs that need to be done. For the 6 jobs, Figure 4.3 gives the activity or operation time in hours (how long it will take to do the job) and the due date in hours from now. To assess the efficiency of their scheduling, SameDay measures the cycle time and the lateness of jobs. In this case, the total cycle time will be the activity time plus the waiting time. Job lateness is defined as being zero if the job is finished exactly at the due date or if it is finished early. Otherwise, the job lateness is the difference between the finish time and the time the job was due. Figure 4.4 shows the cycle times and lateness for two queue discipline rules. The first is for the FCFS rule assuming that the jobs arrived in alphabetical order. The second schedules jobs in terms of their activity times with the shortest times having the highest priority (SAT rule). In both situations we assume that the start is time zero so that the ending time of an activity is also its cycle time. As you can see, the average cycle time and the average lateness are both much lower with the SAT queue discipline than with FCFS. This example shows that the way we schedule work impacts the waiting time of the flow units.

Figure 4.3 Times and Due Dates for Example 4.1

Job	Activity Time	Due Date
A	5	10
B	10	15
C	2	5
D	8	12
E	6	8
F	4	7

Figure 4.4 Results for the FCFS and SAT Queue Discipline Rules

FCFS Queue Discipline

Schedule	Start Time	End (Cycle) Time	Lateness
A	0	5	0
B	5	15	0
C	15	17	12
D	17	25	23
E	25	31	23
F	31	35	28
Averages:		21.33	14.44

SAT Queue Discipline

Schedule	Start Time	End (Cycle) Time	Lateness
C	0	2	0
F	2	6	0
A	6	11	1
E	11	17	9
D	17	25	13
B	25	35	20
Averages:		16.00	7.17

ACTIVITY TIMES

The activity is where the resources of the process perform the process work. Because work takes time, a major consideration is the activity time and the nature of the time distribution. This is similar to the arrival process previously discussed in that we can talk about the length of time the activity takes or the rate at which the resources can perform the activity. For example, if we can process an average of 4 flow units per hour the average activity time is 1/4 hour or 15 minutes. As with arrivals, it is common to assume that the processing follows a Poisson distribution which means the service or activity times follow an exponential distribution.

A critical issue in the queuing situation is often the capacity of the service mechanism, i.e., the number of resources needed to perform the service activities in order to obtain the best performance from the process. We will examine this question in more detail later in this chapter.

PERFORMANCE MEASURES

Before we can address the question of the best service capacity, we need to be able to measure system performance. Although the terms may sound different here, there is a definite connection between the performance measures discussed in this chapter and the process metrics discussed in Chapter 2.

Most of the performance measures in queuing situations relate either to the number of flow units or time. If we further distinguish between the queue and the system as a whole, we get the following measures:

1. N_q is the average number of flow units in the queue
2. N is the average number of flow units in the entire system, i.e. in the queue and in service.
3. T_q is the average time a flow unit spends in the queue

4. T is the average time a flow unit spends in the entire system
5. *Utilization* (ρ) is a measure of efficiency and is calculated as the percentage of time the resources are busy.

The Economics of Queues

As we noted before, in queuing situations, the main question becomes how much capacity, in terms of resources, do we need in the system? In order to make such a decision, we need some criteria in order to evaluate the different alternatives. In a business context, we would hope that the criteria ultimately could be framed in economic terms. However, this is not always easy to do as it requires estimating the costs of waiting. Although we know that waiting is psychologically distasteful for customers, it is very difficult to frame this in dollar terms. However, there are some situations where we can reliably estimate the cost of waiting, e.g., if the flow units that are waiting in line are our own employees who are waiting to use a piece of equipment or particular tools. This leads to two different decision-making situations. If we do have adequate cost estimates, then the capacity decision can be based on minimizing total costs. However, if we cannot reliably estimate the costs of waiting, then we need to consider the psychological aspects of waiting and choose an appropriate capacity level to optimize one or more performance metrics.

THE PSYCHOLOGY OF WAITING

We are all very aware that waiting is psychologically distasteful. As a FedEx advertisement many years ago noted "waiting is frustrating, demoralizing, agonizing, aggravating, annoying, time consuming and incredibly expensive." Many service operations try to provide diversions to counteract the psychological effects of waiting. For example, magazines are left in the waiting room so that patients have something to do while they wait, and background music is played when you are put on hold during a telephone call. Many services have devised some creative and profitable approaches to this problem such as mirrors near elevators or restaurants that have customers wait in the cocktail lounge. Many of these changes were implemented after the appearance of the classic article by Maister (1985), which discussed the psychology of waiting lines. Much of this material is still relevant today and helps us understand why some things have become rather standard in service environments. To understand the principles discussed, we should first start with what Maister (1985) called "The First Law of Science." In equation form, the law is

$$S = P - E$$

where the S stands for satisfaction, the P stands perception, and E for expectation. The implication is that the satisfaction with the service experience is a function of both perception and expectation and can be changed by influencing either aspect of the equation. This "law" helps put the eight basic principles offered by Maister (1985) in context. The eight principles are

1. **Occupied time feels shorter than unoccupied time,** for example reading material in the waiting area. However, the activity used to fill the waiting time should be related to the service or at least pleasurable for the customer (cf. the annoying "muzak" played during phone waits).
2. **People want to get started** (pre-service waiting seems longer than in-service waiting). Moving some aspects of the service forward so that the perception is that the service has started. For example, handing out menus to those waiting in line at a restaurant or the physician's assistant taking patients vitals before they see the doctor.

3. **Anxiety makes waits seem longer.** Alleviating anxiety lowers the perception of wait time, e.g., customer service agents assuring passengers in line for a reschedule due to airline problems that they are indeed in the correct line and that any connecting flights will be held for them.

4. **Uncertain waits are longer than known, finite waits.** One major source of uncertainty is how long the wait will be. For this reason, restaurants now routinely give arriving customers an estimated wait time. Some give a slightly longer estimate so that customers are pleased when they are called early.

5. **Unexplained waits are longer than explained waits.** Not only do unexplained waits seem longer, they also leave the person waiting with a sense of powerlessness.

6. **Unfair waits are longer than equitable waits.** Nothing infuriates a person waiting so much as perceiving that someone who arrives later than they is served before they are. Service managers must do everything they can to insure that those waiting at least perceive that the time-honored tradition of FCFS is maintained. The problem, as we saw in Example 4.1, is that this tradition leads to longer average wait times. Service enterprises have become more sophisticated in devising ways around this problem while maintaining the experience of fairness. Express lanes in supermarkets are one such example.

7. **The more valuable the service the longer the customer will wait.** Some services segregate customer waiting according to the type of transaction and the difficulty and time taken for that transaction, e.g., separate lines for obtaining boarding passes, checking luggage, and buying tickets. Motels also know that the wait in line to check out is perceived to be low value as compared to the check in, so they have worked to minimize this time.

8. **Solo waits feel longer than group waits.** To understand this, contrast the perceived wait for the doctor alone after seeing the physician's assistant with the wait in the waiting area with a crowd of people.

Maister's (1985) paper stimulated a great deal of research and in an unpublished paper, Norman (2008), updated and revised this list into eight design principles for waiting lines[2].

1. **Emotions dominate.** In Norman's view this is the most important principle. Emotions determine how the waiting situation is perceived and how it is remembered (see principle 8 below). Make the surroundings and the employees as cheerful and pleasing as possible. When problems arise handle them immediately. Emotions are contagious.

2. **Eliminate confusion.** Provide a conceptual model, feedback, and explanation. If there are multiple lines they should be clearly labeled with explanations as to their function. Have you ever experienced standing in a long line only to discover at the end that you were in the wrong line? In line with Maister's (1985) principles, a major source of emotional upset is uncertainty.

3. **The wait time must be appropriate.** Those who have to wait should know why and should agree that the wait is unavoidable and appropriate given the situation. The duration of the wait must also be perceived to be appropriate for the situation.

4. **Set expectations, then meet or exceed them.** Provide feedback on expected wait times and make them realistic. If there is uncertainty about the time, provide the upper limit so that you can possibly exceed expectations.

5. **Keep people occupied: filled time passes more quickly than unfilled time.** Psychological perceptions about the passage of time are influenced by activity and events during that time. Time with no activity or events seems much longer.

---

2. A summary of this essay with examples later appeared in a Sloan Management Review article (Norman 2009).

6. **Be Fair.** Emotional reaction to events is heavily influenced by perceived fairness. Waits in which one perceives that others have an unfair advantage are very negative emotionally.
7. **End strong, start strong.** There is considerable evidence that the start and end of an event are most critical in determining one's memory of an event. The beginning and ending of the wait should be the most pleasant experiences.
8. **Memory of an event is more important than the experience.** It is not the actual experience of the event but the memory of it that is important. Since the end of the event is the part remembered most, this is another reason for finishing strong.

THE ECONOMIC COSTS OF WAITING

In some situations, we can appropriately attribute specific costs to waiting in line. These situations usually involve our own employees who are waiting in line. Then, if we are paying those employees a certain wage per hour, the hourly costs of waiting in line are the lost productivity in wages of those employees. The basic problem is to balance the cost of providing the service (capacity costs) with the costs of keeping the flow units waiting in line (waiting costs). Our objective is to minimize the total costs of running the system.

$$TC = \text{Capacity Costs} + \text{Waiting Costs} \qquad (4\text{-}1)$$

The capacity costs are the most straightforward of these costs. Let C_s represent the per unit server costs (i.e. the costs of the resources performing the service). These will usually be per unit of time (e.g., hourly or daily costs). Let S be the number of servers or the number of resources utilized. Then the per-period capacity costs will be

$$\text{Capacity Costs} = C_s S \qquad (4\text{-}2)$$

For example, if we have 4 employees who are each paid $10 per hour, then our capacity costs will be 4(10) = $40 per hour.

We will also assume that we can measure the waiting costs in terms of dollars per unit per time period. Let this cost be C_w. The queuing models we will describe in this chapter provide us with a value for the average number of flow units in the queue (Nq). Although the number of people in the queue will fluctuate over time, the costs will be equivalent to simply having the average number in the queue for the entire period. In other words, the per period waiting costs will be

$$\text{Waiting Costs} = C_w N_q \qquad (4\text{-}3)$$

Putting this all together we will get the total system costs as

$$TC = C_s S + C_w N_q \qquad (4\text{-}4)$$

A typical set of cost curves is illustrated in Figure 4.5. As you can see from Figure 4.5, total costs will decline with increasing capacity up to a point and will then start to increase again. As we will see later, we can use this knowledge to find the optimum (lowest cost) capacity of the system by systematically increasing capacity until the costs increase rather than decrease.

THE NEED FOR QUEUING MODELS

Whether we are going to make the capacity decision on the basis of the psychological aspects of waiting or on the economic costs, we still need a way to derive performance measures for the process. For an existing process and the current configuration, we can obtain historical data on the performance of the process. However, when making decisions about adding capacity or reconfiguring the process, historical data are of little or no use. We need a way to predict the performance of alternative process configurations. Analytical queuing models give us a way of

Figure 4.5 Queuing Costs Curves

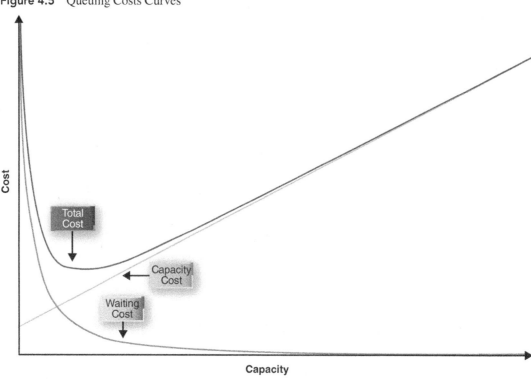

doing precisely that in certain situations. Even if our process does not fit the detailed assumptions of the queuing model exactly, the use of such models can often provide significant insight into the behavior of queues. Therefore, we will now turn to a consideration of a variety of useful queuing models, and following this discussion we will return to the issue of making capacity decisions armed with the tools of analytical queuing models.

Analytical Queuing Models

In this section, we introduce some simple analytical models for a variety of queuing situations. The primary purpose of queuing theory is to provide a system of equations so that probability distributions can be obtained for the states of the system. From these distributions we can then derive the average performance measures. We define the *state of the system* as the number of flow units in the system (both in the queue and in service) at any point in time. We will simplify the presentation here and emphasize the use of the Excel templates that accompany the text to perform the calculations. Mathematical details are available in the appendix to this chapter for those who are interested in them. Before discussing the models, we first need to introduce some notation that will help us classify the situations where the models can be applied.

KENDALL NOTATION

There is a standard notation in queuing theory to help classify the models according to their assumptions. The notation is named the Kendall notation after its developer David George Kendall. The Kendall notation is distinguished by four values generically represented by A, B, C, and D:

$$A/B/C/D$$

The A slot is for the distribution of times between arrivals; the B slot for the distribution of service times; the C slot for the number of servers (i.e. the capacity); and the D slot for the capacity of the queue. If the D slot is omitted, it is assumed to be infinity. In other words, it is assumed that there is no limit on the size of the queue unless stated otherwise. Standard notation is also used for the different possible distributions for slots A and B. Some widely used distributions and their symbols are

> M = exponential distribution
> D = constant distribution
> E = Erlang distribution
> G = general distribution (can be any distribution)

The simplest queuing model is one that assumes exponential arrival and service times, and has a single server and infinite possible queue length. This model, which we will consider next, would then be designated as M/M/1.

THE M/M/1 MODEL

The main parameters of this model are the arrival rate and the service rate. We will designate the arrival rate by the Greek symbol lambda (λ) and the service rate with the symbol mu (μ). Earlier we stated that an analytical queuing model is a set of equations that generate a probability distribution for the states of the system, where the state is the number of flow units in the system. All such models start with an equation for the probability of state 0, in other words, the probability that the system is empty and there are no flow units in the system. The other values are then derived from this root probability. For the M/M/1 model we can state the following equations:

$$P(0) = 1 - \frac{\lambda}{\mu}$$

$$P(n) = P(0)\left(\frac{\lambda}{\mu}\right)^n \tag{4-5}$$

The equations in 4-5 produce the entire probability distribution for the states of the system. What we usually want, however, are just the summary measures like average number in the queue or average time in the queue. Without proof, we can state the following summary results for the M/M/1 model:

Utilization $\quad\quad\quad \rho = \frac{\lambda}{\mu} \tag{4-6}$

Average Number in Queue $\quad\quad\quad N_q = \frac{\lambda^2}{\mu(\mu-\lambda)} \tag{4-7}$

Average Time in Queue $\quad\quad\quad T_q = \frac{\lambda}{\mu(\mu-\lambda)} \tag{4-8}$

Average Number in System $\quad\quad\quad N = \frac{\lambda}{(\mu-\lambda)} \tag{4-9}$

Average Time in System $\quad\quad\quad T = \frac{1}{(\mu-\lambda)} \tag{4-10}$

Notice that the relationship between the arrival rate and the service rate is very important to the behavior of queuing systems. In particular, note what happens if the service rate is equal to the arrival rate ($\lambda = \mu$). The denominator of equation 4-7 will be zero, which implies that the length of the queue will grow to infinity. Similarly the denominators of equations 4-8, 4-9, and 4-10 will also be zero, implying that the system will dissolve into chaos with the queue growing and growing and flow units spending longer and longer times in the queue. The implication of this is that the service rate must be greater than the arrival rate in order to have a *stable system*. What this means, in practice, is that the service facility must have idle time and we must have some "inefficiency" in the service mechanism. This is because idle time built up when arrivals are slow cannot be saved up to be used later. Another implication of this is that since the service rate μ must be greater than the arrival rate λ, the throughput rate of a stable system must be equal to the arrival rate λ. We will first illustrate the simple model with an example and then will look at the Excel templates that come with the text to solve more complex problems.

Example 4.2

The Golden Touch Muffler Shop has a single mechanic who is able to install new mufflers at an average rate of 4 per hour or about 1 every 15 minutes. The distribution of installation times follows an exponential distribution. Customers wanting mufflers installed arrive at the shop on the average of 3 per hour following a Poisson process. There is plenty of parking around the area of the muffler shop so that there is no problem with customers leaving their cars to be worked on. The parameters for the model in this situation are λ = 3 and μ = 4. Although we cannot show the complete probability distribution for the states of the system, since in theory it extends to infinity, we show below the results for n of 0 through 10 and the summary results below the distribution.

n	P(n)
0	0.2500
1	0.1875
2	0.1406
3	0.1055
4	0.0791
5	0.0593
6	0.0445
7	0.0334
8	0.0250
9	0.0188
10	0.0141

$$\rho = \frac{\lambda}{\mu} = .75 \quad N_q = \frac{3^2}{4(4-3)} = \frac{9}{4} = 2.25 \quad T_q = \frac{3}{4(4-3)} = .75 \text{ hrs} = 45 \text{ min}$$

$$N = \frac{3}{(4-3)} = 3 \quad T = \frac{1}{(4-3)} = 1 \text{ hr} = 60 \text{ min}$$

The manager at Golden Touch Muffler Shop can expect his mechanic to be busy 75% of the time and idle 25% of the time. The average number of cars waiting for service at any point in time is 2.25, and the average time a car waits for service is 45 minutes. The average number of cars in the system is 3. Recalling that the average number in the system is the average number in the queue plus the average number in service, we see that 2.25 + .75 = 3 so that our result makes sense. Similarly, the average time in the system (60 minutes) should be equal to the average time in the queue (45 minutes) plus the average time in service (15 minutes).

LITTLE'S LAW

There is a well-known theorem in queuing theory named after its discoverer John D.C. Little (1961). Simply stated, Little's law proves a fundamental relationship between the arrival rate, the time values, and the number measures. The statement is shown in equations 4-11 and 4-12.

$$N = \lambda T \tag{4-11}$$

$$N_q = \lambda T_q \tag{4-12}$$

Although Little's law is simply stated, it has profound implications for processes, as we will discuss later. Moreover, later work has shown that these relationships hold in a broad array of queuing situations. Indeed, Little's law comes as close to a universal law as any result in queuing theory. In Chapter 9 we will examine the process implications of this law and will see that its implications are rather profound.

THE M/M/S MODEL

In this model we still assume that the time between arrivals (interarrival times) and the service times have an exponential distribution, and in addition, we assume that the servers have identical service rates. As can be seen from the appendix, the equations get considerably more complex when multiple servers are allowed in the system. Although it is certainly still possible to solve such problems by hand, there is a good chance of introducing computational errors in doing so. We will use an Excel template that has macro code to solve the problems. The file is called Queue Solver.xlam, and it is included in the software files that accompany the text. The opening screen of the file is shown in Figure 4.6. Note that the program contains macros so that your security settings in Excel should be set to medium so that you are prompted to allow macros in the software. When prompted to do so, click the button to allow macros. If you are using Excel 2007 or later and you do not see such a prompt when you open the file, your security settings are set too high. You will need to go to the Developers section of the Excel ribbon and set the security settings to medium.

The program input section is in the upper left-hand portion of the screen in cells B4 through B7. The arrival rate should be input into cell B4 and the service rate in cell B5. Cell B6 contains the number of servers and cell B7 is for the buffer or queue capacity, K. A value of K greater than 100 is taken to be an infinite queue. Any value of 100 or less will be taken to be a finite queue with a maximum length of K. One final input may be entered in cell B25. If you enter a time here, the macros will return the probability of a wait longer than that time in cell C25. We will demonstrate the usefulness of this result later in this chapter. Once all of your inputs are entered, click the Run button to run the software. The average performance values will be output in cells C10 through C16, the probability distribution will be shown in columns E and F starting in row 5, and the server utilizations will be shown in columns H and I starting in row 6. You may notice that the inputs and results in Figure 4.6 correspond to our results from Example 4.2.

Figure 4.6 The Queue Solver Template

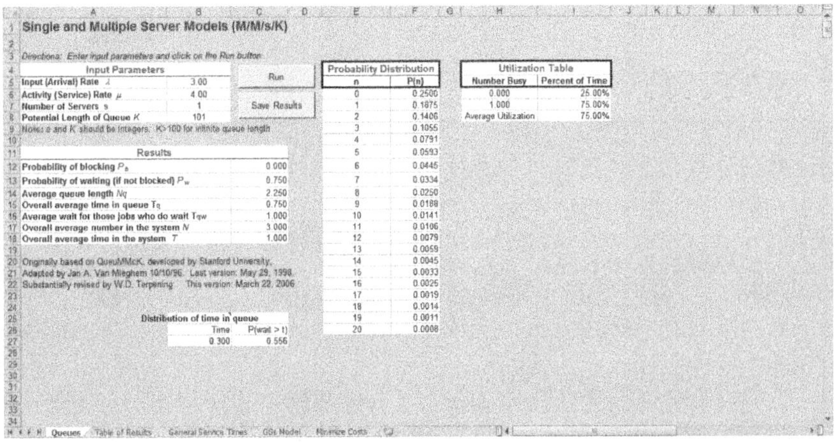

Example 4.3

To illustrate the program, suppose we open a second garage bay and hire a second mechanic for our Golden Touch Muffler shop example of Example 4.2 and that this second mechanic works at the same speed as our current mechanic. After adjusting our input and clicking the Run button, we would observe the results shown in Figure 4.7.

Figure 4.7 Queue Solver Results for Example 4.3

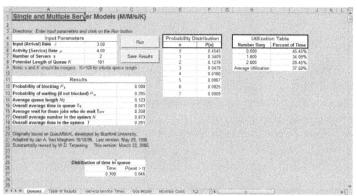

The performance of the system improves dramatically with the addition of the second mechanic. The average queue length drops from 2.25 to .123 and the average time in the queue drops from .75 hrs (45 minutes) to .041 hrs (2.5 minutes). However, the utilization of the mechanics drops from 75% to an average utilization of 37.5%. This illustrates the classic trade-off in queuing situations of reducing waiting time at the expense of increasing the idle time of resources.

THE M/M/S/K MODEL (FINITE QUEUE)

In some situations, the potential length of the queue might be limited. For example, with our muffler shop, there may be a limited space in which to park cars which would limit the number of cars that could be waiting for service. A classic example of a limited queue is a business phone system with a small number of incoming lines so that only so many people can be on hold (in the queue) at a given time; other arrivals will get a busy signal. The equations for this model are even more complex (see the appendix) but our Queue Solver software can easily handle such models. We simply need to change the potential length of the queue in the input parameters section to a value less than 100.

Example 4.4

In our Golden Touch Muffler shop, let's return to the situation of a single garage bay and one mechanic. Further, suppose that we only have space to park three cars that are waiting to be worked on. In other words, the maximum number of customers we can have in the system is 4, one car being worked on and three cars in the queue. If other customers arrive when the system is full, they have to be turned away. We simply need to change the potential length of the queue to 3 and click the Run button. Figure 4.8 illustrates the input and results for this model.

To facilitate the comparison with the original situation, the results of the infinite queue model and the finite queue model are presented side-by-side in Figure 4.9.

Figure 4.8 Queue Solver results for Example 4.4

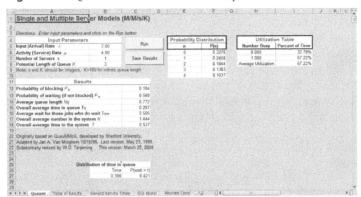

Figure 4.9 Comparison of Results of the M/M/1 and M/M/1/K Models

Measure	M/M/1	M/M/1/K
Probability of blocking P_b	0.000	0.104
Probability of waiting (if not blocked) P_w	0.750	0.569
Average queue length N_q	2.250	0.772
Overall average wait T_q	0.750	0.287
Average wait for those jobs who do wait T_q	1.000	0.505
Overall average number in the system N	3.000	1.444
Overall average time in the system T	1.000	0.537
Utilization	**75.00%**	67.22%

By simply comparing the measures on average times and numbers, it appears that the performance of the limited queue model is better than that of the infinite queue. The average times in the queue and in the system are reduced (0.750 to 0.287 and 1.000 to 0.537, respectively) and the average number in the queue and in the system are smaller (2.250 to 0.772 and 3.000 to 1.444, respectively). Although this seems to be a paradox from what we would expect, if we examine the situation closely, the results make sense. Recall that any customers who arrive when the queue is full are turned away. The probability of blocking (P_b) statistic tells us the percentage of customers who are turned away, in this case about 10.4%. The effect of this is to reduce the number of customers arriving at the system. In effect, the arrival rate is no longer 3 per hour but is now

$$3 - 3(.104) = 3 - .312 = 2.688 \text{ per hour}$$

Given the reduced effective arrival rate, we would expect the performance of the system to improve. However, this improvement comes at the expense of lost customers. The actual losses depend on what customers do when they are turned away. If they take their business elsewhere, then we obviously lose those potential revenues and the resulting profits. We can then calculate the lost business costs, and we must revise the total system costs to take this into account. Our total system costs then become

$$TC = \text{capacity costs} + \text{waiting costs} + \text{blocking costs} \qquad (4\text{-}13)$$

If we assume that the costs of blocking (C_b) are the lost profits on each customer blocked and that we have λP_b customers blocked per hour then our total costs equation from equation 4-4 becomes

$$TC = C_s S + C_w N_q + C_b \lambda P_b \qquad (4\text{-}14)$$

We will illustrate some of these calculations later in this chapter.

THE M/G/1 MODEL (GENERAL SERVICE TIMES)

In all of the models we have considered to this point, we have assumed that the interarrival and service times follow an exponential distribution. In many situations, this is not true. There is a well-known result in queuing theory that shows that we can derive the average performance measures of the system for any service time distribution if we know the standard deviation of the service times. The actual distribution of service times is not important. The equations are given in the appendix and, although they are not too difficult, they have also been incorporated into the General Service Times tab of Queue Solver.

Example 4.5

Going back to the Golden Touch Muffler shop example, assume a single garage mechanic who installs mufflers at a rate of 4 per hour. This implies that the average service time is 1/4 hour. In an exponential distribution, the standard deviation is equal to the mean so that the standard deviation of the service times would also be equal to 1/4 hour. If we do not assume that the distribution of service times follows an exponential distribution, we can use the M/G/1 model to solve the problem. We need to input the arrival rate but this time enter the average service time which is 1 over the service rate or .25. In addition, we need to enter the standard deviation of the service times which we also will assume to be .25 as it would be in the exponential distribution. The input and results are shown in Figure 4.10. As you can see in Figure 4.10, the results here for average time in the queue, number in the queue, time in the system, and number in the system are exactly the same as the results for the M/M/1 model. This does not mean, however, that the two models are identical. Note that we do not know the exact probability distribution for the states of the system, here, so there is additional information gained with the M/M/1 model. What the example does demonstrate, however, is that these five measures depend only on the mean and standard deviation of the wait times, not their exact distribution.

Figure 4.10 Input and Results for Example 4.5

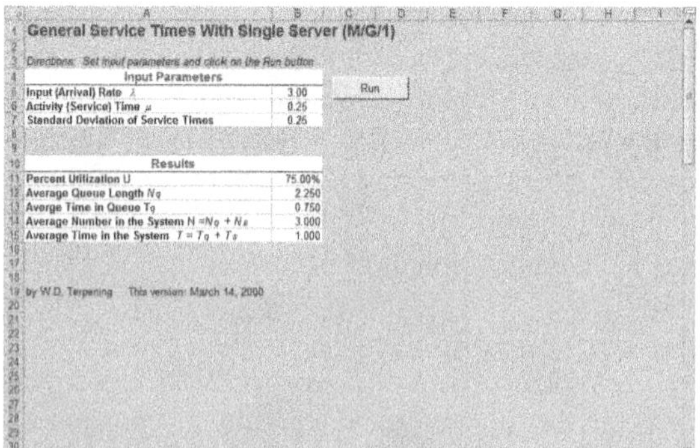

We can use the general service time model to illustrate the effects of variability in queuing situations. Suppose that we are able, through standardization of procedures and possibly some automation, to reduce the standard deviation of the service times from .25 hours to .20 hours leaving the average time at .25 hours. We would then observe the following results:

Percent Utilization U	75.00%
Average Queue Length N_q	1.845
Average Time in Queue T_q	0.615
Average Number in the System $N = N_q + N_s$	2.595
Average Time in the System $T = T_q + T_s$	0.865

Notice that although the utilization is the same, all of the other performance measures are improved. **It is true in general that as the variability of the service times is reduced, the performance of the system will improve.** The same can be said for the variability of the interarrival times as well.

THE G/G/S MODEL (ALLEN-CUNNEEN APPROXIMATION)

A somewhat less well-known approximation exists in the literature that allows for general distributions for both arrival and service times. This is known as the Allen-Cunneen approximation (Allen, 1990). As with the M/G/1 model, we cannot specify the exact probabilities, but we can approximate the average performance measures. The Allen-Cunneen approximation has been adapted from the algorithm that accompanies Albright and Winston (2005) and is incorporated into the Queue Solver software in the GGS Model tab. The approximation utilizes the coefficient of variation of both arrivals and service times. The *coefficient of variation* (CV) is equal to the standard deviation divided by the mean. We illustrate the use of the approximation in Example 4.6.

Example 4.6

Going back to the Golden Touch Muffler Shop problem, let's assume that there are two mechanics at work who install mufflers at a rate of 4 per hour for an average service time of 1/4 hour and that the standard deviation of the service times is .10 hours. We will also assume that the arrival rate is 3 per hour or an average of an arrival every 1/3 hours. Further assume that the standard deviation of arrival times is .20. Then we can calculate the coefficients of variation for both arrivals and service times as

$$CV_A = .20/.33 = .606$$

and

$$CV_S = .10/.25 = .40$$

The entries and results of the model are shown in Figure 4.11.

Figure 4.11 Input and Results for Example 4.6

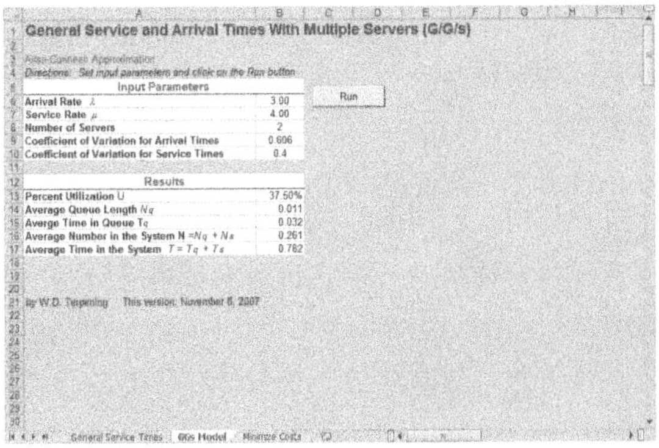

If you compare the results here with the original Golden Touch Muffler Shop problem with two mechanics in Example 4.3, you will see that the system performance is somewhat better, here. That is because the standard deviations of arrival and service times are lower here than with the exponential distribution in Example 4.3.

Queuing Theory and Decision Making

Queuing theory models are an example of *descriptive models* as opposed to *prescriptive models*. Prescriptive models give a "best" or recommended solution to the problem. Descriptive models, on the other hand, merely provide descriptions of the behavior of a system; they do not provide a solution. So how do we use queuing theory to help make decisions about processes? The exact process for doing this goes back to our previous discussion about whether or not we can explicitly estimate the costs involved, particularly the costs of waiting or the costs of being blocked because of a full queue.

COSTS CAN BE ESTIMATED

If we can define the costs of waiting in economic terms, we can use those costs to calculate the optimum capacity of the process. In Figure 4.5 we saw that the total costs decrease as capacity increases up to a point and then increase again with increasing capacity. To find the optimum capacity we therefore have to start with only a minimally acceptable capacity and incrementally add capacity until the costs increase rather than decrease. Although we could do this manually by using equations 4-4 or 4-14 to calculate total costs, the Minimize Costs tab of the Queue Solver software performs the calculations for us. We will illustrate the process in the next example.

Example 4.7

To illustrate the process, let's return to the Golden Touch Muffler Shop and assume that a consultant has done a survey of the shop's customers and analyzed the behavior of customers who cannot get their cars into the queue because it is full. She has calculated that the waiting cost of customers is approximately $50 per hour and that most of the blocked customers go somewhere else to get a new muffler rather than returning to the Golden Touch Muffler Shop. She therefore calculates the blocked customer costs at approximately $80 per customer. Golden Touch Muffler pays its mechanics a flat rate of $30 per hour. Assuming exponentially distributed interarrival and service times and a limited queue length of 3, how many garage bays and mechanics should Golden Touch Muffler employee?

The required inputs to the model are the arrival rate (3 per hour), service rate (4 per hour), maximum queue length (3), wage rate per server ($30), cost of waiting per hour ($50), and cost of a blocked customer ($80). The inputs and results of the Queue Solver software are shown in Figure 4.12. As can be seen, the total costs drop from $71.19 per hour with one mechanic to $65.40 per hour for two mechanics. However, adding a third mechanic increases the total system costs to $90.71, so the optimum number of mechanics is two.

Figure 4.12 Inputs and Results for Example 4.7

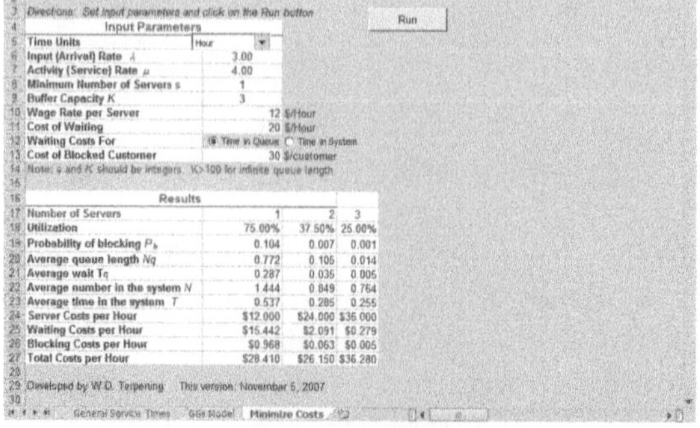

Minimize Total Costs

Directions: Set input parameters and click on the Run button

Run

Input Parameters		
Time Units	Hour	
Input (Arrival) Rate λ	3.00	
Activity (Service) Rate μ	4.00	
Minimum Number of Servers s	1	
Buffer Capacity K	3	
Wage Rate per Server	12	$/Hour
Cost of Waiting	20	$/Hour
Waiting Costs For	Time in Queue	Time in System
Cost of Blocked Customer	30	$/customer

Note: s and K should be integers. K>100 for infinite queue length

Results			
Number of Servers	1	2	3
Utilization	75.00%	37.50%	25.00%
Probability of blocking P_b	0.104	0.007	0.001
Average queue length N_q	0.772	0.106	0.014
Average wait T_q	0.287	0.036	0.005
Average number in the system N	1.444	0.849	0.764
Average time in the system T	0.537	0.285	0.255
Server Costs per Hour	$12.000	$24.000	$36.000
Waiting Costs per Hour	$15.442	$2.091	$0.279
Blocking Costs per Hour	$0.968	$0.063	$0.005
Total Costs per Hour	$28.410	$26.150	$36.280

Developed by W.D. Terpening This version: November 5, 2007

General Service Times GGs Model Minimize Costs

COSTS CANNOT BE ESTIMATED

What happens if we cannot adequately estimate the costs of waiting? This situation is common because waiting costs are often very difficult to estimate. Although we know that waiting is a negative psychological experience for customers and that because of this there are costs associated with it, explicitly stating these costs in dollar terms is usually very difficult to do. Because of this, many managers will formulate a criterion for the design of the process based on one of the process measures. For example, a manager might stipulate that the average wait should be no longer than 10 minutes, or that there should be only a 5% chance of a customer waiting longer than 15 minutes. Any of the process measures can be used as a criterion, including the utilization of resources. In most cases, however, the criterion will be in terms of the waiting behavior of the customers. The logic of using the queuing models to find a satisfactory solution that meets the criterion is similar to the previous economic approach: incrementally add capacity until the criterion is satisfied. The following example illustrates the approach.

Example 4.8

Rockford Savings and Loan Association is opening a new branch in a nearby suburb. They want to know how many savings counselors should be hired at the new branch. It is estimated that counseling time is 15 minutes per customer on the average and that customers are expected to arrive at a rate of 6 per hour. Management has decided that they want the average wait of customers for service to be no more than 10 minutes. How many counselors should Rockford hire?

Noting that the service rate is 4 per hour (15 minutes per customer) and that the arrival rate is 6 per hour, we need at least 2 counselors because 1 counselor would not provide a stable system. Starting with 2 counselors, we would obtain an average wait time of 0.321 hours or a little over 19 minutes. Since this does not satisfy their criterion, let's add a third counselor and calculate the results again. Doing this yields an average wait time of 0.039 hours or a little over 2 minutes. This satisfies the criterion and therefore Rockford should hire 3 loan counselors for the new branch.

The president of Rockford Savings and Loan recently appeared on television ads pledging that Rockford would provide enhanced customer service and promising that virtually no one would have to wait for more than 10 minutes before being helped at any of the Rockford branches. The branch manager of the new bank wants to know if the solution with three counselors will meet this criterion. In particular, he wants the probability of anyone waiting 10 minutes or more for a counselor to be less than .05.

In the lower part of the Queue Solver main screen there is a box to enter a time, and the software will calculate the probability that a customer will wait longer than that amount of time in the queue. Entering (10/60) = .167 in the box produces the results shown in Figure 4.13. The results show that the probability that a customer will have to wait more than 10 minutes is .087, which is not less than .05. As with explicit waiting costs, we must incrementally increase capacity by one unit at a time until the goal is achieved. Unfortunately you must do this manually using the software because Queue Solver does not know what goal you are trying to achieve. In this case, to achieve the .05 goal there would have to be 4 servers when the probability of waiting more than 10 minutes is only .0146.

Figure 4.13 Output for Example 4.8

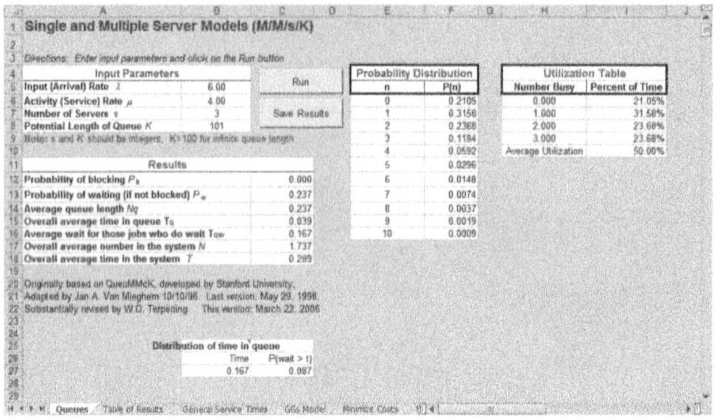

Introduction to Simulation

Although queuing models can be powerful tools in analyzing waiting phenomena, many practical situations are too complex to satisfy the restrictive assumptions of the analytical models. For most complex real world processes, especially those that cross functional boundaries and exhibit complex patterns of variability, we need a more flexible tool. Simulation provides such a flexible and powerful tool for process analysis, design, and improvement. In this section we will introduce the basic principles of simulation and demonstrate with a simulation model of a basic queuing problem.

Simulation is defined in the Merriam-Webster dictionary as

> "The imitative representation of the functioning of one system or process by means of the functioning of another (a computer simulation of an industrial process)"

In other words, simulation is using one system to represent the functioning of another system. Simulation models are usually computer-based models but do not have to be. For example, wind tunnels are commonly used to simulate the effects of an object in flight. Simulation models can be classified along three attributes.

STATIC VERSUS DYNAMIC MODELS

This distinction relates to whether time is a relevant part of the model or not. Static models are those that do not vary with time or where time is not an important variable. For example, at one time during airplane design, plane manufacturers such as Boeing or Airbus created prototypes or physical replicas of the plane to be built. These were static models. Now, manufacturers build such prototypes on the computer but the basic models still tend to be static. Dynamic models, on the other hand, include time as an important variable so that the simulation examines the changes in the system over time.

DETERMINISTIC VERSUS PROBABILISTIC MODELS

Deterministic models do not contain any random events and the behavior of the system is totally determined once the inputs to the model are set. For example, a CAD drawing of a computer modeled component is completely determined when all of the inputs are set. The distinguishing feature of deterministic models is that they will always produce the same result for the same inputs. On the other hand, probabilistic models have at least some variables that are determined by chance. Therefore, in these models, even given the same inputs, the model can produce slightly different results.

DISCRETE VERSUS CONTINUOUS (ANALOG) MODELS

Discrete and continuous models are both dynamic but differ in terms of how they represent the states of the model over time. Continuous models represent systems where the variables of the system change continuously over time. The early work by Forrester (1961) on system dynamics is an example of this type of simulation. Most biological models, such as population growth over time, are also of this type. Such models usually deal with the solution of differential equations as part of the solution process. Discrete event models on the other hand, move the model through time as a chronological sequence of events where each event represents a change in the state of the system. The simulation of queuing models is a good example of discrete event models.

BASICS OF DISCRETE EVENT SIMULATION

Most business simulations, and those that we will examine in this text, are dynamic, probabilistic discrete event simulations. Discrete event simulations involve the following basic elements:

- **Clock:** The simulation clock keeps track of the current time in the simulation and increments the clock as events occur.
- **Event lists:** A simulation keeps at least one, and sometimes two, lists of events. An event list is simply a chronological list of events and when they are to occur, and often when they will end. Some simulations keep separate lists of current and future events. Other simulations maintain only one event list.
- **Simulation executive:** The executive controls the time advance of the clock and executes events. The executive also monitors for the end of the simulation and keeps track of statistics related to performance.
- **Statistics and results:** The simulation maintains statistics related to the performance of the system as it moves through time and presents a summary of these results at the conclusion of the simulation.
- **Random number generators:** Simulations contain routines to generate random numbers to simulate probabilistic aspects of the simulation.

There are two approaches to executing the events in a simulation and moving the clock through time.

1. Time slicing advances the clock a fixed amount of time each time the clock is advanced regardless of whether or not an event has occurred.
2. Next event simulations advance the model to the next event to occur on the events list and increments the clock to that time.

Most simulation languages utilize the next event approach because it is more efficient in most situations. The only disadvantage of the next event simulation approach occurs in systems that use animations as the system moves through time. In these situations, events that occur at different times can appear to occur at the same time in the visualization. This is usually a minor problem, and most simulation languages still use the next event approach. Figure 4.14 illustrates the basic outline of next event simulations.

Figure 4.14 Discrete Event Simulation Using the Next Event Approach

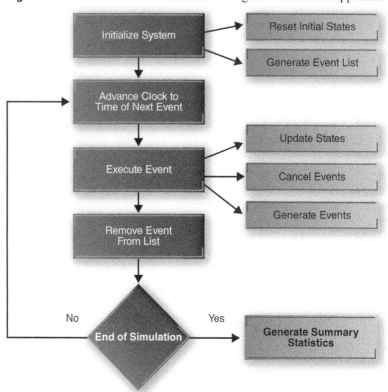

BUILDING A SPREADSHEET SIMULATION

To illustrate the basic ideas of a simulation model, we will build a simple spreadsheet model of the M/M/1 queuing model. Before we build the model, we need to discuss the concept of random numbers and their role in simulation.

Probability Distributions and Random Numbers

In order to generate random events in probabilistic simulation models, we need a way of generating values from a probability distribution. To do this, we need some way of generating random numbers. Actually, such numbers are more appropriately called *pseudo random numbers* because they are generated from a deterministic algorithm. Although the numbers appear to be random, the algorithm will generate exactly the same values each time given the same starting point. This starting point is called a *random number seed*. There is a built-in function in Excel to generate pseudo random numbers, the RAND() function.[3] The RAND function generates random numbers uniformly in the range from 0.0 to 1.0. The numbers are uniform so that 10% of the numbers will be between .00 and .10, 20% between .40 and .60, and so on. Although the RAND function does not have any argument, the parentheses () must be included with the function name.

In most simulations, the random events we want to simulate do not come from a uniform distribution between 0.0 and 1.0. Usually they are derived from a common probability distribution like the normal or the exponential distribution. The standard method for generating events from a probability distribution is to associate the random number generated (between 0.0 and 1.0) with the inverse of the cumulative probability function from the associated probability distribution, which should also have a value between 0.0 and 1.0. Since the exponential distribution is commonly used

---

3. The RAND function in Excel has been criticized by some simulation experts. It is not recommended for scientific work that requires the generation of extremely large sets of numbers. However, the function will work just fine for our purposes of discrete event simulation.

to represent interarrival and service times in queuing models, we will focus on generating values from the exponential distribution, here. For example, if we let λ represent the average arrival rate, then the time of the next arrival to the system can be generated using the following equation

$$\text{Arrival} = \left(\frac{1}{\lambda}\right)\log(r) \tag{4-15}$$

where r is a random number between 0.0 and 1.0. The log is the natural logarithm to the base e which can be calculated in Excel using the LN function where the argument is the value of the random number. Within Excel then, the following would generate a random event from the exponential distribution where the mean rate is λ.

$$A_i = \left(\frac{1}{\lambda}\right) *LN(RAND()) \tag{4-16}$$

To create a simulation model of the simple queuing model, we need to keep track of the following events:

- A job arrives at the system
- A job starts the service process
- A job finished the service process and exits the system

If we track the times of these events then we can calculate the average time in the system and in the queue and the server idle time. Create a spreadsheet similar to that shown in Figure 4.15. The customer numbers in column B of the spreadsheet should run from 1 to 500 to simulate the system for 500 customers. The cells in column D with the red outline are for the input of arrival and service rates. The cells I2 through I5 will contain the simulation results. Note that the arrival and service rates correspond to those in Example 4.2. To complete the model, place the formulas shown in Figure 4.16 in the appropriate cells and then copy the formulas in row 10 down the rest of the table.

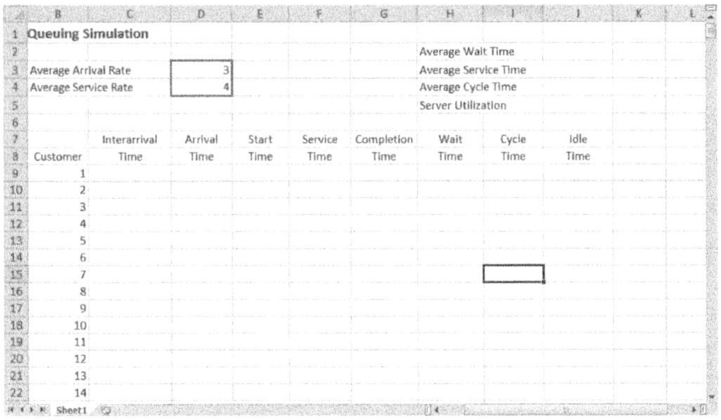

Queuing Simulation

Average Arrival Rate	3		Average Wait Time	
Average Service Rate	4		Average Service Time	
			Average Cycle Time	
			Server Utilization	

Customer	Interarrival Time	Arrival Time	Start Time	Service Time	Completion Time	Wait Time	Cycle Time	Idle Time
1								
2								
3								
4								
5								
6								
7								
8								
9								
10								
11								
12								
13								
14								

Sheet1

Figure 4.15 The Basic Layout of the M/M/1 Simulation Model

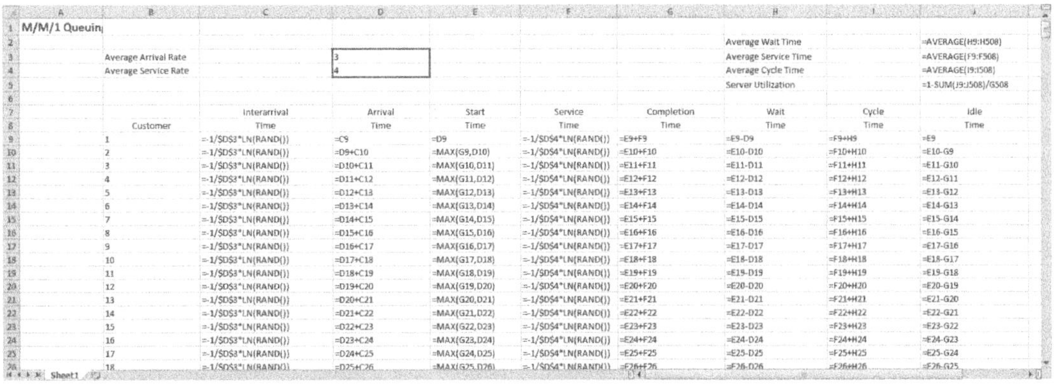

M/M/1 Queuin

Average Arrival Rate	3	Average Wait Time	=AVERAGE(H9:H508)
Average Service Rate	4	Average Service Time	=AVERAGE(F9:F508)
		Average Cycle Time	=AVERAGE(I9:I508)
		Server Utilization	=1-SUM(J9:J508)/G508

Customer	Interarrival Time	Arrival Time	Start Time	Service Time	Completion Time	Wait Time	Cycle Time	Idle Time
1	=-1/$D$3*LN(RAND())	=C9	=D9	=-1/$D$4*LN(RAND())	=E9+F9	=E9-D9	=F9+H9	=E9
2	=-1/$D$3*LN(RAND())	=D9+C10	=MAX(G9,D10)	=-1/$D$4*LN(RAND())	=E10+F10	=E10-D10	=F10+H10	=E10-G9
3	=-1/$D$3*LN(RAND())	=D10+C11	=MAX(G10,D11)	=-1/$D$4*LN(RAND())	=E11+F11	=E11-D11	=F11+H11	=E11-G10
4	=-1/$D$3*LN(RAND())	=D11+C12	=MAX(G11,D12)	=-1/$D$4*LN(RAND())	=E12+F12	=E12-D12	=F12+H12	=E12-G11
5	=-1/$D$3*LN(RAND())	=D12+C13	=MAX(G12,D13)	=-1/$D$4*LN(RAND())	=E13+F13	=E13-D13	=F13+H13	=E13-G12
6	=-1/$D$3*LN(RAND())	=D13+C14	=MAX(G13,D14)	=-1/$D$4*LN(RAND())	=E14+F14	=E14-D14	=F14+H14	=E14-G13
7	=-1/$D$3*LN(RAND())	=D14+C15	=MAX(G14,D15)	=-1/$D$4*LN(RAND())	=E15+F15	=E15-D15	=F15+H15	=E15-G14
8	=-1/$D$3*LN(RAND())	=D15+C16	=MAX(G15,D16)	=-1/$D$4*LN(RAND())	=E16+F16	=E16-D16	=F16+H16	=E16-G15
9	=-1/$D$3*LN(RAND())	=D16+C17	=MAX(G16,D17)	=-1/$D$4*LN(RAND())	=E17+F17	=E17-D17	=F17+H17	=E17-G16
10	=-1/$D$3*LN(RAND())	=D17+C18	=MAX(G17,D18)	=-1/$D$4*LN(RAND())	=E18+F18	=E18-D18	=F18+H18	=E18-G17
11	=-1/$D$3*LN(RAND())	=D18+C19	=MAX(G18,D19)	=-1/$D$4*LN(RAND())	=E19+F19	=E19-D19	=F19+H19	=E19-G18
12	=-1/$D$3*LN(RAND())	=D19+C20	=MAX(G19,D20)	=-1/$D$4*LN(RAND())	=E20+F20	=E20-D20	=F20+H20	=E20-G19
13	=-1/$D$3*LN(RAND())	=D20+C21	=MAX(G20,D21)	=-1/$D$4*LN(RAND())	=E21+F21	=E21-D21	=F21+H21	=E21-G20
14	=-1/$D$3*LN(RAND())	=D21+C22	=MAX(G21,D22)	=-1/$D$4*LN(RAND())	=E22+F22	=E22-D22	=F22+H22	=E22-G21
15	=-1/$D$3*LN(RAND())	=D22+C23	=MAX(G22,D23)	=-1/$D$4*LN(RAND())	=E23+F23	=E23-D23	=F23+H23	=E23-G22
16	=-1/$D$3*LN(RAND())	=D23+C24	=MAX(G23,D24)	=-1/$D$4*LN(RAND())	=E24+F24	=E24-D24	=F24+H24	=E24-G23
17	=-1/$D$3*LN(RAND())	=D24+C25	=MAX(G24,D25)	=-1/$D$4*LN(RAND())	=E25+F25	=E25-D25	=F25+H25	=E25-G24
18	=-1/$D$3*LN(RAND())	=D25+C26	=MAX(G25,D26)	=-1/$D$4*LN(RAND())	=E26+F26	=E26-D26	=F26+H26	=E26-G25

Sheet1

Figure 4.16 The Simulation Formulas

When you have finished the spreadsheet, you should see something similar to Figure 4.17, where the cells have been formatted to four decimal places. Note that your results will not be exactly equal to those given here because of the nature of the RAND function, which uses the numerical value of the time-date stamp from the systems internal clock for the random number seed. If you compare the results here with those from Figure 4.6, they should be roughly the same although they will not be exactly the same because of the nature of the random events.

Figure 4.17 Example Results From the M/M/1 Simulation Model

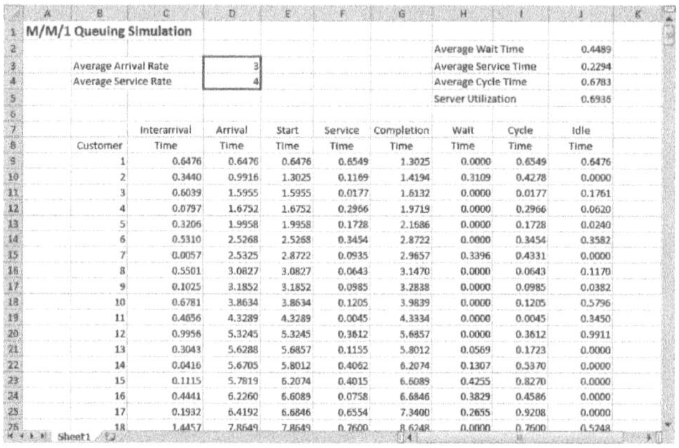

M/M/1 Queuing Simulation

Average Arrival Rate	3
Average Service Rate	4
Average Wait Time	0.4489
Average Service Time	0.2294
Average Cycle Time	0.6783
Server Utilization	0.6936

Customer	Interarrival Time	Arrival Time	Start Time	Service Time	Completion Time	Wait Time	Cycle Time	Idle Time
1	0.6476	0.6476	0.6476	0.6549	1.3025	0.0000	0.6549	0.6476
2	0.3440	0.9916	1.3025	0.1169	1.4194	0.3109	0.4278	0.0000
3	0.6039	1.5955	1.5955	0.0177	1.6132	0.0000	0.0177	0.1761
4	0.0797	1.6752	1.6752	0.2966	1.9719	0.0000	0.2966	0.0620
5	0.3206	1.9958	1.9958	0.1728	2.1686	0.0000	0.1728	0.0240
6	0.5310	2.5268	2.5268	0.3454	2.8722	0.0000	0.3454	0.3582
7	0.0057	2.5325	2.8722	0.0935	2.9657	0.3396	0.4331	0.0000
8	0.5501	3.0827	3.0827	0.0643	3.1470	0.0000	0.0643	0.1170
9	0.1025	3.1852	3.1852	0.0985	3.2838	0.0000	0.0985	0.0382
10	0.6781	3.8634	3.8634	0.1205	3.9839	0.0000	0.1205	0.5796
11	0.4656	4.3289	4.3289	0.0045	4.3334	0.0000	0.0045	0.3450
12	0.9956	5.3245	5.3245	0.3612	5.6857	0.0000	0.3612	0.9911
13	0.3043	5.6288	5.6857	0.1155	5.8012	0.0569	0.1723	0.0000
14	0.0416	5.6705	5.8012	0.4062	6.2074	0.1307	0.5370	0.0000
15	0.1115	5.7819	6.2074	0.4015	6.6089	0.4255	0.8270	0.0000
16	0.4441	6.2260	6.6089	0.0758	6.6846	0.3829	0.4586	0.0000
17	0.1932	6.4192	6.6846	0.6554	7.3400	0.2655	0.9208	0.0000
18	1.4457	7.8649	7.8649	0.7600	8.6248	0.0000	0.7600	0.5248

Sheet1

You may notice that every time you make a change to the spreadsheet, all of the results change. This is because the RAND function recalculates with each change in the worksheet. This can be somewhat disconcerting if you have finalized the model and want to preserve the results for later reference. You can freeze the results by using the following procedure: (1) highlight the table portion in cells B7 through J508, (2) select copy from the Edit menu (or press CTRL+C) and (3) then making sure that the active cell is B7, select Paste Values from the Home tab. Please note however, that this will make your simulation unusable in the sense that the random events will be removed so that changing the input parameters will then have no effect on the results. You may want to save the resulting worksheet under a different name to preserve your simulation model.

Although we can simulate very simple systems within the framework of an Excel spreadsheet, it is not the best approach to simulating processes in general. Even in this simple situation we have no way of gathering statistics on the average number in the queue or average number in the system because these values are a function of time and cannot be easily captured in our model. It also becomes next to impossible to model more complex processes such as those with multiple servers using this approach. For this reason, special purpose simulation software has been developed that can be used to model more complex processes. This specialized software has the additional advantage of being easier to use because we do not have to develop complex formulas to track and record events. We will introduce an example of such as system in the next chapter, the XLSIM package that accompanies the text.

Chapter Glossary

Balking The refusal of a customer to enter a queue because the line is too long

Blocking When a customer is denied entry to a queue because it is full

Calling population A collection of people or things that might need the activities provided by the service mechanism and therefore be potential arrivals to the queuing process.

Coefficient of variation A measure of relative variability that is equal to the standard deviation divided by the mean.

Descriptive model A model that simply describes the behavior of a system but does not suggest a best solution.

Jockeying When customers move from one line to another in hopes of finding a faster moving line.

Prescriptive Model A model that prescribes a best solution to a problem.

Pseudo random numbers Numbers that appear to be random but that are systematically generated by an algorithm.

Queue configuration The physical arrangement of the queue.

Queue discipline The rule that determines the order in which customers or jobs are selected from the queue for service.

Random number seed The starting point for the generation of random numbers.

Reneging When a customer enters a queue but then decides to leave the system before being served.

Stable System System in which the service rate exceeds the arrival rate so that the throughput rate of the system is equal to the arrival rate.

Simulation Building and manipulating a model of a real world system or process.

State of the system Refers to the number of customers or flow units in the system, both in the queue and being served.

Utilization The percentage of time the service mechanism is busy.

Discussion Questions and Problems

1. The drive thru window at the Hot Dog Emporium has an average arrival rate of 40 customers per hour. If the average time to service a customer is 1 minute
   a. How many customers, on average, are waiting in line?
   b. How long does the average customer wait in line?
   c. What is the average utilization of the drive-thru window?

2. On average, 100 customers per hour arrive at the Two Dot National Bank. Management wants to ensure that there is less than a 5% chance of a customer waiting more than 5 minutes for a teller. How many tellers should the bank schedule to meet this policy?

3. An average of 30 cars per hour arrive at the drive-thru window of the Java Express espresso stand. If it takes an average of 1.5 minutes to mix a drink
   a. How many customers, on average, are waiting in line?
   b. How long does the average customer wait in line?
   c. What is the average cycle time for the system?
   d. What is the average utilization of the drive-thru window?

4. The main office of the Medford Insurance Company employs a large number of claims adjusters who heavily utilize the available copy equipment. Recent complaints of long waits at the machines have lead senior management to propose that a new copy center be designed and equipped with new copy machines. Adjusters are paid $35 per hour and the cost of new copiers including purchase costs, maintenance and supplies will be about $20 per hour depreciated over the life of the equipment. Previous studies show that adjusters arrive at the copy center at an average rate of 30 per hour, and it takes, on average, about 1.5 minutes for the average copy job. How many copiers should Medford buy for the new copy center to minimize total costs?

5. The Murphysboro airport has a single security check-in station that is manned by 2 employees. If passengers arrive at a rate of 10 per minute and if it takes an average of 13 minutes to process each passenger,
   a. What is the probability that a customer will have to wait to be checked at security?
   b. What is the average length of time that a customer is in the queue?
   c. Of those customers who have to wait, what is the average length of the wait?
   d. What is the average length of the queue at the security check-in?

6. Merkle Drug Company employs a team of technical writers to complete FDA applications for the approval of new drugs. It takes an average of 5 months for the team to complete an application. The company estimates that it costs about $120,000 for each month that an application is delayed. A team of technical writers costs about $60,000 per month. If applications arrive at a rate of 2 per year, should the company hire a second team of technical writers?

7. Dan Jones runs a small barber shop that is located in a small space in a strip mall. The space only has room for 3 chairs for waiting customers. Dan knows that customers who come in for a haircut and see all of the chairs full leave and go somewhere else for a haircut. Customers generally arrive at a rate of 4 per hour. Dan can perform 5 haircuts per hour on average. If Dan keeps his shop open 8 hours per day and makes $15 per haircut, how much money is he losing each day in lost customers?

8. The Lube N' Tube corporation markets a line of industrial lubricants throughout the United States. Lube N' Tube employees a 40 person sales force that calls on its manufacturing customers and gets feedback on their products as well as take orders for products. Lube N' Tube still utilizes a sales force because of the quality of the feedback they get from the sales force and the number of ideas it generates for new products. When a salesperson calls in an order they have to confirm pricing, check on availability of product, and obtain an estimated delivery date. The calls last on average about 10 minutes but some calls can last much longer. Salespeople call in on average about once every 2 hours over a 12 hour time period. Lube N' Tube employs specially trained order schedulers to handle the calls and they are paid at a rate of $20 per hour. The time for the highly skilled salespeople is valued at $100 per hour. If the phone lines of all of the order schedulers are occupied, an incoming call is put on hold. There is no limitation on the number of calls that can be put on hold. Assuming that both the call times and the times between orders follow an exponential distribution, how many order schedulers should Lube N' Tube have?

9. Arnie owns a small auto repair shop that he has owned and operated for 10 years. Arnie can only work on one car at a time and there is limited space for customers to leave their cars for repair work. Currently Arnie can only park about 5 cars outside his facility. Customers arrive at a rate of 10 per day, it takes Arnie about 40 minutes to work on a car, and he works for 8 hours per day. Arnie knows that customers who arrive at his shop and find the parking area full will most likely go to another shop to get the work done. Arnie makes an average of $45 dollars in profit per car, and that profit is lost if the customer goes elsewhere. Arnie recently received an offer from the owner of the lot next door. He can lease the space at a rate of $30 per day, and this would double his parking area. Should Arnie lease the lot next door?

10. Marjorie Cummings started selling crocheted and knitted animals on Etsy about 5 years ago. Business has been so good that she has hired several friends to help with the crocheting and knitting but is having trouble getting orders shipped. She is considering renting a

small warehouse space and hiring some local high school students to pick and ship orders from the inventory of animals created by the production group. Orders average about 20 per day, and Marjorie estimates that the students, who will work 2 hours each day after school, can each fill about 4 orders per day. How many students should Marjorie hire if she wants to ensure that all of the orders get processed each day?

11. Create a simulation model of the Hot Dog Emporium from Problem 1. Based on a simulation of 1,000 customers, compare the simulation results with the theoretical predictions from the single server queuing model in terms of the average wait time, average cycle time, and average utilization. Why are the simulation results not exactly as predicted by the queuing model?

12. Create a simulation model of Java Express from Problem 3.

    a. Based on a simulation of 100 customers, compare the simulation results with the theoretical predictions from the single server queuing model in terms of the average wait time, average cycle time, and average utilization. Why are the simulation results not exactly as predicted by the queuing model?

    b. Run the simulation for 1,000 customers. How do these results compare with the theoretical predictions? Would you expect these results to be more like the theoretical predictions or less like them? Explain your reasoning.

13. Joe Delgado operates the Flying Pig, a mobile food cart in the downtown area of Seattle. Joe knows that customer arrivals vary depending on the time of day. He also knows that he can serve about 22 customers per hour. He wants to build a spreadsheet model so that he can predict the behavior of the waiting line at the cart depending on the arrival rate. Build a model for Joe that will simulate 1,000 customers.

    a. Joe estimates that at the beginning of the lunch hour (around 11:00 AM) customers arrive at a rate of 15 per hour on average. Run the simulation for 1,000 customers. Describe the behavior of the system especially the wait and cycle times of customers and the idle time of Joe.

    b. During the peak of the lunch hour, Joe estimates that the customer arrivals average about 20 per hour. Compare the behavior of the system at the peak time versus that of the system at the beginning of the lunch hour.

References

Allen, A.O. *Probability, Statistics and Queueing Theory: With Computer Science Applications*. 1990, Boston, MA: Academic Press

Albright, S.C. & Winston, W.L. *Spreadsheet Modeling and Applications: Essentials of Practical Management Science*, 2005, Belmont CA: Brooks/Cole

Forrester, J.W. *Industrial Dynamics*, 1961, Waltham, MA: Pegasus Communications.

Little, J.D.C. A proof of the queuing formula $L = \lambda W$, *Operations Research*, 1961, 9, 383–387.

Maister, D. The Psychology of Waiting Lines. In J.A. Czepiel, M.R. Solomon & C.F. Surprenant (Eds.), *The Service Encounter: Managing Employee/Customer Interaction in Service Businesses*. 1985, Lexington, MA: Lexington Books.

Norman, D.A., *The Psychology of Waiting Lines*, Unpublished Paper, 2008, Available at http://www.jnd.org/ms/Norman The Psychology of Waiting Lines.pdf, last referenced 8/1/2016.

Norman, D. A. Designing Waits That Work, 2009, *MIT Sloan Management Review*, 50, 4, 23–28.

Appendix

This appendix contains the equations for many of the formal queuing models discussed in the text.

M/M/1 Model

$$P(0) = 1 - \frac{\lambda}{\mu} \qquad P(n) = P(0)\left(\frac{\lambda}{\mu}\right)^n$$

$$\rho = \frac{\lambda}{\mu}$$

$$N_q = \frac{\lambda^2}{\mu(\mu-\lambda)} \qquad T_q = \frac{\lambda}{\mu(\mu-\lambda)}$$

$$N = \frac{\lambda}{(\mu-\lambda)} \qquad T = \frac{1}{(\mu-\lambda)}$$

M/M/s Model

$$P(0) = \frac{1}{\sum_{i=0}^{s-1}\frac{\left(\frac{\lambda}{\mu}\right)^i}{i!} + \frac{\left(\frac{\lambda}{\mu}\right)^s}{s!\left(1-\frac{\left(\frac{\lambda}{\mu}\right)}{s}\right)}}$$

$$P(n) = P(0)\left(\frac{\left(\frac{\lambda}{\mu}\right)^n}{n!}\right) \text{ for } n \leq s \qquad P(n) = P(0)\left(\frac{\left(\frac{\lambda}{\mu}\right)^n}{s!s^{n-s}}\right) \text{ for } n > s$$

$$\rho = \frac{\lambda}{s\mu}$$

$$L_q = P(0)\left(\frac{\left(\frac{\lambda}{\mu}\right)^{s+1}}{(s-1)!\left(s-\frac{\lambda}{\mu}\right)^2}\right)$$

$$L = L_q + \frac{\lambda}{\mu} \qquad W_q = \frac{L_q}{\lambda} \qquad W = W_q + \frac{1}{\mu}$$

M/M/s/K Model (Finite Queue)

$$P(0) = \frac{1}{\left(\sum_{i=0}^{s} \frac{\left(\frac{\lambda}{\mu}\right)^i}{i!}\right) + \left(\frac{1}{s!}\right)\left(\sum_{i=s+1}^{K} \frac{\left(\frac{\lambda}{\mu}\right)^i}{s^{i-s}}\right)}$$

$$P(n) = P(0) \left(\frac{\left(\frac{\lambda}{\mu}\right)^n}{n!}\right) \text{ for } 0 < n \leq s$$

$$P(n) = P(0) \left(\frac{\left(\frac{\lambda}{\mu}\right)^n}{s! s^{n-s}}\right) \text{ for } s < n \leq K$$

$$L_q = \left(\frac{P(0)\left(\frac{\lambda}{\mu}\right)^{s+1}}{(s-1)!\left(s-\frac{\lambda}{\mu}\right)^2}\right)\left(1 - \left(\frac{\left(\frac{\lambda}{\mu}\right)}{s}\right)^{K-s} - (K-s)\left(\frac{\left(\frac{\lambda}{\mu}\right)}{s}\right)^{K-s}\left(1 - \frac{\frac{\lambda}{\mu}}{s}\right)\right)$$

$$L = L_q + \left(\frac{\lambda}{\mu}\right)(1 - P(K))$$

$$W_q = \frac{L_q}{\lambda(1 - P(K))}$$

$$W = W_q + \frac{1}{\mu}$$

M/G/1 Model (General Service Times)

$$P_0 = 1 - \frac{\lambda}{\mu}$$

$$L_q = \frac{\lambda^2 \sigma^2 + \left(\frac{\lambda}{\mu}\right)^2}{2\left(1 - \frac{\lambda}{\mu}\right)}$$

$$L = L_q + \frac{\lambda}{\mu}$$

$$W_q = \frac{L_q}{\lambda}$$

$$W = W_q + \frac{1}{\mu}$$

Chapter 5

Using XLSim in Process Simulation

"In my teaching, I enjoyed creating models to clearly communicate my thoughts."
—Erno Rubik

"The purpose of science is not to analyze or describe but to make useful models of the world. A model is useful if it allows us to get use out of it."
—Edward de Bono

As the quotes above imply, building models is an excellent way to communicate and is, at least in de Bono's mind, the purpose of science. Modeling is certainly a helpful way to begin to understand a process and can be extremely useful in the design and improvement of processes. It is much simpler, and certainly less expensive, to experiment and try out ideas with a model of a process rather than tinkering with the real thing. In the last chapter we introduced the topic of queues and the concept of simulation. In this chapter, we will introduce a software tool that allows us to model and simulate much more complex processes than we could in the last chapter. We will employ this tool in later sections for designing and improving processes. The software is contained in an Excel file called XLSim.xlam that accompanies this text. XLSim is a discrete-event simulation system designed for pedagogical purposes and is not a professional simulation system. However, it has most of the capabilities of professional simulation packages and in fact is designed to have many of the capabilities of the ProModel software.[1] XLSim will run in any version of Excel version 12 (Office 2007) or later on Windows-based computers.

---

1. Promodel software is produced by ProModel Corporation which can be found at www.promodel.com.

92 PART ONE Metrics and Tools in Business Process Management

Running the Software

XLSim is written in Visual Basic for Applications (VBA) which is the macro language of Microsoft Office. To protect against potential dangerous computer viruses Microsoft Office requires that you specifically enable macros in software that you know is safe and does not contain viruses, such as XLSim. You can do this in two different ways.

SET MACRO SECURITY SETTINGS

If you set the macro settings properly, Excel will ask your permission before running any code embedded in an Excel workbook. Each time that you run XLSim with these settings, Excel will notify you that it contains macros and ask if you want to enable them. There are two ways of setting the security settings in Excel. For either option, you need to click File in the ribbon and select Excel Options from the menu on the left of the screen (Figure 5.1). This leads to the option menu shown in Figure 5.2. At this point there are two ways of setting the security settings. The first way is to add the Developer tab to your Excel ribbon. To do this select Customize Ribbon in the options menu. This will result in the screen shown in Figure 5.3. Check the box that says Developer and then click the OK button. This will add the Developer tab to your Excel ribbon. Click on this tab, and you will see the ribbon shown in Figure 5.4. In this tab, click on Macro Security in the Code section of the ribbon. This will display the macro security settings dialog shown in Figure 5.5.

Figure 5.1 Selecting Excel Options

In the dialog, select the Disable all macros with notification option and click the OK button to save the macro settings. **Do not select the Enable all macros option**. This could expose your computer to dangerous macro viruses.

If you do not want to put the Developer tab on your Excel ribbon you can use another approach. In the Excel Options dialog (Figure 5.2), select Trust Center. This action results in the screen shown in Figure 5.6. In this screen, click the Trust Center Settings button, which shows the settings in Figure 5.7. Then select Macro Settings from the list of options. This will produce the same dialog shown in Figure 5.5. Select the Disable all macros with notification option and click the OK button to save the macro settings. After you have set the macro settings correctly, you can open the XLSim software. When the software opens

Figure 5.2 Excel Options

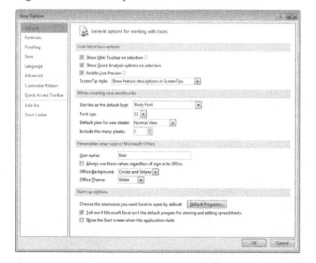

Figure 5.3 Customize Ribbon Dialog

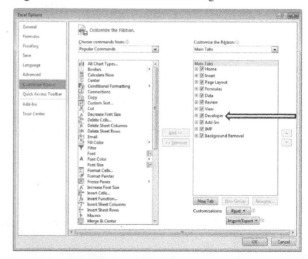

you will see the screen shown in Figure 5.8. Just above the formula bar in Excel is the warning that this problem contains macros. If you want to run the program, click the Enable Content button to enable the XLSim software.

Figure 5.4 The Developer Tab in the Excel Ribbon

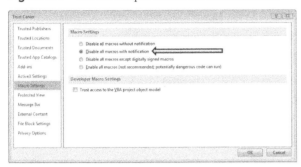

Figure 5.5 Macro Security Settings Dialog

Figure 5.6 Excel Trust Center

Figure 5.7 Trust Center Settings

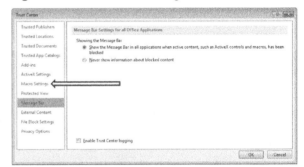

Figure 5.8 XLSim Opening Model Page

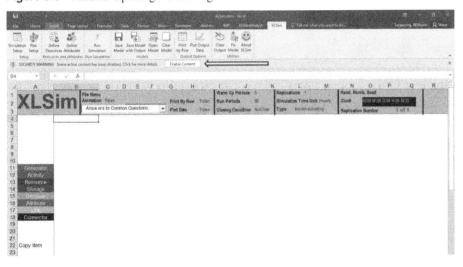

USE TRUSTED LOCATIONS

A second way of enabling macro software like XLSim to run is to store the software in a trusted location. Microsoft Excel has some trusted locations by default, but you can also create your own trusted locations. You can set up a folder that contains your trusted macro software, or you can create a folder for each Excel macro program that you use. For example, you could create a folder on your hard drive called XLSim. You can then tell Excel to trust macro programs stored in this location as follows.

Go to Excel Options as described in Figure 5.1, and in the options menu select the Trust Center option. Click the Trust Center Settings button as discussed previously. Rather than selecting Macro Settings from the options menu, select Trusted Locations. This will result in the dialog shown in Figure 5.9. You can see that there are several default trusted sites already in Excel. You can add your XLSim folder to the trusted locations by clicking the Add new location button. You then can add the location directly as shown in Figure 5.10, or you can click the Browse button to browse your hard disk to find the appropriate folder. Once you have done this, any Excel workbooks with macros located in this folder will start automatically when double clicked and will not display the warning as in Figure 5.8 but will directly open to the default worksheet.

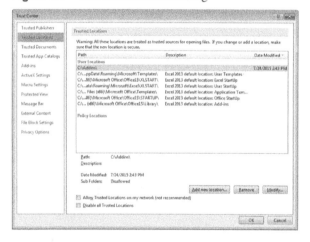

Figure 5.9 Trusted Locations Dialog

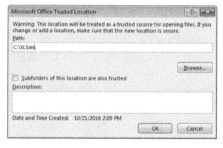

Figure 5.10 Entry of Trusted Location

The XLSim Working Environment

The main screen of XLSim is the Model view, which is shown in Figure 5.11, with the four major areas of this screen labeled here for discussion purposes.

AREA 1—THE XLSIM RIBBON

Area 1 of XLSim is the ribbon tab, which is added to the end of the Excel ribbon. If this tab is not displayed when XLSim is opened, simply click on the ribbon tab named XLSim. The ribbon contains the main commands of the software.

The first section of the tab contains two set-up buttons. The first button sets up the simulation by allowing the user to specify the various parameters of the simulation. These parameters are displayed at the top of the worksheet in Area 2. You will most likely want to change some or all of these parameters before running the simulation, and we will discuss them in more detail later

Figure 5.11 The Model Building Environment of XLSim

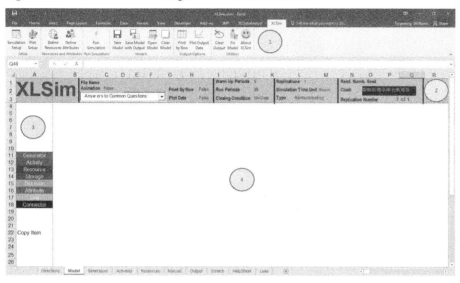

in this chapter. The second button in this section sets up the snapshot function to capture data to plot in a graph if you choose to plot the output. Whether or not you plot the output is determined by Plot Output Data in the Output Options section of the ribbon tab. When you click the Plot Setup button, the dialog shown in Figure 5.12 will appear.

Only two items of information are required in this dialog. First, you need to select the process metric which is to be plotted. XLSim will plot any one of the five common metrics: inventory, throughput, cycle time, wait time, or resource utilization. Second, you must specify how often the data snapshots are to be taken. Select the units (minutes, hours, days, weeks, or months) from the drop-down list and enter the number of periods in the text box. For example, entering a 10 in the dialog as pictured would take a snapshot of inventory every 10 minutes.

The second section of the XLSim ribbon tab is used to define either resources to be used in the model or attributes that can be assigned to flow units. Both resources and attributes have to be defined before they can be used in any models. We will discuss how to define them in detail later in this chapter.

The third section of the ribbon tab contains a single button that, when clicked, will run the simulation using the current model and the current parameters shown in area 2 of the screen.

The fourth section of the ribbon contains four buttons that relate to the model displayed in area 4 of the screen, which is currently blank. The first button saves the current model but does not save the output sheet. The second button saves the current model and also saves the current output sheet. This should only be used if the output sheet contains information based only on the current model. The third button in this section opens a model that has been previously saved to disk, and the fourth button clears the model portion of the window so that you can begin design of a new model.

Figure 5.12 Plot Setup Dialog

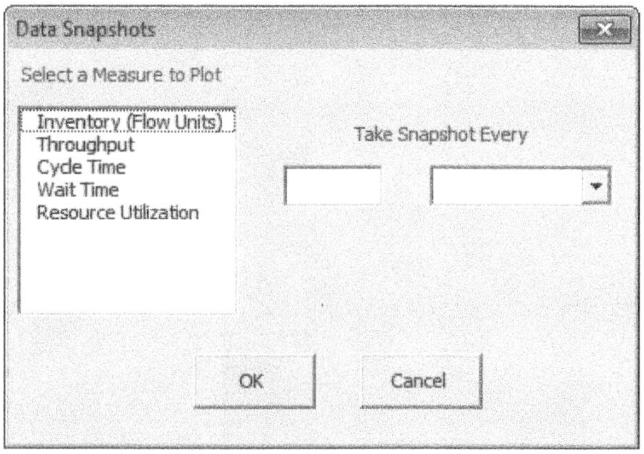

The fifth section of the ribbon labeled Output Options contains two toggle buttons that control two different aspects of the simulation output. Normally the results of a simulation run are output in an easy-to-read row-and-column format. Sometimes it may be desirable to print the entire output in one row. For example, this may be used to make it easier to compare outputs from different simulation models of the same process because the corresponding outputs for the different models are in the same column. Clicking the Print by Row button will turn this option on, and clicking it again will turn it off. The default is the off position. The other toggle button is the Plot Output Data option. When you turn this option on XLSim will take snapshots of selected data to plot in a graph. You must use the Plot Setup button described above to specify the needed information before taking these snapshots.

The sixth and final section of the ribbon contains three utility buttons to quickly perform certain tasks. The first button clears the output sheet. When this button is clicked, you will be warned that all previous output will be lost and asked to confirm that you want to delete this information. The second button labeled Fix Model requires a little more explanation. XLSim is a complex program and sometimes strains the limits of Excel. This means that in rare cases, errors can occur in the software which will render it unable to perform its editing functions. When this happens, double clicking a building block in the model may not have any effect, or you may not be able to drag a model element to a new location. If this happens, or if the cursor remains stuck in the "circling" icon, which means Excel is continuing to execute when it is not doing anything, click the Fix Me button. Normally this will reset the software to respond to your commands once again. Clicking this button is perfectly safe and will not do any harm to your model or and any unsaved output. The final button in this section brings up a simple About XLSim dialog box.

AREA 2—THE SIMULATION PARAMETERS SECTION

Area 2, located across the top of the screen, contains the name of the currently open model file—if there is one—information about the parameters of the simulation, some common questions and answers about XLSim, and a simulation clock. You cannot enter any information in this section. XLSim will display information here when you change the setup and while the simulation is running.

The question-and-answer drop-down list is designed to answer common questions about the simulation and XLSim models. When you select the drop-down arrow, you will see a list of questions, as shown in Figure 5.13a. When you select a particular question, an answer screen will pop up, such as that shown in the Figure 5.13b.

At the right side of Section 2 is the simulation clock. The clock is colored with a black background and a green foreground, as can be seen in Figure 5.11. This clock changes while a simulation is running to show the current status of the simulation clock.

The remaining information in this section relates to the setup of the simulation and is described in more detail later in this chapter.

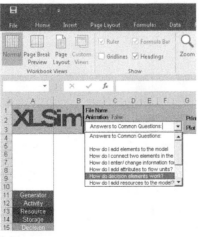

Figure 5.13 Question and Answer Box

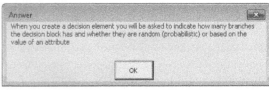

(a)　　　　　　　　　　　　　　　　(b)

AREA 3—THE MODEL BUILDING BLOCKS

Area 3 contains the model building blocks that are used to build a simulation model in XLSim. The block types are color coded for easy identification. The building blocks are Generators (red), Activities (green), Resources (dark blue), Storages (purple), Decisions (light blue), Attributes (brown), Links (gray) and Connectors (black). A building block is added to the model by double clicking that block in Section 3. That block is then copied in cell A23, where it is labeled Copy Item, so that you can see which block you are working with. If you then click anywhere in Section 4, the Model Canvas, that block is added to the model, and a corresponding dialog will be displayed to enter information for that block. The model building process and the use of the individual blocks is described in much greater detail later in this chapter.

AREA 4—THE MODEL CANVAS

Area 4 of the model worksheet contains the model itself. Although the model will contain some drawing objects such as arrows, it is very important that the model be built through the software rather than using the drawing objects in Excel. In that way, the elements of the model will be correctly cataloged in the software. **You should never add elements to the model using the drawing tools of Excel**. We will see in the next section how to add elements to a model.

You may move blocks in a model by clicking on the cell where the block is located and then hovering the mouse over one of the sides of the cell until the cursor turns into the familiar move symbol (the crosshair ⇠⇡⇢). Hold down the left mouse button and drag the block to the desired position. It is usually best to move blocks around in the diagram before you connect the blocks with arrows because moving blocks also affect the positioning of the arrows and can create a confusing diagram.

Building a Model

A model is built out of the eight basic building blocks in Area 3 of the layout. To place one of the blocks in the model, double click on the block in Area 3. When you do this the building block should appear below the Copy Item label. This is an indication that this block is ready to be pasted into the model area of the worksheet. Simply click on the location in the model area where you want to place the block. That building block should then appear in that cell and a dialog for that block type should pop onto the screen so that you can enter the relevant information for that block. You do not have to enter information for the block at this time. You can go back and change or enter new information at any time you wish. If you do not enter a name for the block it will be given a default name such as Activity1 or Resource3, depending on the block. Again, you can go back and change this later. If you click the cancel button of the dialog box, the block will be erased from the model. If you want the block to remain in the model, make sure you click the OK button. The dialogs will be discussed in the appropriate section when that model block type is discussed.

CONNECTING BLOCKS

To simulate the process, XLSim must know how the flow units move through the blocks of the model. You do this within the model by connecting the blocks with *connectors*. Connectors are added using the Connector element. Double click the Connector element so that it appears in the Copy Item area. Then click, first on the block that the connector starts from, and then click on the block that the connector goes to. An arrow will then appear in the model, indicating that flow units move from the block at the end of the arrow to the block at the head of the arrow. **Although connectors show up as arrows, you should never directly add arrows from the drawing tools in Excel to your model.** Connectors added in this way will not be properly recorded in the model.

THE LINK BLOCK

There is a special element in XLSim for linking blocks without drawing an arrow. The *Link block* is usually used to indicate backward looping in a model, typically in the case of rework after a quality test. Therefore, Link elements are commonly used after a Test block in the model. Link blocks can also be used to connect elements separated in the model by considerable distance. The primary purpose of the Link block is to promote clarity in the model. It can be used any time that drawing a direct connection would make the model look awkward. It is usually recommended that you use Link blocks only when necessary because they disguise the linkages of the model. Therefore, you should rearrange your model as much as possible so that you do not have to use them.

ATTRIBUTES AND RESOURCES

There are two elements in XLSim that must be defined before they are used in a model. The two elements are attributes and resources.

Attributes are characteristics that can be assigned to flow units in the model. Attributes can be discrete values, such as a type of surgery (major, minor or outpatient), or continuous, such as weight of a pallet of materials. Attributes are usually used to determine activity times or to determine the path taken when leaving a decision block. Attributes must be defined using the Define Attributes ribbon item before they can be used in a model. Transactions can then be assigned attribute values in Generator or Attribute blocks.

Resources are equipment or people that perform the work of activities. Therefore, resources are always associated with an activity. Resources are defined using the Define Resources ribbon item. The creation of attributes and resources is described in more detail in a later section of this chapter.

MODEL BUILDING BLOCKS

This section describes the eight building blocks of XLSim and the required information associated with each block.

Generator Blocks

Generator blocks create flow units for the model. Usually there are very few Generators and many models have only one generator. **However, every model must have at least one Generator**. In most cases, the Generator will be the first block in the model because nothing can happen in a model until a flow unit is generated. When you create a Generator block, the dialog shown in Figure 5.14 will appear.

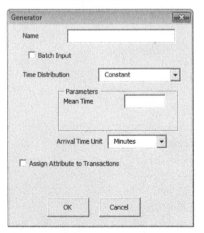

Figure 5.14 Information Dialog for the Generator Block

For a Generator, the requested information is a name, a distribution for the arrival times, the parameters of that distribution, and the time units of the distribution. If you do not enter a name for the Generator, XLSim will assign a generic name such as Generator1. There are four options for the arrival time distribution. These same four options, all continuous distributions, are available for other blocks that use distributions in XLSim, so we will discuss them in some detail here.

The *constant distribution* generates flow units at a constant rate. The only parameter is the constant time between arrivals of the flow units. For example, a constant distribution with a Time parameter of five minutes will generate a new flow unit in the simulation every five minutes. This is the simplest, but least realistic, arrival time distribution.

The *uniform distribution* is the continuous distribution in which each value is equally likely to occur. It has two parameters, a minimum and a maximum value. A uniform distribution with a minimum of 5 and a maximum of 10 is shown in Figure 5.15. If the time units of this distribution were minutes, the Generator would generate flow units at random times between 5 and 10 minutes.

The *exponential distribution* is the most commonly used distribution for arrivals in simulation models. The exponential distribution is a positively skewed distribution with a single parameter that represents the average time between arrivals. For example, an exponential distribution with a mean time of 5 minutes would generate flow units on average every 5 minutes, but sometimes it might be considerably longer between arrivals. An example of an exponential distribution with a mean of 5 minutes is shown in Figure 5.16.

Figure 5.15 Uniform Distribution with a Minimum of 5 and a Maximum of 10 Minutes

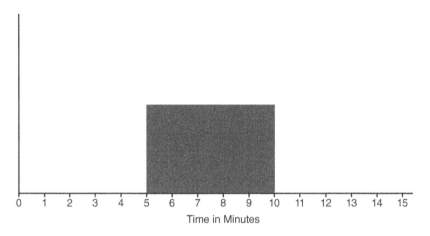

Figure 5.16 Exponential Distribution with a Mean of 5 Minutes

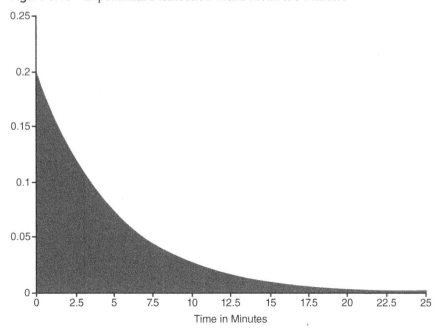

Figure 5.17 Example of a Normal Distribution with a Mean of 5 and a Standard Deviation of 1

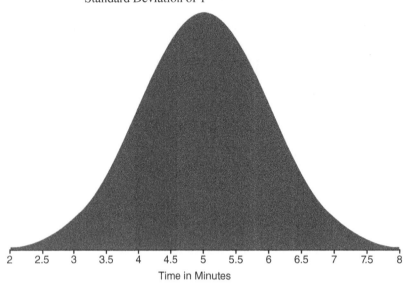

The *normal distribution* is the familiar symmetrical bell-shaped distribution from statistics. It has two parameters, a mean and a standard deviation. An example of a normal distribution with a mean of 5 minutes and a standard deviation of 1 minute is shown in Figure 5.17.

Activity Blocks

The heart of XLSim models are the activities of the process. Activities utilize resources to perform the work of the process. Each *Activity block* has a built-in queue so that normally no queues need be specified for an activity. The exception is when several activities utilize a common queue and then a Storage block described later can be used. When an Activity block is created, the dialog box shown in Figure 5.18 will appear.

The Activity block has the most input options of any block in XLSim. Besides the name for the activity, there are four tabs of information for the Activity block. When the dialog is first presented, the third tab labeled Task is showing. This tab has input for the Activity time distribution, the fixed cost and value-adding type of the activity, and the capacity of the activity. The default capacity is a finite capacity of 1. If you check the Unlimited box, the capacity will be unlimited. The fixed cost is entered as a number and is the cost per time unit of operating the activity. The options on the type of activity are VA for value-adding, NVA for non-value-adding, and BVA for business-value-adding, and are set by using the drop-down list. The activity time distribution is similar to the arrival time distributions. The distribution choices are constant, uniform, exponential, and normal. Again, the parameters that need to be input depend on the distribution chosen. For the Constant choice, simply enter the constant time to perform the service. The Uniform distribution requires minimum and maximum values. The Exponential distribution requires an average activity time, and the Normal distribution requires a mean and a standard

Figure 5.18 Task Tab of the Information Dialog for the Activity Block

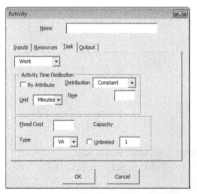

deviation. The last drop-down at the top of the tab is for the type of activity. Activities can be Work, the most common and the default, or they can be Delays. Delays are used to represent activities that are not important to the model but take time. For example, in a simulation of an operating room the cleanup of the room for the next surgery would take time, but the activity itself is not important to the modeling of the surgery activities and could be modeled as a delay.

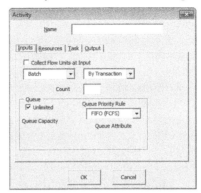

Figure 5.19 Inputs Tab of the Activity Block Information Dialog

The first tab of the Activity block dialog deals with information regarding how inputs to the activity are handled. This tab is shown in Figure 5.19.

The Collect Flow Units at Input check box determines whether or not the flow units are combined in some way before they are processed. If the box is checked units are combined according to the selections in the drop-down boxes below the check box. If the box is not checked, flow units are not combined. The two options for combining flow units are Batch and Join. *Batching* flow units are the most common situation and are the default. Batched flow units are combined but maintain their individual identity so that they can be unbatched later. Batching operations are quite common. Some examples might be loading pallets onto a truck, loading loaves of bread into an oven to be baked, or placing documents into a folder. *Joining*, on the other hand, combines flow units so that their identity is lost. Sometimes a flow unit may be split or copied for parallel work paths. These flow units would later be joined back into a single transaction. An example might be a patient at a medical clinic who has an x-ray taken. Following the x-ray process the patient and the x-ray may take different paths but come together again in the doctor's office, where the doctor reviews the x-ray with the patient. If you are modeling the flow of patients you would no longer need the x-ray as a separate flow unit, and we could join the two as one flow unit. The important point about batching and joining is that they affect the timing of flow units. When flow units are collected, they may need to wait for other flow units to form a batch or collection. For example, we may not be able to load the truck until all pallets have arrived at the loading dock. Or in our medical clinic example, the doctor cannot see the patient until both the x-ray and the patient have arrived at the office.

In addition to specifying whether the combining of flow units is a Batch or a Join, you also need to specify how to combine the units. Options are By Transaction, By Count, and By Attribute. By Transaction waits until all flow units from the same transaction arrive at the activity. This is usually after a flow unit has been split or copied, as with our patient and the x-ray. The By Count waits until a specified number of flow units are present before combining and processing the items. For example, loading the loaves of bread into an oven would occur when there were enough loaves to fill the oven. The By Attribute type is used when flow units are split or copied and assigned different values on the basis of some attribute. The By Attribute option waits until flow units with all of the relevant attributes arrive at the activity. An example might be in a manufacturing process where all parts and subassemblies have to be present in order for a product to be manufactured.

The bottom portion of the Inputs tab specifies information about how the queue operates. The first box indicates whether the queue size is unlimited or of finite length. The default is an unlimited queue length. If this box is unchecked, another box will appear for input of the capacity of the queue and two option buttons to indicate what happens to a flow unit when the queue is full. The two options are to exit the system or to wait. If incoming flow units must exit the process when the queue is full, select the exit option. This would be the case, for example, for incoming phone calls when a limited number can be put on hold. The other option might exist in a manufacturing facility or in a hospital where there is a limited amount of space to wait but flow units do not exit the system. In effect, in this case flow units have to wait at a prior point in the process. This waiting point is always the block that the flow unit was in just before trying to enter this activity. The last element of the Inputs tab, the drop-down box, is used to specify the queue discipline (priority rule). The alternatives are the default FIFO (first-in-first-out), which is essentially FCFS (first-come-first-served), LIFO (last- in-first-out), Minimum of Attribute, and Maximum of Attribute. These last two options can be used for a variety of priority rules such as earliest due date or shortest operation time. Of course, the relevant attributes such as due date or operation time would have to be specified to use the Minimum and Maximum options.

The tab labeled Resources can be used to specify the resources utilized in performing the activity. This tab is shown in Figure 5.20. Up to four different types of resources can be assigned to an activity. Multiple units of each type can be assigned, however. Only resources that have already been defined (see the section on Defining Attributes and Resources later in this chapter) can be assigned in this tab. If no resources have been defined, only the None option will appear in each drop-down box. If any resources have already been defined they will appear in the drop down list along with the None option. By default, no resources are assigned to an activity. When you assign a resource, you must also specify when the resource is occupied and how it is freed when the activity is finished. This is done in the drop-down next to the resource. The three options are Acquire/Release, Acquire, and Release. The default is Acquire/Release. The normal behavior is that a resource is "acquired" or becomes busy when the activity begins and is then "released" or becomes free when the activity is finished. However, sometimes a resource performs several activities in sequence and is not free until all of the activities are finished. In this case the activity would be set to Acquire at the first activity and would then be set to Release at the last activity in the sequence. The last box for each resource is to specify how many units of each resource are utilized for that activity. Sometimes multiple units of a resource might be used as with nurses in an operating room.

The final tab for an activity is the Output tab (Figure 5.21). This tab is quite simple: it consists of only three options that specify how flow units leave the activity. The default outputs the individual flow units. However, you can also duplicate flow units when they are output. This can be used when a job goes through parallel activities. For example, earlier we discussed the situation of a patient and the patient's x-ray following different paths. This can be simulated by duplicating the flow unit when it leaves an activity, and the two flow units would branch over different paths. Another example might be when files or documents are duplicated and sent to

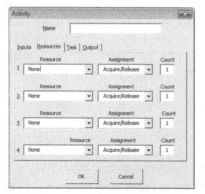

Figure 5.20 Resources Tab of the Activity Block Information Dialog

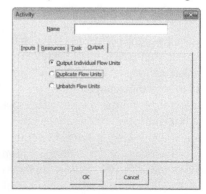

Figure 5.21 Output Tab of the Activity Block Information Dialog

different locations. The last option is to unbatch flow units that have been previously batched in the Inputs tab of an activity.

Resource Blocks

Resources are normally added through the Activities block as described previously, but they can also be added directly through the *Resource block*. When you add the Resource block to a model a pick list like that shown in Figure 5.22 will appear on the screen with a list of defined resources. Only a defined resource may be associated with the Resource block. If you need to add resources to the resource pool, you must use the Define Resources ribbon item. If you try to add a resource to the model before any resources have been defined, you will receive an error message notifying you that no resources have been defined.

To add a resource to the model, select the resource name from the list and click the OK button. Note that this adds the resource to the model but does not connect it to an activity. When you add a resource this way, you need to explicitly connect it to an activity using a connector.

The same resource can be used in multiple locations in the model. However, when the simulation is run, a given resource can only be involved in one activity at a time. Therefore, if a resource is busy on another activity, a second activity may have to wait until that resource is released before it can begin. If a resource has multiple versions, such as several nurses with the same basic skills, then different instances of that resource could be performing different activities. The number of units of a resource is specified when the resource is defined and must be changed via the Define Resources button.

Storage Blocks

Since queues are automatically associated with each activity in a model, you do not usually have to explicitly define a queue. However, there are situations when you do need to explicitly define a queue. For example, when multiple different activities share a common queue, you cannot use the separate queues of the different activities. The *Storage blocks* are designed for such situations. When you insert a Storage block in an XLSim model the dialog shown in Figure 5.23 will appear on the screen.

Since a Storage block is just a queue, it should not surprise you to find that the input dialog for this block is virtually the same as the Inputs tab of the Activity dialog, which defines properties of the queue for that activity. After entering a name for the Storage, or assuming the default name, you will need to specify whether or not incoming flow units are combined or not and provide the details about the queue. These inputs are described in detail in the previous section on the Activity block and are not repeated here.

Figure 5.22 Example of a Resource Pick List

Figure 5.23 Information Dialog for the Storage Block

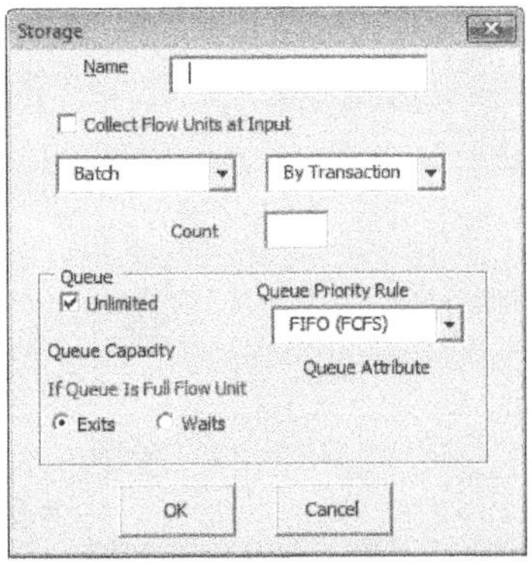

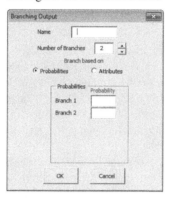

Figure 5.24 Information Dialog for the Decision Block

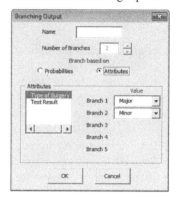

Figure 5.25 Dialog for the Decision Block with the Attributes Branching Option

Decision Blocks

A *Decision block* is used to transfer flow units down alternative paths based on some criterion. When a Decision block is created in a model, the information dialog shown in Figure 5.24 will appear on the screen. As usual, you can assign a name to the block, or XLSim will assign a default name for you. The primary input item in the Decision block is the basis of the branching. Branching can be on the basis of probabilities or on the basis of an attribute. Probabilistic branching is for those situations where a known percentage of the flow units follow each path. By default, there are two branches, but it is possible to have up to five branches out of a Decision block. Increasing the number of branches by entering a value in the text box, or using the spinner button, will automatically add new branches to the Probabilities frames. No matter how many branches are used with the Decision block, the sum of the probabilities must be equal to 1.0. In other words, a flow unit must follow one of the branches after it passes through the Decision block. If Attributes have been defined, you can elect to branch on the basis of an attribute by selecting the Attributes option. **If no attributes have been defined, this option will not be active**. If you select the Attributes option the dialog will change and a list of defined attributes will appear. Then you can select the branches that will be taken based on the value of an attribute associated with the flow unit. An example is shown in Figure 5.25. Selecting an attribute on the left will cause the number of branches to change, reflecting the number of values defined for that attribute.[2] XLSim will assign the attribute values to branches as shown in the figure, but you can change these assignments using the drop-down lists for each branch. With this option, you will no longer be able to change the number of branches using the text box or the spinner because the number of possible values for an attribute are defined when the attribute is defined. The only way to change this is to use the Define Attributes ribbon button to edit the attribute.

Attribute Blocks

The *Attribute block* can be used to assign an attribute value to transactions. Attributes can be assigned in a Generation block as well. Attributes can be used for a variety of different purposes in XLSim. Like resources, attributes must be created before they can be used in the model. Attributes are created using the Define Attributes ribbon button. Attributes and their creation will be discussed in detail later in the chapter.

---

2. Continuous attributes can also be used in a decision block. In that case you would specify cut-off values rather than probabilities for the various branches.

Discrete and continuous attributes are treated differently in XLSim and the specific information in the dialog box when an attribute block is created depends on what type of attribute is currently selected.

Discrete Attributes

For *discrete attributes,* values are assigned to transactions based on probabilities or percentages. These probabilities are specified each time a transaction is assigned a value in a Generator or Attribute block. Therefore, the assignment of probabilities could be different at different points in a model. However, the possible values of a discrete attribute cannot be changed in the model. To redefine the possible values of a discrete attribute, you must use the Define Attributes ribbon button.

When a discrete attribute is selected in the Attribute block, the predefined values for that attribute will be displayed along with text boxes to enter probabilities for each possible attribute value. An example for types of surgery is shown in Figure 5.26. When assigning probabilities to attribute values, keep in mind that the probabilities must sum to 1.0. In other words, one of the attribute values must be assigned to a transaction.

Continuous Attributes

Continuous attributes are assigned to transactions on the basis of a predefined function. A continuous attribute can be assigned an initial value when it is defined using the Define Attributes ribbon button. This initial value will be used for the attribute until the value is redefined in a Generator or Attribute block. The specific function used and the parameters of that function can be different in different Generator or Attribute blocks. When a continuous attribute is selected, the dialog will change to one such as that shown in Figure 5.27. You may then select a distribution to be used in the assignment and the parameters of that distribution. The distribution choices are the same as those for the Generator and Activity blocks: constant, uniform, exponential, and normal.

Link Blocks

As discussed briefly earlier, a Link block can be used to create a connection to a block in a different part of the model. The Link block should be used when the blocks are located far apart in the model and creating a regular link would cross other links and make for a confusing model. Link blocks are often used in rework cycles when a transaction needs to be sent back to a prior block to be reprocessed. When a Link block is created, the dialog shown in Figure 5.28 will appear on the screen.

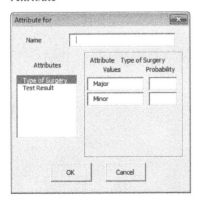

Figure 5.26 Dialog for the Attribute Block with a Discrete Attribute

Figure 5.27 Dialog for the Attribute Block with a Continuous Attribute

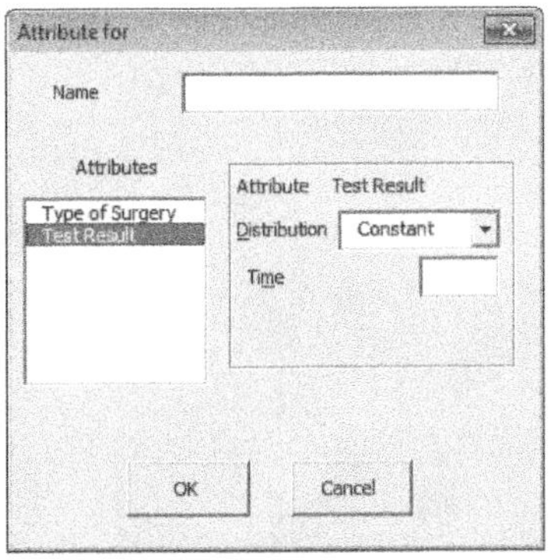

Figure 5.28 Sample Dialog for the Link Block

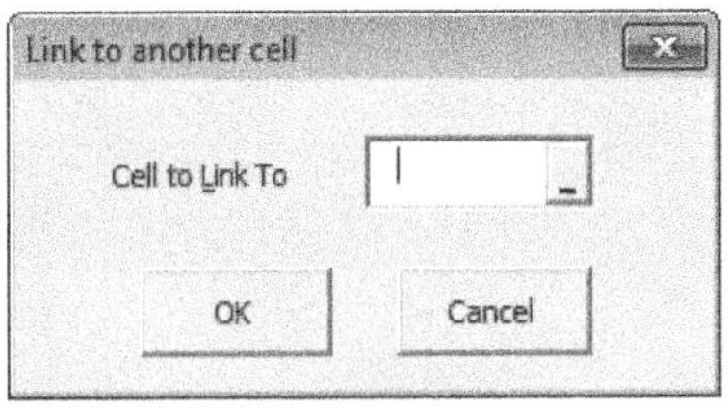

This dialog is very simple. The only information required is the location of the cell to link to. You can either enter the cell manually in the box, or you can click on the cell in the model to create the link. After you have entered the link, click on OK to exit the dialog. XLSim will not draw an arrow between the two cells but will record that link to be used in the simulation. You can always go back and change which cell is linked by double clicking on the Link block.

Connector Blocks

The final building block in XLSim is not really a model block at all. The *Connector block* is used to create links between model elements represented by arrows in the diagram. When the simulation is run, flow units proceed through the process following these links. To create connectors double click the Connector element so that it appears in the Copy Item area. Then click first on the block that the connector starts from and then click on the block that the connector goes to. An arrow will then appear in the model indicating that flow units move from the block at the end of the arrow to the block at the head of the arrow. **Although connectors show up as arrows you should never directly add arrows from the drawing tools in Excel to your model.** Connectors added in this way will not be properly recorded in the model.

Defining Attributes and Resources

As we have stated several times, attributes and resources must be defined before they can be used in the model. In this section we will describe how to create attributes and resources.

DEFINING ATTRIBUTES

Attributes are defined and modified using the Define Attributes ribbon button in XLSim. When this button is clicked the dialog shown in Figure 5.29 will appear on the screen.

Click the Add button to add an attribute. When you click the Add button an input box will appear for you to enter the name of the Attribute. If you click the Cancel button or do not enter a name, the attribute will not be added. When you enter a name for the attribute, that name will be added to the list of existing attributes. You can then designate whether the value is continuous or discrete by selecting the appropriate option. For continuous attributes you can input an initial value if you desire. In most cases, continuous attributes are assigned using one of the built-in functions in XLSim. These functions can be assigned in a Generator or Attribute block as described previously in this chapter. If you specify the discrete option, the dialog will change so that you can enter up to five possible values for the discrete attribute as shown in Figure 5.30. These values can be numeric but in most cases will be text descriptions of that attribute, such as a type of surgery or a product type. You can save the changes you have made to an attribute

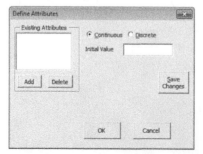

Figure 5.29 Sample Dialog for Defining Attributes

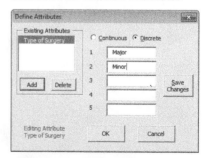

Figure 5.30 Dialog for Defining Attributes for Discrete Attributes

at any time by clicking the Save Changes button. When you make changes to an attribute you must save them before making changes to other attributes or adding another attribute. When changes have been made to an attribute a message is displayed in the lower left corner of the dialog stating which attribute is being edited. If you click on another attribute in the list without saving the changes you will be warned and asked if you want to save your changes. When you have finished defining or editing attributes click the OK or Cancel buttons to exit.

DEFINING RESOURCES

Resources are defined and modified using the Define Resources ribbon button. When you select this option the dialog shown in Figure 5.31 will appear. To add a resource, click the Add button. When you click the Add button an input box will appear for you to enter the name of the resource. If you click the Cancel button or do not enter a name, the resource will not be added.

When you enter a name for the resource, that name will be added to the list of existing resources. You can then enter the information for that resource such as its costs, its type, either labor or equipment, and the number of that type of resource available. The default value for the number of resources is 1. You can either set this value to a different number, or check the unlimited box if there is an unlimited amount of this resource. You can save the changes you have made to a resource at any time by clicking the Save Changes button. When you make changes to a resource, you must save them before making changes to other resources or adding another resource. When changes have been made to a resource, a message is displayed in the lower left corner of the dialog stating which resource is being edited. If you click on another resource in the list without saving the changes, you will be warned and asked if you want to save the changes. When you have finished defining or editing resources, click the OK or Cancel buttons to exit.

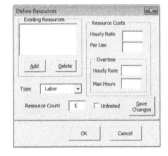

Figure 5.31 Sample Dialog for Defining Resources

Setting Up and Running the Simulation

In this section, we will assume that the model has been built and you are ready to run the simulation. Before running the simulation you will need to tell XLSim more about how you want to run the simulation and what kinds of output you want at the end of the simulation run.

SIMULATION SETUP

Before you can run the model, you first need to set up the simulation and its parameters. To set up the simulation, click the Simulation Setup button in the first section of the XLSim ribbon. The dialog shown in Figure 5.32 will then appear. The title is optional but may help you differentiate between different simulation runs since the title is printed on the output each time. The next items of input are for the number of warm-up periods and the number of run periods. To understand the role of warm-up periods it is necessary to understand the distinction between transient-state and steady-state systems. This distinction is made in a variety of subject areas ranging from chemistry and biology to engineering and economics.

Figure 5.32 Sample Dialog for Simulation Setup

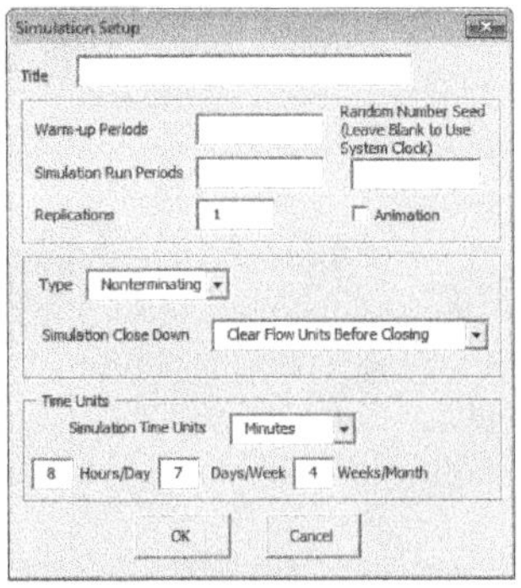

A *transient-state* system is one in which the average values of the variables that define the system change over time. In other words, the system is in a state of flux. In contrast, a *steady-state* system is one in which the average values of the system variables do not change over time; the system is in a state of equilibrium. In simulation, the system is always in a transient-state at the beginning, and its behavior tends to be quite erratic. If our interest is in the steady-state behavior of the system, then we may not want the statistics from the transient-state to influence the performance measures. If you specify a certain number of warm-up periods in the simulation setup, statistics will not be kept during this period. Statistics are always kept during the simulation run period and will cover the number of periods specified for this parameter. The time units will be those specified in the bottom portion of the dialog. The next parameter specifies the number of replications. Since the performance of any simulation depends to a certain extent on the starting random number seed, it is usually a good idea to perform several replications of each simulation condition and then use statistical analysis to test for significant differences in performances between scenarios.

The next input item is to specify a starting random number seed. In some cases you may want to compare simulations using different conditions with the same pattern of random events for a more direct comparison. You can do that by using the same random number seed each time. In most cases, however, you will not care about the random number seed, and you can leave this parameter blank. When the value is omitted, the system clock is used to set the random number seed. In most situations this is what you want.

The check box for Animation will turn on animation if checked. The default is to have animation turned off. Since the animation adds little to the analysis this will usually be left at the default.

The next section specifies what type of system we are dealing with (terminating or nonterminating) and what to do when the simulation finishes. A very important distinction in simulations is whether the process is terminating or nonterminating. *Terminating processes* are those that have a natural end point where all flow units are cleared from the system while *nonterminating processes* have no natural end point. Technically, terminating processes reach an end point at the end of the cycle (typically a day) where the system is cleared out and the process starts from scratch the next cycle. Nonterminating processes, however, never clear the system. Even if they stop for the day, they resume where they left off the next day with the queues and other system components in the same states as they were the day before. In the real world, terminating processes are usually those that shut down every day and everyone, including customers, leave the system. Examples include retail stores and medical clinics. These systems start the next day with zero flow units in the system. Nonterminating processes may be systems that operate 24 hours a day, 7 days a week, such as hospital emergency wards, but they do not necessarily have to run 24/7. For example, most manufacturing facilities can be considered to be nonterminating processes because when they shut down, the state of the system remains the same until they start again. In other words, there is no natural condition where the system empties and starts over. Therefore, simulating such a process for 240 hours would be equivalent to simulating 30 eight-hour days. In general, many terminating processes never reach a steady state condition. Nonterminating processes, on the other hand, usually reach a steady-state and it is the steady-state behavior that we are usually interested in when evaluating such systems. The drop-down box labeled Type is used to indicate the type of process being modeled.

For terminating systems, we also need to specify when the process terminates (i.e., what is the shut down cycle for the process). This is done by entering a value in the Close Down Every box and selecting a unit from the drop-down combo box. For example, if the system closed every day after eight hours, you would enter a value of 8 in the text box and select a unit of hours.

The drop-down box for Simulation Close Down determines what XLSim does with flow units within the system when the run time expires and how it calculates the statistics. The default is to clear all of the flow units before closing the simulation. This option effectively extends the run time until all units are processed. This option would be most relevant in a retail context because all customers have to be out of the store before it closes. Other options are to calculate statistics as they are at the end of the designated time without clearing the flow units and to calculate statistics only for those flow units that have completed the process.

The last entries in the simulation setup are to specify the time units of the simulation, how many hours the facility being simulated is open per day, and how many days are in a work week. You can also specify the number of weeks in a typical month. These values are only important if you use different time units in different points in the simulation, and the simulation time unit that you specify is days, weeks, or months. If the simulation time units are in minutes or hours, then these values have no effect on the simulation. For example, if the simulation time unit is weeks, and one of the activity times is specified in hours, then this information is used by XLSim to make the conversion.

RUNNING THE SIMULATION

After the model is built and the simulation setup parameters have been specified, you are ready to run the simulation. You can start the simulation by clicking the Run Simulation ribbon button. The simulation will begin and the simulation clock will indicate the current simulation clock time. When the simulation is finished, the output of the run will be displayed on the Output window, and you will automatically be transferred to view the output. Of course the actual output will depend on the model and the parameters specified, but in general, the output follows the outline shown in Figure 5.33.

Results are shown for each queue in the simulation, both those associated with activities and separate Storage blocks. Output is also shown for each resource and activity. Lastly, summary statistics are shown for the flow units and costs incurred in the simulation. We will examine some sample output in the next section when we look at a sample model.

To return to the model window, scroll to the top of the output window and click the Return to Model button or just click on the Model sheet tab at the bottom of the page. You can save the output to a file by clicking the Save Output button.

Figure 5.33 Outline of the Output from an XLSim Simulation

Category								
Generators	Transactions							
Queues	Transactions	% Blocked	Max Content	Current Contents	Avg Content	Num Zeros	Avg Wait	Avg Nonzero Wait
Resources	Count	Type	% Utilization					
Activities	Type	Transactions	Current Contents	Avg Time	Max Cap Used			
Flow Units	Count	Avg Cycle Time						
Costs	Per Flow Unit	Per Hour	Total					

OUTPUT OPTIONS

You can control how results are presented in the Output window. The options are to print an output summary in the format described in Figure 5.33, or to print the output as one long row. The default is to print a summary as shown in the figure. However, if you run multiple replications and want the data in a form suitable for copying to statistical software, then the print-by-row option would be best. This is controlled by the Print by Row option, which is a toggle button in the output options of the XLSim ribbon whose current value is also indicated by entry in the parameters section at the top of the screen. When this option is activated (the parameter section indicates True), output is printed by row. When the option is deactivated (the parameter section indicates False), the printed output will again be in summary format.

If you run many simulation runs, the Output sheet can become very full. If you want to clear the output and start over with a clean output sheet, select the Clear Output ribbon button. This will clear all of the results from the Output window. If you want to preserve some of the output make sure that you copy it to another worksheet or to another workbook or application, such as Microsoft Word, before clearing the output. Alternatively, you can use the Save Output ribbon button to save the output to an Excel file.

A Sample Model

To illustrate the operation of XLSim, consider a simple process consisting of three activities: Activity 1, Activity 2, and Activity 3. There are three resources involved in this process, Sam, John, and a Computer. The first activity occurs when the flow units first arrive at the process. This activity (Activity 1) is done by Sam using the Computer. Then 60% of the flow units go to Activity 2, which is performed by John, and 40% of the flow units go to Activity 3, which is performed by Sam.

Arrivals at the process are normally distributed with an average time between arrivals of 15 minutes with a standard deviation of 2 minutes. The activity times for Activity 1 follow an exponential distribution with a mean of 20 minutes, for Activity 2 the times are a constant 5 minutes, and for Activity 3 the times are normally distributed with a mean of 10 minutes and a standard deviation of 2 minutes. The model diagram is shown in Figure 5.34.

Figure 5.34 Model Diagram for the Sample Model

You may notice that the resources do not appear directly in the model diagram. This is done to simplify the diagrams and reduce clutter. For more complex models the inclusion of the resources for each activity can greatly increase the complexity of the diagram and make it difficult to interpret. However, the resources are there and have been associated with the activities. If you hover the mouse over an activity in an XLSim model, the resources, if any, will appear next to the activity as shown in Figure 5.35. To further clarify, the role of the resources in the model XLSim always contain a worksheet labeled Resource Table, which holds a table of the resources along with the average service times of the activities associated with each resource, and a total load for each resource. The resource table for our sample model is shown in Figure 5.36. Notice that Sam has the largest load with a total load of 35 minutes. This indicates that Sam may well be the bottleneck resource of this process.

The model was simulated as a nonterminating system with a warm-up period of 1,000 minutes and a run period of 1,000 minutes. The simulation close down was set to "Calculate

Figure 5.35 The Sample Model with Resources Displayed

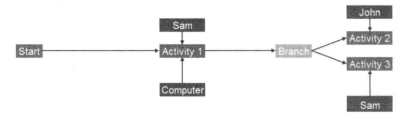

Figure 5.36 The Resource Table for the Sample Model

	A	B	C	D	E	F
1	Minutes	Activity 1	Activity 2	Activity 3	Total Load	
2	Sam	20	5	10	35	
3	Computer	20			20	
4	John		5	10	15	
5						

Figure 5.37 Sample Output for the Sample Model

	A	B	C	D	E	F	G	H	I	J
1	*Sample Model*									
2	Replication 1		Time Units in: Minutes							
3	Arrivals		Flow Units							
4	Start		110							
5	Queues		Flow Units	% Blocked	Max Content	Current Contents	Avg Content	Num Zeros	Avg Wait	Avg Nonzero Wait
6	Activity 1		55	0.00%	33	33	4.364	0	948.482	948.482
7	Activity 2		13	0.00%	0	0	0.000	13	0.447	0.447
8	Activity 3		8	0.00%	0	0	0.000	8	0.000	0.000
9	Resources		Count	Type	% Utilization					
10	Sam		1	Labor	100.00%					
11	Computer		1	Equipment	92.27%					
12	John		1	Labor	65.70%					
13	Activities		Type	Flow Units	Current Contents		Avg Time	Max Cap Used		
14	Activity 1		VA	21	1		16.398	1		
15	Activity 2		VA	13	0		5.000	1		
16	Activity 3		VA	8	0		9.657	1		
17	Completed Flow Units		Count	Avg Cycle Time						
18			43	267.197						
19	Run Periods		Specified	Actual						
20			1,000.000	1,000.000						
21	Costs		Per Flow Unit	Per Hour	Total					
22	VA(Based on Activity Times)		$0.00	$0.00	$0.00					
23	BVA(Based on Activity Times)		$0.00	$0.00	$0.00					
24	NVA(Based on Activity Times)		$0.00	$0.00	$0.00					
25	Labor(Per Hour or Per Use)		$0.00	$0.00	$0.00					
26	Equipment(Per Hour or Per Use)		$0.00	$0.00	$0.00					
27	Other(Per Hour or Per Use)		$0.00	$0.00	$0.00					
28	Standard		$0.00	$0.00	$0.00					
29	Overtime		$0.00	$0.00	$0.00					

Statistics Without Clearing." The output for this sample run is shown in Figure 5.37. Conceptually, the output of XLSim consists of eight different sections. The first section of the output contains the simulation title, the replication number, and the time units of the simulation, in this case minutes. The next section shows the number of flow units generated overall by each generator in the model. In this case there is only one generator named Start which generated 110 flow units over the entire simulation. The rest of the output relates only to the run periods and ignores the statistics from the warm-up period.

The next section shows the results for each of the queues in the model. The only queues in this example are those associated with the three activities. You can see that 55 transactions entered the queue for the first activity during the run period. There were still 33 flow units in the queue at the end of the simulation. Only 21 units were processed through the first activity and passed on to Activities 2 and 3, 13 to Activity 2, and 8 to Activity 3. The average wait time in the queue for Activity 1 is a little over 948 minutes or almost 60 hours. The average weight for Activity 2 is less than .5 minutes or a little less than 30 seconds. There is no waiting for Activity 3.

The next section shows the utilization of the resources used in the model. The busiest resource was, of course, Sam who was at 100% utilization during the run period. The computer was also busy over 90% of the time but John was only busy about 66% of the time. The third section shows the number of flow units processed by each activity and the average service time of the activities. These average activity times are fairly close to the given average times of 20, 5, and 10 minutes.

The fourth section shows that 43 flow units were completed during the run period. The average cycle time was approximately 267 minutes, or almost 4 and one-half hours. Obviously this process is not functioning very well, and the obvious bottleneck is Sam.

Chapter Glossary

Activity block A block where resources are used to perform the work of the process in transforming the flow units.

Attribute A characteristic of flow units in the simulation that can be used for routing in Decision Blocks and for activity times in Activity Blocks.

Attribute block Model block where flow units are assigned a value for an attribute.

Batching Action in which flow units are grouped together but maintain their individual identities.

Connector blocks Model building blocks which connect two other model blocks, and which indicate the direction of flow of the flow units.

Constant distribution Values are constant with no variation.

Continuous attribute An attribute that can take on any value in an interval of values. Usually defined by a function.

Decision block A model block where flow units may take alternative routes with branching either based on an attribute or determined probabilistically.

Discrete attribute An attribute that can take on only a limited number of values.

Exponential distribution A positively skewed distribution of times from a Poisson process.

Generator block A model block that generates flow units that move through the simulation.

Joining Action in which flow units are grouped together in such a way that they lose their individual identity.

Link blocks Link blocks are used to connect model blocks that would be awkward to connect with a regular connection.

Nonterminating process A process that never ends or never clears out the system and starts over.

Normal distribution A symmetrical bell-shaped distribution with two parameters: a mean and a standard deviation.

Resource block Place where resources are assigned to an activity.

Resources Labor and equipment that are used in the performance of an activity.

Steady State When a system is in steady state, the average values of variables that define the state of the system are constant over time.

Storage block A model block that represents a queue or waiting area.

Terminating process A process that ends after a certain number of periods and clears out the system to start over again the next period.

Transient state When a system is in a transient state, the variables that define the state of the system vary over time. The behavior of the system is erratic.

Uniform distribution Situation in which values are distributed uniformly across a range of values.

Discussion Questions and Problems

1. Simulate a single-server queuing model with exponential arrival and service times under the following conditions:
   a. The mean interarrival time and the mean service times are both equal to 5 minutes. Run the simulation for 100, 500, 1000, 2,000 and 5,000 hours. Plot the average queue times. What conclusions can you draw from this plot? (Hint: Perform the simulation runs with the same random number seed and turn on the Print Output By Row option)
   b. Simulate the same conditions when the mean service time is 3 minutes. How do the results compare with those in part a?

2. Perform a simulation analysis of problem 3 in Chapter 4. How do your answers here compare with the analytical answers from Chapter 4?

3. The ticket counter at Skyways Airlines currently is configured to allow customers to queue up in front of each ticket agent. Customers arrive at a rate of 12 per hour. Service times for the ticket agents are uniformly distributed between 2 and 10 minutes.
   a. Develop a simulation model for Skyways and determine the minimum number of ticket agents that will result in an average wait time of 5 minutes or less.
   b. A consultant has suggested that Skyways would be better off having a single queue form before the ticket agents and the customer at the front of the line going to the next available ticket agent. Simulate this arrangement to determine the minimum number of ticket agents that will result in an average wait of less than 5 minutes. How does this answer compare with your answer in part a?

4. The audit process at the Womack accounting firm follows a four-step process: Preliminary Review, Fieldwork, Audit Report, and Follow-up Review. Different groups in the organization handle the different phases of the process. The following table shows the activities, their associated times, and the resources involved in each. Assuming that audit clients arrive at a rate of 2 per day, build a simulation model to answer the following questions. You can assume 8-hour days for purposes of the simulation.

Activity	Distribution	Parameters	Resources
Preliminary Review	Normal	Mean = 5 hours Standard Dev = 1 hour	Junior Accounting Team
Fieldwork	Exponential	Mean = 20 hours	Student Intern
Audit Report	Exponential	Mean = 35 hours	Senior Accounting Team
Follow-up Review	Normal	Mean = 3 hours Standard Dev = 1 hour	Junior Accounting Team Senior Accounting Team

   a. What is the average resource utilization for the various resources?
   b. What is average cycle time of the audit?

c. Which activity seems to have the most problems as evidenced by the length and time in the queue?

5. Rockford National Bank currently operates its teller windows on the basis of separate queues for each teller. The daughter of the bank president, a student at the local university, has told her dad that according to what she learned in her Process Management class, a single queue would be more efficient. Assume that customers arrive at the bank every minute on average and the that the times follow an exponential distribution. Service times also follow an exponential distribution with a mean of 4.5 minutes. Simulate both systems with the appropriate number of tellers for 20 days (Assume 8 hours per day). What would you recommend to the bank president?

6. The Arrowsmith Manufacturing Company produces custom manufactured plastic parts for other manufacturing companies in the area. A key aspect of the manufacturing process at Arrowsmith is a plastic extruder that forces hot plastic through a die to produce parts of various shapes and thicknesses. When this machine breaks down and requires repairs, the entire production process comes to a halt. Arrowsmith employs a single repair technician who works on the extruder and other equipment used in the manufacturing process. Currently, Arrowsmith performs maintenance on the extruder only when it breaks down and requires repairs. The average time between failures of the extruder is 400 minutes, with the times following an exponential distribution. When repairs are required on the extruder, they take an average of 90 minutes, with the service times also following an exponential distribution. Jobs arrive at the extruder at a rate of 10 per hour, and it takes an average of 5 minutes to finish a job. All times follow an exponential distribution. Arrowsmith management is considering revising its maintenance policy on the extruder to performing maintenance on the extruder every 8 hours. The maintenance takes 60 minutes but extends the time between failures to an average of 700 minutes. What would be the impact of this new policy on the overall output of the extruder as compared with the current policy? What would you recommend to Arrowsmith management?

7. Antigua Inc. manufacturers upscale watches that are sold in the stores of large retailers such as Target and Walmart. The watches are assembled utilizing an assembly line process with five work stations. Antigua's manufacturing engineers have designed the assembly line so that it is perfectly balanced, with each work station taking 5 minutes on average to perform its part of the watch assembly. Antigua management, therefore, expects that a watch will be produced every five minutes or at a rate of 12 watches per hour. That means that the assembly process should produce 96 watches per 8-hour shift.

   a. Assuming that the times at each work station follow a normal distribution with a mean of 5 minutes and a standard deviation of 1 minute, simulate the watch assembly process for 1,000 8-hour shifts. Does the performance of the assembly line meet management's expectations? Why might the performance be different from what is expected?
   b. Simulate the process for 1,000 8-hour shifts assuming that the times at each work station follow an exponential distribution with a mean of 5 minutes. Is the performance of the assembly process better or worse than it was before? What could explain this result? (Hint: Compare the standard deviation of the exponential distribution with that of the normal distribution).

Part II
Process Analysis and Design

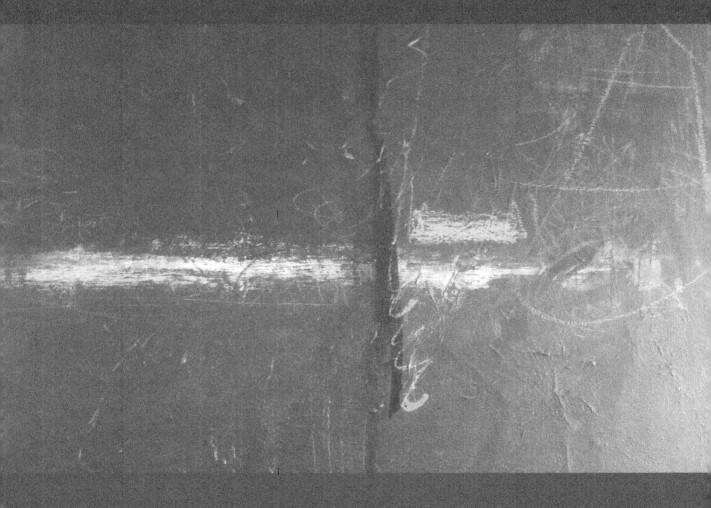

Chapter 6
Objectives and Strategy in Business Process Design

"However beautiful the strategy, you should occasionally look at the results."
—Winston Churchill

"You have to be fast on your feet and adaptive or else a strategy is useless."
—Charles de Gaulle

"If you automate a mess you get an automated mess."
—Amy Wold

Although the literature on business process design is in the nascent stage, one thing in the literature is clear: Well-designed business processes must be connected to the strategic goals of the organization. It is also clear from the far more extensive literature on goals and objective setting, that any design that does not begin with well-established goals and objectives has little chance of ultimate success. This chapter lays out the key linkages between business process design and business strategy and provides some basic principles and objectives for business process design that have been gleaned from the literature. Process design can relate to both design of entirely new processes or the redesign of existing organizational processes. Since it is unlikely that most readers of this text will ever design an organization and its processes from scratch, our primary emphasis here will be on process redesign.[1]

---

1. The term redesign seems to imply that the process was designed in the first place. As is often said in the reengineering literature, the assumption that the process was engineered or rationally designed in the first place is likely erroneous. Most processes seem to simply evolve over time with little apparent rational design taking place.

Strategy and Process Design

The concept of strategy was borrowed from military use and adapted to a business context. Although most business scholars would agree that strategy is important to any organization, there is little agreement on what strategy means or how one goes about devising a strategy. At the simplest level, a strategy is simply a plan of action designed to achieve a particular goal. In a military context, a strategy is a plan of action designed to win a particular battle or an entire war. In a business context, the main goal of a strategy is to achieve a competitive advantage over competing organizations (Porter 1996). Mintzberg (1994) has pointed out that writers use the term strategy in at least four ways:

1. Strategy as a plan: How do we get from where we are to where we want to be? This is the basic idea of strategic planning (Steiner, 1979).
2. Strategy as a pattern of actions over time: Even before it adopted the catch phrase it was very obvious that WalMart was pursuing a low-cost strategy. This is what Mintzberg (1994) called the realized, or emergent, strategy.
3. Strategy as a position: A position in the market that reflects decisions about the products and services offered and the markets entered (Porter 1996).
4. Strategy as perspective: The vision and direction point of view.

No matter how we define strategy, it is obvious that the strategy reflects the direction that senior management believes the organization should go and how resources should be allocated. Therefore, everything that the organization does, including process design, should be done with the overall strategy in mind.

Of course, not every process in an organization is of strategic importance. This implies that different processes may need to be treated differently when it comes to process design. The process-strategy matrix shown in Figure 6.1 demonstrates this. The matrix has the strategic importance of the process on the horizontal axis. The vertical axis encompasses two factors: process complexity and the dynamic nature of the process. The dynamism of the process is an indicator of how often the process has to change. Processes located in the lower left quadrant of the graph are simple processes with little strategic impact that do not change often. Such processes are prime candidates for automation. Processes in the upper left quadrant are complex dynamic processes that are of little strategic importance to the organization. Such processes are prime candidates for outsourcing. For many organizations, processes related to information technology have been judged to be in this quadrant. Processes in the upper right corner of the matrix are complex dynamic processes that are highly important strategically. These processes are the core processes that provide an organization with its competitive advantage. These processes must be designed with the utmost care. Processes in the lower right quadrant are relatively simple processes but have high strategic importance. Although in most cases not many processes fall into this quadrant, the design of those that do is important. They should be automated (digitized), if possible, and optimized with respect to metrics that are important to the customer. Examples of this type of process are the customer-facing processes that increasingly occur via the Internet. As Desmet et al. (2015) reported, a leading energy company reduced customer churn among customers who moved by 40% by making service renewal a simple two-click process online, and a bank cut its new mortgage costs by 70% and reduced preapproval times from several days to one minute by digitizing its mortgage application and approval process.

SELECTING PROCESSES TO REDESIGN

In most cases, the first logical question is which process or processes should the organization redesign and improve? Ultimately, the answer to this question depends on the organization, its

Figure 6.1 The Process-Strategy Matrix

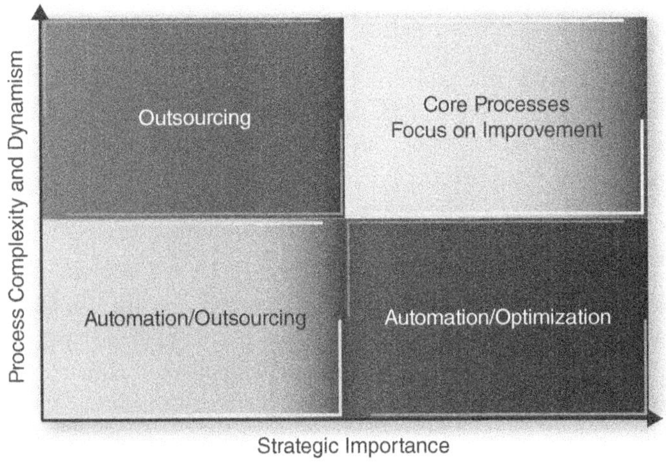

Y-axis: Process Complexity and Dynamism
X-axis: Strategic Importance

- Top-left: Outsourcing
- Top-right: Core Processes — Focus on Improvement
- Bottom-left: Automation/Outsourcing
- Bottom-right: Automation/Optimization

Source: Adapted from Harmon, 2003, p. 82

core processes, and its strategy. As we have argued before, process design must be done in the context of the overall strategy of the organization, and this includes selecting processes to redesign as well as how they are designed. Although the choice of processes to redesign depends on the nature and strategies of the organization, there are some useful guidelines that can be gleaned from the literature.

Broken or Dysfunctional Processes

Although fairly obvious, the most likely candidates for process redesign are those processes that are not performing well currently, i.e., those that are in the most trouble. But this begs the question of how can we tell a process is broken or not performing well? In their reengineering book Hammer and Champy (1993) outline some useful indicators of broken processes:

- Extensive information exchange
- Reentering of data in information systems
- High ratio of checking, inspection, and control to value adding activities
- Rework and work looping
- Numerous inventories and buffers
- Process complexity
- Numerous exceptions and special cases

The first three indicators arise because of the fragmentation of the process, usually between functional units of the organization. This fragmentation often necessitates extensive information exchange and the unnecessary entry of data in redundant data systems.

Important Processes

Redesigning and implementing process change often involves significant resources, so ideally we would want to make those investments in the most important or core processes of the organization. Any customer-facing process could certainly be considered important, but the core processes or distinctive competencies of the organization would also be considered to be important processes.

Process Improvement Potential

Along with how dysfunctional and important a process is, we should also consider the feasibility of being able to successfully redesign the process to achieve positive results. The feasibility of process improvement involves considering the organizational climate, the number of different organizational units involved, and the individuals involved in the process, among other factors. Certainly the likelihood of gaining key management support for the effort would be an important factor in the improvement potential.

UNDERSTANDING THE PROCESS

Although there are subtle differences between redesigning an existing process and designing an entirely new process, in both cases a critical need is to understand the purpose of the process and, in particular, what the customer of the process desires from that process. Every process has a customer or set of customers and what they want from the process should be a critical starting point of the process design or redesign. If the process is an existing process, we need to also understand how the process is currently functioning and why the performance of the process is unsatisfactory. Business process benchmarking as discussed in Chapter 3 can be very helpful in gaining process understanding. If the benchmarking is done on a global basis with organizations that perform that process very well, benchmarking can also generate ideas for creative new process designs. In all cases, it is important to understand both the existing process and the customers and their needs.

It is important to keep in mind that processes can be described at different levels. Every high-level process consists of different *subprocesses*. Each subprocess consists of smaller subprocesses and so on. In fact, we can describe an individual activity as a process. This implies that the individual activity is the smallest component level of a process. For example, a process like order fulfillment consists of many subprocesses such as order entry, order picking, packaging, shipping, and so on. Each of these subprocesses can also be further broken down into subprocesses. The point of all of this is that when you are trying to understand an existing process, it is often easiest to start at the highest level and work your way down to more detailed levels as necessary.

Many of the tools that we will discuss in Chapter 7 are useful for process understanding, especially such tools as flowcharting and process mapping. The 5w2h framework[2] can also be very helpful in understanding an existing process or the process of another organization as part of a benchmarking effort. This framework involves asking five *w* questions (who?, what?, when?, where?, and why?), and two *h* questions (how? and how much?). The framework is shown in more detail in Figure 6.2

Figure 6.2 The 5w2h Framework

Classification	5w2h questions	Description
People	Who?	Who is performing the activity? Why is this person doing it? Could/Should someone else perform the activity?
Subject matter	What?	What is being done in this activity? Can the activity in question be eliminated?

---

2. The 5w2h framework is derived from the 5w1h, which is widely used to analyze situations in areas as diverse as police work, journalism, and Web design. This 5w2h framework adds the second *h* for how much it costs.

Classification	5w2h questions	Description
Sequence	When?	When is the best time to perform this activity? Does it have to be done at a certain time?
Location	Where?	Where is this activity carried out? Does it have to be done at this location?
Purpose	Why?	Why is this activity needed? Do we really need to perform this activity? (Because we have always done it is not a good answer)
Method	How?	How is the activity carried out? Is this the best way or are there alternatives?
Cost	How much?	How much does it currently cost? What would be the estimated cost after improvement?

Source: Adapted from Robinson 1991, p. 245.

Answering these questions can be a great help in process understanding and may also generate ideas for process improvement. The 5w2h framework is especially useful in distinguishing between value-adding and non-value-adding activities in the process.

EVALUATE ENABLERS OF PROCESS REDESIGN

Once you have gained a basic understanding of a process, you are in a position to evaluate key factors that may enable innovative design or redesign of the process. Enablers can generally be classified into three categories: new technologies, human resources, and organizational enablers.

Technology as a Design Enabler

New technologies, and especially information technologies, have been a key enabler of successful process redesign over the past 10 to 20 years. However, creative process design is more than just applying new technologies to an old process. Automation is not the same thing as redesign, as the quote from Amy Wold at the beginning of this chapter indicates. Hammer and Champy (1993) offered two questions that a redesign team should ask with respect to new technologies:

- How can new technologies be used to enhance, streamline, or improve what we are doing now?
- How can new technologies enable us to do things that we are not currently doing or do things in totally different ways?

The first question comes closest to the automation answer, but the second one can lead to more innovative solutions. One should always ask how new technologies can be used to enable us to do new things or do things in entirely new ways. One only has to look at the massive changes in the financial services sector over the last decade to appreciate the potential impact of information technologies on the performance of processes and the types of products and services that can be offered. According to Hammer and Champy (1993) the largest potential of new information technologies is to break traditional rules of how work should be done. Figure 6.3 outlines some of the "old rules" that information technologies have allowed organizations to break and replace with new rules.

Figure 6.3 Technology as a Means to Break Old Work Rules

Old Rule	New Technology	New Rule
Information can appear in only one place at a time.	Shared databases	Information can appear simultaneously in as many places as needed.
Only experts can perform complex work.	Expert systems	Almost anyone can do the work of an expert.
Organizations must choose between centralization and decentralization.	Telecommunication networks	Organizations can simultaneously obtain the benefits of centralization and decentralization.
Managers make all the decisions.	Decision support tools	Decision making is part of everyone's job.
Field personnel need offices where they can receive, store, retrieve, and transmit information.	Wireless data communication Portable computing	Field personnel can send and receive information from wherever they happen to be.
The best contact with a potential buyer is personal contact.	Interactive media and Web pages	The best contact with a potential buyer is an effective and convenient contact.
People must find where things are.	Automatic identification tracking technology RFID	Things tell you where they are.
Plans get revised periodically.	High performance computers	Plans get revised instantaneously.

Source: Adapted from Hammer & Champy (1993)

Human Resource Enablers

Human resource enablers relate to job skills, motivation, and human resource policies. Specific skill sets possessed by employees involved in the process can be utilized to advantage in process design. Training is also another important enabler. Hammer and Champy (1993) and Davenport (1993) both noted that structuring work as a process usually requires different skills than traditional functionally-oriented work. Therefore, training becomes a significant factor in the ultimate success of the new process. Compensation and employee evaluation become issues in process-oriented work when the traditional functional organizational structure is maintained. How are employees to be compensated when working as part of a process, especially in a work team environment? Who evaluates the workers in such a system and how do we resolve differences in goals and objectives between functional areas of the organization? Because of the significant human resource issues involved, most organizations will want to ensure that the human resource function is adequately represented on the process design team.

Organizational Enablers

Davenport (1993) classified organizational enablers as either structural or cultural. An example of a structural enabler might be the existence of work teams. Work teams can provide many benefits to an organization (Kinlaw, 1991). Of particular relevance to process management and design are cross-functional teams. Cross-functional teams are known to be beneficial to the process design effort, but they can also be a significant benefit in performing the work of the process as well. This is not to say that setting up and managing cross-functional teams is an easy process or that there are not problems with such teams. One of the most significant difficulties is that team members often still have functional affiliations and are usually evaluated by functional managers. This can create considerable conflict for individual members of the team who have split allegiances between the team and a functional area of the organization. Nonetheless, empowered, autonomous work teams form the basis of the case management approach to process work described by Davenport (1993).

Organizational enablers can also be cultural. For example, over the past decade, there has been movement toward more empowerment of workers and greater participation in the decision-making process. This participative approach fits well in a process environment. Empowered workers have been a major factor in many customer-facing processes as evidenced by the case management movement. An organization with a cultural history of empowerment is better situated to implement cross-functional processes.

Basic Principles of Process Design

Although effective process design is a creative process and the ultimate success often depends on the skills and creativity of the individuals involved with the design team, there are some general principles that can aid in the design process. Many of these principles come from the recent literature on reengineering and the organization of manufacturing facilities (Hammer and Champy, 1993; Hyer and Wemmerlov, 2002; Laguna and Marklund, 2005). Other principles are more technical and work-flow oriented and have been known for some time in the fields of operations management and industrial engineering.

1. **Organize work around outcomes, not tasks:** The goal here is to move toward more horizontally integrated activities and away from fractionalized specialized activities. Applying this principle means that several tasks previously performed by different individuals in the organization will be combined into a single activity. An important enabler of this principle is cross-functional training. This principle has led to the case management approach (Davenport and Nohria, 1994). The *case management approach* utilizes a case manager who oversees a complete work process to deliver an entire product or service to the customer. The case manager is typically located where the customer and other functional areas of the organization intersect. The case manager has complete authority to make decisions and resolve customer issues. IBM Credit utilized such an approach to great success.

2. **Let those who use the process output perform the process:** The easiest way of stating this principle is to do the work where it makes the most sense. The goal is to avoid excessive delegation of responsibility and is similar in spirit to the first principle of horizontal integration of work.

3. **Merge information processing and data-gathering activities:** According to this principle, the individuals who gather the data should also process it and turn it into useful information. Eliminating a second group that processes data that it did not gather eliminates additional handoffs and reduces the risk of errors.

4. **Capture the information once—at the source:** This is similar in spirit to the previous principle. The aim of this is to eliminate information redundancy and the resulting errors that inevitably result. Data should be entered into a system only once, when it is first gathered.

5. **Put the decision point where the work is performed and build control into the process:** This principle involves the vertical integration of work in that additional layers of supervisory work are eliminated and the decision-making power and responsibility for quality and control of the process is integrated into the process where the work is performed. The result is a flattening of the organizational structure.

6. **Treat geographically dispersed resources as though they were centralized:** With modern information systems, geographically dispersed workers need no longer be automatically considered as decentralized. This provides extra flexibility for the design team to make the best decision regarding the centralization/decentralization issue.

7. **Link parallel activities instead of just integrating their output:** Parallel activities in a process often operate independently, and their results are not integrated until the point where the separate paths merge again. This can lead to expensive rework and waste. This principle implies that there should be linkages and coordination between the parallel activities to ensure that this does not happen.

8. **Design the process for the dominant flow, not for the exceptions:** All too often, processes focus too much on special cases and exceptions, which makes the process overly complicated. The IBM Credit Corporation case discussed in Hammer & Champy (1993) is a great example of a process complicated by exceptions and special cases.

9. **Mistake-proof the process if possible:** This principle implies that we should look for ways to design the process so that it becomes virtually impossible for mistakes to occur. This principle derives from the work of the famous Japanese industrial engineer Shigeo Shingo and because of its origins is often called *Poka-Yoke*. This deceptively simple principle has been widely adopted in consumer product design and is evident in everyday life, e.g., cars that make a noise when the door is opened with the headlights still on, self-flushing public toilets, and ATMs that start buzzing if you do not remove your card are all examples of this principle.

10. **Examine the interactions with other processes and avoid suboptimization:** Earlier we noted that a process consists of subprocesses and that the subprocesses themselves consist of subprocesses and so on down to the level of the individual activity. In fact, any process can be viewed as a subprocess of a higher level process and all processes are input into some other process. This means that a process always interacts or is interfaced with other processes. The danger in process design is that we can optimize the process we are designing but cause harm to another process that interfaces with it. If the process being designed is a subprocess within an organization this is called suboptimization. Suboptimization simply means that when we optimize a subprocess we cause the overall process to perform more poorly.

11. **Minimize sequential processing and handoffs:** Sequential processing is a vestige of the division of labor approach, which is, in many ways, the opposite of the process approach to work. Sequential processing has two disadvantages: (1) Handoffs between activities often lead to buffers and waste, and (2) the activities are dependent on one another and therefore are constrained by the slowest activity. To illustrate the problems, consider a process that consists of four activities A, B, C, and D. The activities take 6, 4, 10, and 7 minutes respectively. In a sequential process, the activities would be performed in order sequentially, likely by four different individuals, as shown in Figure 6.4. The throughput rate is constrained by the slowest activity, in this case activity C which takes 10 minutes.

    Therefore the throughput would be (60/10) = 6 per hour. Moreover, because activity B operates at a faster rate than activity C, there would need to be a buffer in front of activity C unless activity B has some idle time. Similarly, activities B and D would have significant idle time because they operate at faster rates than the preceding activities. If we arrange the work in parallel with each individual performing all four activities, which should take 25 minutes (6+4+10+5), then the throughput rate will become (60 / 25) $\times$ 4 = 9.6 per hour.

12. **Minimize multiple paths through the process:** Multiple paths in a process often lead to unnecessary complexity and are difficult to manage and schedule. Most of us have probably called a company with a problem and been put through the torture of being passed from one employee to another in what seems to be an endless cycle to get the problem resolved. With each new person you are forced to repeat the problem all over again. This is also another example of minimizing handoffs as in principle 11.

Figure 6.4 Illustration of Parallel Versus Sequential Activities

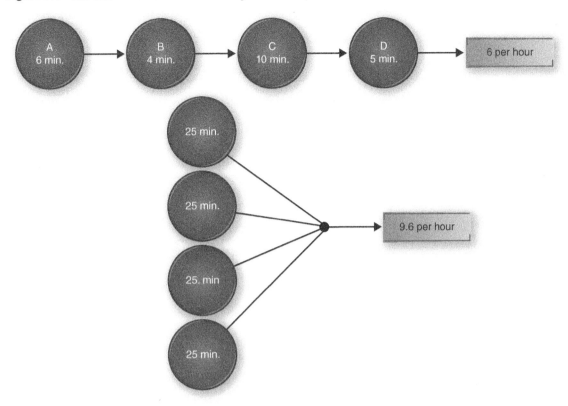

Chapter Glossary

Case management approach Organizational design where a case manager or a team complete the entire process.
Poka-Yoke Mistake proofing a process so that mistakes cannot be made.
Subprocess A part of a larger process which is also a process itself.

Chapter Questions and Problems

1. Discuss how benchmarking can be useful in business process design efforts.
2. Discuss why the improvement potential of a process should be one of the criteria used in deciding which processes to improve. How might this factor relate to the other criteria of a broken process and an important process?
3. Identify similarities and differences among the 12 design principles. Do the principles make sense? Why or why not?

4. Explain how the strategy would impact the process design in each of the following scenarios:
   a. The organizational strategy is to be a low-cost provider of its service and you are designing a customer service process.
   b. The organizational strategy is to increase financial returns to shareholders, and you are designing an accounts receivable process.
   c. You are designing an admissions process to a School of Nursing that has a strategic goal of increasing enrollments by 25% over the next three years.
5. What is the role of top management in the process design or redesign process? Does it matter if it is the design of a new process or the redesign of an existing one?
6. Discuss the difference between using technology as an enabler in process design and using technology to reduce cost, such as with automation.

References

Davenport, T.H. *Process Innovation: Reengineering Work Through Information Technology*, 1993, Boston: Harvard Business School Press.

Davenport, T.H. & Nohria, N. Case Management and the Integration of Labor, *Sloan Management Review*. 1994, 35, 2, 11–23.

Desmet, D., Duncan, E., Scanlan, J., & Singer, M. Six Building Blocks for Creating a High-Performing Digital Enterprise. *Insights & Publications*, McKinsey & Company, September 2015. http://www.mckinsey.com/Insights/Organization/Six_building_blocks_for_creating_a_high_performing_digital_enterprise?cid=digital-eml-alt-mip-mck-oth-1509. Last accessed on 9/15/2015.

Hammer, M. & Champy, J. *Reengineering the Corporation*, 1993, New York: Harper Business.

Harmon, P. *Business Process Change: A Manager's Guide to Improving, Redesigning, and Automating Processes*, 2003, San Francisco: Morgan Kaufmann.

Hyer, N. & Wemmerlov, U. *Reorganizing the Factory: Competing Through Cellular Manufacturing*, 2002, Portland, OR: Productivity Press.

Kinlaw, D. *Developing Superior Work Teams*, 1991, Lexington, MA: Lexington Books.

Laguna, M. & Marklund, J. *Business Process Modeling, Simulation, and Design*, 2005, Upper Saddle River, NJ: Pearson Prentice Hall.

Mintzberg, H. *The Rise and Fall of Strategic Planning*, 1994, Basic Books.

Porter, M. What is Strategy? *Harvard Business Review*, 1996, 74, 6, 61–78.

Robinson, A. (Ed) *Continuous Improvement in Operations: A Systematic Approach to Waste Reduction*, 1991, Cambridge, MA: Productivity Press.

Steiner, G. *Strategic Planning*, 1979, New York, NY: Free Press.

Chapter 7

Tools for Process Design

"Man is a tool-using animal. Nowhere do you find him without tools; without tools he is nothing, with tools he is all."

—Thomas Carlyle

"People who don't use the tools given to them only injure themselves."

—Debra Wilson

In this chapter we will explore some of the tools that are useful in understanding and designing business processes. Most of these tools involve visual diagrams and are fairly basic and easy to use. As with most tools, it is the intelligent use of them that is important.

Process Mapping

Process design begins with a process map. There is general agreement that a *process map* is simply a graphical representation of the steps involved in the process. It is also generally agreed that process maps can serve several useful functions:

- Developing a process map leads to better understanding of the process
- A process map serves as documentation of how work gets done in the organization
- A process map provides the starting point of discussion for any improvement effort.
- A good process map can provide the basis for a simulation model to help in process design

Although there is agreement on these basic points, there is very little agreement on what specific types of information should be included in the map and how the different components are to be represented. If you search the Internet for examples of process maps, you will find many examples. All of the examples will be graphical in nature and will generally looks something like a flowchart, but they will vary widely in the specific details included in the map and how they are represented. We will first present some of the different types of process maps categorized by whether they show the flow of work through the process (flow-oriented diagrams) or the flow of data (data-oriented diagrams). There are no right or wrong ways of mapping a process, but some will be more useful in a given situation than others.

Flow-Oriented Diagrams

The tools discussed in this section generally involve the depiction of the flow through a process. The differences between them are sometimes subtle but important. Each tool has strengths and weaknesses, and all are useful for particular purposes.

RELATIONSHIP MAPPING

Relationship mapping is a useful tool in determining the boundaries of a process and in marking the interaction of the process being mapped to other processes, both internal and external to the organization. In Chapter 6 we discussed the dangers of suboptimization if the interaction of the process with other processes is not taken into account. *Relationship maps* help in this regard by delineating the relationships between the process and other entities and processes. Relationship maps do not consider the activities involved in the process but only the main actors in the process, other processes that interact with the process of interest, and the nature of this interaction. Relationship mapping is a general tool that has been used in a variety of contexts including negotiations, information systems design, political affairs, and knowledge management. The basic process to construct a relationship map is to

1. Identify all of the internal and external organizational units or individuals that play a part in the process.
2. Identify the type of relationship, if any, between all pairs of units identified.
3. Diagram the units with identified relationships, indicated with arrows, that show the nature of the relationship.

Example 7.1

The order-fulfillment process at Evergreen Florist begins when a customer comes into the store, phones in an order, or places an order through the company's website. A few standard floral arrangements are prepared in advance in the morning, with the types of arrangements depending on the time of the year and special holidays that may be occurring at that time. If flowers are needed for orders that are not in stock, they must be ordered from a wholesaler by Sam, the owner. The wholesaler delivers to the floral department twice a day, in the morning and in the afternoon. All floral arrangements are done in the floral department located in the back of the store. Debbie takes all phone orders and extracts the orders from the website. Counter employees take customer orders in the store if the customer does not want one of the prepared arrangements and passes them on to Debbie. Debbie takes all of the orders and enters them into the computer system. The floral department accesses the orders in the system and produces the arrangements according to the time when the orders need to be delivered or when they will be picked up. Once the arrangements are finished, they are picked up by the counter employees and placed in glass cases in the front of the store where they will be picked up by customers or by delivery employees who deliver flowers using company delivery vans.

Solution

The primary agents in this process are the customer, Sam, Debbie, the floral department, the wholesaler, the counter employees, and the delivery employees. The primary relationships are in terms of order flow and the flow of materials, i.e., flowers. A sample relationship map is shown in Figure 7.1.

Figure 7.1 A Sample Relationship Map for Evergreen Florist

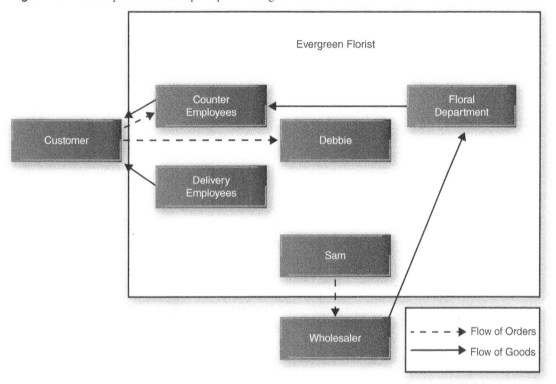

Although the relationship map does not identify the specific activities involved in the process, it does provide information on all of the interactions of the key resources involved in that process, including the key interactions with the customer.

PROCESS-FLOW DIAGRAMS

Process-flow diagrams are commonly used in the physical arrangement of facilities, but they are also very useful in analyzing traffic patterns between individual workers or work centers. These traffic patterns can be important in understanding and designing a process. Process-flow diagrams combine flow information, called load, with distance information to form a load distance score for each pair of items being located within a facility.

$$LD_{ij} = Load_{ij} \times Distance_{ij}$$

Locations are indicated by pairs of XY coordinates, $X_i Y_j$. Distances can be calculated as either rectilinear distances or Euclidean. If one item is located at position $X_1 Y_1$ and a second at position $X_2 Y_2$ the distances would be calculated as

Rectilinear: $D_{12} = |X_1 - X_2| + |Y_1 - Y_2|$

Euclidean: $D_{12} = \sqrt{(X_1 - X_2)^2 + (Y_1 - Y_2)^2}$

The rectilinear distance is measured by going over so many units on the x-axis and then going up or down so many units on the y-axis. The Euclidean distance is measured as the length of a straight line between the two points. Alternate physical layouts of the process are then evaluated in terms of their total load distance scores where the total load distance score is the sum of the load distance scores of all pairs of elements.

Example 7.2

Philco Advertising Agency has four departments in its agency: the art department, the administrative department, the design department, and the marketing department. Philco is moving into a new building soon and wants to know if their present arrangement of the facilities is the best way to arrange things or if the departments should be rearranged in the new facilities. Philco hired a group of college students to monitor traffic between the departments and record when someone traveled from one department to another. The average weekly traffic was then put into a load matrix as show in Figure 7.2. The current arrangement of the departments is shown in Figure 7.3, along with a proposed arrangement for the new facility suggested by a consultant. Philco wants to evaluate the two arrangements to see which is best with regard to traffic flow using rectilinear distance.

Figure 7.2 Load Matrix for Philco

Art		To Department		
		Administrative	Design	Marketing
From Department	Art	—	25	75	15
	Administrative	5	—	10	35
	Design	25	7	—	18
	Marketing	10	30	15	—

Figure 7.3 Current and Proposed Arrangements

Current

Administrative | Design
Art | Marketing

Proposed

Design | Administrative
Art | Marketing

Distances

	Art	Administrative	Design	Marketing
Art	--	1	2	1
Administrative	1	--	1	2
Design	2	1	--	1

Load Distance Score 435

	Art	Administrative	Design	Marketing
Art	--	2	1	1
Administrative	2	--	1	1
Design	1	1	--	2

Load Distance Score 333

Therefore the best arrangement is the proposed new arrangement. Note that the SUM-PRODUCT function in Excel makes it very easy to calculate the load distance scores.

FLOWCHARTS

Undoubtedly the most widely used tool in process design is the flowchart. Flowcharts show the activities of the process and the order in which they occur. The symbols used in flow charting vary widely from simple shapes to complex icons. The most common types of symbols and their meaning are shown in Figure 7.4.

Figure 7.4 Common Flowchart Symbols

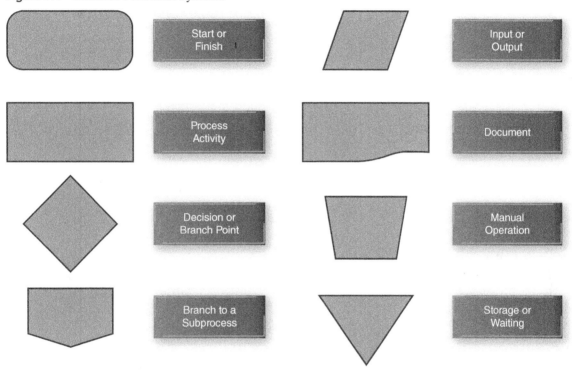

The most important point of flowcharts is not the particular symbols used but the clarity of the resulting document. Figure 7.5 shows an example flowchart of an accounts receivable process. Note the addition of notes to the side of figures in the flowchart to add additional information.

PROCESS ACTIVITY CHARTS

Although process flowcharts are very useful for understanding the flow of a process, they do not usually contain information on the amounts of time spent at each stage of the process, nor do they indicate whether this time is value-adding or waste. A *process activity chart* provides this additional information. Process activity charts usually include the following components for each step in the process: activities, inspections, transportation, delays, and storages (waiting). In addition to adding new elements, the standard symbols in a process activity chart differ slightly from those used in standard flowcharting. The symbols used in process activity charts and a process activity chart of an order-fulfillment process for an online store are shown in Figure 7.6. In Chapter 9 we will discuss the concept of cycle-time efficiency. Process activity charts are very useful in calculating this value.

Figure 7.5 Sample Flowchart of an Accounts Receivable Process

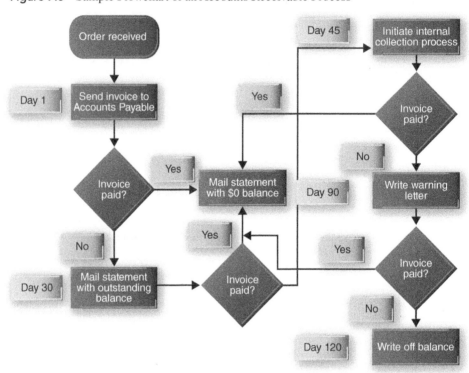

Figure 7.6 Process Activity Chart for an Order-Fulfillment Process.

Date: 3/1/2008		Process: Order Fulfillment		
Analyst: T.A. Anderson				
Step	Description	Time (Min)	Value Code	Symbol
1	Order entered on Web	5	VA	
2	Orders wait to be picked	120	NVA	
3	Order picked in warehouse	25	VA	
4	Order transported to shipping	7	NVA	
5	Wait for Inspection	45	NVA	
6	Order inspected for accuracy	5	BVA	
7	Order loaded and shipped	20	VA	

Symbols: ● Operation ▷ Delay ■ Inspection → Transport ▼ Storage

CROSS-FUNCTIONAL FLOWCHARTS

Flowcharts and process activity charts generally do not show the departments or functional areas involved in the activities of the process. A cross-functional flowchart shows the department or function involved, along with any relevant suppliers and the customer of the process. The departments or functional areas are listed across the top of a column with the steps in the flowchart of the process shown in the appropriate column. These columns are sometimes called *swim lanes* because of their similarities to swimming lanes in a pool during competitive swimming events. Such charts are especially useful in highlighting the customer "touch points" (places when the customer comes in contact with the organization). These points require special attention in the design of a process because they can be very influential in terms of the customers' perceptions of the organization and their satisfaction with the product or service provided. Many practitioners in business process management recommend the use of swim lanes in flowcharting because they also indicate the points where the process crosses functional boundaries. Boundaries between different functional areas of the organization are typically where process problems are most likely to arise.

Besides the activities involved, additional information can be contained along the bottom of the swim lanes such as an estimate of the time involved, the value-adding classification, costs, or other relevant information. A cross-functional chart of the order-fulfillment process described in the process activity chart is shown in Figure 7.7.

SERVICE SYSTEM MAPPING AND SERVICE BLUEPRINTS

The techniques described in this section, are closely related to the cross functional flowcharts described previously. The concept of *service blueprinting* was first proposed by Lynn Shostack (1984). Shostack proposed that the marketing of services could be improved by adopting a systematic process orientation to the design of services (Shostack, 1987). The blueprinting methodology devised by Shostack (1984, 1987) basically involved flowcharting the service process from the customer point of view with two additional components:

- The line of visibility that separated the customer interactions from the internal workings of the service provider.
- The inclusion of what Shostack called the facilitating goods and services, which are physical "products" sold to the customer during the provision of the service or physical items used during the provision of the service.

Figure 7.7 A Cross-Functional Flowchart of the Order-Fulfillment Process

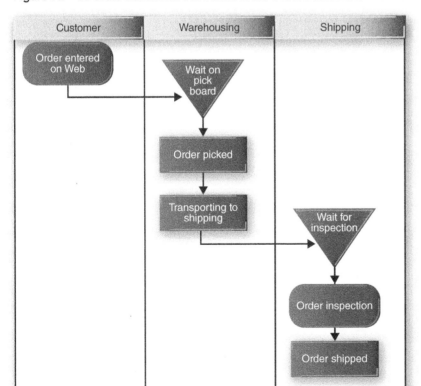

The service blueprinting concept has been expanded and refined over the years to include distinguishing between customer interactions that take place with the customer physically present (onstage contacts) from customer interactions that take place without the customer being present, e.g., via telephone, Internet, or other communication methods. Blueprinting has also been refined to include support processes of the organization that support the customer interactions and physical evidence, which is similar to Shostack's facilitating goods and services. An example of a service blueprint from Bitner (1993, 2008) is shown in Figure 7.8.

A similar concept, called *service system mapping*, has been described by Cross et al. (1994) and Laguna and Marklund (2005). The basic components of the service system map are shown in Figure 7.9. The primary differences between a service blueprint and a service system map are in terms of the addition of an information systems band and a supplier band in the diagram. The information systems band is very similar to support processes in the service blueprint. Service systems maps are designed to address manufacturing processes as well as service processes and give a more prominent place to information systems in the diagram. It should be noted that the horizontal placement of the bands in both Figures 7.8 and 7.9 is arbitrary. If it makes the presentation of the map easier, a vertical orientation may be used.

It should be noted that the functional aspects of the organization can also be superimposed on the service system map, if desired, to provide information similar to the cross-functional flowchart. Service systems mapping and service blueprinting have several advantages over traditional flowcharting.

- Service blueprinting is very versatile and flexible and can be used in many different ways (Bitner, Ostrom, and Morgan, 2007).
- By detailing the points of customer contact, it focuses management attention on factors that may increase customer satisfaction.

Figure 7.8 Service Blueprint of a Hotel Service

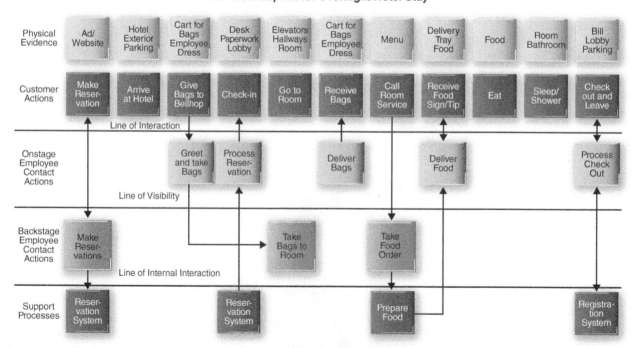

Source: Adapted from Bitner (1993) and Bitner et al. (2008)

Figure 7.9 Components of a Service System Map

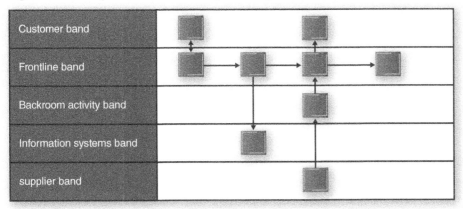

- Information systems and other support processes can be focused more strategically on factors that increase process efficiency and enhance the customer experience.
- Critical performance measurement points can more easily be identified within the horizontal view of the process flow without the vertical (functional) divisions of the organization (Cross, Feather, and Lynch, 1994).

MULTILEVEL FLOWCHARTS

At times, flowcharts of business processes can become extremely complex and difficult to understand. In addition, sometimes a design team will need to view the details and at other times they need to focus on the higher level strategic implications of the design. One solution to this dilemma is to design the flowchart at different levels of detail (Anderson, 2007). This can be done for regular or cross-functional flowcharts.[1] The following example will be used to illustrate the concept of a *multilevel flowchart*.

Example 7.3

A small contract manufacturer produces plastic parts for other manufacturers to use in their products. Raw materials and necessary parts are not kept in inventory but are ordered when production is about to begin. Figure 7.10 illustrates the highest level of the flowchart, level 0. At this level only general categories are entered into the flowchart. Of course, each of the activities shown in this flowchart contains a lot of detail that is hidden at this level. An example of the next level of the flowchart (level 1) for the procure parts activity is shown in Figure 7.11. Items at this level can also be further detailed at the next level. For example, selecting a supplier could involve a number of steps and itself be a subprocess. Modern software could make this type of flowcharting a very useful tool for process design as the process design team could work at the higher levels during more strategic aspects of the planning process and drill down to more detailed levels as needed.

---

1. Although the author is not aware of any such examples, at least in principle, multilevel charts can also be done for service blueprints and service systems maps.

Figure 7.10 Level 0 Flowchart for Example 7.3

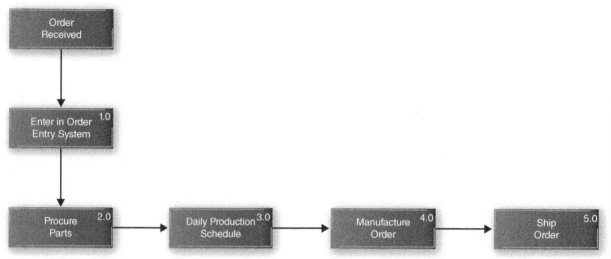

Figure 7.11 Level 1 Flowchart for Procure Parts Activity of Example 7.3

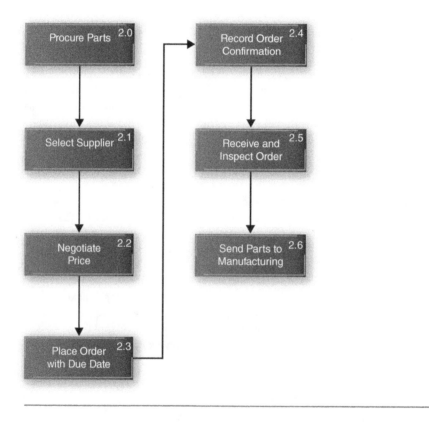

Data-Oriented Diagrams

As Kock (2007) has pointed out, traditional process diagrams of all types suffer from one serious deficiency in that they usually fail to include anything about the web of communications activities that make up a substantial portion of most modern business processes. Given that information technology is often a primary enabler of business process redesign, as discussed in Chapter 6, this may be a critical limitation. As argued by Kock (2007), with the possible exception of manufacturing processes, communication flow representations may provide a more complete view of the elements that should be considered in business process redesign than activity representations for most modern processes. Information system design has traditionally had its own set of diagramming tools for communication and information flow, most popularly the data-flow diagram.

DATA-FLOW DIAGRAMS (DFDs)

The Gane-Sarson approach to information system design (Gane & Sarson 1977) is one of the more popular approaches to structured systems analysis and design. The notation for the Gane-Sarson approach is very simple, as shown in Figure 7.12. Notice that there are no symbols for decisions or branches in data-flow diagrams (DFDs). Most adherents of structured systems analysis and design view decisions or branching as inappropriate in DFDs and are best left to supporting flowcharts if necessary. Figure 7.13 shows a data-flow diagram of the process of applying to a university.

Figure 7.12 Symbols for Gane-Sarson Data-Flow Diagrams

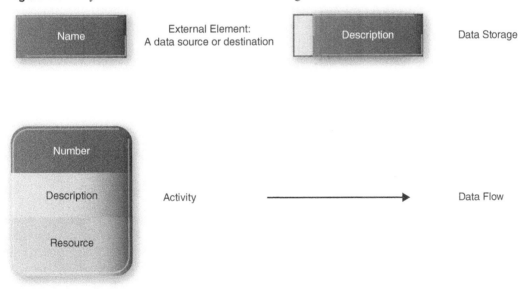

Figure 7.13 A Data-Flow Diagram of a University Application Process

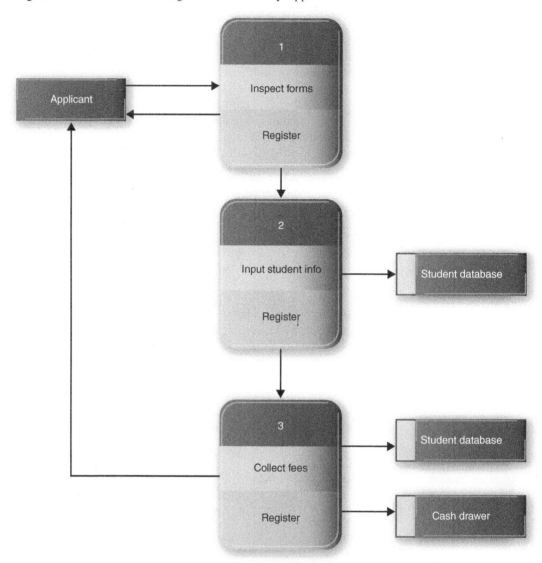

Creatively Combining Different Methods

There are many different flowcharting and diagramming methods described in the literature. We have discussed only a few of them here. It is important to keep in mind that how a design team works should not be dictated by a particular method. There is no reason that a design team cannot combine different methods, use mixed symbols from the different methods, or even develop new ones. The important point of using flowcharts and diagrams in process design is to provide a clear picture of the current process and to encourage creative thinking about how to redesign the process. For example, the cross-functional flowchart in Figure 7.2 might utilize some of the data-flow elements of data-flow diagrams to present a more detailed flowchart like that shown in Figure 7.14. Remember, the purpose of the diagramming process is to help the redesign effort, not to satisfy someone's idea of what should be legitimate in certain types of diagrams.

Figure 7.14 An Example Mixing Different Methods

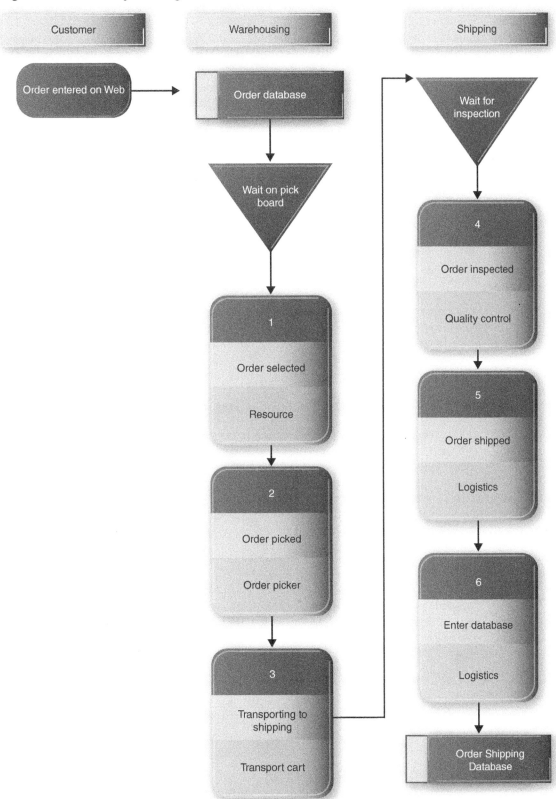

Interface Mapping

Bevington & Samson (2012) argue that process mapping, by itself, is insufficient in that it misses a significant portion of organizational activity. These normally undocumented activities are what Bevington & Samson (2012) call *interfacing activities*. Interfacing activities are the activities associated with preparing data, forms, product, transactions, and other items to enable the next step in the process to be performed. Bevington & Samson (2012) maintain that many of these activities remain hidden from normal process mapping yet often account for a significant portion of total resource time expended in performing the process[2]. Some of this interfacing activity is necessary as support activity, some of it is discretionary as a result of management policy usually related to risk management, but the remainder is waste, what Bevington & Sampson (2012) call *interface activity noise*. Noise is the checking, correction, and chasing of information because of a failure to perform process activities correctly. In the 117 firms studied by Bevington & Samson (2012) interface activity noise accounted for approximately 33 percent of the total resource time allocated to organizational processes, i.e., 33 percent of the work time was waste. *Interface mapping* is designed to account for all of the activities of a process, both the core process activities and the interface activities. Like process mapping, interface mapping documents the functional activities of a process in the order in which they are performed. It differs from the normal process mapping in (1) recording the normally hidden, situationally determined, interfacing activity, and (2) documenting the resources and their time associated with each activity. Interface mapping also differs in practice from the way process mapping is normally performed. Process mapping is normally done by management personnel or "experts" knowledgeable about the process. Interfacing mapping is done in bottom up fashion by those actually engaged in performing the work of the process.

Customer Input and Quality Function Deployment

At many points in this text, we have reiterated the position that all process design efforts start with the customer. Therefore, it is important in discussing tools for process design that we also discuss tools for gathering customer input about the process and their requirements for the product or service. In Chapter 2 we discussed the technique of quality function deployment and customer surveys as methods for gathering customer input. We will not go over these methods again in detail here, but only point out that these techniques could just as easily have been discussed in this chapter as tools of process design.

Flowcharting with Microsoft Office and Visio

There are a variety of flowcharting software tools available in the market. Their prices vary widely from relatively cheap to very expensive. In fact, many people and most businesses already have an easy-to-use flowcharting tool installed on their computers, namely Microsoft Office.

FLOWCHARTING WITH EXCEL

Several applications in the Office suite have drawing tools that can be used to produce most of the flowcharts and diagrams described in this chapter. Word, Excel, and PowerPoint all have built-in drawing tools that work much the same across all three applications. Which application you use

---

2. In the Bevington & Samson research, the undocumented activities outnumbered the documented activities by a ratio of over 5 to 1 (Table 3.2 p. 69).

to prepare flowcharts is largely a matter of preference. However, the available space for constructing a flowchart is somewhat restricted in Word and PowerPoint. In PowerPoint, you are restricted by the size of the slide and in Word, by the size of the page and drawing canvas, if it is used. Excel essentially offers the entire worksheet space for the drawing which provides considerable more flexibility. Therefore, we will use Excel here to illustrate the flowcharting process. However, since the drawing tools operate much the same in all three applications, what we discuss here can be easily adapted to the Word or PowerPoint applications. Our discussion will focus on Office 2007 and later and will use Excel 2016 for the illustrations.

The drawing tools are accessed through the Shapes option in the Illustrations section on the Insert tab of the Office ribbon as shown in Figure 7.15. You can use the basic shapes or the special flowcharts section to create your flowcharts or other diagrams. Select the shape that you want and click in the position of the workbook where you wish to place that shape. You can always move the shape later if you wish. You can add other shapes to your flowchart in the same way. To connect the shapes in the flowchart, select one of the line shapes from the lines section. Click in

Figure 7.15 The Shapes Options of the Insert Tab in Excel

the worksheet where you want the line to begin and drag to the position where you want it to end.

You can always change the formatting of the shape objects in your flowchart using the Drawing Tools formatting capabilities. When you click on a shape in your drawing, the Drawing Tools tab appears as shown in Figure 7.16. You can change the fill color of the shape by selecting a different color from the Shape Fill drop-down box. You can also add special effects, such as shadowing using the Shape Effects drop-down. The Drawing toolbar also contains an Insert Shapes section that you can use to add shapes and lines to your flowchart.

Figure 7.16 Formatting Options of the Drawing Toolbar

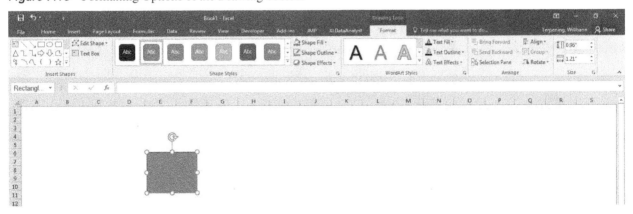

When you finish your flowchart, or before if you desire, you should eliminate the gridlines in the worksheet so that it appears more like a white sheet of paper. You can do this by going to the Page Layout tab of the ribbon and unchecking the box labeled View under Gridlines in the Sheet Options section. You can also remove the row and column headers, if you want, by deselecting the View box under the Headings section.

There are two issues that often frustrate new users of the diagramming tools in Microsoft Office. One is the limited set of symbols included in the drawing toolbox. More complex symbols can always be created out of these basic building blocks, however. For example, the activity block in the data-flow diagrams shown in Figure 7.12 was created from a rounded flowchart symbol by adding two lines and two text boxes. The problem remains that these are still separate drawing elements, and if you try to move one of them the others will not "follow." You can get around this problem by using the grouping option in the drawing toolbar. Select all the items that you want to group together and then click the Group option in the Arrange portion of the Drawing Tools tab of the ribbon. This will then create one drawing object from the separate components that can then be moved, copied, and manipulated as one unit. You can always "ungroup" back into the separate units if necessary by using the Ungroup option.

The second issue arises when you try to move symbols that have been connected by arrows or lines in the diagram. Unless they are properly "connected," the arrows and lines do not follow the moving symbol. Simply connecting a point on one shape to a point on another is not sufficient to make sure that they are "connected." This has been improved in Excel 2016, but you still need to take care in connecting shapes. When you properly connect two drawing objects, the connections remain when the objects are moved. When you click on a drawing shape in Excel, a square or a rectangle appears around the object, with clear circles on the corners and sides of the square or rectangle as shown in Figure 7.17(a). If you then click on a line or arrow shape in Insert Shapes connection and hover the mouse over the selected shape, you will notice that some of the circles turn black in color (red in Excel 2010). Press and hold the left mouse button over one of these colored circles. You can then drag the line to another shape. When the mouse is over the second shape, you will see the black (red in Excel 2010) circles appear on that second object, as shown in Figure 7.17(b). If you draw a line from the colored dots in the first object to any of the colored dots in the second object they will be "connected" and will remain so when they are moved. If you connect a colored dot in the first object to any other point in the second figure, the objects will not be properly connected.

Figure 7.17 Properly Connecting Drawing Objects in Excel

(a)   (b)

FLOWCHARTING WITH VISIO

One of the most popular drawing packages on the market is Microsoft's Visio. Unlike Excel, which has a limited number of flowcharting symbols, Visio has a large collection of different shapes organized into Stencils by type of use. Although the classification underlying the Stencils is not always intuitive, almost all of the shapes and features discussed in this chapter can be found somewhere within the collection. Although we do not have space here for an extensive tutorial on the use of Visio, we will give you a brief introduction. The software is quite easy to use and has an excellent help system. If you want to explore Visio further you can get a free trial version on the Microsoft Office website.

When you first open Visio you will see a blank canvas with a standard Office-type ribbon, as shown in Figure 7.18. The first step is to create a new document. Clicking on the File tab in

Figure 7.18 Opening Screen of Visio

the upper left-hand corner opens a screen where you can chose the type of document that you want to produce, including a Blank Drawing. A portion of this screen showing the available templates is shown in Figure 7.19.

These templates group stencils that are typically used in a particular type of drawing along with a beginning diagram to get started. There are other templates that can be viewed by scrolling down the screen, and you can also search for additional templates using the search box shown in Figure 7.19. The most relevant templates for our purposes are the Business Process Model and Notation (BPMN) Diagram, the Basic Flowchart, and the Cross-Functional Flowchart. BPMN is a diagramming standard for business processes that is specifically oriented toward software development. This standard is discussed later in this chapter. Here we will look at the Cross-Functional Flowchart template, which is shown in Figure 7.20.

As can be seen in Figure 7.20, this template automatically creates a sample diagram of a process with two swim lanes, as shown in the drawing canvas on the right. The template also selects shape stencils commonly used in such diagrams, which are shown in the panel on the left. The two primary stencils are the Cross-Functional Flowchart Shapes (to create swim lanes) and Basic Flowchart Shapes for diagraming the process. You can also load other shape stencils by clicking on "More Shapes." Shapes are again organized into stencils and grouped by function. The most widely used for process diagraming are the stencils in the Business—Business Process section shown in Figure 7.21(a) and the Flowchart group shown in Figure 7.21(b).

As you can see, there are many options for creating diagrams in Visio, and adding and connecting objects in the diagram is very simple. To add objects, simply drag the object from the Stencils on the left-hand side of the screen to the drawing area. In some cases, Visio will automatically connect the new object to an existing object. To connect objects manually, right

Figure 7.19 Visio Templates

Figure 7.20 The Cross-Functional Flowchart Template

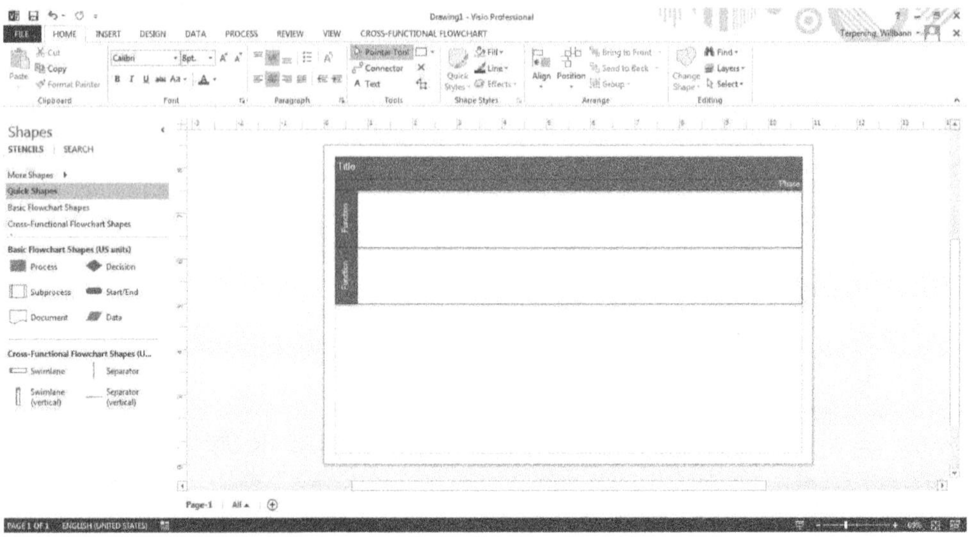

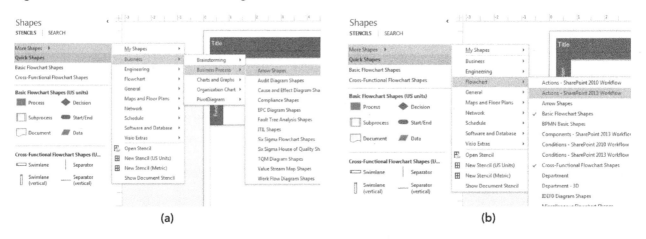

Figure 7.21 Common Process Flowcharting Stencils in Visio

(a)   (b)

click on the connector object in the tools section of the ribbon. When you mouse over a diagram object, it will be highlighted with connector points. If you place the mouse over a connector point and drag to a connector point of another object, Visio will connect the two objects. See Figure 7.22 for an illustration.

BPMS Software and Process Design

Diagramming tools such as Excel or Visio are adequate for diagramming simple processes and are easy for most business users. However, there are three difficulties with these tools:

1. There is no central repository for storing these documents that can be easily accessed by everyone in the organization.

2. The documents are static and hard to maintain. For example, what happens when a department changes its name? Usually a large number of documents have to be tracked down and changed to reflect the new name.

Figure 7.22 Adding and Connecting Objects in Visio

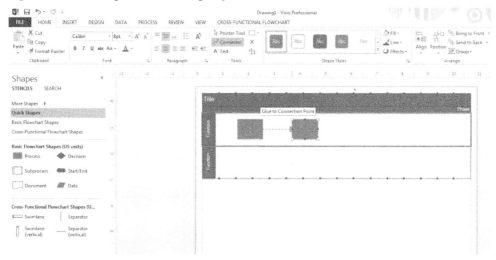

3. There are no connections to the software that supports the processes. When a process is designed or redesigned, IT must provide resources to modify existing systems or to write new applications to incorporate the changes designed into the process. This often takes a great deal of time and a lot of interaction between the process managers and IT personnel to insure that the supporting software operates as intended.

Business process management suites contain a variety of tools to aid in process design, which overcome most of these difficulties. We will consider some of the primary concerns here. Figure 7.23 shows the BPMS components described in Chapter 1, with the components to be discussed here colored in light blue.

Figure 7.23 Components of BPMS for Process Design

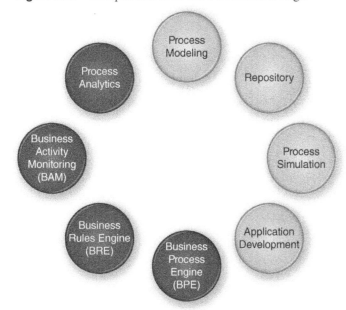

PROCESS MODELING TOOLS AND REPOSITORIES

Since process models are at the heart of BPM, their development, storage, and use are important concerns. Most BPMS software contains tools for modeling processes and a repository that functions as a database for the storage and retrieval of these process models. As Franz & Kirchmer (2012) point out, the choices of modeling tools and repositories are important enough that they require a systematic strategy to guide these decisions. The key components of such a strategy are shown in Figure 7.24, which is adapted from the model in Chapter 8 of Franz & Kirchmer (2012).

Central to the strategy is the value outcome anticipated from the software. In other words, what are you going to use the tools and repository for? Are they to be used primarily to drive a BPM transformation, enhance compliance, improve risk management, or for some other purpose? Content refers to the type of content that needs to be modeled and stored. Format is the choice of the many possible formats you want to use. Any of the many formats described in this chapter, along with many other formats, are possible. Governance involves answering the "who" questions. Who can see the repository content? Who can modify the content? Who makes sure that process changes are reflected in the repository? Finally, what software tools do we choose? As you might expect, the decisions made for any one of these issues impacts our decisions for the other components of the strategy. For example, the choice of software tools will obviously impact the formats chosen for the content and vice versa. Since the processing modeling tools and repository are at the heart of the technological support of BPM, these tools should be selected carefully to be in sync with the value outcome of the strategy.

REFERENCE MODELS

Rather than starting process modeling from scratch, many organizations use reference models as a starting point. Reference models are generic models intended to have wide applicability. Reference models are designed to represent best business practices and are intended to be applicable to a wide variety of organizations. They are structured to be easily adaptable to a variety of circumstances. Some reference models are designed for specific industries. For example, Accenture is reported to have models available for 71 different industries (Franz & Kirchmer, 2012). The APQC process classification framework discussed in Chapter 1 has been used to define reference

Figure 7.24 Modeling and Repository Strategy Components

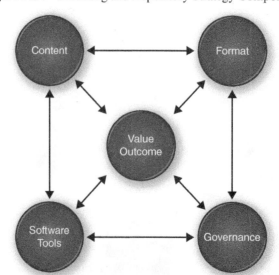

Source: Adapted from Franz & Kirchmer (2012), Figure 8-1, p. 151.

models in a variety of industries that are available to its members. Other reference models are designed to apply to all organizations for a specific domain. The Supply Chain Reference Model (SCOR) from the Supply Chain Council is an example of this type of model. Other reference models are designed as part of a software product, such as SAP or Oracle.

Reference models can be invaluable in guiding discussions about processes and process improvement or as a starting point in process analysis. However, it should be kept in mind that such general models are meant to be used as guidelines not as "the" process design for a specific context.

PROCESS DESIGN AND SIMULATION

Simulation is so important to process design that every modern BPMS contains a simulation component. There are also a number of good standalone simulation languages available on the market. One obvious advantage of using a simulation language that is part of a BPMS is the ease of connecting the final design to the execution portion of the BPMS. Another advantage, especially in redesign of existing projects, is that the key metrics for the process are already available in the BPMS to use in the simulation. To further emphasize the importance of simulation to BPM, Chapter 8 is dedicated to the topic of simulation in process design.

DEVELOPING SOFTWARE APPLICATIONS

Most complex business processes consist of both human tasks and automated computer tasks. This means that designing business processes usually has an IT element as well. Most BPMS software also contains tools for developing custom applications to support these complex processes. Although this is not a software book, business managers should be at least familiar with the key concepts at this intersection of business and IT. Service-oriented architecture (SOA) is one of these concepts. SOA is a set of design principles for software development, which is an outgrowth of the component-based view of software development. In this view, reusable software components that provide basic services are strung together to produce software applications. Modern SOA is also generally associated with Web services that integrate components from diverse software systems. In this way, new applications can be connected to and communicate with legacy systems and enterprise-level software systems, as well as with software systems outside the organization itself.

The importance of this is that SOA has become the de facto standard for designing the automated computer elements of business processes, and many in the technology sector envision BPM and SOA as being very closely intertwined. It is essentially this partnership of BPM and SOA that Smith and Fingar (2003) call "The Third Wave" of BPM. BPMS software can use SOA to help bridge the gap between the process designer (usually a business person) and the software developer (an IT person). It is important in selecting a BPMS system to ensure that it has distinct tools to support both the business person and the IT developer. There are a variety of standards that have been developed to make this possible. One of those is Business Process Model and Notation (BPMN) which is a graphical notation that can be used to diagram business processes. BPMN 2.0 is the latest version of the BPMN standard maintained by the Object Management Group.[3] The advantage of BPMN is that it can be directly translated into a processing metalanguage, such as business process modeling language (BPML) or business process execution language (BPEL), which is designed to directly translate into software applications. Although these metalanguages are not yet standardized, it is the hope that in the future these solutions will be able to directly translate visual process diagrams into software components that automate the computer services components of the process. At the current time, however, those selecting a BPMS system must make sure that the appropriate tools are available to support both the business designer and the IT developer by helping translate from the language of one into the language of the other.

---

3. See http://www.omg.org/spec/BPMN/2.0.2/ for the current version of the standard.

Chapter Glossary

Cross-functional flowchart A flowchart with the functional departments of the activities superimposed.
Data-flow diagrams Diagrams out of the structured systems analysis and design approach that show the flow of data rather than the flow of materials or customers.
Interfacing activities The steps taken to prepare data, forms, products, transactions, etc. so that they are in a form suitable for processing at the next stage of the process.
Interface activity noise Interface activity that is waste, i.e., is not necessary to support the activities of the process nor is it business-value-adding in the sense of being related to compliance and reducing risk.
Interface Mapping Like process mapping, specifies the activities involved in a process and the sequence in which they are performed but also records the resources utilized in performing the primary activities and the interfacing activities performed in the process.
Multilevel flowchart A set of flowcharts that uses different charts to show different levels of detail.
Process activity chart A chart that shows the sequence of activities but also shows the activity times, value-adding classification, and other information.
Process map A graphical representation of the activities and flows involved in a process.
Relationship map A diagram that shows the interrelationships of the entities involved in a process along with the relationships to outside entities and other processes.
Service blueprinting A technique to show customer interactions along with the sequence of activities involved in a process and the facilitating goods involved in the provision of the service.
Service system mapping A diagram similar to a service blueprint that also highlights information systems and suppliers involved in the process.
Swim lanes The columns representing the functional departments in a cross-functional flowchart.

Chapter Questions and Problems

1. Discuss why swim lanes, such as those in cross-functional diagrams, or indicators of organizational boundaries, such as those in service blueprints, may be important in process design.
2. Why are process repositories important to an organization? Identify some potential organizational impediments to the implementation of a process repository.
3. Describe a business or other process that you are familiar with in enough detail so someone could create a flowchart from your description. Use Excel to create a flowchart of your process.
4. Draw a cross-functional chart of your process from question 3.
5. An advertising agency has six departments A, B, C, D, E, and F. A month long study revealed the traffic patterns shown in the load matrix below.

	B	C	D	E	F
A	10	30		43	17
B	—	50	110	15	20
C	—	—	13	32	41
D	—	—	—	55	7
E	—	—	—	—	27

a. Given only the previous information, what two departments should be located closest to one another?
b. Given the layout shown below, what is the load-distance score?

A	B	C	D
E	F	G	H

c. Devise a layout better than that shown in part b by swapping the location of two departments. What is the load-distance score of this layout?

6. The College of Business Administration at Big Western University has six departments: Accounting, Finance, Marketing, Operations, Management and Information Systems. Traffic between departments consists of faculty who do research with faculty in other departments and departmental staff who carry documents between the departmental units. The load matrix is shown below.

	Accounting	Finance	Marketing	Operations	Management	Info Systems
Accounting	—	120	5	10	15	90
Finance	—	—	10	15	32	65
Marketing	—	—	—	84	71	15
Operations	—	—	—	—	74	96

a. Given the layout shown below, what is the load-distance score?

Accounting	Operations	Informaton Systems
Management	Marketing	Finance

b. Devise a better layout. What is the load-distance score of your layout?

7. As any academic knows, the submission process to academic and scientific journals can be a daunting process. The following steps describe a typical sequence of events for such a submission.

1. The author(s) submit a manuscript to the editorial office (EO).
2. The EO sends a letter to the author(s) acknowledging receipt of the manuscript and sends a copy of the manuscript to the editor-in-chief (EIC).
3. The EIC decides on the appropriate department and the associated departmental editor (DE) notifies the EO.
4. The EO sends a copy of the manuscript to the appropriate DE.
5. The DE reads the manuscript, selects three reviewers to review the paper, and notifies the EO.
6. The EO sends copies of the manuscript to the referees.
7. The referees review the manuscript and send their reports to the DE.
8. After reading the referees comments, the DE decides whether the article should be accepted, rejected, or revised. The DE sends his/her decision to the EIC.
9. If the manuscript is accepted, the EIC notifies the EO who sends the manuscript to production to be published according to the schedule.

10. If the manuscript is rejected, the EIC sends a letter to the author(s) notifying them of the decision.
11. If the manuscript is to be revised, the EIC sends a letter to the author(s) along with the referees' comments and invites them to revise and resubmit the manuscript.
12. The author(s) revise the manuscript and send the revised manuscript back to the EO.
13. The EO sends copies of the revised manuscripts directly to the appropriate DE, who decides if the manuscript should now be accepted or sent to referees for further review.

a. Construct a flowchart of the process.
b. Construct a service system map or service blueprint of the process. Which of these representations, the flowchart or the service system map (service blueprint), do you think provides the best representation of the process?
c. Can you identify any opportunities for improvement of the process?

References

Anderson, B. *Business Process Improvement Toolbox,* 2nd Edition, 2007, Milwaukee: Quality Press.

Bevington, T. & Samson, D. *Implementing Strategic Change: Managing Processes and Interfaces to Develop a Highly Productive Organization*, 2012, London: Kogan Page.

Bitner, M.J. Managing the Evidence of Service, in E.E. Scheuing and W.F. Christopher, (Eds.), *The Service Quality Handbook*, 1993, New York, NY: American Management Association

Bitner, M.J., Ostrom, A.L. & Morgan, F.N. Service Blueprinting: A Practical Tool for Service Innovation, 2008, *California Management Review*, 50, 3, 66–94.

Cross, K.F., Feather, J.J. & Lynch, R.L. *Corporate Renaissance: The Art of Reengineering*, 1994, Cambridge, MA: Blackwell Business.

Franz, P. & Kirchmer, M. *Value-Driven Business Process Management: The Value-Switch for Lasting Competitive Advantage*, 2012, New York: McGraw-Hill.

Gane, C. & Sarson, T., *Structured Systems Analysis and Design, 1977,* New York: Improved Systems Technologies Inc.

Kock, N., *Systems Analysis & Design Fundamentals: A Business Process Redesign Approach*, 2007, Thousand Oaks, CA: Sage Publications.

Laguna, M. & Marklund, J. *Business Process Modeling, Simulation, and Design*, 2005, Upper Saddle River, NJ: Pearson Prentice Hall.

Shostack, G.L. Designing services that deliver. *Harvard Business Review* 1984, 62, 1, 133–139.

Shostack, G.L. Service positioning through structural change. *Journal of Marketing*, 1987, 51, 1, 34–43.

Smith, H. & Fingar, P. *Business Process Management: The Third Wave*, 2003, Tampa: Meghan-Kiffer.

Chapter 8

Simulation and Process Design

"Let's take flight simulation as an example. If you're trying to train a pilot, you can simulate almost the whole course. You don't have to get in an airplane until late in the process."

—Roy Romer

"He did not arrive at this conclusion by the decent process of quiet, logical deduction, nor yet by the blinding flash of glorious intuition, but by the shoddy, untidy process halfway between the two by which one usually gets to know things."

—Margery Allingham

As the quote from Roy Romer illustrates, simulation has long played an important role in training areas of all types, and the primary advantage is that you can do most of the learning before you get to the dangerous part. The same principle holds in using computer simulation in process design. You can test many of the ideas for process improvement before you get to the dangerous part—implementing the changes. The quote from Margery Allingham is relevant in this context because simulation is not a process of logical deduction, nor does it usually involve a flash of brilliant intuition. Rather simulation is a powerful tool in the lengthy and untidy process of getting to know a process and experimenting and trying out new ideas for possible design improvements.

In Chapter 5, we introduced XLSim and the basic simulation process. In this chapter, we will explore more features of the simulation language and discuss how simulation can be utilized in the design process. At the end of the chapter we will present several case studies to allow you to practice your skills at the art of simulation.

The Role of Simulation in Process Design

Simulation has long been utilized in engineering for the design of chemical processes (Dimian, 2003), embedded systems (Deprettere, Teich, & Vassiliadis, 2002), and even building design (Clarke, 2001). More recently, discrete event simulation has proven useful in process design in manufacturing and service environments. In Chapter 6 we discussed some general principles of process design. In this section, we expand on these ideas to develop a framework for business process design and the role of simulation in that framework. The framework is presented in Figure 8.1. The first three steps of the process were discussed in Chapter 6. The fourth step, generating ideas for process design, is situation-specific and really a creative activity. This step is vital because the success of the entire process design depends on the quality and creativity of the potential solutions proposed for the design. However, given the situation-specific nature of this process, there is very little that we can say about this stage in this text.

The last step in the process, the implementation step, is also very important and will be treated in more detail in Chapter 12 when we discuss the topic of managing change. In the current chapter, we will deal with step 5 of the process, where proposed design changes are

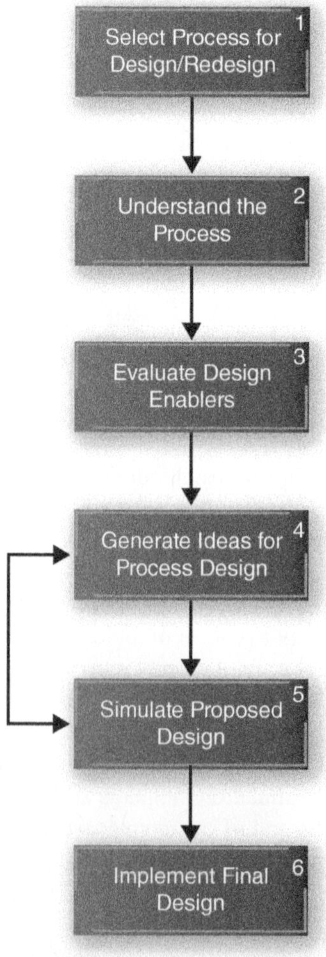

Figure 8.1 A Framework for Business Process Design Using Simulation

simulated and tested. Here we will address many technical and practical aspects of using simulation in process design. At the end of the chapter we will present several cases that will allow you to test your skills in applying simulation to process design issues.

Using Time Units in XLSim

Time units are set in XLSim at a global level but can be varied within individual activity and generator blocks. The global time unit is set by clicking the Simulation Setup button in the Setup tab of XLSim. The resulting dialog is shown in Figure 8.2. The frame labeled Time Units contains the input data for time units in XLSim. The drop-down box for Simulation Time Units sets the global time unit for the current model. This can be set to minutes, hours, days, weeks, or months. The default is minutes. The global time unit is the time unit used in the simulation and in the output results of the simulation. It can be, and often should be, overridden within a specific activity or generator block. The time unit for these individual blocks is the time unit specified within that block. Differences between individual block time units and the global time unit for the simulation are adjusted when the simulation is run.

Run Length and Replications

The simulation setup shown in Figure 8.2 also requires the specification of the number of warm-up periods, simulation run periods, and the number of replications. The values for these three parameters depend on a number of issues but the two most critical are

- whether the process is terminating or nonterminating and
- whether the objectives of the simulation are to estimate long-term performance of a process or to evaluate alternative process designs.

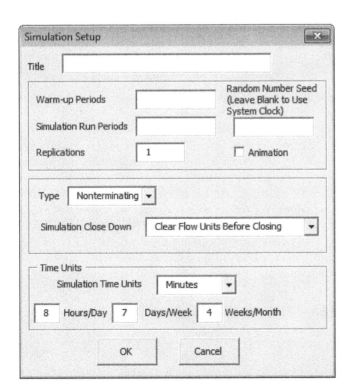

Figure 8.2 The Simulation Setup Dialog Box

TERMINATING VERSUS NONTERMINATING PROCESSES

Recall from our discussion in Chapter 5 that terminating processes are those that have a natural end point where all flow units are cleared from the system, while nonterminating processes have no natural end point. Technically, terminating processes reach an end point at the end of the cycle (typically a day) where the system is cleared out and the process starts from scratch with the next cycle. Nonterminating processes, however, never clear the system. Even if they stop for the day, they resume where they left off the next day with the queues and other system components in the same states as they were the day before.

Terminating Processes

Since terminating processes never reach a steady state condition, the warm-up periods are usually not relevant and can be set to zero for such processes. An exception would be if you were only interested in the behavior of the system during a particular time of the day. For example, in a fast-food restaurant, we might be particularly interested in the performance of the system during the lunch hour, from 11:00 to 1:00. If the restaurant opened at 7:00 AM, we could then set the simulation run periods to 6 hours and the warm-up periods to 4 hours and only collect statistics during the last 2 hours.

The simulation run periods for terminating processes should be set to a number that is related to the simulation cycle, i.e., the time when the process terminates. This will usually be the number of minutes or hours in a day with the unit, depending on the time unit of the simulation. Since the results from a single day depend on the random number seed used to start the random number sequence and may not be representative of typical performance, you should run a terminating simulation for multiple cycles. This can be done in one of three ways.

One way is to determine the number of cycles (usually days) that you want to simulate and set the run periods to the number of time units to equal that number of cycles. For example, if the process operates for 8 hours per day, your simulation time unit is hours, and you want to simulate the process for 100 days, then set the run periods equal to $100 \times 8 = 800$. If your simulation time unit is minutes, then you would set the run periods to $100 \times 8 \times 60 = 48,000$ minutes.

A second procedure is to set the simulation time unit to the length of the cycle, e.g., days. Then set the simulation runs to the number of cycles you wish to simulate. The third way to add multiple cycles to the simulation is to set the run length of the simulation to 1 cycle (for example 8 hours for a daily cycle) and set the number of replications to a value greater than 1. The number of replications that you want to specify also depends on your objectives in running the simulation, as discussed later in this chapter.

Nonterminating Processes

For nonterminating processes, interest usually centers on steady-state performance. Since behavior at the beginning of the simulation is very dependent on the random number seed used and the initial state of the system at the start of the simulation (usually empty), we normally do not want the results at the beginning of the simulation to influence our estimate of the performance of the system in steady state. For this reason, we will normally run the simulation for a certain number of warm-up periods before starting to gather statistics. For nonterminating processes you will want to set the number of warm-up periods to be large enough to ensure that the process is in steady state and then run it only for enough simulation run periods to get statistics. It may take some trial and error in running the model to determine how many warm-up periods will be enough.

ESTIMATING PERFORMANCE VERSUS EVALUATING ALTERNATIVE DESIGNS

The second factor that affects the run length and replication parameters is the objective of the simulation. The objective is likely to be either to estimate the long-term performance of the system or to evaluate alternative process designs. In general, estimation of performance would involve longer runs to insure stable estimates, whereas evaluating alternative designs would normally involve several replications of short runs to enable statistical testing. In general, if statistical tests are to be performed to determine if there are statistical differences between different alternatives, replications are more important that the length of the runs. Our discussion concerning replications and run periods is summarized in Table 8.1

Table 8.1 Replications, Warm-Ups, and Run Periods by Type of System and Purpose

		Purpose of Simulation	
		Estimating Performance	Evaluating Alternatives
Type of System	Terminating	Replications: 1 Warm-up Periods: 0 Simulation Time Unit: Cycles Run Periods: Large value	Replications: Greater than 1 Warm-up Periods: 0 Simulation Time Unit: Cycles Run Periods: Small value
	Nonterminating	Replications : 1 Warm-up Periods: Large value Simulation Time Unit: Natural units Run Periods: Large value	Replications: Greater than 1 Warm-up Periods: Large value Simulation Time Unit: Natural units Run Periods : Smaller values but more than 1

Model Verification and Validation

Before models can be used to estimate performance or test alternative process designs, they should be verified and validated. *Model verification* means that the model is operating as expected, i.e., there are no errors in the model. *Model validation* means that the model is an accurate representation of the real-world process that it is designed to model. Model verification is a necessary but not sufficient condition for model validation. In other words, a model must be free of errors to be a valid model, but a model that is free of errors is not necessarily a valid model of the real world process.

MODEL VERIFICATION

There is no magic answer for model verification, and there is no way of ensuring that your model does not have errors. However, we can give some tips to help test your model to increase the odds that it is working properly.

- For large, complex models, break the model up into pieces (subprocesses) that you can test independently. It is much easier to test smaller pieces for accuracy than to test large, complex models. In computer programming terms, this is design by modularization.
- Use dummy input to check for accuracy. For example, it is easier to test the accuracy and behavior of a model with constant input parameters rather than probabilistic input. Even though the inputs to the real-world system may be random, checking the model design with constant parameters initially will be more likely to reveal any errors that may be present.
- Test extreme cases. If a model has errors, they are most likely to show up at the extremes rather than under average conditions. In a simulation model, this may involve reducing resources to extremely low levels to check for problems. If demands on the system vary over time, make sure that you test the model with the highest demands on the system.
- Test all input types. If there are different types of inputs make sure that you test the model using all input types. Do not assume that, because the model works correctly with one type of input, it will work correctly with all input types.

MODEL VALIDATION

Once your model has been verified, it should be validated. At the very least, individuals familiar with the process should be asked if the model is a reasonable representation of the process. If historical data are available for the process, the best way of validating a model is by comparing the performance of the process with performance of the real process under similar conditions. In other words, given the same inputs, the model of the process should produce the same outputs as the process itself. The key to validation is making sure that the conditions are similar in both the model and the process itself and that the performance metrics are calculated in the same way in both cases. It is not necessary that the results be exactly the same, and rarely will that happen. However, they should be substantially the same, although admittedly that can be a subjective judgment. One can also do a statistical test to make sure that they are not statistically different.

Analysis of Simulation Inputs

There are many parameters that need to be set in a simulation model. Among the most important of these are the parameters for arrivals of flow units and the service times of the activities of the process. Both arrivals and service times are most likely random in nature and are best described by probability distributions. For probability distributions, you need to both select a distribution type and then set the parameters of that distribution. But how do you determine what type of distribution to use and the parameters of that distribution? Sometimes the expert judgment of those involved in the process can be used for this purpose, but the best way to determine these values is with the use of historical data if it is available. We will first discuss the issue of type of distribution and then the estimation of the parameters.

FINDING THE APPROPRIATE PROBABILITY DISTRIBUTION

There are a wide variety of probability distributions that can be used in simulation models, and it is rarely obvious which one would be best in a given situation. A starting point is to plot a histogram of the historical data and visually determine what type of distribution might be most appropriate.

Creating a Histogram

Histograms can be easily created with Excel using the following process:

1. Sort the data and find the minimum and maximum values.
2. Decide on how many class intervals should be in the histogram. There are no hard-and-fast rules for the number of intervals but, in general, it should be between 5 and 15. Taking the square root of the number of values in the data usually gives a reasonable answer.
3. Divide the sample data into bins, with the range for each bin based on the number of intervals calculated in step 2. The first bin should start with a low enough value to include the minimum value in the data, and the maximum value should fall in the last bin. Place these bin values in a column of the Excel worksheet.
4. Determine the frequency count of data points that fall in each bin and record this value in the column next to the appropriate bin values.
5. Select the range of cells that contain the frequencies, click the Insert tab of the Excel ribbon, and select the Column chart in the Charts section.
6. Right click on one of the columns in the chart and chose Select Data from the menu.
7. Click the Edit button under Horizontal (Category) axis labels and select the bin values for the horizontal axis. Click OK twice to add the labels.

8. You can also give your chart a title if you wish, and you can format the chart to your liking. If you want to remove the spacing to create a true histogram, right click on one of the columns and select Format Data Point. Slide the slider for Gap Width all the way to the left for No Gap.

Example 8.1

Over the course of the few days, Mary has kept track of the time between arrivals at her espresso stand. She has 50 observations, as shown in Table 8.2. She would like to determine an appropriate distribution to describe the arrival pattern of customers at her business.

Table 8.2 Historical Data on Interarrival Times

7	16	43	8	38	34	33	5	8	14
2	7	31	16	9	75	1	26	4	40
2	33	36	26	33	3	83	20	30	17
35	4	8	24	1	56	33	21	24	48
9	29	6	10	8	13	19	2	14	11

Solution

Sorting the data you will find that the minimum value is 1 and the maximum is 83. Taking the square root of 50 (the number of observations) yields a value of about 7 for the number of intervals. The overall range of values is from 1 to 83. If we divide 83 by the 7 intervals we get an approximate interval width of 12. Therefore each interval should include 12 values. The resulting bins and the corresponding frequencies are shown below and the resulting histogram is shown in Figure 8.3.

Bin	Frequency
1-12	20
13-25	11
26-38	13
39-51	3
52-64	1
65-77	1
78-90	1

Figure 8.3 Histogram of the Interarrival Times for Example 8.1

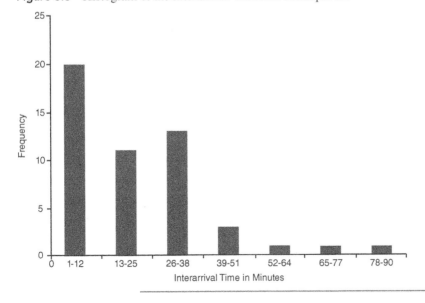

From Figure 8.3 it is evident that a symmetric distribution like the Normal does not fit the data very well at all, but a positively skewed distribution like the Exponential may fit the data fairly well. We will see in the next section how we can determine if the Exponential distribution is a good fit for the data.

Goodness of Fit Tests

Goodness of fit tests are used to determine how closely observed frequencies agree with the frequencies that would occur if the values were derived from some specified theoretical distribution. For example, tests can be used to determine whether empirical data actually conform to a statistical distribution such as the Uniform, Exponential, or Normal distribution. The most widely used goodness of fit test is the chi-square test. The chi-square test compares the observed frequencies with the expected frequencies. The Excel file Goodness of Fit.xlsx can be used to conduct goodness of fit tests for several theoretical distributions. The opening sheet of the Excel file is shown in Figure 8.4. To perform the chi-square test you need the observed frequencies from the historical data and the expected frequencies from the appropriate theoretical distribution. The Goodness of Fit.xlsx file provides worksheets to derive the expected frequencies for five distributions: Exponential, Normal, Uniform, Triangular, and Beta. In Example 8.1 we speculated that the data may have come from an exponential distribution. To test this, we need the expected frequencies from the Exponential distribution to compare with our observed frequencies. Figure 8.5 shows the appropriate worksheet for this example. To use this worksheet, you need the limits of the intervals for the frequency distributions. The appropriate values from Example 8.1 are illustrated in Figure 8.5. You also need to supply the sample size, 50 in this case, and the mean of the distribution. For our example, we can use the mean of the sample data which is 21.5 for Example 8.1. The template will then generate the expected frequencies as shown in Figure 8.5.

Figure 8.4 Goodness of Fit Opening Worksheet

Frequencies				
Observed	Expected			
20	19.114	Number of Categories	7	
11	11.6826	Number of Estimated Parameters	1	
13	6.38181	Chi-Square Value	7.7711	
3	3.48616	Degrees of Freedom	5	
1	1.90437	p-value	0.1693	
1	1.04029			
1	0.56827			

Figure 8.5 Exponential Distribution Worksheet

Distribution Intervals		Expected			
Lower Limit	Upper Limit	Frequencies		Number of Observations	50
1	12	19.1140		Mean of Distribution	21.5
13	25	11.6826		Constant e	2.71828
26	38	6.3818			
39	51	3.4862			
52	64	1.9044			
65	77	1.0403			
78	90	0.5683			

These expected frequencies can then be copied and pasted into the Goodness of Fit worksheet as shown in Figure 8.4. Since the cells for the expected frequencies are formulas, make sure that you use Paste Special and select the Values option to paste the values into the Goodness of Fit worksheet so that you copy only the values, not the formulas. You also need to enter the number of estimated parameters into the Goodness of Fit worksheet. In this case we have only estimated the mean of the distribution, so we enter a value of 1. The chi-square results are then calculated by the template, as shown in Figure 8.4. It is important to note that this version of the chi-square test is different from the normal hypothesis testing procedure in statistics. Here the null hypothesis (that the model fits the data) is what we are trying to demonstrate. In other words, we are trying to support the null hypothesis rather than reject it. Therefore, we cannot "prove" that the data support the model but merely that the data do not refute the model. In Example 8.4, the p-value of .1693 provides support for the hypothesis that the data come from an Exponential distribution. In contrast, if you try to fit the Normal distribution to the same frequencies, the p-value of .0000 clearly indicates that the data do not support that hypothesis.

ESTIMATING PARAMETERS

Once the type of distribution has been established, the estimation of parameters is usually fairly straightforward. In the case of the Exponential distribution, there is only one parameter, the average. If the sample size is reasonably large, the sample mean provides a good estimate of this value. For the normal distribution, the sample mean and standard deviation will provide acceptable estimates of the corresponding parameters of the normal distribution. For the Uniform distribution, the minimum and maximum values can be used. The triangular and beta distributions both have three parameters, which are usually best estimated by the minimum and maximum values from the data along with the mean value.

Analysis of Simulation Outputs

The purpose of a simulation is generally to estimate the performance of a process or to evaluate different possible process designs. In either case, the statistical analysis of the outputs of the simulation is an important part of the simulation process.

ESTIMATION OF PERFORMANCE

Statistical estimates of the performance measures of a process typically take one of two forms: point estimates and interval estimates. A *point estimate* is a single value that represents our best estimate of a characteristic of the performance of the process. Estimates might be statistical measures of central tendency (mean, median, or proportion), variability (variance or standard deviation), or measures of shape, such as skewness. These estimates can be obtained for any performance measure output by the simulation software. The point estimate is simply the value of the appropriate measure provided by the simulation software. For example, a point estimate of the average cycle time of the process would be the average cycle time output by XLSim.

However, we know that the estimate is not exactly correct because it depends on the random events in the simulation, and therefore, on the random number stream that was created in the simulation. Therefore, we may want to provide an *interval estimate* such that we are fairly confident that the true population value is within that interval.

The confidence intervals for means and proportions typically involve the normal, or t, probability distributions. Table 8.3 gives the confidence intervals for means, proportions, and variances. The appropriate values from the probability distributions can be found using the Excel functions shown in the last column of Table 8.3.

Table 8.3 Table of Confidence Intervals

Parameter	Sample Estimate	Confidence Interval	Excel Functions
Mean	$\bar{X}$	$\bar{X} \pm t_{n-1,\alpha/2} \frac{s}{\sqrt{n}}$	$t_{n-1,\alpha/2}$ = T.INV(α, n−1)
Proportion	P	$p \pm Z_{\alpha/2} \sqrt{\frac{p(1-p)}{n}}$	$Z_{\alpha/2}$ = NORM.INV(1−α/2)
Variance	s^2	$\frac{(n-1)s^2}{x^2_{\alpha/2}}, \frac{(n-1)s^2}{x^2_{\alpha/2}}$	$X^2_{\alpha/2}$ = CHISQ.INV(α/2)

As we discussed earlier, if you are estimating the performance of a nonterminating process, it is important that you utilize a warm-up period so that the system reaches steady state before deriving the data that you use to estimate the confidence interval. Otherwise, the estimates will be distorted somewhat by the conditions at startup and the random number seed used. If you are estimating the performance of a terminating process, you should use a substantial number of replications, usually at least 25 or 30, and average the resulting outputs to estimate performance.

COMPARING ALTERNATIVES

Comparing alternative designs involves testing hypotheses about the differences between groups. With two alternative designs, this involves a simple t-test for the difference between two means, a Z or chi-square test for the difference between two proportions, and an F-test for the difference between two variances. For three or more alternative designs, one must go to Analysis of Variance for means and a chi-square test for proportions. The key to comparing alternatives is to have replications for each design, whether they are terminating or nonterminating processes. These replications then serve as the sample sizes for the hypothesis tests. You should consult a statistics book if you are unsure about what type of analysis to perform on the simulation output.

Chapter Glossary

Goodness of fit tests Statistical tests used to determine whether or not a specified probability distribution reasonably fits the observed frequencies.
Interval estimate A range of values that we are confident includes the estimated value.
Model validation Determining that the model is a true representation of the real world system being modeled and that it behaves in the same way.
Model verification Verifying that the model works correctly, that there are no errors.
Point estimate A single numerical value that is our best estimate of an unknown quantity.

Chapter Questions and Problems

1. Compare and contrast terminating and nonterminating processes. Give at least two examples of each.
2. Describe the difference between model verification and model validation. Which logically comes first?
3. What is the purpose of a warm-up period in a simulation? For what type of processes might it be necessary to use warm-up periods?

4. The following 100 times represent the time between job arrivals at work center. What is the best distribution to represent these arrival times, and what are the parameters of that distribution?

5	4	3	5	5	5	4	5	4	8	3	9	5	5	5	8	7	7	5	7
5	10	8	6	7	4	4	8	3	4	3	10	6	5	5	4	5	4	8	5
7	4	5	10	10	7	5	6	4	4	4	7	6	5	7	5	4	4	6	6
5	5	5	4	5	7	5	9	7	6	8	3	5	9	15	6	4	6	3	8
5	8	4	4	4	8	4	5	12	5	12	3	5	9	5	4	5	5	5	5

5. The following 60 times represent order fulfillment activity times at a small online retailer. What is the best distribution to represent these arrival times, and what are the parameters of that distribution?

Order Fulfillment Activity Times														
21	8	40	36	28	21	21	26	44	32	21	17	33	27	31
22	19	42	28	39	28	26	18	20	51	31	14	37	29	33
33	27	42	40	50	28	33	22	19	28	39	30	25	28	28
19	30	28	33	19	17	24	24	19	29	46	26	13	22	24

6. The following cycle times in minutes were obtained over 20 replications of a simulation of a process.

Cycle Times										
321	357	363	314	315	396	327	409	293	404
344	354	366	352	389	360	401	349	357	352

a. What is the best estimate of the average cycle time for this process?
b. Give a range of values that you are pretty sure that the average cycle time is within that range.

7. The company in problem 6 is particularly concerned about cycle times over 400 minutes. What is the best estimate of the percentage of times that the cycle time will exceed 400 minutes? What are the 95% confidence limits for this proportion?

Cases Projects

Case 1—Phase III Physical Therapy

Joe owns and operates a small physical therapy practice called Phase III Physical Therapy. Joe has about 25-years of physical therapy experience, ranging from working as a physical therapist in a practice to now owning and operating his own physical therapy practice.

Currently Joe employs a receptionist, Stacy, who schedules and queues patients for their physical therapy treatments. Joe also employs a physical therapy aide, Christie, who prepares patients for their treatments and monitors their exercises. (Note: Due to licensing requirements, the physical therapy aide cannot deliver the actual physical therapy treatments. As such, the aide is limited to preparing the patients for their treatments and monitoring their exercises.) Finally, Joe himself delivers the actual physical therapy treatments to the patients.

Currently Phase III Physical Therapy has four treatment rooms. Each treatment room has an adjustable bed with a muscle stimulation device.

Despite his 25-years of experience, Joe is unsure if he should add a second physical therapist to his practice or not. While he has a sufficient queue of patients who are waiting for physical therapy, he wonders if his facility in its current configuration has the capacity to handle the additional patient load that a second physical therapist will generate. If he adds a second physical therapist, will he need to expand the number of treatment rooms, hire an additional physical therapy assistant, or both?

QUESTIONS

1. Based on the following information, use XLSim to create a simulation model for the current situation at Phase III Physical Therapy:
   - Starting at 8 AM patient appointments are scheduled to start on the hour and on the half of an hour until 5 PM with an hour off for lunch. As such, Phase III Physical Therapy sees 30–40 patients per day.
   - While many patients are generally on time, quite a few patients are late (exponential distribution, mean = 30 minutes).
   - Depending on the patient, on average it takes Stacy about 5 minutes to check-in a patient (normal distribution, mean = 5 minutes, standard deviation = 2 minutes).
   - Depending on the patient's treatment plan, on average it takes Christie about 5 minutes to place the patient in their assigned treatment room and set the patient up for exercises (Note: Once the treatment room is assigned, it is retained for the patient's use until check-out.) (normal distribution, mean = 5 minutes, standard deviation = 2 minutes).
   - On average each patient exercises for 30 minutes prior to treatment. Christie is required to monitor these exercises to ensure that the patient is doing the exercises correctly (normal distribution, mean = 30 minutes, standard deviation = 10 minutes).
   - Depending on their treatment plan, on average Joe spends 30 minutes with each patient providing their physical therapy treatment (normal distribution, mean = 30 minutes, standard deviation = 10 minutes).
   - After their physical therapy treatment, each patient uses a muscle stimulation device for 15 minutes to help reduce the patient's post treatment stiffness and soreness (As a reminder, each treatment room has an assigned stimulation device.) (constant = 15 minutes).
   - On completion of a patient's treatment, on average it takes Christie about 5 minutes to prepare the treatment room for the next patient (normal distribution, mean = 5 minutes, standard deviation = 2 minutes).
   - On completion of a patient's treatment, on average it takes Stacy 5 minutes to check the patient out and schedule their next appointment (normal distribution, mean = 5 minutes, standard deviation = 2 minutes).

2. Simulate the current situation for 10 business days (80 hours) and collect the following data: utilization of the receptionist, aide, physical therapist, treatment rooms (e.g., beds and muscle stimulation devices), waiting time, and cycle time. Note: Processes terminate each day and no patients remain in physical therapy after the end of each day.

3. Assuming that Phase III Physical Therapy has sufficient space for patients waiting for physical therapy treatments, modify your XLSim model to simulate the addition of a second physical therapist. Repeat question 2 for your new model. Compare the performance of the two situations by analyzing the data collected from the simulation runs. What does your analysis of the data show? Should Phase III Physical Therapy hire a second physical therapist? Does Phase III have capacity to handle the additional patient load? If not, should they expand the number of treatment rooms, hire another physical therapy aide, or both?

Case 2—An Apple a Day Keeps the Doctor Away

Doctors Smith and Jones operate a small family medicine practice. As part of their practice Smith and Jones employ a receptionist, patient scheduler, two registered nurses (RNs), and a practice manager. While 85 percent of their patients come in for minor medical issues such as a cold or the flu, about 15 percent come in with far more serious medical issues. In general, patients with serious medical issues require more time with the doctor than do patients with minor issues. Additionally, as part of a patient's office visit on average 25 percent of the patients require a diagnostic blood draw after their visit with the doctor. Finally, about 35 percent of the patients require a drug prescription.

Smith and Jones' practice is usually very busy. Currently they have four examination rooms and one blood draw area. Smith and Jones suspect that they may be nearing maximum capacity for their current facility. Just last week the real estate company that manages the office complex where Smith and Jones' practice is located contacted the practice manager regarding a soon-to-be available larger location, within the same office complex. This larger location can accommodate eight examination rooms and two blood draw areas, along with larger areas for doctors offices and other administrative areas.

Smith and Jones' practice manager has contacted you and would like you to model their current operations, as well as what would happen if they moved to the proposed new larger location. Assuming that the waiting areas for patients is sufficient in both locations, should Smith and Jones stay in their present location or move to the new larger facility?

QUESTIONS

1. Based on the following, create an XLSim simulation model for the current situation at Smith and Jones' family medicine practice.
    - Two patient appointments are scheduled on the hour starting at 8 AM and then two more appointments are scheduled in 15 minute increments throughout the day until 4 PM. As such doctors Smith and Jones see between 60 and 70 patients per day.
    - While many patients are generally on time, quite a few patients are late (exponential distribution, mean = 15 minutes)
    - Depending on the patient, on average it takes .the receptionist about 3 minutes to check in a patient. This includes obtaining the patient's insurance co-payment and queuing the patient's chart for the nurses.(exponential distribution, mean = 3 minutes).
    - Once checked in, a patient waits on average about 15 minutes in the doctor's waiting room (exponential distribution, mean = 15 minutes)
    - On average it takes the nurse about 10 minutes to we.igh the patient and take the patient to an available examination room. Once in the examination room, the nurse completes a standard patient interview, along with measuring their blood pressure and taking their temperature (normal distribution, mean = 10 minutes, standard deviation = 2 minutes).
    - On average the required doctor time with a patient with a minor medical issue is usually about 10 minutes. However, the required doctor time with a patient with a serious medial issue can last 30 minutes or longer (minor medical issue: normal distribution, mean = 10 minutes, standard deviation = 2 minutes. major medical issue: normal distribution, mean = 30 minutes, standard deviation = 6 minutes).
    - On average it takes 5 minutes to complete a blood draw. Based on who is available, one of the two nurses performs the blood draw (normal distribution, mean = 5 minutes, standard deviation = 1.5 minutes).
    - On average it takes the doctor about 5 minutes to verify what medicine should be prescribed and then write a prescription (exponential distribution, mean = 5 minutes).
    - At the completion of a patient's visit, the patient checks out with the receptionist which takes about 3 minutes (exponential distribution, mean = 3 minutes).

2. Simulate the current situation for 10 business days (80 hours) and collect the following data: utilization of the receptionist, nurses, doctors, examination rooms, waiting time, and cycle time. As a note, processes terminate each day as no patients remain in treatment after the end of each day.

3. Assuming that Smith and Jones have a sufficient space for waiting patients, modify your XLSim model to simulate the move to the proposed larger location. Repeat question 2 for the new model. Compare the performance of the two situations by analyzing the data collected during the simulation runs. What does your analysis of the data show? Should Smith and Jones relocate to the larger facility or not? If they choose not to relocate to the larger facilities, what other options do they have to handle their patient backlog?

Case 3—A Trip to the Dentist

Dr. Williams has successfully operated a small dental practice for years. You are one of her many loyal patients. Currently she employs a receptionist, two dental technicians and a dental hygienist who cleans teeth and provides teeth whitening services. Dr. Williams has four dental chairs each equipped with the appropriate dental instruments, including a foldaway X-ray machine. Nevertheless, with all of the recent teeth whitening marketing push by a number of large dental care companies, Dr. Williams is experiencing increased demand for her dental hygienist services. Whereas in the past she averaged a 1-in-5 request by her patients for oral hygiene services, or 20 percent, now about 70 percent are requesting hygienist services. All of the patients who request dental hygienist services require cleaning, and roughly 50 percent of those patients also request teeth whitening services. In fact to keep up with the oral hygienist services demand, Dr. Williams has had to fill in as a dental hygienist more than she would like. Nevertheless, while her gut tells her that she needs to hire a second dental hygienist immediately, she is not sure.

On your recent trip to see Dr. Williams, she tells you all about her dental hygienist dilemma. In between her probes inside your mouth, you mention that you are taking a process improvement class and are looking to test out your skills using XLSim on a real world problem. (As an incentive, the professor has offered extra credit to students who attempt to model a real world problem in XLSim.) As a result of your interest in her situation, Dr. Williams has asked you to model her current practice and what the practice would look like if she hires a second dental hygienist.

QUESTIONS

1. Based on the following, create an XLSim simulation model for the current situation in Dr. Williams's dental practice.
    - Patient appointments are scheduled starting at 8 AM and in 15-minutes increments throughout the day until 4 PM. As a result Dr. Williams sees about 32 patients per day. Her dental hygienist provides services to about half of the patients, or 13–16 patients per day.
    - While many patients are generally on time, quite a few patients are late. (exponential distribution, mean = 15 minutes)
    - Depending on the patient, on average it takes the receptionist about 3 minutes to check in a patient including queuing the patient's chart for the dentist. (exponential distribution, mean = 3 minutes)
    - Once checked in, a patient waits on average about 15 minutes in the dentist's waiting room. (exponential distribution, mean = 15 minutes)
    - Prior to a patient having their teeth cleaned, Dr. Williams conducts an oral exam. On average these exams take about 15 minutes to complete. (normal distribution, mean = 15 minutes, standard deviation = 3 minutes)

- On average it a takes the oral hygienist an hour to clean a patient's teeth and, if requested, another 30 minutes to apply a commercial dental whitening product to the patient's teeth (teeth cleaning: normal distribution, mean = 60 minutes, standard deviation = 12 minutes. teeth whitening: normal distribution mean = 30 minutes, standard deviation = 5 minutes).
- At the completion of a patient's visit, the patient checks out with the receptionist. On average this takes about 3-minutes (exponential distribution, mean = 3 minutes).

2. Simulate the current situation for 10 business days (80 hours) and collect the following data: Utilization of the receptionist and dental hygienist, waiting time, and cycle time. As a note, processes terminate each day and no patients remain in the office at the end of the day.
3. Assuming that Dr. Williams has sufficient space for waiting patients, modify your XLSim model to simulate adding a second dental hygienist to Dr. Williams' practice. Repeat question 2 for the new model. Compare the performance of the two situations by analyzing the data collected during the simulation runs. What does your analysis of the data show? Should Dr. Williams hire a second dental hygienist or not?

Case 4—Mac's Barbershop

Mac has been operating a small barbershop for years in Smithsville, OR. Everyone around town knows and likes Mac. Mac is open Tuesday–Saturday from 9:00 AM to 5:00 PM. Mac typically does not close for lunch. Depending on the flow of customers, when he can, Mac will take intermittent breaks to eat something. Recently a bargain barbershop moved into Smithsville and is offering haircuts at very low prices: $9.95 for a men's haircut, while Mac charges $12.95. While in general Mac's customers acknowledge they like Mac's haircuts better than the bargain shop, still saving $3 is tempting for some of his less loyal customers.

Besides offering cheaper haircuts, the new competition guarantees no more than a 15-minute wait for a haircut or the customer's next haircut is free. Because he did not have any competition, Mac had become accustomed to his customers waiting up to an hour for a haircut. While some of Mac's customers are retired and are willing to wait for a haircut, many of his other customers are just too busy to wait.

As a result of the new competition from the bargain barbershop, Mac is considering adding a second chair and a new barber to his shop. While he cannot directly compete with the 15-minute-wait-or-your-next-haircut-is-free promotion, he hopes to significantly reduce his waiting times and at least help stabilize his once-prosperous business.

QUESTIONS

1. Based on the following, create an XLSim simulation model for the current situation at Mac's Barbershop.
   - On busy days a customer arrives nearly every 15 minutes. However, on slow days only one customer per hour arrives. Mac opens at 9 AM and closes at 5 PM. He is open Tuesday–Saturday. Mac does not take appointments. As a result haircuts are on a first-come, first-serve basis (exponential distribution, mean = 30 minutes).
   - On average Mac can cut one customer's hair every 15 minutes (normal distribution, mean = 15 minutes, standard deviation = 3 minutes).
   - Mac charges $12.95 per haircut while paying himself a salary of $25 per hour.
   - Mac's fixed costs for his shop each month are as follows:
     - Rent: $1,000 per month
     - Utilities: $150 per month (electric, gas, water, sewer, waste removal)
     - Marketing: $100 per month (website, yellow pages, newspaper ad)

2. Simulate the current situation for 10 business days (80 hours) and collect the following data: utilization of Mac, waiting time, and cycle time. As a note, processes terminate each day and no one remains in the barbershop after the end of each day.

3. Assuming that Mac has a sufficient queue of loyal customers who plan to stay with him, and he decides to add a second barber station with a new barber, modify your XLSim model to simulate having two barbers available to cut hair versus having one barber available. Repeat question 2 for the new model. Compare the performance of the two situations by analyzing the data collected during the simulation runs. What does your analysis of the data show? Will adding a second barber reduce Mac's average waiting time for a haircut to less than 15 minutes to allow him to be competitive with the new bargain barbershop? Considering the one-time cost of adding a second barber chair as well as fixed and variable costs, can Mac still be profitable by charging $12.95 per haircut or will he need to increase his haircut prices? Consider the following in modifying your XLSim model:
   - Mac expects to pay the new barber $25 per hour. (Customary barber tips are not included.)
   - Mac's onetime costs to add a second barber service station are as follows:
     - Barber Chair: $600
     - Barber Equipment: $400 (barber clippers (2), hair cutting scissors (3), styling combs (12), straight edge razor (2), razor sharpening belt, shave cream machine, towel heater, wall mirror ,and sterilization equipment)
     - Note: Mac expects to recoup these one-time costs within the first year of operating with a second barber.

Case 5—Al's One-Stop Garage Quick-Lube Service

Al Green, and accomplished mechanic, has a small garage where he specializes in doing anything from minor automobile repairs to engine overhauls. Besides himself, Al currently employs a master mechanic, two journeymen mechanics, and an apprentice mechanic. Additionally, Al has four service bays with hydraulic lifts to hoist vehicles to provide access for repair or maintenance work. For all practical purposes, each vehicle that Al services requires a hydraulic lift for at least part of the service.

Some weeks Al's One Stop Garage is very busy, while other weeks, things are rather slow. Al recently attended a business seminar sponsored by the local Chamber of Commerce. During the seminar, the speaker suggested that one approach to filling in gaps in capacity is to diversify services. Not wanting to send his employees home early without pay on slow days Al wonders if he offered a cost-competitive quick-lube service on a walk-in basis, could he fill in some of his excess capacity without straining his other services during times of high demand?

Based on his years of experience, Al figures that it takes on average 30 minutes to put a vehicle on a lift, hoist it up, drain the oil, replace the filter, and grease any required fittings. Nevertheless, depending on the vehicle, a lube service can take as few as 20 minutes or as many as 40 minutes.

As a way to help his customers and also increase business, Al's mechanics also perform a top-to-bottom safety inspection on each vehicle that is in the garage for service. Al does not charge for this service and generally his customers appreciate the safety inspection especially if they are planning a long trip. On average these safety inspections take about 15 minutes to complete.

QUESTIONS

1. Design and build a sample XLSim model of current operations based on the following:
   - Assume that customers (cars) arrive at Al's One Stop Garage arrive at a rate of 1 per hour and that the time between arrivals follows an exponential distribution.

- With regard to normal operations, most of the work is performed by Al, the master mechanic, and the two journeymen. Al and his master mechanic mostly perform the complex level tasks in the garage such as engine and transmission repairs. His journeymen mechanics perform the medium level tasks such as brake work, radiator work, and transmission flushes. The apprentice mostly helps the mechanics by getting tools and parts and also does the test drives.
- The following table lists typical day-to-day garage tasks, the resources required, and the percentage breakdown of tasks.

Task	Required Resource	Average (Mean)	Standard Deviation	Percent of Jobs
Brake Repair	Journeyman or above	2 hours	.25 hours	20%
Engine Repair	Al or Master mechanic	7 hours	2 hours	5%
Engine Tune-Up	Journeyman or above	2 hours	.5 hours	35%
Radiator Flush	Journeyman or above	1 hour	.25 hours	15%
Radiator Replacement	Journeyman or above	3 hours	.5 hours	5%
Safety Inspection Note: Required for all vehicles serviced	Journeyman or above	.25 hours	.05 hours	100%
Test Drive Note: Required for all vehicles serviced	Apprentice or above	.25 hours	.05 hours	100%
Transmission Flush	Journeyman or above	1 hour	.2 hours	15%
Transmission Repair	Al or Master mechanic	10 hours	4 hours	5%

2. Simulate the situation for 10 business days (80 hours). Collect the following data: utilization of Al, the master mechanic, the two journeymen mechanics, and the apprentice mechanic, waiting time, and cycle time. As a note, processes do not terminate each day as some cars may remain in the garage at the end of each day. [Hint: Use the part of the auto being worked on as an attribute of the flow units (brake, ending, radiator, or transmission)]. On the basis of your results, do you think that Al's Garage can handle more traffic by adding the lube service? Who in the shop should perform the lube service work? Support your answer.

3. Using the XLSim model that you created for Al's One-Stop Garage, modify the model to add a quick lube service. Assume that cars requiring the lube service will arrive at a rate of 5 per hour and it takes, on average, 30 minutes to complete the job with a standard deviation of 3 minutes. Can Al's One Stop Garage handle this level of increased traffic? If not, how much additional traffic can the shop support?

Case 6—Frogmore Medical Center

The Frogmore Medical Center (FMC) is a regionally based medical facility that serves a five-county area. The FMC operates a 200-bed hospital along with an emergency room facility.

Recently FMC has added a number of surgeons specializing in different types of surgery and is in the planning stages for adding a new surgical center to the medical center. Given demand for surgeries and their staffing resources, FMC is planning on performing 25 to 30 operations a day following a uniform distribution. Patients for surgery are to be checked into the facility the night before their scheduled surgery and remain in their rooms until their surgery is to begin. The major decision facing FMC is the capacity of the surgical area, i.e., the number of operating theaters and the capacity of the recovery room in terms of the number of recovery beds. Figure 8.6 shows patient flow along with the essential details of the surgical theaters and the recovery room. Patients wait in their rooms in the general ward until time for their surgery. They are prepped for surgery in their rooms, but this time is not relevant to the decision facing FMC. When a surgical theater comes open, the patient is transported to the surgical theater which is then busy and cannot accommodate another patient. Operations take on average 65 minutes and follow an exponential distribution. When the surgery is finished, the surgical theater must be cleaned before another patient can be moved in. After the cleaning is finished, the room is free, and another patient can be moved in for surgery. Meanwhile, the patient whose operation was just completed, is normally moved to the recovery room. However, about 30 percent of minor surgeries do not require a recovery room. If all of the recovery beds are occupied when a patient arrives, the patient must wait in the hallway outside the recovery room until a bed becomes available. When a bed is available, the patient is moved into the recovery room bed until they are recovered, at which time the patient is transferred back to their room or discharged from the

Figure 8.6 Patient Flows for Surgical Patients at FMC

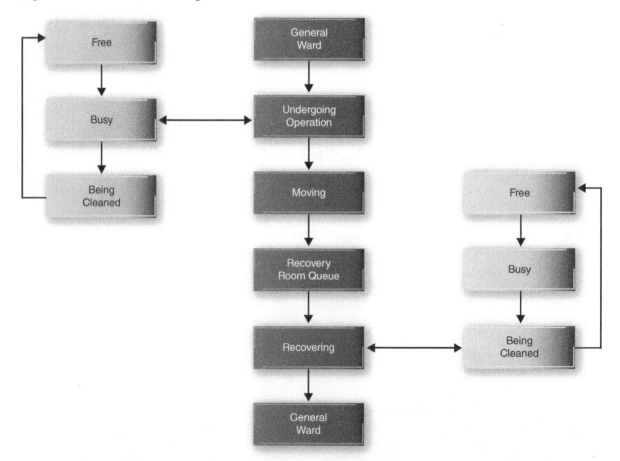

hospital. After the patient is transferred, the recovery room bed must be cleaned before it is free to accommodate another patient.

Surgeries longer than 45 minutes are considered to be major surgeries, and surgeries of 45 minutes or less are considered minor surgeries. Recovery times for minor surgeries average 60 minutes and follow an exponential distribution, while major surgeries have a recovery time of 150 minutes on average and also follow an exponential distribution. Clean-up times average 20 minutes in the operating theater and 15 minutes in the recovery room. Both times follow a normal distribution with a standard deviation of 4 and 3 respectively.

Hospital administration has set a goal of finishing all surgeries within an 8-hour period from 8:00 AM to 4:00 PM. However, hospital administrators are aware that this will not always be possible, but want to ensure that this will happen at least 95% of the time. The policy established for the recovery room is that there be will be no queue with patients waiting for a recovery bed. Of course in the event of a local disaster, this may not be possible, but under normal circumstances they want the chance of a queue forming here to be basically zero. Determine what capacity is necessary for both surgical theaters and recovery room beds to meet the administrators' policy goals.

References

Clarke, J.A. *Energy Simulation in Building Design*, 2nd Edition, 2001, Oxford: Butterworth-Heinemann.
Deprettere, E.F., Teich, J. & Vassiliadis, S. (Eds.), Embedded Processor Design Challenges: Systems, Architectures, Modeling, and Simulation-SAMOS, 2002, New York: Springer.
Dimian, A.C., *Integrated Design and Simulation of Chemical Processes*, 2003, Elsevier.

Part III
Process Management

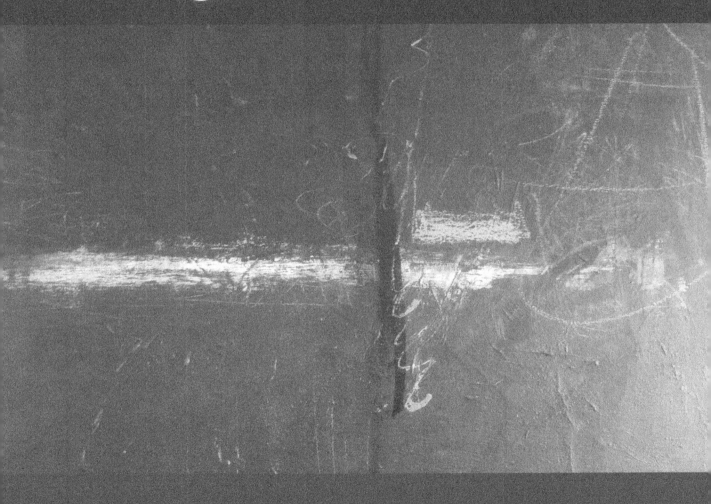

Chapter 9

Managing Process Flows

"Technology speeds the process, makes it simpler—and you can view the entire transaction as an automated work flow."

—Todd Costigan

"Because manufacturers can accurately follow the overall process flow, they can find out critical process steps and adjust them accordingly to increase yield, and end users will get products where performance variations are smaller."

—Lari Kytölä

"Time is the scarcest resource and unless it is managed nothing else can be managed."

—Peter Drucker

In this section of the text, we cover the topic of process management, which is the ensemble of activities of planning and monitoring the performance of a process, especially in the sense of business processes (Becker et al., 2003). In Chapter 9 we will talk about managing process flows and in Chapter 10 we will cover the monitoring and controlling aspects of business process management. Although much of this material comes from the operations management literature, in particular the quality management literature, the application of this material is universal to any type of process from the manufacturing floor to a CPA auditing process to the recruiting and hiring process. The material in this chapter is closely related to the material in Chapter 4 on queuing and simulation, and it may be worthwhile to briefly review that material before starting this chapter.

The Concept of Process Flow

To truly understand a process, you must understand the flow of the flow units within that process. To manage a process, you must know the most important measures related to that flow and the critical factors that affect it. It is these topics that we will discuss in this chapter.

Different sources use different terms for the units that flow through a process such as jobs, orders, work, or items. We will use the general term flow unit to refer to the items that flow through a process. Flow units can be jobs or products in manufacturing, information or paperwork in a knowledge-based service, patients in medical facility, money in a financial services firm, or data in an information processing service. There are three primary flow patterns in processes:

- **Divergent flows**: A single input flow unit diverges along several paths. Divergent flows occur in manufacturing when a single raw material is converted into multiple products. An example is crude oil, which is refined into multiple products.
- **Convergent flows**: Multiple input flow units converge into a single flow unit. An example, again from manufacturing, is when multiple component parts converge at final assembly to be assembled into a product.
- **Linear flows**: A flow unit goes through a linear sequence of steps without branching. Assembly line production in manufacturing is an example of a linear flow.

Most processes are a mixture of the three types of flow, although a process may be dominated by one or the other flow types. So-called job shops lack a dominant type of flow and exhibit a seemingly random pattern of the three types of flow. Batch production has somewhat more consistent flow and sometimes exhibits one or more dominant flow patterns. Assembly lines and continuous production are characterized by consistent linear flow patterns. Umble and Srikanth (1990) defined different types of manufacturing plants depending on their dominant flows. Redefined in process terms, the types are

- V-Plant: a process dominated by divergent flows,
- A-Plant: a process dominated by convergent flows,
- I-Plant: a process dominated by linear flows, and
- T-Plant: a hybrid process that is primarily linear but diverges into a large number of different flow units in the last few stages.

No matter what the nature of the process, the essence of process flows can be captured with three key performance measures: flow rate, flow time, and inventory. These three measures answer three critical questions about a process:

1. On average, how many flow units pass through the process per unit of time (flow rate)?
2. On average, how long does it take a flow unit to move through the process (flow time)?
3. On average, how many flow units are within the process boundaries at any given time (inventory)?

We will discuss these key concepts and their interrelationships in the following sections.

FLOW RATES

An important concept in discussing flow dynamics in processes is the *flow rate*. Flow rates are defined as the number of flow units per unit of time. For example, an auditing group may be able to perform five audits a month. Recalling from Chapter 1 that a process takes inputs and transforms them into outputs, both the inflow rate (R_i) and the outflow rate (R_o) are important to describing flows. Since inflow and outflow rates vary over time, we can define the time varying flow rates as

$R_i(t)$: the inflow rate of flow units from all input sources at time period t.

$R_o(t)$: the outflow rate from all output points at time period t.

Figure 9.1 shows an example of the fluctuating inflow and outflow rates over time.

Although inflow and outflow rates vary over time, a *stable process* is one in which the average inflow rate is equal to the average outflow rate. That means we do not need to distinguish between the inflow rate and the outflow rate in a stable process because they are the same. We call this value *throughput* (TH), the average outflow rate of the process stated in flow units per time period. In Figure 9.1 the average inflow and outflow rates, and therefore the throughput, are 100 units per time period.

Figure 9.1 Fluctuating Inflow and Outflow Rates

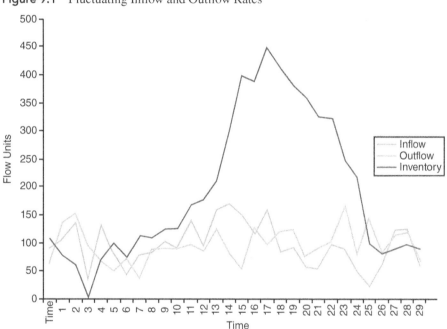

INVENTORY

If we take a snapshot of a process at any particular moment in time, we would find that there are flow units at different stages in the process. In a manufacturing context these flow units are called *work-in-process inventory*, or WIP. We will use the term *inventory* (I) to represent those flow units that have entered the process but not yet exited. Keep in mind that this meaning of inventory in not necessarily the same as the traditional meaning of inventory, which defines inventory as "physical items that are used to make other products or to satisfy demand." In the process sense, flow units, and therefore inventory, can be physical items, but they can also be information, data, money, or people.

The amount of inventory in a process is directly related to the inflow and outflow rates of the process. Just as the inflow rates and outflow rates vary over time, so does the amount of inventory. Figure 9.1 shows the inventory levels over time as well as the inflow and outflow rates. In periods where the inflow rate exceeds the outflow rate, inventory increases. Conversely, in periods where the outflow rate exceeds the inflow rate, inventory decreases. More specifically, the inventory at the end of time period t [I(t)] is

$$I(t) = I(t-1) + R_i(t) - R_o(t) \qquad (9\text{-}1)$$

Since in a stable system, the average inflow rate is equal to the average outflow rate, the average inventory in a stable system remains the same. In Figure 9.1 the beginning inventory was 90 units and the ending inventory is also near that same amount, despite some large fluctuations.

FLOW TIMES

Flow times are the times it takes a flow unit to move from one part of a process to another. Different flow units will have different flow times. *Cycle time* (CT) refers to the time that it takes a flow unit to go through the entire process. Since flow time and cycle time are basically the same concept, differing only in how much of the process is being referred to, we will use the two terms interchangeably in this text. Any reference to flow time will apply to cycle time as well and vice versa.

Flow times can have several different components to them depending on the situation. The major components are

- activity, or processing time,
- waiting time,
- transportation or move time,
- inspection time, and
- setup time.

Of these different components of the flow time, only the first, the activity or processing time, is usually regarded as value-adding time as discussed in Chapter 1. The other components are at best business-value-adding, and most are non-value-adding. Unfortunately, in many processes, activity time, the value-adding portion, is only a small percentage of the total cycle time. Often, process improvement efforts focus on reducing the non-value-adding components of the flow time.

LITTLE'S LAW: THE RELATIONSHIP OF THROUGHPUT, INVENTORY, AND CYCLE TIME

In Chapter 4, we discussed Little's law as a basic principle of queuing situations. Little's law basically states the relationship between queuing measures arrival rate, average number in the system, and average time in the system. In brief,

$$N = \lambda T \qquad (9\text{-}2)$$

where N is the average number in the system, λ is the average arrival rate, and T is the average time in the system. In process terms, the average number in the system is inventory (I). The arrival rate corresponds to the inflow rate, which in a stable system is equal to the outflow rate, or throughput (TH). The average time in the system is the cycle time (CT). Therefore, in process terms Little's law becomes

$$I = TH \times CT \qquad (9\text{-}3)$$

In words, Little's law states that the average inventory in a process is equal to the throughput rate times the cycle time. The implication of Little's law is that if we know any two of these values, we can calculate the third.

$$TH = I/CT \qquad (9\text{-}4)$$

$$CT = I/TH \qquad (9\text{-}5)$$

It is important to keep in mind that Little's law relates not only to the process as a whole, but also to any part of the process down, to each individual activity.

> **Example 9.1**
>
> The credit approval process at an auto company handles an average of 3,000 applications a month. It is estimated that there are an average of 500 applications at various points in the process at any one point in time. What is the average cycle time of the process?
>
> *Solution*
>
> TH = 3,000
>
> I = 500
>
> $CT = \frac{I}{TH} = \frac{500}{3000} = \frac{1}{6}$ month
>
> If there are on average 30 days in a month, then the cycle time is approximately 5 days.

Little's law dictates what we must do if we want to increase or decrease one of the measures when a second measure must remain fixed. For example, if we wish to reduce cycle time while maintaining the same level of throughput, we must reduce inventory. Conversely, if we reduce the inventory level, we will automatically reduce the cycle time for a given throughput rate. This is the basic principle behind just-in-time or lean philosophies.

In terms of process management, this implies that if we control two of these factors, we control the third. Which factors we control depends on the situation. For example, in many service environments, the inflow rate, and therefore throughput, is dictated by the customer and is outside of process control. Therefore, if we wish to reduce the number of customers in the system (inventory), we must reduce the cycle time. This is a basic principle that some fast-food companies forget periodically. For example, increasing the menu variety tends to increase order and preparation times, which increases cycle times. With a fixed throughput rate, this inevitably means more customers in the system, and therefore longer wait times. This is not really fast food.

There are other implications of Little's law as well. For example, if you want to increase throughput for a process, you must either increase inventory, reduce cycle time, or both. To reduce inventory, you must either reduce throughput, reduce cycle time, or both. Finally, to reduce cycle time, you must either reduce inventory, increase throughput, or both.

PROCESS MEASURES AND FINANCIAL MEASURES

The process measures can also be directly linked to financial measures of the organization. The most obvious connection is with cash flow. Real throughput for any profit making organization should be measured as sales, not just as output of goods or services (Goldratt & Cox, 1992). Real throughput is therefore positively related to positive cash flow. An increase in throughput directly increases cash flow. In many businesses, inventory is negatively related to cash flow (positively related to negative cash flow). Reducing inventory reduces an organization's need for working capital, which lowers its interest expense and therefore reduces negative cash flow. Operating costs are also related to negative cash flow, and if a reduction in cycle time reduces the resource requirements to produce a given throughput, then cycle time reductions are positively related to negative cash flow. Also, if a reduction in cycle time leads to increased throughput it will be positively related to positive cash flow. As Goldratt and Cox (1992) and others have noted, there are three questions that determine whether process-related improvements will translate into bottom-line improvements:

1. Has process throughput (as measured in sales) increased without any corresponding increase in inventories or process costs?
2. Has process inventory been reduced without any corresponding reduction in throughput or increase in operating costs?
3. Have process costs been reduced without any corresponding reduction in throughput or increase in inventory?

Another important measure with financial implication that is used by many companies is *inventory turns* or *turnover ratio*. The turnover ratio is a measure of how many times inventory is converted into sales during a specific period of time. In accounting terms, inventory turnover is defined as "cost of goods sold divided by inventory." In other situations, turnover is calculated as the average sales per period divided by the average inventory level. In either case, the numerator is basically throughput and the denominator is inventory. Therefore

$$\text{Inventory turns} = TH/I \qquad (9\text{-}6)$$

Since TH/I is just the reciprocal of I/TH, which is cycle time, we can also write the relationship as

$$\text{Inventory turns} = 1/CT \qquad (9\text{-}7)$$

In the remainder of this chapter, we will discuss each of the three performance measures in more detail and examine some of the factors that impact each of them.

The Analysis of Flow Times

Flow times or cycle times are important measures that are widely used to select processes for improvement efforts and in documenting the effects of those improvements. This is not surprising when you consider some of the benefits of shorter flow times:

- Provide quicker delivery time of products and services to customers, which is often an important determinant of customer satisfaction
- Often mean less inventory and lower associated costs
- In new product and service development, give an organization a competitive edge by being first to market
- Allow forecasting horizons to be reduced which increases forecast accuracy
- Allow for faster feedback and correction of quality problems
- Are indicative of a process that is functioning efficiently without a lot of rework or waste

In this section we want to explore the concept of flow, or cycle, time and the factors that affect it. We will also introduce the concepts of theoretical cycle time and cycle time efficiency.

MEASURING FLOW TIME

The average flow time for a process can be measured directly or indirectly through Little's law. Direct measurement of flow time involves observing the process over an extended period and for each flow unit, or a random sample of flow units, recording the time of arrival at the process and the time of departure. Flow time or cycle time is the difference between the arrival and departure times. The average over many such measurements is an estimate of the average cycle time.

Indirect measurement of flow time involves observing the process over an extended period and counting the number of flow units that exit the process. This count can then be used to calculate the throughput rate. Also, at random intervals, the number of flow units in the process is recorded, and the average of these counts estimates the average inventory level. The average cycle time could then be calculated using Little's law.

There are several issues in measuring flow times in real world processes. For example, the flow units handled by most processes are not homogeneous and many of these differences are quite important to the organization. For example, credit application for a large amount of money from a major repeat customer is not the same as a credit application for a small amount from a new customer. Most organizations produce multiple products and/or services, and these different products and services generate different amounts of revenue. Also, different flow units may be treated differently, take different paths through the process, and require different resources in the process. Some of these differences in processing can be accounted for in calculating flow times for the process, as we will see shortly. Other differences must be considered in terms of defining the flow unit itself.

Heterogeneous Flow Units

How we deal with heterogeneous flow units depends to a great extent on the process being examined, particularly its scope, on the extent of the differences between the flow units, and the objectives of the process, among other things. If the flow units differ only slightly, we may simply decide to weight them equally in calculating flows. However, if the flow units differ greatly in terms of their costs, revenues, or other factors, we may want to take these differences into account. This is the *product mix* problem in defining flow units. The product mix is the percentage allocations of the different types of flow units. There is no right or wrong answer to the issue of heterogeneous flow units, and it is very much a matter of managerial judgment. An example may help illustrate some of the issues.

Example 9.2

The Robinson Ad Agency develops radio, TV, and print advertisements for its customers. They charge $1000 for a TV ad, $500 for a radio ad, and $250 for a print ad. They typically do 10 TV ads, 15 radio ads, and 40 print ads a month. It usually takes 6 working days to create a TV ad, 4 working days to create a radio ad, and 1 working day to create a print ad. What is the average flow time for the advertisements at Robinson Agency?

Solution

One approach would be to weight the ads equally and take the weighted average of the flow times, where the weights are the number of ads done of each type. Then the average flow or cycle time would be

$$\text{Average Flow Time} = \frac{10(6) + 15(4) + 40(1)}{10 + 15 + 40} = \frac{160}{65} = 2.46 \text{ days}$$

However, Robinson might also consider the revenues that derive from the ad and the resources that have to be expended in producing the ad. Using revenues as a surrogate for both, they may calculate that a radio ad is worth twice what a print ad is worth and a TV ad is worth four times a print ad. Weighting the frequencies this way means that the 10 TV ads would be worth 40 (10 × 4), the 15 radio ads would be worth 30 (15 × 2), and the 40 print ads worth 40 (40 × 1). The average flow time would then be

$$\text{Average Flow Time} = \frac{40(6) + 30(4) + 40(1)}{40 + 30 + 40} = 3.64 \text{ days}$$

We should point out that neither approach is necessarily right or wrong. They are just different ways to approach the problem.

Process Boundaries

In measuring flow units, we must also decide on the location of the process boundaries. Recall that the definition of flow time or cycle time is the amount of time a flow unit is within the process boundaries from start to finish. This means that where we locate the process boundaries can have a profound effect on cycle times. For example, with the Robinson Ad Agency in Example 9.2, where does the ad process start? Does it start when someone in the agency begins work on the project, when the contract to do the ad is signed, or when the initial meeting with a prospective client takes place? Similar options exist on the output end of the process. Does the process end when we finish working on the ad, when the client approves the ad, when we bill the client, or when we receive payment for the ad? The answers to these questions will certainly affect the cycle times we calculate. Also the definition of inventory must match that of the cycle time definition. Again, there is no right or wrong answer to these questions.

Where we draw the boundaries will depend on our objective in doing the analysis and what parts of the process we feel need to be monitored or improved. The important thing to keep in mind is that the different boundaries result in different interpretation of the three measures, cycle time, inventory, and throughput.

REWORK

Some situations present two additional factors that must be taken into account in calculating cycle times. The first, addressed in this section, is the existence of rework. The second, addressed in the next section, is the existence of multiple paths in the process.

In some processes, there is the possibility of errors or defects in the process that must be reworked to remove the problem. This rework will certainly affect the cycle times of those items that need to be reworked, but it is likely that not all items will need this additional time. How then, do we account for these effects? The answer takes into account the percentage of those items that must go through the rework loop (that portion of the process that must be repeated). If we let rw% represent the percentage of flow units that have to be reworked and T represent the sum of the activity times within the rework loop, then the cycle time of the rework loop will be

$$CT = T(1 + rw\%) \qquad (9\text{-}8)$$

This, however, assumes that the rework only needs to be done once. In other words, that the probability of an error the first time through the process is rw% but the probability of an error the second time is 0.0. If the probability of an error remains the same the second, third, fourth, or any time through the process, then the cycle time would be computed as

$$CT = \frac{T}{1 - rw\%} \qquad (9\text{-}9)$$

An example may help to illustrate the calculations.

Example 9.3 The expense reimbursement process at Logsdon Enterprises is graphed in Figure 9.2. The procedure begins when the employee fills out the expense form after incurring a business-related expense, usually within 3 days of the expense. Errors are sometimes made in the expense reports that are not caught until the supervisory inspection, with about 15% of all forms having at least one error. Returned forms are almost always correct after the first correction. How long is the cycle time for expense reimbursement at Logsdon Enterprises?

Figure 9.2 Expense Reimbursement at Logsdon Enterprises

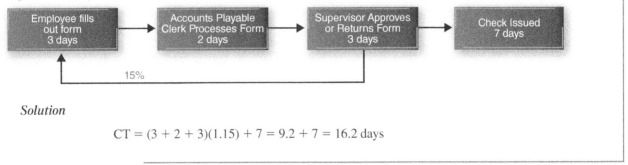

Solution

$$CT = (3 + 2 + 3)(1.15) + 7 = 9.2 + 7 = 16.2 \text{ days}$$

MULTIPLE PATHS

In most real-world processes, there are multiple paths through the process. These different paths can arise for two reasons. The first is because of heterogeneous flow units that may require different paths through the process. This is the product mix problem mentioned earlier. The second is because of parallel activities that may be performed at the same time. These different reasons for the multiple paths have different solutions in calculating cycle times.

Heterogeneous Flow Units

When different types of flow units follow different paths through the process, the calculation of the flow times is straightforward if we know the product mix. The average cycle time is then simply the weighted average of the separate cycle times of the different flow units where the weight is the percentage for that type in the product mix.

Example 9.4

In Example 9.2 we discussed the Robinson Ad Agency. They typically do 10 TV ads, 15 radio ads, and 40 print ads a month. Therefore the product mix is approximately 15% TV, 23% radio, and 62% print. The ad development process is shown in Figure 9.3. What is the average cycle time to develop an ad at Robinson Ad Agency?

Figure 9.3 Ad Development at the Robinson Ad Agency

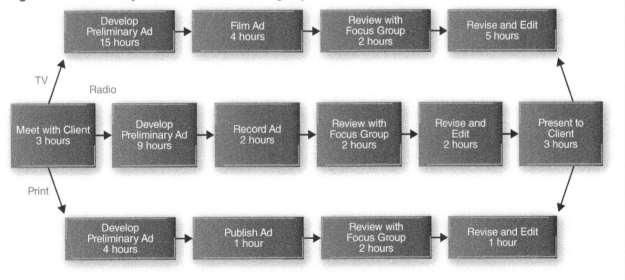

Solution

$$CT = 3 + .15(15 + 4 + 2 + 5) + .23(9 + 2 + 2 + 2) + .62(4 + 1 + 2 + 1) + 3$$

$$= 3 + .15(26) + .23(15) + .62(8) + 3 = 3 + 12.31 + 3 = 18.31 \text{ hours}$$

Parallel Activities

Graphically, the situation with parallel activities looks similar to that of heterogeneous flow units. In both cases, there are branching paths in the graphs that later converge. However, the underlying logic is quite different. With heterogeneous flow units, different flow units branch along different paths because they differed on some characteristic, e.g., the types of ads in Example 9.4. Each flow unit goes along only one of the paths indicated in the graph. With parallel activities, branching occurs because certain activities are performed at the same time. In this case, each flow unit (or a portion or copy of that flow unit) follows all of the branching paths that later converge. In other words, parallel activities are like divergent flow that later becomes convergent flow to become a single path again. The problem is how to account for the multiple paths in calculating the cycle time. This is similar to the project scheduling problem in the project management literature, and the answer is the same. The cycle time depends on the lengths (sum of the activity times) of the separate paths and, in fact, is the largest of these sums. In other words, the cycle time, like the "critical path" in project scheduling, is the longest path through the process. We will call the activities on the critical path *critical activities,* because they impact the overall cycle time. Non-critical activities do not impact that cycle time. An example may help illustrate the calculations.

Example 9.5

Morgan Insurance Group receives application packets from homeowners seeking to insure their homes. Each packet contains a homeowner form and a property form. The homeowner form contains information on the homeowner: their employment history, credit history, and other information. The property, form contains information about the property: its location, size of the property and information about the house including its age and size. A clerk processes the application and checks for completeness of the information. The homeowner packet is then sent to the credit department, where a clerk first checks and verifies the employment history of the applicant that then sends it to another clerk who does a detailed credit history report. The packet is then sent to a senior manager, who evaluates the application for approval or denial. The property form is sent to an assessor, who verifies the information about the property and assesses the value of the home. The assessor then sends the completed packet to the senior manager to be combined with the homeowner information for a decision. The process is diagrammed in Figure 9.4. Calculate the average cycle time of the application process.

Figure 9.4 Processing a Homeowner Insurance Policy at Morgan Insurance Group

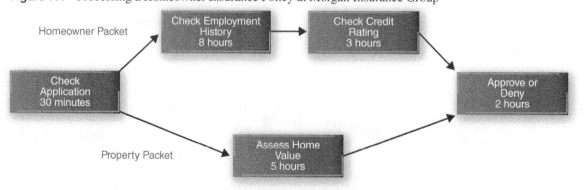

Solution

$$CT = .5 + \max[(8+3), 5] + 2 = .5 + 11 + 2 = 13.5 \text{ hours}$$

THEORETICAL CYCLE TIME AND CYCLE-TIME EFFICIENCY

Up to this point, we have only included activity times in the calculations of flow time. However, as we noted in the beginning, there are often many non-value-adding or business-value-adding components of flow times, especially wait times. We will define the theoretical cycle time as the average flow time excluding wait time, rework, and other non-value-adding components.[1] *Cycle-time efficiency* is then defined as the ratio of the theoretical cycle time to the average cycle time.

$$\text{Cycle-Time Efficiency} = \frac{\text{Theoretical Cycle Time}}{\text{Average Cycle Time}} \quad (9\text{-}10)$$

In effect, cycle-time efficiency is a measure of how close we are coming to achieving 100% value-adding time. Any further improvements in the process would have to come from reengineering the process to reduce the activity times or shorten the critical path. Early reengineering studies showed that cycle time efficiencies in many service industries were often less than 5%.

Example 9.6

Returning to the Morgan Insurance Group from Example 9.5, suppose that it normally takes 7 working days to process an application for homeowner's insurance and that there are 8 hours in a working day. What is the cycle-time efficiency of the process?

Solution

$$\text{Cycle-Time Efficiency} = \frac{\text{Theoretical Cycle Time}}{\text{Average Cycle Time}} = \frac{13.5}{7(8)} = 24.11\%$$

LEVERS FOR MANAGING FLOW TIMES

Now that we have discussed different aspects in calculating cycle times, we turn to the question of how we can improve them. There are basically three approaches for reducing flow or cycle time.

Reduce the Times for Critical Activities

One obvious approach is to try to reduce the times of the critical activities. These activities may contain non-value-adding components that can be eliminated and thereby reduce the cycle time. Whether this approach will indeed lower cycle time can be determined by examining cycle-time efficiency. If this measure is less than 100%, then there is room for improving the cycle time by eliminating wasteful aspects of these activities. If rework is a major cause of inefficiency, we may look for ways of fool-proofing the activities involved in the rework loop, i.e., the concept of Poka-Yoke. If transportation times are a problem, a redesign and physical rearrangement of the process may help to reduce cycle times. More resources at some critical activities may reduce wait times and thereby also reduce the cycle time.

---

1. Anupindi et al. (2006) include rework in their definition of theoretical flow time. However, we believe that the theoretical time should be an "ideal" time and should not include non-value-adding activities. Process activity charts discussed in Chapter 7 are a great source for the values used in calculating cycle-time efficiency.

In any case, knowing which activities are critical activities helps focus our attention on the activities that are capable of leading to lower cycle times. However, we need to keep in mind that when we reduce the times for the critical activities, a different path may become the critical path, i.e., different activities may become critical activities. Therefore, there is always a point where decreasing the times for the current critical activities will not reduce the cycle time of the process because at least some of them will no longer be critical activities.

Move Work off the Critical Path

Another way to reduce the cycle time is to move some of the work on the critical path to other noncritical activities or outside the process boundaries.

Moving critical path activities to noncritical paths can be done in one of two ways: (1) reassign work to those currently performing other activities if possible, or (2) change activities that are currently done sequentially to being performed in parallel. The first approach requires that there be sufficient resources available to perform the additional activities. Otherwise, we would simply be shifting the critical path from one point to another. The second approach of performing activities in parallel is a better approach if the opportunities exist. Sequential processing is necessary because of *precedence requirements*, which dictate that one activity has to finish before another can begin. Precedence requirements are sometimes logical, and there is nothing that can be done to change them. For example, in building a house, we cannot put up the walls before the foundation is poured. There is no physical way that this can be done. However, even with logical requirements, it may be worthwhile to consider if there are new technologies available that may eliminate these requirements. This relates back to the fact, noted in Chapter 6, that technology is often a key enabler for improving process design. Other precedence requirements, however, may be due to limited resources. In other words, two activities may have to be performed in sequence because both activities involve some of the same resources, which are in limited supply. Reconfiguring resources and tasks may eliminate such requirements and allow us to perform the activities in parallel. Finally, there may not actually be any requirements that dictate that the activities be performed sequentially. For example, at one time new product design activities were performed sequentially primarily because they were performed in different functional departments of the organization. The concurrent engineering movement broke down these organizational barriers and allowed many of the previously sequential activities to be performed in parallel, allowing for improvements in product design and greatly reduced cycle times.[2]

Moving work outside the process boundaries refers to accomplishing some of the tasks before the process begins or after it ends. These approaches are sometimes called *pre-processing* or *post-processing*. However, great care must be taken in pre-processing or post-processing that we do not simply move the work to another process within the organizational boundaries. We do not gain anything by simply moving the cycle time from one part of the organization to another. However, there are times when this approach can be very useful in reducing cycle times. For example, in medical clinics, often one part of the process is having the patient fill out an information form before seeing a doctor. If the patient is sent this form in advance, or better yet, is directed to a website where they can enter the required information, then the patient's cycle time at the clinic may be reduced.

Change the Product Mix

As noted earlier in this chapter, all flow units are not necessarily the same, and we may be able to reduce the overall cycle time by changing the mix of products or services performed by the process. An example will help illustrate this.

---

2. An interesting, although not terribly practical, example of moving from sequential to parallel processing is the story that the scientific-management pioneer Frank Gilbreth reportedly trained himself to shave both sides of his face at the same time by holding razors in both hands (Gilbreth & Gilbreth, 1949).

> **Example 9.7**
>
> In Example 9.4 we examined the impact of product mix on the ad development cycle time at the Robinson Ad Agency. Recall that the product mix was 15% TV, 23% radio, and 62% print. TV ads took an average of 26 hours to develop, radio ads took an average of 15 hours, and print ads an average of 8 hours. There was an additional 6 hours of client meeting times that did not depend on the type of ad. Senior management has been contemplating getting out of the television ad business because of the expense and the fact that this is not their particular expertise. They estimate that doing this will change their product mix to 25% radio ads and 75% print ads. How will this impact the ad development cycle time?
>
> $$CT = 6 + .25(15) + .75(8) = 6 + 3.75 + 6 = 15.75$$
>
> The cycle time will be reduced from 18.31 hours to 15.75 hours for a reduction of approximately 14%.

The Analysis of Flow Rates and Capacity

In this section we will look at the relationship between flow rates and capacity. Flow rates and capacities are closely interrelated because the amount of flow or throughput that can be obtained in a process depends on the capacity of the resources available in that process. Unlike flow times and cycle times which are determined by activity times, flow rates and capacities are functions of the resources in the process that performs the activities. Both flow rate, or throughput, and capacity are expressed in terms of number of flow units per time period. For example, they might be expressed as customers per hour or tons per day or dollars per month.

MEASURING FLOW RATES AND CAPACITY

The average flow rate, or throughput, of a process can be calculated by observing the process over an extended period of time and counting the number of flow units that exit the process, or a particular point in the process, each time period. The average of these values is the average flow rate or throughput. The *capacity* is the maximum sustainable flow rate of the process. However, there are different ways to define capacity as we will explore in the following sections.

RESOURCES AND CAPACITY

The activities of a process are performed by resources, primarily labor and equipment. Each activity may utilize one or more resources, and a given resource may perform one or more activities. For example, consider a bakery and the bread-making process. In making bread, several inputs such as flour, salt, butter, water, and yeast are transformed into loaves of bread. During this process there are several activities that are done such as mixing ingredients, kneading the dough, forming it into loaves, placing the loaves in the oven, and removing them from the oven. These activities, in turn, use resources such as mixers, ovens, and bakers. A resource, such as a baker, may be used for several activities such as mixing, kneading, and forming loaves. A given activity, such as mixing the ingredients, may use several resources, such as a baker and a mixer. A *resource pool* is a collection of similar resources that can perform the same activities. Each unit in a resource pool is called a *resource unit*. The key aspect of a resource pool is that the resource units are totally interchangeable; that is, they perform the same activities and at roughly the same speed and efficiency. In the bakery, for example, you might have three bakers who can all mix ingredients, knead the bread, and form the loaves. These three bakers form a resource pool with three resource units. On the other hand, if the bakers were specialized so that one only mixed ingredients, another only kneaded the dough, and the third formed the loaves, then there would be three separate resource pools with one resource unit in each.

When a resource unit is utilized to perform an activity, it is occupied for the length of time that it takes to perform that activity and is unavailable to perform other activities. The total time that it takes a resource to process one flow unit for all the activities that utilize that resource is the *unit load (UL)* for that resource. The UL for a resource is calculated by adding the activity times for all activities that use that resource.

Example 9.8

The Wheat Montana Bakery employs several bakers and bakers helpers in the bread-making process. Some of the bakers (we will designate them as Bakers) mix the ingredients, form the loaves, and place them in the oven. An oven can bake up to 5 loaves at a time. Other bakers (we will designate them as Kneaders) do all of the kneading of the dough, which is done twice for each batch. The bakers helpers (designated as Helpers) help the Bakers place the loaves in the oven and remove them when they are done. The helpers then place the finished loaves on the conveyer to the wrapping machine, where the loaves are wrapped for delivery, and remove them from the machine when they are wrapped. The activities, their resources, and the associated activity times are shown in Table 9.1, where all times are in minutes.

Table 9.1 Activities Times for Wheat Montana Bakery

Activity	Resources	Time (Min)
Mixing ingredients	Baker	6
Kneading dough	Kneader	15
Forming a loaf	Baker	1
Placing loaves in oven	Baker, Helper, Oven	1
Removing loaves from oven	Oven, Helper	1
Wrapping the loaves	Helper	4
Baking the bread	Oven	30

Given the description of which resources perform which activities, we can calculate the unit load for each resource. The unit loads are shown in Table 9.2.

Table 9.2 Unit Loads for the Wheat Montana Bakery

Resource	Unit Load (Min)
Baker	8
Kneader	15
Helper	6
Oven	32

Theoretical Capacity

If we observe a resource over time, we would note that at certain times the resource may be busy performing an activity of a process, unavailable either for scheduled or unscheduled reasons, or available for use but idle because there is no work to perform. Most resources have some scheduled times when they are not available. Human resources need breaks, and equipment will normally have certain periods when it is scheduled for routine maintenance. The *scheduled availability* of a resource is the amount of time it is supposed to be available for work, taking into account breaks, maintenance, and other controllable factors. The *theoretical capacity* (TC) of a resource unit is the maximum sustainable flow if it were fully utilized during its scheduled availability. The maximum flow rate depends on the unit load, the load batch, and the scheduled availability of the resource. The *load batch* is the number of flow units that the resource can process at one time. In Example 9.8, the oven could bake up to 5 loaves at a time, so its load batch would be 5. The theoretical capacity can be calculated as

$$TC = \left(\frac{1}{\text{Unit Load}}\right)(\text{Load Batch})(\text{Scheduled Availability}) \qquad (9\text{-}11)$$

The theoretical capacity of a resource pool is the sum of the theoretical capacities of the individual resource units in that pool. The *bottleneck* is the slowest resource pool, i.e., the resource pool with the smallest capacity. Since flow units must be processed by all of the resources in a process, the theoretical capacity of a process is the theoretical capacity of its bottleneck resource. An example may help illustrate the concepts.

Returning to the Wheat Montana Bakery problem in Example 9.8, suppose that the employees are given four scheduled 15-minute breaks during the 8-hour work day. The half-hour lunch break is not considered to be part of the 8-hour work day and can be ignored. The oven operates continuously over the 8-hour period, except it is down for 15 minutes in the middle of the day for cleaning. Bread is mixed in batches of 5 loaves each, which is the capacity of the oven. There are 2 Bakers, 3 Kneaders, 2 Helpers, and 2 Ovens. Using the unit loads from Table 9.2, we can calculate the theoretical capacities of each of the resource units and the corresponding resource pools. The results are shown in Table 9.3. It is obvious from the capacities of the resource pools that the ovens are the bottleneck of the process and, therefore, the theoretical capacity of the process is 144.15 loaves per day. Table 9.3 illustrates all of the calculations involved in determining capacities. In many cases, the load batch will be 1 unit, and the scheduled availabilities can be ignored, which simplifies the calculations considerably.

Example 9.9

Table 9.3 Theoretical Capacities for Example 9.9

Resource	Unit Load		Scheduled Availability (min per day)	Load Batch	Theoretical Capacity of a resource unit (units/day)	Number of Units in Resource Pool	Capacity of Resource Pool
Baker	8	(1/8) = .125	450	5	281.25	2	562.50
Kneader	15	(1/15) = .067	450	5	150.75	3	452.25
Helper	6	(1/6) = .167	450	5	375.75	2	751.50
Oven	32	(1/32) = .031	465	5	72.075	2	144.15

Effective Capacity

Rarely does a process actually achieve its theoretical capacity. There are a number of issues that prevent this. One problem is that the availability of resources often falls short of their scheduled availability. Machines break down; people do not show up for work or get sick during the day. For these, and a variety of other reasons, the net availability of resources may be less than their scheduled availability. The *net availability* of a resource unit is the actual time that the resource is available to process flow units. The *effective capacity* (EC) of a resource unit is then the maximum sustainable flow if it were fully utilized during its net availability. Effective capacity can be calculated as

$$EC = \left(\frac{1}{\text{Unit Load}}\right)(\text{Load Batch})(\text{Net Availability}) \quad (9\text{-}12)$$

Note that the effective capacity cannot exceed the theoretical capacity and may indeed be less if the net availability is less than the scheduled availability.

Process Capacity

Sometimes a resource may be idle even when it is available to process flow units. For example, a billing clerk may be available and ready to work but simply has nothing to work on. This is known as *starvation*. Or a work center may have finished a job but cannot send it on to the next work center because there is no room at the next work center. Therefore the previous work center cannot start on another flow unit until that last one is cleared, a situation called *blocking*. Blocking and starvation lead to resource idleness, which means that the resource may be idle even though it is available. *Process capacity (PC)* is therefore the capacity of a resource taking into account resource idleness and it is calculated as

$$PC = \left(\frac{1}{\text{Unit Load}}\right)(\text{Load Batch})(\text{Net Availability} - \text{Resource Idleness}) \quad (9\text{-}13)$$

It is also the case that process capacity cannot exceed effective capacity and may indeed be less if there is any starvation or blocking of resources.

Throughput

Finally, throughput may be less than process capacity because of external constraints. Sometimes the external constraints are in terms of the process output. For example, if there is not enough demand for the products or services of the firm, then the throughput rate may be less than the process capacity. At the other end of the process, if inputs are suddenly reduced, for example by a strike or natural disaster, then the throughput rate will also be less than the process capacity.

Putting all of these factors together we have the following relationships:

$$\text{Throughput} \leq \text{Process Capacity} \leq \text{Effective Capacity} \leq \text{Theoretical Capacity} \quad (9\text{-}14)$$

Capacity Utilization

Although a resource pool rarely works at its theoretical capacity, it is useful to know how close it is coming to that theoretical limit. *Capacity utilization* for a resource pool (ρ_p) is the ratio of throughput for that resource pool to its theoretical capacity and is a measure of how effectively we are utilizing process resources.

$$\rho_p = \frac{\text{Throughput}}{\text{Theoretical Capacity}} \quad (9\text{-}15)$$

Each resource pool has a capacity utilization measure, and the process utilization is the capacity utilization of the bottleneck resource. An example may help clarify these concepts.

> **Example 9.10**
>
> Sam's Dry Cleaners process can handle 10 batches of clothes per hour, and each batch can include up to 5 articles of clothing. Sam is open 8 hours a day, but the dry cleaning equipment is down for 30 minutes for scheduled maintenance in the morning. Sometimes employees do not show up for work, or they come in late. This costs Sam about 10 minutes per day on average. Sam has kept careful historical records that indicate that the dry-cleaning machines are idle an average of 20 minutes per day, in addition to scheduled maintenance and absenteeism. The main difficulties are that sometimes staff personnel do not notice that a previous batch has finished and the equipment sits idle until someone puts in the next batch. The company that supplies the chemicals necessary for the dry-cleaning process recently had a fire that damaged part of their plant, so that they can supply only enough chemicals for 300 units a day. Find the theoretical, effective, and process capacity of Sam's Dry Cleaners along with the throughput and capacity utilization.
>
> *Solution*
>
> Unit Load = 6 minutes
>
> Load Batch = 5
>
> Theoretical Capacity = (1/6)(5)(450) = 375 units per day
>
> Effective Capacity = (1/6)(5)(440) = 366.67 units per day
>
> Process Capacity = (1/6)(5)(420) = 350 units per day
>
> Throughput = 300 units per day
>
> Capacity Utilization (ρ) = 300/375 = 80%

LEVERS FOR MANAGING THROUGHPUT

The relationships expressed in 9-14 make it clear that throughput is constrained by capacity so that ultimately, the only way to increase throughput is by increasing capacity. It should be no surprise then that the levers for managing throughput are all related to capacity issues.

Improve Theoretical Capacity

The best way to improve throughput is to increase the theoretical capacity of the process. Since the theoretical capacity of a process depends on the capacity of the bottleneck resource, we should focus on the capacities of bottleneck not on non-bottleneck, resources. The equation for theoretical capacity gives some clues about increasing bottleneck capacity.

$$TC = \left(\frac{1}{\text{Unit Load}}\right)(\text{Load Batch})(\text{Scheduled Availability})$$

Decrease the Unit Load

In our discussion of cycle time, we noted that one way to improve cycle time was to move work from activities on the critical path. Similarly, to increase the capacity of the bottleneck resource we can reduce the unit load for that resource pool. Analogous to our discussions with cycle times, we can take the following actions:

- Decrease the work content of activities performed by the bottleneck resource pool
- Move work from a bottleneck resource to non-bottleneck resources
- Modify the product mix

Essentially then, the levers here are the same as they were for cycle time. The only difference is the focus of the improvement efforts. For cycle time we focus on activities on the critical path, and with throughput we focus on activities performed by the bottleneck resource pool. In both cases we need to reduce the work content by working faster, working smarter, doing things right the first time, and doing the right things (i.e., product mix).

Increase the Load Batch

Besides reducing the unit load on the bottleneck, we could increase capacity by increasing the load batch of the bottleneck resource. If the bottleneck resource is equipment related, we may be able to increase capacity by replacing the equipment with new equipment having a larger capacity. In the Montana Wheat example, we could immediately increase the capacity of the process by buying new ovens that could bake 10 loaves at a time instead of 5.

Increase Resource Availability

Often, we cannot change the scheduled availability because workers need breaks and equipment needs maintenance. In some cases, we may be able to move maintenance activities to times that the process is not operating. We could also extend the period of time that the bottleneck operates by working overtime or working the bottleneck equipment for extra hours. We can also try to increase net availability by working on the sources of the availability issues. If the problem is equipment breakdown, we may want to explore better preventative maintenance options or perhaps replace aging equipment. If the problem is absenteeism in the labor force, then this problem should be addressed. We may also want to address scheduling issues so that a resource is not starved for work during its net availability. We certainly want to insure that the bottleneck resource is never starved for work. This may involve placing a buffer before a critical activity performed by the bottleneck resource.

Increase the Number of Units of the Bottleneck Resource

Perhaps the most obvious way to increase the capacity of the bottleneck resource is to add more resource units. However, we need to be cognizant of the fact that in adding resources to the bottleneck, the problem may shift to another resource. In other words, the current bottleneck will no longer be a constraint on throughput, but another resource will be. This requires a careful consideration of costs and the likelihood of the bottleneck shifting.

The Analysis of Inventory

Inventory is the number of flow units in the process at a given time. The average inventory level (I) is the average number of flow units in the process. The nature of the inventory depends on the process and the flow units. Inventory in a manufacturing process or in a service context where the flow units are data or forms, is quite different from that in service environments (e.g., medical facilities) where the flow units are human beings. Obviously managing inventories in these two environments is quite different. However, many service industries have to manage physical inventories as well. It has been estimated that the typical hospital in the United States spends between 15% and 25% of its budget on medical, surgical, and pharmaceutical supplies, or between $113 billion and $188 billion annually across all hospitals (Anupindi et al., 2006). The management of physical inventories is an important, well-covered topic in the operations management literature. We will focus on inventory as process flow units here and discuss some of the significant levers for reducing it.

LEVERS FOR MANAGING INVENTORIES

Reduce Cycle Time and Throughput

Recall from Little's law in an earlier section of this chapter that inventory is a function of throughput and cycle time. This is important because inventory, in a process sense, is best managed by trying to reduce cycle time and speed the flow through the process. Therefore, some common ways of reducing inventories are the following:

- Reducing work content of critical activities
- Eliminating non-value adding components of the process
- Moving work from critical activities to noncritical activities
- Replacing sequential processing with parallel processing
- Reducing the throughput rate

The last option, reducing the throughput rate, although effective in reducing inventory, is often not an attractive option because it may well also reduce revenues. However, there is one sense in which this is a viable option. That is through scheduling arrivals. By scheduling and controlling the arrival rate to a process, you can smooth the flow of flow units through the process and greatly reduce inventories. There are two aspects of controlling arrivals to minimize inventories. The first is to reduce the throughput rate which, by Little's law, will obviously reduce inventories. The second aspect of controlling arrivals is in reducing variability. It is this second function of controlling arrivals that may be the most important lever of reducing inventories.

Reduce Variability

Perhaps the most important lever for reducing inventories in a process is to reduce process variability. There are two aspects of this variability. The first, variability in arrivals, leads to longer queues and therefore more inventory in the process. Simply reducing the variability of the arrivals through scheduling, if possible, can improve inventories without lowering throughput. The second aspect, variability of the activity times in the process, is perhaps even more controllable from a process point of view. The problem is compounded if there is variability in both arrival times and activity times. Moreover, the effects of variability are magnified as capacity utilization increases. These effects are explored in the next section.

The Effects of Variability and Utilization

It makes intuitive sense that capacity utilization would have an effect on process inventories and therefore on cycle times and throughput. The less slack capacity we have in the process to absorb fluctuations in demand for that capacity, the more congested the process will become. We also know, from our study of queues in Chapter 4, that increased variability in arrivals, service times, or both will also increase the inventories in the process. However, these two effects are not independent of one another, and in fact magnify each other. Hopp & Spearman (1996) have shown that the inventories in a process are **approximately** related to variability and capacity utilization, as shown in equation 9-15. This is what Anupindi et al. (2006) refer to as the queue-length formula.

$$I = \frac{\rho^{\sqrt{2(s+1)}}}{1-\rho} \times \frac{C_i^2 + C_p^2}{2} \qquad (9\text{-}15)$$

This relationship states that the average inventory is a function of two factors. The first might be called the capacity-utilization effect. Recall that ρ is the capacity utilization of the process. The value s in the equation refers the number of servers in a queuing context, or the number of identical resources in the process. Equation 9-15 clearly indicates that inventories will increase as capacity utilization increases. The other component captures the variability effect. The C_i and C_p terms are the coefficient of variation for the inflow times and process times, respectively. The coefficient of variation is simply the standard deviation divided by the average or mean.

Capacity-Utilization Effect $\quad \dfrac{\rho^{\sqrt{2(s+1)}}}{1-\rho}$

Variability Effect $\quad \dfrac{C_i^2 + C_p^2}{2}$

The variability effect term also clearly indicates that as the variability of inflows or process time increases, as measured by the standard deviations, inventories will also increase. Also note that the relationship in equation 9-15 is multiplicative. In other words, the effects of capacity utilization are magnified by increased variability and vice versa. This is shown graphically in Figure 9.5, which shows the flow times of a process as a function of capacity utilization. Figure 9.5 shows that as utilization get closer to 100% that the average flow time increases exponentially. Moreover, the larger the process variability, the sooner this happens. In other words, as process variability increases, the exponential increase comes at lower and lower levels of utilization. Of course, as flow or cycle times increase, so does inventory.

Figure 9.5 The Effects of Utilization and Variability on Flow Times

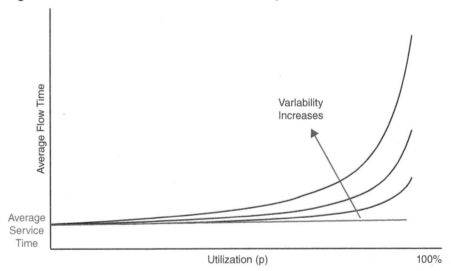

Source: Adapted from Anupindi et al. (2006), Figure 8.6, p. 216

Chapter Glossary

Blocking A resource is finished with a job but cannot send it on to the next stage and is prevented from working on another flow unit.

Bottleneck The slowest resource pool in the process, i.e., the resource with the largest unit load.

Capacity The maximum sustainable flow rate of a process.

Capacity utilization The ratio of throughput to theoretical capacity.
Critical activities Activities on the critical or longest path through the process.
Cycle time The average time it takes a flow unit to move through the entire process.
Cycle-time efficiency The ratio of the theoretical cycle time to the actual cycle time.
Effective capacity The maximum sustainable flow for a resource unit if it is fully utilized during its net availability.
Flow rate The number of flow units that flow through a point in the process per time period.
Flow time The time it takes a flow unit to move from one part of the process to another.
Inventory Flow units that have entered the process but not yet exited.
Inventory turns or **turnover ratio** The number of times inventory is turned into output per units of time.
Load batch The number of flow units that a resource can process at the same time.
Net availability The actual time that the resource is available to process flow units within its scheduled availability.
Post-processing Moving work to a point after the process ends.
Precedence requirements Requirements that dictate that one activity be completed before another can begin.
Pre-processing Moving work to a point before the process begins.
Process capacity The maximum sustainable flow for a resource unit, taking into account resource idleness during its net availability.
Product mix The percentages of different types of heterogeneous flow units that are output by the process.
Resource unit A resource, labor or equipment, necessary to perform an activity.
Resource pool A group of similar resources that are interchangeable with regard to performing activities.
Scheduled availability The amount of time for which a resource is scheduled to be available for work, taking into account breaks, maintenance, and other known factors.
Stable process A process in which the average inflow rate is equal to the average outflow rate.
Starvation A resource is ready and available to work but there are no flow units available.
Throughput The average number of flow units that complete a process during a specified period of time.
Unit load The total time it takes a resource unit to process one flow unit for all the activities performed by that resource.
Work-in-process inventory (WIP) Partially completed flow units in a manufacturing process.

Chapter Questions and Problems

1. You don't have to be a racing fan to marvel at the efficiency with which the pit crew changes flat tires and performs other tasks during a pit stop. Explain pre-processing and post-processing in this context.
2. The theoretical capacity of a process is the reciprocal of the theoretical flow time of the process. Do you agree? Explain.
3. The main office of Worldwide Credit Union processes 4,000 car loan applications per year. On average, loan applications are processed in 2 weeks. On average, how many car loan applications can be found in the various stages of processing at any given time?

4. Dick's Hamburgers processes on average 1,300 customers per day. At any given time, 60 customers are in the restaurant waiting to place an order, placing an order, waiting for the order to be ready, eating, and so on.
   a. What is the average time that a customer spends in the store?
   b. How often can the manager of Dick's expect the entire group of 60 customers to be replaced with new customers?

5. At the drive-thru window at Dick's Hamburgers, there is an average of 10 cars in line during the lunch hour. The manager is concerned about people seeing the long line of cars and refusing to enter the line. Over the course of several weeks she monitors the arrivals at the drive-thru and finds that a car arrives on average every 3 minutes, but that 20% of the cars are discouraged by the long line and leave immediately. Assuming a stable process, how long does a car spend in line on average?

6. At the emergency room of Providence General Hospital entering patients initially go through a registration process that takes 3 minutes on average. When his or her turn comes, the patient is seen by a doctor and is either given detailed instructions for further care of the injury or illness, written a prescription, or admitted to the hospital. Time with the doctor averages 8 minutes for those given a prescription, 12 minutes for those given detailed instructions, and 30 minutes for those admitted to the hospital. Historically about 10% of patients are admitted to the hospital, 20% are given detailed instructions, and the remainder receive prescriptions. On average about 70 patients per hour arrive at the emergency room. An average of 10 people are waiting to be registered at any time, and 40 are registered but waiting to see a doctor. Assuming that the average inflow rate is equal to the average outflow rate (the system is stable)
   a. On average, how long does a patient spend in the ER?
   b. On average, how many patients are being examined by doctors?
   c. On average, how many patients are there in the ER?

7. The Elbonian Hotel caters to business travelers and is very proud of its reputation for excellent service. As part of catering to busy traveling business executives, room service at the Elbonian is available 24 hours a day. When a guest calls room service, the room-service manager on duty takes the call and submits the food-ticket order to the kitchen for food and nonalcoholic drinks. Orders for wine and other alcoholic drinks are submitted to the bar, when it is open, or are prepared by the room-service manager when the bar is closed. The manager also assigns the order to one of 10 waiters. Taking and submitting the order to the kitchen and assigning the waiter takes about 5 minutes. If the bar is open, filling the drink order takes about 10 minutes, which may include some wait time. When the bar is closed, the manager takes about 4 minutes on average to fill the drink order. The time to prepare the food part of the order depends on how busy the kitchen is. During busy periods, there may be a wait before the order is prepared. After preparation begins, it takes an average of 20 minutes to prepare the food portion of the order. While the food and drinks are being prepared, the waiter assigned the order prepares a cart for delivery by covering the cart with a fresh tablecloth, gathering the silverware, and filling orders for nonalcoholic drinks such as coffee, tea, or soda. This takes about 10 minutes on average. When the food and drinks are finished and the waiter is available, the waiter delivers the order to the guest room. If the waiter is unavailable, the food waits in a warming area until the waiter is available. After the waiter returns from delivering the order, he or she enters the order into the

computer system, which charges the meal to the guest's account. On average it takes about 15 minutes for the waiter to deliver the order and about 2 minutes to enter the order into the computer.

   a. Draw a process map for the room-service process.
   b. What is the theoretical flow time of the process?
   c. The average flow time of the process was measured to be 60 minutes. What is the flow-time efficiency?

8. A consultant is studying the flow through traffic court in the local courthouse. She takes a random sample of 10 defendants during a Monday morning and records their arrival time, their departure time, the time actually spent talking to the judge, and the time spent paying their fine in minutes. The data is shown below.

Defendant	Arrival	Departure	Time with Judge (Min)	Time Paying Fine (Min)
1	8:45	9:30	3	5
2	8:45	9:45	2.5	2
3	8:45	12:05	4	3
4	8:50	12:55	1.5	5
5	8:50	10:35	2	2
6	8:55	9:20	1	0
7	8:55	11:35	2	2
8	9:00	10:45	3	0
9	9:00	12:55	2	4
10	9:00	9:20	1.5	3

   a. Estimate the average theoretical cycle time of the process.
   b. Estimate the average actual cycle time of the process.
   c. What is the flow time efficiency?

9. The U.S. Transportation Security Administration (TSA) is concerned about the airline passenger experience at their security sites. They decide to monitor the screening times at a small airport in the northwest. The security setup at this airport has a single screening station with a single waiting line, which has one X-ray scanner with an operator, a body scanning machine, and three screening officers. Arriving passengers form a line at the X-ray scanner and place their bags on the scanner belt when it is their turn. Each passenger can have from 0 to 3 bags including luggage, purses or carry-on bags, and possibly medical devices. The average number of bags per customer is 1.8. The X-ray scanner can handle 15 bags per minute. After their bags are scanned, 90% of passengers leave the security checkpoint, and 10% of customers selected at random are asked to undergo additional manual screening by one of three screening officers. A manual screening takes on average 2 minutes per passenger.

   a. What is theoretical flow time through the security check for an average passenger?
   b. A random sample of 25 passengers was timed at the securing check and an average flow time of 150 seconds was calculated. What is the flow-time efficiency of the system?

10. The following flow chart of a process shows the activity times, including wait times, in minutes.

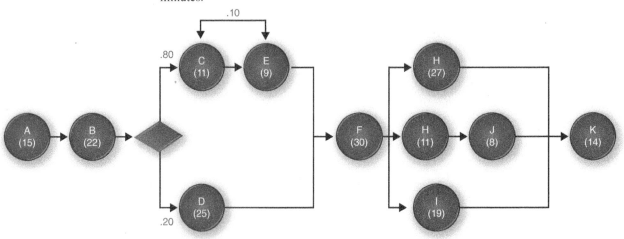

a. Calculate the average cycle time
b. Using the actual activity times (no waiting) shown in the following table, calculate the theoretical cycle time and the cycle time efficiency.

Activity	Processing Time	Activity	Processing Time
A	13	G	21
B	17	H	8
C	9	I	14
D	20	J	6
E	5	K	10
F	22		

c. Four resources are needed to perform the activities in the process as shown in the following table. If there are 2 units of resource 1, 2 units of resource 2, 3 units of resource 3 and 3 units of resource, 4 calculate the capacity of the process.

Resource	Activities
1	A, E, G
2	B, D, K
3	C, I
4	F, H, L

d. If the actual throughput for the process is 2.5 flow units per hour, what is the capacity utilization?

11. Three teams (T1, T2, and T3) work in the following process where the numbers in each activity indicate processing times in minutes. The activities that each team works on are given in the table following the diagram. Calculate the capacity utilization of the process assuming that the throughput is one job per hour.

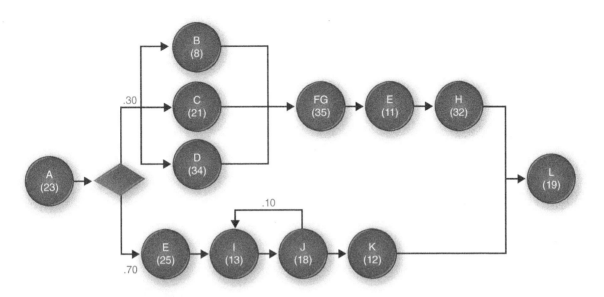

Team	Activities
T1	A,D,G,H
T2	B,F,I,L
T3	C,E,J,K

12. The activity times for the process in problem 11 have been broken down into activity and wait times in the following table. Use cycle-time efficiency to compare this process with a redesigned version where the rework between activities I and J has been eliminated and the activities G and H are now performed in parallel rather than sequentially.

Job	A	B	C	D	E	F	G	H	I	J	K	L
Total Time	23	8	21	34	25	35	11	32	13	18	12	19
Activity Time	18	4	13	22	17	26	7	24	9	13	5	14

References

Anupindi, R., Chopra, S., Deshmukh, S.D., Van Mieghem, J.A., & Semel, E. *Managing Business Process Flows*, 2nd Edition, 2006, Upper Saddle River NJ: Prentice-Hall.

Becker, J., Kugeler, M. & Rosemann, M. (Eds.), *Process Management*, 2003, Heidelberg: Springer-Verlag.

Gilbreth, F.B. & Gilbreth Carey, E.G. *Cheaper by the Dozen*, 1949, New York: T.Y Crowell.

Goldratt, E. & Cox, J. *The Goal: Excellence in Manufacturing*, 2nd Edition, 1992, Great Barrington, MA: North River Press.

Hopp, W.J. & Spearman, M.L. *Factory Physics: Foundations of Manufacturing Management*, 1996, Chicago: Irwin.

Umble, M. & Srikanth, L. *Synchronous Manufacturing: Principles for World Class Excellence*, 1990, Wallingford, CT: Spectrum Publishing.

Chapter 10

Implementing, Executing, and Monitoring the Process

"However beautiful the strategy, you should occasionally look at the results."

—Sir Winston Churchill

"Vision without execution is just hallucination."

—Henry Ford

"Nothing exceptional was ever accomplished without positive mental attitude, enthusiasm, hard work, perseverance, and monitoring."

—David Gyimah Boadi

Once a process has been designed to achieve an organization's objectives, it then must be implemented, executed, and monitored to make sure that it is operating properly. In this chapter, we will discuss the steps necessary to actually use the process once it has been designed, with special emphasis on process monitoring.

Implementation

The literature on BPM has much to say about process design and improvement but is notably silent on the issue of how to implement a new process or an improved design of an existing process. Implementation is by no means a simple matter. The complexity and difficulty of implementing a process will depend on a number of factors, among them

- the number of steps in the process,
- the number of different organizational units involved in the process,

- whether or not elements outside the organization are involved in the process,
- whether it is a new process or the redesign of an existing process, and
- the mix of human and technological elements involved in the process.

The number of steps in the process and the number of different organizational units involved are rather obvious factors that increase the difficulty of implementation. For more complex processes, the tools and skills for managing projects become more critical. The literature on project management is voluminous and beyond the scope of this text. Suffice it to say that if the organization is facing a complex implementation situation and it does not have the internal expertise to manage such projects, it should seek outside help for the implementation.

The implementation effort, and the need for project management skills, becomes even more important if the process involves elements external to the organization, either suppliers to the firm or customers of the organization's products or services. Involving external elements in implementation efforts will be especially difficult and will likely fail unless they are involved in the process design from the beginning.

Process redesigns are typically more difficult to implement than clean new processes and are an even more delicate matter if they involve employees already using an existing process. In this situation implementing a new process design involves changing the way that employees perform their job. As is the case with external elements, the implementation will be much easier if the employees are also fully involved in the redesign of the process.

The final factor of the mix of human and technological elements requires a little more discussion. Following Chang (2006), we can categorize processes, and subparts of a process, into three types:

- Person to person
- Person to system
- System to system

The implementation issues involved are quite different, depending on which type of situation we are dealing with.

PERSON TO PERSON

These are usually the most complex processes and the ones that most closely resemble the traditional definition of a business process. These types of processes are the most sensitive during process redesign efforts because they involve changing the way in which employees do their jobs. Implementation efforts generally proceed more smoothly if the employees involved with the process were also involved in the design of the process. Implementation efforts generally involve training and a lot of educational efforts through dissemination of documents related to the new process design. Implementation is often gradual with employees requiring time to get used to the new way of doing things. Process performance often declines at first as employees struggle with the new procedures, but should rebound over time and eventually improve if the new process design is more efficient than the old way of doing things.

PERSON TO SYSTEM

Person to system processes involve human participants interacting with technological components that are part of the process. It is difficult to envision organizational processes anymore that do not involve at least some person-to-system components. Implementation issues tend to revolve around designing effective human/computer interfaces and training employees in the use of new technology. In most cases, the old process will continue as training in the new system takes place and at a specific point in time the switchover to the new process occurs. From an IT perspective, implementing a new person-to-system process often involves designing new applications and, in some cases, implementing new computer systems.

SYSTEM TO SYSTEM

From a business perspective implementing this type of process is relatively straightforward. However, from an IT perspective, implementing a new system-to-system process can be a very complex undertaking, almost always involving a good deal of application and system development activity. As with many software projects, the new and old systems are often run in parallel until management is sure that the new system is working properly.

The implementation process can become particularly difficult when the process involves systems external to the organization. Recent widespread adoption of Web-based standards such as HTTP and XML and technological advances such as service-oriented architecture (SOA) have made this kind of implementation less difficult than it was in the past. As discussed in Chapter 7, SOA has become so important on the IT side of BPM that for many in the technology sector SOA is nearly synonymous with BPM. However, these are distinctly different concepts: BPM is a business management philosophy and approach to increase organizational effectiveness and flexibility; SOA is a software-development principle that leads to software systems composed of well-defined and reusable components. However, these two concepts get their real value when used together (Frantz & Kirchmer, 2012 and Smith & Fingar, 2003).

Execution

From a BPM perspective, process execution was discussed extensively in Chapter 9. There we discussed the key performance measures of process execution and how they are related to one another and are impacted by different design factors. From an IT perspective, many of the modern BPMS are an outgrowth of the earlier work flow systems of the 1990s, which were designed primarily to control the execution of processes in terms of managing documents. These aspects of BPMS are discussed later in this chapter.

Monitoring

The normal day-to-day monitoring of a process is important to maintain efficient functioning of all processes. However, there are times when this monitoring is especially important. One of those is after a process has been changed to improve its performance, which has lasting effects only if we monitor the performance after the changes to insure that the performance improvements are maintained. As has been noted (Hall, 2008), maintaining process improvements has been much more difficult than was originally thought. One reason for this is because of inadequate monitoring to insure that improvements are maintained.

Monitoring is also important in knowing when the process has stabilized so that performance measures are meaningful. This cycle of process improvement, then stabilization, and finally recalibration of the process measures, is an important topic in the last section of the text on process improvement.

THE PURPOSE OF PROCESS MONITORING

A hallmark of statistical process thinking is that all processes exhibit variability and that a key managerial task is to monitor and control that variability (Hoerl & Snee, 2002). By variability, we mean simply deviations of performance from the expected or average performance. As we discussed in Chapter 4, variability has a negative impact on wait times in queuing situations and generally has a negative impact on process performance overall (see Chapter 9). However, for monitoring purposes, it is important to distinguish between different types of variability. *Common cause variability* is the inherent random variability in a process that results from many small, unknown sources. *Special cause variability*, on the other hand, comes from sources outside the process itself or is an indication that something in the process has changed (Deming, 1986).[1] A process is said to be in control, or stable, if there are no special causes of variability present, i.e., the only source of variability is common cause variability. The distinction between common and special cause variability is critical to understanding process monitoring and is at the heart of statistical process control (SPC). There are some subtle, but important, implications of this distinction:

- Common cause variability appears to be random because we do not know the causes of this variability.
- To reduce common cause variability, we must change the process itself and to do this we must understand the process in much more detail and must learn at least some of the causes of this source of variability.
- Workers can do nothing to eliminate common cause variability
- Special cause, or as Shewart called it, assignable cause, variability comes from specific identifiable sources that can and should be identified and removed.
- Common cause variability arises from many small sources of variability, while special cause comes from a single, or very few, major sources of variability.
- The primary purpose of process monitoring is to discover special causes of variability when they occur.

The tools for monitoring processes are primarily designed to distinguish between these two sources of variability. In particular, they are designed to detect special cause variability when it occurs.

There is a third type of variability that is identified in the forecasting literature, which Anupindi et al. (2006) call structural variability. *Structural variability* is the systematic change in a process measure over time. Examples of structural variability are trend and seasonal effects. Structural variability cannot be eliminated in most cases, but should be isolated from other sources of variability for process monitoring and decision making.

PROCESS-MONITORING TOOLS

The tools useful in process monitoring have a long history in the quality management literature and in practice. Most of the tools discussed in this chapter fall under the rubric of statistical process control (SPC) and have played a large part in the quality management movement of the 1980s and beyond, especially in the work of W. Edwards Deming (1986, 1993). Although the tools originated in the field of quality control, there is nothing that restricts their use to the quality area, and they can be used with any process metric that has been discussed in Chapter 2 and throughout the text.

FEEDBACK CONTROL PRINCIPLE

The use of feedback to control a process has a long history in engineering and manufacturing, as well as biology, in the study of dynamic systems. The basic idea is to collect performance measures over time and take corrective actions if necessary, based on that feedback, in order to guide the process to achieve the goals established for it. The basic principle is shown in Figure

---

1. Deming (1993) credits Walter Shewart with the original conceptualization of common and special cause variation although Shewart used the terms "chance" and "assignable" causes which Deming later changed to common cause and special cause.

10.1. A good example of this type of system is the cruise-control system on a modern vehicle. In the case of the cruise control, periodic readings on the speed of the vehicle are compared with the designated speed set for the cruise control, and if there is a significant discrepancy, corrective action is taken.

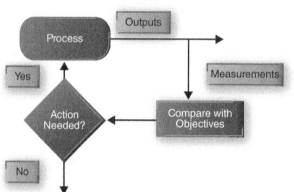

Figure 10.1 The Feedback-Control Principle

The control of a business process is similar except for the additional complexity of the process. In the cruise-control example, the cause of the discrepancy, and therefore the action that needs to be taken, are obvious from the nature of the deviation. If the speed is too fast, let up on the gas; if it is too slow, increase acceleration.

In business processes, however, often the cause of the discrepancy is not immediately obvious because there may be multiple causes for performance deviations. Thus a major issue in business processes is discovering the source of the problem. However, the basic concept still applies. Conceptually, the feedback control principle is very similar to Deming's plan-do-check-act cycle (PDCA) that we explore in the next section of the text.

TYPES OF DATA

The type of monitoring tool used depends somewhat on the type of data that we have. We can classify metrics as either qualitative or quantitative.[2] A *qualitative* metric is one that is inherently nonnumeric such male/female, defective/nondefective, or major surgery/minor surgery. With qualitative data all we can do is count occurrences and calculate proportions or percentages. *Quantitative* metrics are inherently numerical in value. Most of the metrics that we have discussed previously are of this type. For example, cycle time, inventory, and throughput rates are numerical quantities. In a business context, anything measured as height, weight, distance, speed, or dollars are quantitative metrics.

TOOLS FOR QUALITATIVE DATA

We will first look at tools for qualitative data, and then at similar tools for quantitative data. Recall that qualitative data are inherently nonnumeric so that all we can do with such data is count occurrences and calculate proportions for different categories. Therefore, the tools in this section deal with counts or proportions.

---

2. In the quality control literature these are called attribute data and variables data.

Check Sheets

Check sheets are commonly used in the quality control area to record the types of defects that occur. They can also be used in process control to tally such metrics as the type of customer complaints or causes of long wait times. Check sheets are simply tally sheets for recording the occurrences of a particular qualitative value. An example for customer complaints at an airline is shown in Figure 10.2.

Figure 10.2 A Check Sheet of Airline Complaint Data

Type of Complaint	Number of Occurences
Flight Delay	|||| |||
Lost Luggage	|||| |||| ||||
Seating Arrangements	||||
Discourteous Staff	||
Cleanliness of Plane	||||	

Pareto Charts

Pareto charts show the same information as check sheets except in graphical form. Pareto charts are named after the Italian economist Vilfredo Pareto who studied the distribution of wealth in Italian society in the later part of the seventeenth century. Pareto's law, also called the 80/20 rule, states that 80% of the wealth is concentrated in the hands of 20% of the people. Adapted to process terms, Pareto's law roughly means that most of the problems with a process are due to a few causes. The Pareto chart is simply a bar chart of the frequency counts in order of frequency from highest to lowest. Sometimes a line graph of the cumulative frequency is also superimposed on the graph. An example using the airline complaint data is shown in Figure 10.3.

Process Control Charts

Process control charts are an important tool in implementing the feedback control principle that we discussed earlier in this chapter. Control charts are used to see whether or not a process is stable, or in control. Recall that a process is in control when the only source of variability is random, common cause variability. Process control charts are a plot of the feedback data over time, along with control limits that determine when action should be taken. The control limits are established based on what is expected in terms of common cause variability which is measured by the standard deviation of the metric when the process is known to be stable. Thus, the basic control chart simply consists of the lower and upper control limits with room to plot the observed metric calculated from the sample data. The different control charts differ primarily in the types of data that are plotted rather than in the basic concept involved. The basic concept of control limits is

$$\text{Control Limits} \quad \text{Normal Metric Value} \pm Z \times \text{Standard Deviation} \quad (10\text{-}1)$$

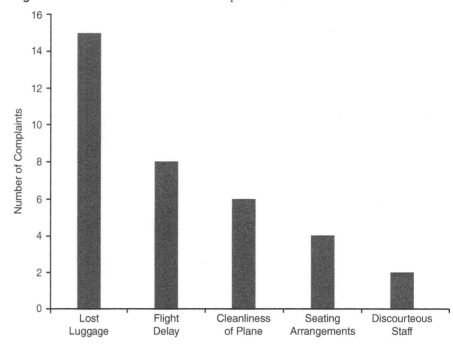

Figure 10.3 Pareto Chart of Airline Complaint Data.

The upper control limit is the normal value of the metric plus a Z value times the standard deviation, and the lower control limit is the normal value minus a Z value times the standard deviation. But how do we get these values?

The commonly used value for Z is 3, although 2 is sometimes used. The value of 3 is usually selected because in the standard normal distribution, almost all of the distribution (actually 99.7%) is within 3 standard deviation units of the average value. Almost 95% is within 2 standard deviation units.

The normal value for the metric may be obtained from process design specifications or estimated from sample data. In actual practice, the normal value is usually estimated from sample data when the process is known to be stable.

The standard deviation is usually dictated by the type of variable for which we are establishing limits. For quantitative variables, it is usually established like the normal value, from the process design specifications or estimated from a sample. For count and proportion data, the standard deviation is calculated from the count or proportion itself.

Process charts for qualitative variables are of two types: p-charts and c-charts. Both types of charts deal with count values for a qualitative variable that can take on only one of two possible values. The p-chart is used for binomial situations to plot the proportion (or number in an np-chart) of "successes" in a sample. The c-chart is used for Poisson-type variables where the interest is in the number of occurrences per opportunity. For example, the number of calls to a call center per day.

P-charts

Let π represent the proportion of successes under normal conditions and n be the size of the samples that are to be taken from the process. From statistical theory, it is known that the standard deviation of the sample proportion is given by

$$\sigma_p = \sqrt{\frac{\pi(1-\pi)}{n}}$$

If there is a target value (π) for the proportion, the p-chart control limits are calculated as

$$\pi \pm Z\sqrt{\frac{\pi(1-\pi)}{n}} \qquad (10\text{-}2)$$

You can see that equation 10-2 follows the basic format outlined in equation 10-1. Unless the proportion comes from the design specification, however, we will not normally know the value of π and must estimate it from a sample. Therefore, in practice, the control limits of the p-chart are usually given by

$$\bar{p} \pm Z\sqrt{\frac{\bar{p}(1-\bar{p})}{n}} \qquad (10\text{-}3)$$

An example may help illustrate the process.

Example 10.1

Humanix Hospital monitors the utilization of some of its most expensive and technologically advanced equipment to make sure that it is being used as much as prudently possible. Humanix management knows that they cannot operate the equipment 100% of the time because of maintenance requirements and patient cancellations. They also need to allow slack times for emergency use of the equipment. Their goal is to achieve 70% usage of the equipment under normal circumstances. They propose to visually determine at random intervals 50 times a week whether the equipment is being used or not. The proportion of times during the week that the equipment is busy will be plotted on the control chart. Establish control limits for the process control chart.

Solution

Since 70% is the goal for the population proportion, we can use this as the population value. The control limits then become

$$.7 \pm 3\sqrt{\frac{(.7)(.3)}{20}} = .7 \pm .19$$

or Lower Control Limit (LCL) = .51

Upper Control Limit (UCL) = .89

The graph of the control chart is shown in Figure 10.4. The proportion of times that the equipment was busy in the 50 weekly samples would be plotted as points in the chart each week. If a point falls between the control limits, we would infer that the process is stable, or in control. If a point falls outside the control limits, that would be evidence of special cause variability or an out-of-control, or unstable, process. In this case we would investigate to identify the source of the problem.

C-charts

The process of establishing c-charts follows closely that for p-charts except that with Poisson variables, and therefore with the c-chart, the standard deviation is equal to the square root of the average. Let λ be the population number of occurrences per opportunity, i.e. the occurrence rate. Then the control limits for the c-chart are

$$\lambda \pm Z\sqrt{\lambda} \qquad (10\text{-}4)$$

Figure 10.4 Control Chart for Example 10.1

As with p-charts, the parameter for the average λ may come from a goal or objective for the process, or it can come from a sample of observations.

Example 10.2

Humanix Hospital is concerned with long wait times in the emergency room (ER) at the hospital. Their ultimate goal is to have no patients wait more than 15 minutes before being seen by a nurse or physician's assistant (PA). Humanix hired a group of students from the local university to periodically monitor the wait times of patients in the ER for 2-hour periods. The average number of patients who had to wait for more than 15 minutes in the periods observed was 4.3. Assuming that this value is the average of the current system, what are the control limits for the number of patients who have to wait more than 15 minutes during a 2-hour time period using a Z value of 2?

Solution
Using the 4.3 as the value of λ the control limits are

$$4.3 \pm 2\sqrt{4.3} = 4.3 \pm 4.1$$

or

$$\text{LCL} = 0.20 \qquad \text{UCL} = 8.4$$

TOOLS FOR QUANTITATIVE DATA

Quantitative variables are numeric in nature and represent most of the metrics that we have discussed in this text. Quantitative data contain much more information than qualitative data, which means that much more can be done with this data in terms of analysis.

Histograms

Histograms are used to graphically display the general distribution of values for a quantitative variable. With histograms you can observe where the middle value lies and discern the general shape of the distribution of values. For example, are the values symmetrically distributed around a central value or are they skewed in one direction or another?

Bob's Hamburgers has hired a student intern to record the cycle time in minutes of randomly selected customers during the specific times of the day. The averages of these cycle times over 20 days are shown in Table 10.1 below. The time measures are in minutes. Develop a histogram of the data.

Example 10.3

Table 10.1 Cycle Time Averages for Example 10.3

Day Time	1	2	3	4	5	6	7	8	9	10
8:00 AM	7	6	4	7	6	11	3	6	7	8
10:00 AM	3	4	3	4	4	3	4	5	3	3
12:00 PM	7	8	11	12	4	6	8	13	8	12
2:00 PM	3	3	3	4	4	5	3	3	4	4
4:00 PM	4	6	3	4	4	3	4	3	6	8
6:00 PM	8	10	8	10	11	5	10	11	5	13

Day Time	11	12	13	14	15	16	17	18	19	20
8:00 AM	3	6	9	6	3	6	11	3	7	7
10:00 AM	5	5	4	3	5	3	6	7	4	6
12:00 PM	14	12	9	12	9	9	10	5	10	12
2:00 PM	3	3	4	3	3	3	4	3	4	3
4:00 PM	6	4	3	7	7	3	5	5	6	5
6:00 PM	11	15	9	9	8	8	10	14	5	14

Solution

The solution is shown in Figure 10.5. From this graph we can see that the distribution of cycle times is positively skewed with most of the times being four minutes or less but some of the times being as long as 15 minutes.

Figure 10.5 Histogram of Cycle Times for Example 10.3

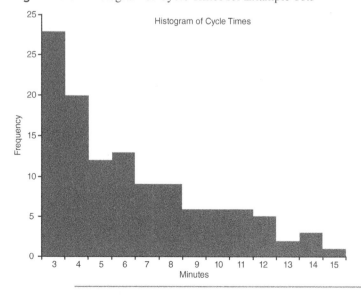

Run Charts

Run charts plot data as a function of time. They are primarily useful for identifying structural sources of variation such as trends or seasonal effects. A run chart of the data from Example 10.3 sorted by time of day is shown in Figure 10.6.

In Figure 10.6, you can see that there seem to be periods where the cycle times are quite long, and alternate periods where cycle times are much shorter, i.e., there appear to be seasonal effects. To see seasonal fluctuations more clearly, it is sometimes useful to highlight the different time periods in the seasonal cycle. This is done in Figure 10.7.

You can see from the pattern of data in Figure 10.7 that the cycle times vary by time of day. For example, the first 20 observations were made at 8:00 and the second 20 at 10:00. Clearly, the average cycle time is higher at 8:00 than at 10:00 because of increased traffic during the breakfast hour. A similar pattern can be seen at 12:00 and 6:00, where the cycle times increase because of the increased traffic. There even seems to be evidence for slightly higher cycle times at 4:00, possibly from those leaving work earlier.

Figure 10.6 Run Chart for the Example 10.3 Data

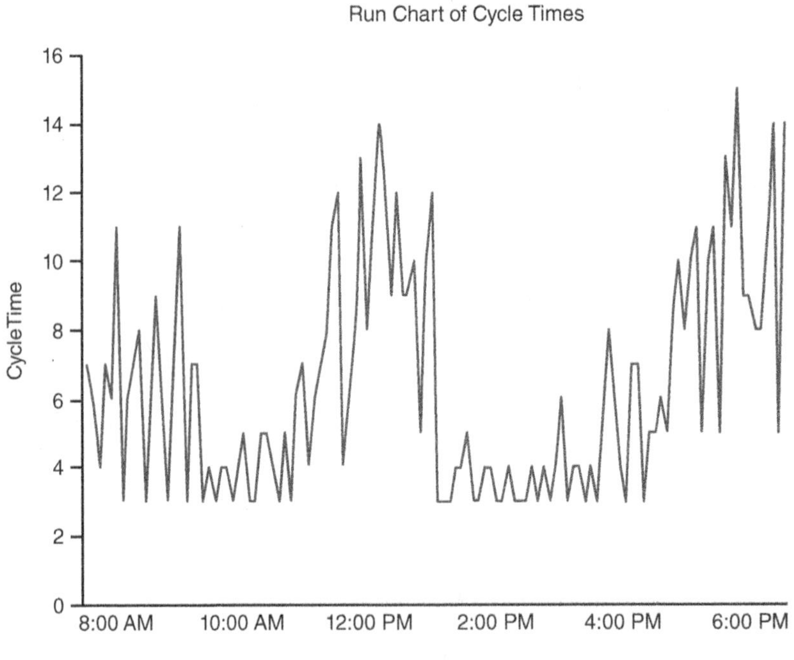

Multi-Vari Charts

A multi-vari chart is a tool that graphically displays patterns of variation. It is used to identify possible factors that impact variability such as structural effects or other outside factors that cause differences in variability. A multi-vari chart typically plots high, low, and average values for a variable as a function of time or some other factor. Figure 10.8 shows a multi-vari chart of the times from Example 10.3 where the data are grouped by time of day. This figure clearly shows that the average cycle time varies by time of day and also that the variability increases during the peak periods as well.

Process Control Charts

Process control charts for quantitative data follow the same logic as those for qualitative data. However, for quantitative data, the standard deviation must be calculated separately since it is not a function of the normal value. There are two types of process charts for quantitative variables:

- averages or means charts, and
- charts of variability, typically a range or standard deviation chart.

Figure 10.7 Run Chart for the Example 10.3 Data with Time Periods Highlighted

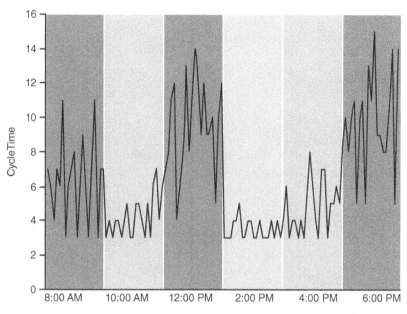

Figure 10.8 Multi-Vari Chart of Example 10.3 Data

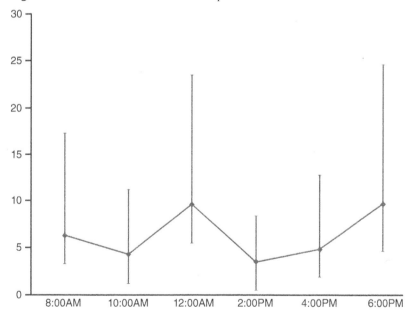

X-bar charts

The x-bar ($\overline{X}$) chart plots the average of a quantitative variable. The general form of the control limits follows that outlined in equation 10-1.

$$\mu \pm Z\frac{\sigma}{\sqrt{n}} \qquad (10\text{-}5)$$

Again, the Z value is usually 3, and if the population or normal standard deviation (σ) is not known, the sample standard deviation (s) can be used instead. The nominal value (population mean μ) may be given by the design of the process or, more likely, estimated by the average from a sample of observations from the process. When sample values are used to estimate the mean and the standard deviation, the control limits become

$$\bar{X} \pm Z \frac{s}{\sqrt{n}} \qquad (10\text{-}6)$$

R charts and s Charts

The R in R charts stands for the range, which is defined as the maximum value minus the minimum value. The range is a very simple measure of variability and has been widely used in SPC charts. The s in s charts stands for standard deviation. Conceptually, R and s charts are constructed in the same fashion as the other control charts. The major difficulty with R and s charts is finding the standard deviations of R or s that are more complicated than for p, c or x-bar charts. Special tables or software can be used to calculate these values. We can also estimate the values from sample data. We will illustrate these calculations within the context of an example.

Example 10.4

Humanix Hospital is concerned about waiting times in the emergency rooms of the 10 hospitals in the chain. They decide to monitor the wait times of 8 randomly selected patients on 20 different occasions over a 10-day period. As a result, they will have 20 different samples with 8 people in each sample. The results are shown in Table 10.2.

Table 10.2 Wait Times for Example 10.4

Samples	Patient 1	2	3	4	5	6	7	8	R	s	$\bar{X}$
1	39	52	23	41	30	32	17	24	35	11.36	32.25
2	39	15	24	33	26	41	18	17	26	10.07	26.63
3	43	20	38	33	10	31	39	27	33	10.91	30.13
4	30	20	16	43	33	37	37	27	27	9.10	30.38
5	24	35	27	29	8	35	34	27	27	8.86	27.38
6	55	32	28	30	36	29	27	40	28	9.32	34.63
7	16	30	32	35	12	25	33	33	23	8.62	27.00
8	34	33	41	30	6	59	38	31	53	14.64	34.00
9	24	27	29	33	47	46	21	40	26	9.93	33.38
10	24	33	36	36	33	48	21	45	27	9.21	34.50
11	34	29	15	12	9	39	29	16	30	11.21	22.88
12	44	34	22	26	36	58	32	29	36	11.38	35.13
13	10	41	26	43	3	33	24	19	40	14.10	24.88
14	27	19	31	31	29	30	33	23	14	4.70	27.88
15	24	28	24	46	26	19	25	24	27	8.09	27.00
16	53	27	12	10	26	21	12	31	43	14.12	24.00
17	31	21	15	26	23	36	22	38	23	7.91	26.50
18	51	27	25	37	14	39	29	34	37	10.99	32.00

Samples	Patient 1	2	3	4	5	6	7	8	R	s	$\overline{X}$
19	27	19	24	23	38	20	36	35	19	7.55	27.75
20	29	23	27	32	41	37	39	22	19	7.23	31.25
Average									29.65	9.97	29.48
Standard Deviation									9.13	2.48	3.78

Note that the averages of the three statistics (R, s, and $\overline{X}$) are estimates of the population value and the standard deviation of these values is an estimate of the standard deviation of those statistics in the population. Given a Z value, we can then estimate the control limits for the three charts.

R chart

$$LCL = 29.65 - 3(9.13) = 2.27$$
$$UCL = 29.65 + 3(9.13) = 57.03$$

s chart

$$LCL = 9.97 - 3(2.48) = 2.51$$
$$UCL = 9.97 + 3(2.48) = 17.42$$

X-bar chart

$$LCL = 29.48 - 3(3.78) = 18.13$$
$$UCL = 29.48 + 3(3.78) = 40.82$$

The problem with this example is the small sample sizes used to estimate the variability of the standard deviation (s) and the range (R). The mean of the process can be estimated fairly well from smaller samples, especially if we have multiple samples as in this example. However, estimating variability requires larger samples. For this reason, traditionally only R charts are produced from smaller samples and both the X-bar and R charts typically use special tables to calculate the control limits. These charts are illustrated in a later section of this chapter when we discuss the use of the SPC Templates. Charts for the standard deviation have been rarely used in practice primarily because they require large sample sizes.

Using Process Control Charts

As we stated earlier, process control charts are used to determine whether a process is in control, or stable. But how do we know if a process is out of control, or unstable? Certainly one way is if a point on the control chart is above the upper limit or below the lower limit. This would be an indication that the process is unstable or out of control since this is highly unlikely to happen if there is only common cause variability present. However, there are other patterns that can also indicate that a process is unstable. Most of these patterns use three different zones in the control chart where the zones are determined by the standard deviation. Zone C is plus or minus 1 standard deviation from the normal values, Zone B is plus or minus 2 standard deviations, and Zone A is plus or minus 3 standard deviations. This division of the control limits is shown in

Figure 10.9. There are seven patterns that can be identified which indicate that the process is unstable or not in control. These seven patterns are:

- Any point falls outside the control limits
- Any 2 out of 3 consecutive points fall in one of the A zones on the same side of the centerline
- 4 out of 5 consecutive points fall in one of the B zones or beyond on the same side of the centerline
- 8 or more consecutive points line on one side of the centerline
- 8 or more consecutive points move upward in value or move downward in value
- An unusually small number of runs above and below the centerline are present (saw-tooth pattern)
- 13 consecutive points fall within zone C on either side of the centerline

Figure 10.9 Control Chart with Zones

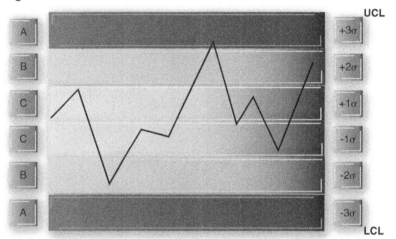

If a process is found to be out of control, then we need to search for the sources of the special cause variation. Once the problem is found and corrected, then the process should again be stable. However, as we will explore in the last section of the text, when we make process improvements, our control limits will no longer be appropriate for the new process, and we will need to recalibrate the control limits and monitor the process until it stabilizes again.

Process Capability

Sometimes there are specified limits within which a process metric should fall. In the quality area, these are called design specifications and are part of the design of a product or service. However, even with non-quality related metrics, management may specify that a metric should fall within a certain range. For example, management may specify that the cycle time for a process should be between 4 and 6 hours. We will call these *specification limits* and designate them as LSL and USL for lower specification limit and upper specification limit, respectively. If we assume that the metrics follow a normal distribution and that the process is stable, then we can define common cause variation as the standard deviation of the metric designated as σ. We can then define the *process capability index* which is a measure of how well the process can maintain the chosen metric within the specification limits. Recall that in a normal distribution, virtually all values fall within plus or minus 3 standard deviations. This means that the total range of the likely values of the process metric is 6σ. The process capability index is then defined as the ratio of the difference between the specification limits to the width of the normal process variability.

$$\text{Process Capability Index} \qquad C_p = \frac{USL - LSL}{6\sigma} \qquad (10\text{-}7)$$

The higher the value of the capability index, the more capable the process is of staying within the specification limits. However, this index assumes that the process is centered at the average of the upper and lower specification limits. If this is not the case, then we have to compute a slightly different index. Assume that μ is the point at which the process is centered. In other words, μ is the average value of the metric. Then we need to compute an upper and lower value and the process capability index (now called C_{pk}) is the minimum of these two values.

$$C_{PU} = \frac{USL - \mu}{3\sigma}$$

$$C_{PL} = \frac{\mu - LSL}{3\sigma}$$

$$\text{Process Capability Index} \qquad C_{pk} = \min(C_{PL}, C_{PU})$$

In the next section of the text we will discuss the Six Sigma movement that was popularized by Motorola. This movement gets its name from the process capability index and it basically means a process capability of 2. This means that the specification limits are twice as wide as the normal variability of the process or that there is virtually no way that the process would go outside the specification limits. In fact, in a centered process, it should happen only about 2 times in a billion.

Example 10.5

Xandu operates a large call center in eastern Colorado. Xandu has just signed a large contract with an important client that will add over 100 jobs. As part of this agreement, they have agreed that all incoming calls, even if put on hold, will be answered by a customer-service representative within 10 minutes. Based on Xandu's previous experience, the average time to answer a call is 6 minutes with a standard deviation of 2.5 minutes. Based on the agreement, the VP of Operations at Xandu estimates that design specifications for the call answering process for the new client should have an average time of 5 minutes with a design tolerance of ±5 minutes. This means that the lower specification limit is 0 and the upper specification limit is 10. What is the process capability index of the current process with the new design specifications?

Since the current process is not centered on the design specification, we have to compute both an upper and lower index.

$$C_{PL} = \frac{\mu - LSL}{3\sigma} = \frac{6 - 0}{3(2.5)} = 0.80 \qquad C_{PU} = \frac{USL - \mu}{3\sigma} = \frac{10 - 6}{3(2.5)} = 0.533$$

Then $C_{pk} = \min(0.80, .533) = .533$.

Using the SPC Templates

You can use the SPC Charts.xlsx workbook that accompanies the text to produce SPC charts and calculate process capability. The workbook will produce any of the charts discussed in this chapter. We will illustrate a few of them here to give you an idea how they work. All of the charts are easy to use and simply require that you input the data and key items of information.

Example 10.6

Like all hospitals, Humanix Hospital is concerned about errors in administering drugs to patients. Errors can include administering an incorrect drug or an incorrect dosage of the correct drug. To monitor these types of errors, Humanix takes daily random samples of 100 instances in which drugs are checked out and administered to patients. The following data show 30 such daily samples. Plot a p-chart showing the control limits and indicate any instances where the process may be out of control.

Sample	1	2	3	4	5	6	7	8	9	10	11	12	13	14	15
Defects	3	4	4	6	3	5	7	4	6	4	6	15	3	7	6
Sample	16	17	18	19	20	21	22	23	24	25	26	27	28	29	30
Defects	1	1	9	7	6	7	7	5	4	0	4	3	6	8	5

The worksheet for p-charts is shown in Figure 10.10 with the data for the example already entered and the chart produced. All of the worksheets follow a similar pattern. Cells in which data can be entered are outlined in red. All other cells are locked and will not allow data entry.[3] For the p-chart, the data on defects must be entered (If you paste data into the worksheet use the paste values option so that the red outline of the cells is preserved). You also need to enter a value for Z, which helps determine the width of the control limits, and the size of the samples (n), in this case 100. The graph automatically adjusts as you change any of these factors or enter new data. In Figure 10.10 you can see the tabs for the various types of charts on the bottom of the screen. There is a tab for each type of chart discussed in this chapter.

Figure 10.10 Input data and P-Chart for Example 10.6

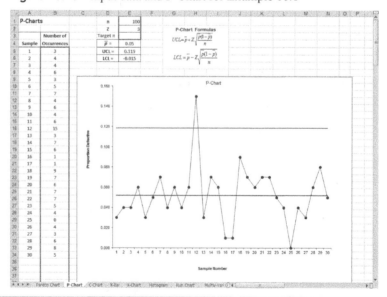

---

3. The worksheets in this file have been protected to protect the formulas of the worksheet. There is no password for any of the worksheets so you can unprotect the sheets if you want. Instances where you might want to do this are to make the chart larger or to change colors of other aspects of the chart. Just be careful not to overwrite any formulas in the worksheet and protect the sheet again when finished.

From Figure 10.10 we can see that the average is 5 errors out of 100 administrations. The control limits are from 0 (-.015) to .119. There is one period where the process may have been out of control. In Period 12 there were 15 errors, which should be investigated to determine what circumstances led to such a high error rate. One other period is also unusual. Although the calculated lower bound is -0.015, the effective lower bound is 0.0 since there cannot be a negative number of errors. There were zero errors in period 25, which would lie on this practical lower bound. Although having zero errors does not seem to be a problem, it is an indication that something different is going on in the process and should be investigated. Perhaps something happened during this period that should be incorporated into the process to improve performance and lower the error rate.

In example 10.4, we mentioned that X-bar and R charts are normally designed using table values rather than the standard deviations of the two statistics. The SPC templates incorporate these table values as we will illustrate here. Figure 10.11 shows the SPC template with the data and results from Example 10.3.

Figure 10.11 Data and Results for Example 10.4 with the X-bar Template

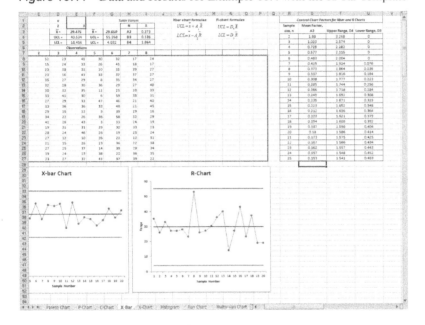

The data for this template is entered into columns B through P in rows 8 through 27. This allows for 20 samples of up to 15 observations in each sample. There are two other cells in which values can be entered. Cell E1 allows for the entry of a value for the standard deviation of the process. If a value is entered here, that value is used to produce the control limits in the X-bar chart. If this cell is blank, then the table values shown on the right of the screen are used to produce the X-bar chart. The table values are always used to produce the R-chart. If the standard deviation is to be used, a Z value can be entered into cell E2. If no value is given here, then a value of 3 is assumed.

Both the X-bar and R charts in Figure 10.3 seem to indicate that the process is under control both for the average value and for variability.

Our last example of using the SPC templates utilizes the process capability tab of the templates. In Example 10.4, we calculated a process capability index of .533 for the Xandu call center. The top officials at Xandu agree that this capability index is much too low and have decided that they want a process capability of at least 1 and want the process average to be 5 minutes, not 6. Figure 10.12 shows the process capability template with the current situation, which has the same value as we calculated earlier. The figure also shows that slightly more than 5% of the calls will exceed the upper specification limit. In other words, slightly more than 5% of the calls will take over 10 minutes before they are answered.

Figure 10.12 The Original Process Capability

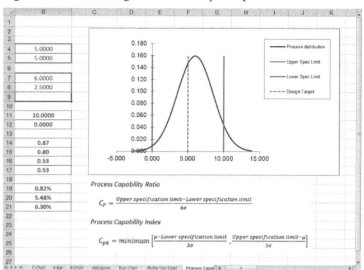

The supervisors of the call center are confident that the average time can be reduced to 5 minutes by adding a single employee on each shift. This increases the process capability to .67, still well short of the target. Recognizing that they are going to have to use additional resources and possibly better technology to reduce the standard deviation of the process times, the question becomes what standard deviation would be necessary to produce a process capability index of 1. Changing the standard deviation to 2.0 raises the capability index to .83, and reducing it to 1.75 raises the index to .95, which is very close. Further reducing the standard deviation to 1.5 produces a capability index of 1.1, as shown in Figure 10.13. Figure 10.13 also shows that now less than one half of one percent of the calls (.04%) will exceed the upper limit.

Figure 10.13 A Capability Index Above 1.0

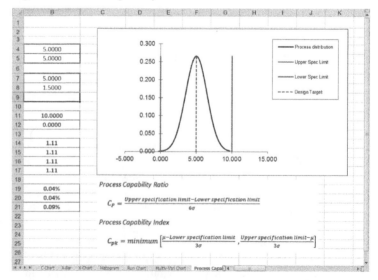

Implementation, Execution, and Monitoring with BPMS

Given the origins of many business process management suites in work flow systems, it is not surprising that these software systems contain many tools for the execution and monitoring of

Figure 10.14 Components of a BPMS and Process Implementation, Execution, and Monitoring

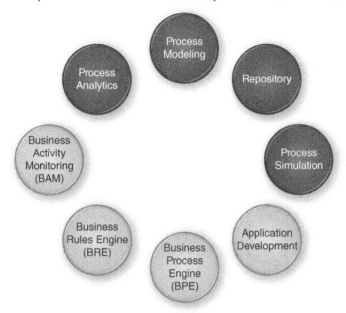

processes. Figure 10.14 shows the components of a BPMS first introduced in Chapter 1, with the components relevant to this chapter highlighted in light blue.

APPLICATION DEVELOPMENT

You may notice that the application development component was highlighted in Chapter 7 and again here as well. Application development is relevant to both process design and process implementation. The design aspects of application development such as designing user interfaces were of most concern in Chapter 7, while the development of the applications themselves is of most importance in the implementation phase. Of course, all application development must be completed before process execution can begin as designed.

For some time, the vision of BPMS software vendors has been to have a standardized graphical business process modeling language, such as BPMN 2.0, which could be used by business users to build process models, and a standardized business process execution language (BPEL), such as BPEL4WS, which could be translated into executable code. The vision was that models designed in BPMN could be directly translated into BPEL that could be understood by the business process engine (BPE). However, this "automatic" generation of executable code has been very difficult to achieve, and some doubt that it will ever be possible to do this in any general way. Despite this, many BPM suites have components that attempt to translate a process designed by a business analyst into some form of business process notation that can then be translated into a standard BPEL that the BPMS can use. This certainly helps in the application development process but still has a long way to go in terms of become a standard solution.

BUSINESS PROCESS ENGINE (BPE)

The business process engine (BPE) is at the heart of BPMS. The BPE, sometimes called the workflow engine, performs the following activities among others:

- Creates a *process instance* when a work flow unit is initiated
- Manages the routing of the process instance to relevant employees or systems to work on

- Maintains basic information about the process instance such as key performance indicators (KPIs)
- Stores current state of the process instance for monitoring and reporting
- Executes those parts of the process that can be automated using the business rules engine
- Manages versioning for processes with different versions
- Handles process exceptions and failures

BUSINESS RULES ENGINE (BRE)

Most businesses have literally hundreds, if not thousands, of business rules that are designed to guide employee behavior and decision making in their day-to-day work. Examples of business rules are "Supervisors must approve all purchase requisitions over $500" or "All purchases must be made from an authorized vendor." The business rules engine (BRE) serves as a tool to maintain and modify these rules and as a method of implementing the rules in practice. For example, the BPE would consult the BRE when making decisions in an automated process, or user interface software would use the BRE in accepting input from users of the BPMS during process execution. The advantage of the BRE located in a BPMS is that it provides a central repository for all business rules, a mechanism for quickly changing business rules, and a way to ensure that business rules are not in conflict with one another. The principal advantage of having the rules built into the BPMS is that the businesses can define, change, and manage business rules without waiting for IT to do software modifications.

BUSINESS ACTIVITY MONITORING (BAM)

The process of managing key metrics as defined by management is automatically performed by the monitoring functions of BPMS. Real-time, online information about process performance is available to everyone in the organization. Within BPMS, performance dashboards can be designed for each individual. The data gathered by BAM can also be easily used for benchmarking purposes by comparing current process performance both to process objectives and to the performance of other organizations. Control mechanisms, such as the control limits discussed in this chapter, can be easily maintained by BPMS, and appropriate individuals can be notified if a process appears to be having problems or if bottlenecks are developing in the process. Since BPMS keeps track of the current state of each process instance, management can actually smooth the flow of work by directly changing the state of the process instance to direct the work to other resources.

Chapter Glossary

Common cause variability The normal random variability inherent in the process.
Process capability index A measure of how well the process can maintain a measure within its specification limits.
Process instance An item created by BPMS when a flow unit is initiated in the system, which is tracked and monitored as it flows through the process.
Qualitative data Data that are inherently nonnumeric.
Quantitative data Data that are numerical in nature.
Special cause variability Deviations caused by sources outside the process or by a change in the process itself.
Specification limits A range that a performance measure should fall within in order to meet the organizational objectives.
Structural variability A systematic change in a process metric over time.

Chapter Questions and Problems

1. Discuss the factors that increase the difficulty in implementing a process design. Which factors present the most difficult hurdles to implementation?

2. Assuming that the specification limits remain unchanged as process improvement efforts improve the value of the process capability index, what happens to the difference between the upper and lower control limits (UCL − LCL)? Does this difference remain unchanged, increase, or decrease? Explain why.

3. The Waters End Clothing Company sells outdoor clothing through a catalog and a specially designed website. A recurring problem for the company is the wrong items being shipped to customers. This has led to an increasing number of customer complaints. The company has performed a random sample of 100 orders each over a 30-day period and counted the number of orders that had shipping errors. The data are shown in the following table. Construct a p-chart and note if there are any samples where the process seems to be out of control. Provide supporting evidence for your answers.

Sample	Bad Orders	Sample	Bad Orders	Sample	Bad Orders
1	11	11	18	21	17
2	11	12	14	22	13
3	15	13	10	23	20
4	14	14	10	24	18
5	13	15	24	25	14
6	10	16	15	26	14
7	19	17	12	27	17
8	15	18	12	28	10
9	10	19	18	29	12
10	9	20	15	30	17

4. The FreshWater Fish Company has a highly automated process for smoking fresh clams and packaging them into 10-oz tins for shipping to the retail market. They want to develop a control chart to monitor the process, especially the packaging part of the operation. They have carefully weighed and recorded the weights for 15 random samples of 10 tins each. The resulting observations are shown in the following table. Construct an R, S, and $\bar{X}$ chart for the data. Are there any samples that seem to indicate that the process is not in control?

Sample	Weight in Ounces									
1	9.88	10.02	9.81	9.98	10.12	9.93	9.86	9.93	10.15	9.98
2	10.16	10.02	9.95	9.98	9.97	9.76	9.90	10.14	10.04	10.00
3	10.16	9.89	9.98	9.93	9.85	9.90	9.94	9.92	9.90	9.90
4	10.02	10.10	9.95	9.98	9.89	10.14	10.24	10.12	9.93	9.90
5	9.89	10.00	9.91	9.81	9.77	10.10	10.06	10.08	10.03	10.00
6	9.95	10.03	9.97	9.91	9.86	9.95	10.15	9.89	10.09	10.11
7	10.15	10.05	10.00	10.17	9.96	9.90	9.94	9.94	10.06	9.94
8	9.98	9.92	9.94	10.11	9.78	10.02	9.97	10.09	10.09	9.95
9	9.96	9.94	9.97	9.93	9.99	9.88	9.94	9.85	10.21	10.20
10	9.93	9.90	10.09	9.91	10.14	10.08	9.92	10.03	9.90	10.17

Sample	Weight in Ounces									
11	10.00	9.92	10.04	9.95	9.87	9.98	9.90	9.92	10.00	9.83
12	10.04	9.81	9.97	10.02	9.98	9.91	9.93	10.15	10.06	10.05
13	9.86	10.20	10.01	10.03	10.09	10.03	9.96	10.12	10.01	10.00
14	10.10	9.94	9.91	9.96	9.95	10.00	10.13	9.99	10.01	10.06
15	10.01	9.89	9.89	10.00	9.89	9.84	9.91	10.00	9.99	10.02

5. The Big Valley Medical Clinic is always concerned about the wait time of patients to see their doctor. Recently the VP of Operations has suggested that they maintain control charts on wait times in the reception areas to help maintain control. They decided to initiate a pilot study in the neurology area of the clinic, and they hired an intern from the local university to measure wait times for patients in neurology. The intern took 20 random samples with 8 patients in each sample. The data are shown below. Construct an R, S, and $\overline{X}$ chart for the data. Are there any samples that seem to indicate that the process is not in control? Explain your answers with supporting documentation.

Sample	Wait Times (Minutes)							
1	19.9	17.6	14.1	11.9	14.0	2.9	16.9	12.5
2	3.1	18.4	21.8	19.3	16.2	4.5	12.4	11.4
3	14.0	10.1	14.7	19.0	20.4	16.5	16.5	23.7
4	10.7	10.9	13.1	16.6	16.5	15.4	15.1	14.6
5	21.9	17.7	17.7	15.8	14.8	12.5	18.5	22.3
6	20.8	15.1	8.5	14.5	15.8	21.7	15.4	4.4
7	13.1	11.1	19.1	22.4	15.0	12.6	12.5	15.7
8	9.8	8.6	22.9	18.1	6.3	25.0	9.5	12.0
9	17.6	19.1	17.9	9.8	10.4	14.3	13.4	12.3
10	21.7	9.7	12.9	15.8	15.5	25.9	14.6	17.7
11	9.6	22.7	12.6	14.1	15.7	9.5	13.7	16.3
12	6.3	9.6	13.1	17.0	14.2	7.5	15.0	12.6
13	15.9	21.4	14.6	15.4	17.8	14.7	13.5	10.2
14	18.8	17.2	16.2	18.9	14.9	9.1	10.0	15.6
15	19.5	12.3	19.1	10.1	19.9	16.7	6.9	12.9
16	9.1	20.0	21.6	17.4	18.8	8.6	18.1	12.6
17	11.3	17.4	16.4	15.3	15.3	9.9	23.3	14.4
18	15.3	21.3	14.4	10.5	15.9	17.1	23.5	6.9
19	11.3	23.9	12.6	8.6	4.1	14.9	10.5	8.6
20	13.1	13.9	13.3	21.8	6.7	12.0	17.6	12.2

6. A large national retail chain employees "mystery shoppers" to visit their stores and evaluate the quality of the service, cleanliness of the stores, and the maintenance and orderliness of the merchandise layout. The mystery shopper evaluates the store with a checklist that asks if each item is acceptable or not. The data for the number of unacceptable marks given a particular store over 20 different visits are shown in the following table. Given that the retail chain wants to maintain an average of 5 or fewer unacceptable marks, is the store in question in control? Explain why or why not.

Visit	Unacceptable
1	10
2	12
3	5
4	9
5	9
6	12
7	7
8	7
9	6
10	14
11	9
12	6
13	5
14	6
15	7
16	6
17	9
18	10
19	6
20	10

7. Rawlings is the official supplier of baseballs to Major League Baseball (MLB). The standards for baseballs require that they be a certain size and a certain weight. The weight requirement is that the ball must weigh no less than 5 ounces and no more than 5.25 ounces. In order to maintain their position as the supplier of baseballs to MLB, it is vital that Rawlings maintain the quality of its baseballs in terms of meeting specifications. The current process at Rawlings is designed to produce baseballs with an average weight of 5.125 ounces with a standard deviation of .05 ounces. To monitor the quality of the process, Rawlings takes periodic samples of 10 baseballs from the process and carefully weighs each ball. The results from the last 10 samples are show in the following table. Should Rawlings be concerned about the production process? Support your answer with documentation.

Sample	Observation									
	1	2	3	4	5	6	7	8	9	10
1	5.13	5.13	5.11	5.11	5.11	5.24	5.20	5.30	5.20	5.28
2	5.17	5.13	5.12	5.20	5.20	5.31	5.23	5.21	5.08	5.16
3	5.17	5.20	5.18	5.05	5.15	5.22	5.03	5.15	5.31	5.22
4	5.08	5.07	5.10	5.17	5.18	5.18	5.24	5.31	5.26	5.18
5	5.08	5.19	5.18	5.10	5.14	5.18	5.20	5.09	5.34	5.23
6	5.15	5.16	5.20	5.16	5.12	5.17	5.26	5.25	5.24	5.18
7	5.10	5.07	5.14	5.10	5.17	5.21	5.34	5.16	5.08	5.23
8	5.08	5.18	5.15	5.11	5.17	5.05	5.18	5.25	5.19	5.12
9	5.07	5.08	5.05	5.13	5.18	5.22	5.13	5.27	5.17	5.13
10	5.08	5.02	5.15	5.05	5.15	5.34	5.22	5.30	5.09	5.25

8. The offices of MLB have recently entered into discussions with Rawlings about improving the quality of the baseball in terms of meeting the design specifications. MLB officials have requested that Rawlings provide baseballs with less than .5% of them outside the design specifications. What process capability ratio must Rawlings attain with their process to achieve this level of quality? Approximately what is the implied process standard deviation that will allow this level of capability?

9. You have started a new delivery service called El Rapido, which promises prompt delivery of goods in the local area with friendly service. A large charity organization has approached you about delivering meals from their kitchens to distribution centers around the city. The meals will then be distributed to senior citizens and other low-income clients. The charity is very proud of the quality of their meals, and much of that quality depends on quick delivery to the distribution locations. It is also a problem if the meals are delivered too quickly because the distribution facilities do not have equipment to keep the food warm for extended periods of time. The specifications call for deliveries to be made in 45 minutes with a tolerance of ± 20 minutes. The proposal calls for a $50 penalty for deliveries that are outside this range. You hired a college friend to work for you at El Rapido because of his analytical skills, and he has analyzed traffic patterns in the city and has come up with two alternative route structures. Both alternatives would deliver the meals to the distribution centers in an average of 45 minutes. However, one alternative (Route A) calls for considerable travel on streets through the heart of the city, where traffic patterns can fluctuate considerably, leading to a standard deviation of 12 minutes in delivery times. However, this alternative uses the shortest routes to the distribution centers, and the daily fuel costs would average only $40 per day. The second alternative (Route B) would route the deliveries primarily around the city center in areas where traffic patterns are more predictable, which would reduce the standard deviation of delivery times to 8 minutes. However, since the routes are longer for this alternative, the fuel costs are projected to average about $60 per day. If El Rapido is going to make 10 deliveries per day, which alternative would be most cost effective? Explain your reasoning.

10. The Sisters of Poor Claire Hospital has recently suffered a number of complaints from patients about errors in their bills. The VP of Operations has ordered a statistical audit of the billing process during the last month. For each day's patient dismissals, a sample of 30 bills are taken and carefully scrutinized to see if any errors have occurred. The number of errors that occurred in the sample of 30 bills for each day is shown in the following table.

Day	Bills with Errors	Day	Bills with Errors	Day	Bills with Errors
1	2	11	3	21	11
2	2	12	4	22	3
3	3	13	3	23	1
4	2	14	8	24	3
5	0	15	1	25	3
6	1	16	1	26	4
7	9	17	4	27	3
8	3	18	5	28	9
9	2	19	2	29	2
10	4	20	4	30	5

a. Is there cause for concern about the billing process at the hospital?
b. If you were told that Day 1 was a Monday and that the hospital operates 7 days a week as all hospitals do, what can you conclude from the pattern of errors?

11. The Alcan Aluminum Company produces large rolls of thin aluminum for use in producing cans for the beverage and food industries. The production process is highly automated and produces continuous sheets of aluminum at a high rate of speed. The sheets are wound into large rolls that are then shipped to the customers. A high speed scanner at the end of the process detects weak spots (defects) in the aluminum as it passes the scanner. The numbers of defects spotted per day over the last 25 days of production are shown in the following table. Is the process under control? Explain why or why not.

Day	Defects	Day	Defects	Day	Defects
1	15	10	9	19	6
2	14	11	15	20	6
3	9	12	9	21	18
4	6	13	7	22	7
5	13	14	9	23	18
6	9	15	12	24	10
7	9	16	10	25	8
8	11	17	11		
9	15	18	6		

References

Anupindi, R., Chopra, S., Deshmukh, S.D., Van Mieghem, J.A. & Semel, E. *Managing Business Process Flows*, 2nd Edition, 2006, Upper Saddle River, NJ: Prentice-Hall.

Chang, J.F. *Business Process Management Systems: Strategy and Implementation*, 2006, Boca Raton, FL: Auerbach Publications.

Deming, W.E. *Out of the Crisis: Quality, Productivity and Competitive Position*, 1986, Cambridge, MA: Cambridge University Press.

Deming, W.E. *The New Economics for Industry, Government and Education*, 1993, Cambridge, MA: MIT Press.

Franz, P. & Kirchmer, M. *Value-Driven Business Process Management: The Value-Switch for Lasting Competitive Advantage*, 2012, New York: McGraw-Hill.

Hall, R.W. The Vigorous Learning Enterprise, *Target: Innovation at Work*, 2008, 24, 1, 5-14.

Hoerl, R.W. & Snee, R.D. *Statistical Thinking: Improving Business Performance*, 2002, Pacific Grove, CA: Duxbury.

Smith, H. & Fingar, P. *Business Process Management: The Third Wave*, 2003, Tampa FL: Meghan-Kiffer.

Part IV

Process Improvement

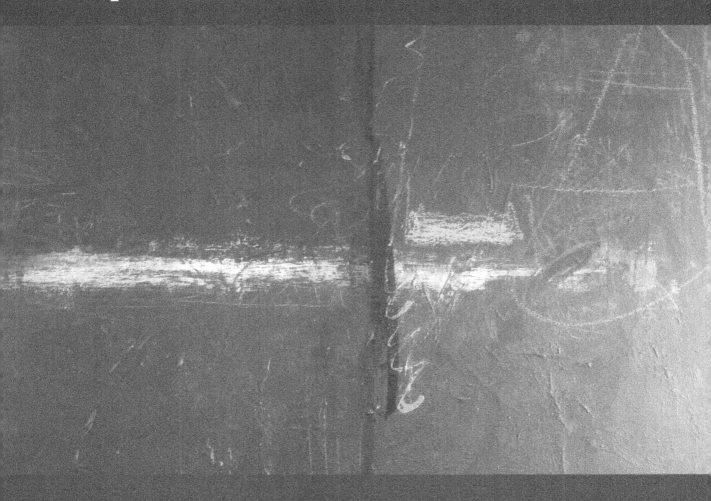

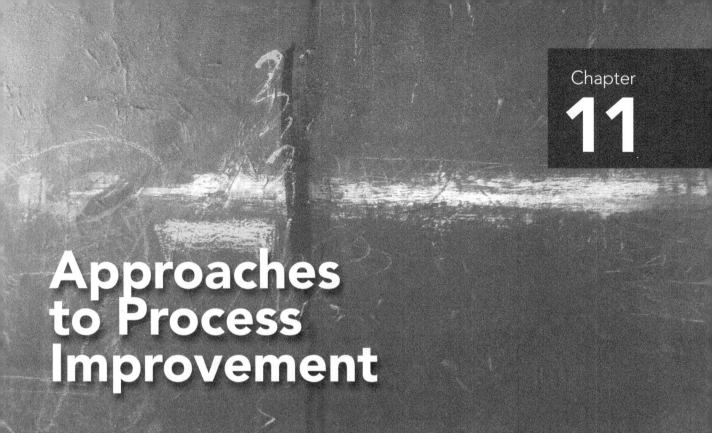

Chapter 11

Approaches to Process Improvement

"The most damaging phrase in the language is: "It's always been done that way."
—Grace Hopper

"To improve is to change; to be perfect is to change often."
—Winston Churchill

"You can't do today's job with yesterday's methods and be in business tomorrow."
—Anonymous

In this last section of the text, we will cover the topics of process improvement, managing change, and building the process enterprise. In this chapter, we will deal the topic of process improvement including the ongoing debate about whether we should focus on continuous process improvement or whether we should focus on radical innovation to gain quantum leaps in performance improvement. We will also address some of the approaches to process improvement, including some of the major buzzwords of the last 40 years. In Chapter 12 we will attempt to tackle the million-dollar question of how to manage the change process. In the final chapter we will address some of the major issues in the still unresolved question of how to build a process-oriented enterprise.

Before discussing the tools and approaches to process improvement, we will first consider some of the issues in the ongoing debate between advocates of *continuous improvement* efforts and those who feel that a more *radical innovation* approach is necessary. In the quotes at the beginning of the chapter, Winston Churchill seems to land on the side of continuous improvement, while our anonymous sage seems to side with the radical innovation group. There is quite likely not a right or wrong answer in this debate, and indeed, as we will consider later, perhaps both sides are right at different points in time. Nevertheless, it is good to consider the pros and cons of this debate because it brings into focus the key points of the best known process-oriented movements of the past 40 to 50 years, which we will discuss later in this chapter.

Continuous Improvement

We will first present the case for continuous incremental improvements in processes, starting with the modern historical origins of these arguments which go back almost 40 years.

HISTORICAL ORIGINS OF CONTINUOUS IMPROVEMENT

Many treatises on the origins of modern business ideas trace their antecedents far back in time to the Greeks, Romans, or Egyptians, or even earlier. Certainly the origins of continuous improvement efforts could also be traced back at least that far and certainly as far back as the scientific management movement started by Frederick Taylor and his followers. However, we start our story at a more recent time since this is the beginning of a movement that is still going strong in the American business scene. In the late 1970s the United States' business community became acutely aware of the growing competitive threat from foreign manufacturers, especially those in Japan. By the early 1980s, articles started to appear in the academic literature extolling the virtues of what was then called just-in-time techniques that were pioneered in Japan, primarily by Toyota (Kimura & Terada, 1981; Rice & Yoshikawa, 1982; Schonberger, 1982a, 1982b, 1983a, 1983b; Hall, 1983b; Hay, 1983; Ritzman, King & Krajewski, 1984). These and many other articles were joined by three highly influential books by Hall (1983a) and Schonberger (1982c, 1986). All of these articles and books extolled the virtues of the just-in-time manufacturing philosophy with its three cornerstones:

- Elimination of waste
- Total quality control
- Continuous improvement

The continuous improvement efforts in Japan heavily involved what Toyota called small group improvement activities, which, when imported into the United States, were termed quality circles. However, in Japan, the idea of continuous improvement, or *kaizen*, was a philosophy that permeated the entire organization, not just a few group activities. Everyone in the organization was expected to be continually looking for opportunities to improve the way work was performed.

In the mid-1980s, the total quality management movement (TQM) became prominent in the United States. This era of focusing on quality was prompted by the growing realization that the quality of American goods and services was not up to world-class standards, and that quality was becoming an increasingly important factor in consumer buying decisions. The founding of the Malcolm Baldridge Quality award in the United States in 1987 stimulated further interest in TQM. Although largely American in origins, TQM borrowed heavily from the ideas embodied in the just-in-time philosophy, including an emphasis on continuous improvement. The archetypal representation of this notion in TQM was Deming's PDCA cycle, which will be covered in more detail later in this chapter.

In 1990, Womack, Jones, and Roos published *The Machine that Changed the World*, an influential book detailing the Toyota production system and its impact on the global auto industry. In this book they popularized the term *lean*, which grew in popular usage and eventually came to subsume the major characteristics of both just-in-time and TQM with some additional twists. The lean concept is so popular now that there is a Lean Enterprise Institute, which was founded by Jim Womack, one of the authors of the book. The Association for Manufacturing Excellence (AME), founded in 1985 by Robert Hall and several manufacturing executives, has publicized the lean philosophy through their publication *Target*, which is available online at their web site.[1] Again, the concept of kaizen, or continuous improvement, plays a central role in

---

1. The AME web site is located at www.ame.org

this philosophy. The concept of lean, although originally a manufacturing concept, has broadened and been applied to service environments (Liker & Morgan, 2006), product development (Schipper & Schmidt, 2006), healthcare (Spear, 2005), the environment (Kidwell, 2006), and even to the consumer (Womack & Jones, 2005). It appears that the principles of elimination of waste and continuous improvement are applicable in most any situation.

THE CASE FOR CONTINUOUS IMPROVEMENT

At first blush it may seem unnecessary to make a case for the benefits of continuous improvement. After all, who would not want to get better at what they do? However, the continuous improvement as practiced at Toyota and other lean companies is much more than always trying to improve performance—it is a way of life. Besides always striving to improve performance, a lean company is also constantly learning how to better perform the improvement effort. In other words, they are learning how to learn. As Hall (2008) has stated, perhaps the biggest benefit of the adherence to a continuous improvement regimen is the creation of a learning organization, as envisioned by Senge (1990). Hall argues that employees in lean organizations become great problem solvers, able to handle new challenges as they arise.

In addition, lean organizations that are continuously improving make for moving targets and thereby make life difficult for competitors. Once a lean organization gains a competitive advantage, it is difficult to catch because it's continuously getting better and better. A culture of continuous improvement, by focusing on processes as the target for improvement, also fosters process-oriented thinking in the organization and helps build a process enterprise. Many have noted the difficulty of building a process-oriented enterprise on top of an organizational structure based on functions. Continuous improvement activities may well be a path to doing so by building a process orientation in all organizational employees. Finally, even if an organization does succeed in achieving radical innovation, such gains are rarely sustained without continuous improvement activities to support them (Hall, 2008). In the final analysis, the main benefit of continuous improvement may well be in building an organizational culture that values processes, problem solving, and learning and adapting to a rapidly changing environment.

Radical Innovation

We will now explore the arguments for radical innovation, which holds that continuous improvement is no longer sufficient in the rapidly changing world of global business, and that only radical changes leading to quantum improvements in performance will give an organization true competitive advantage. These arguments have generally been subsumed under the rubric of reengineering and are more closely tied to the use of technology, in particular information technology.

HISTORICAL ORIGINS OF RADICAL INNOVATION—REENGINEERING

Although the concept of radical innovation and change is certainly not new, its importance in the world of business is quite recent. While Toyota has been developing and improving the central ideas of lean and continuous improvement since the early 1950s, the principles of radical innovation are more recent and can trace their origins to two seminal articles by Michael Hammer (1990) and Thomas Davenport (Davenport & Short, 1990), which were soon followed by books authored by Hammer and Champy (1993) and Davenport (1993). These publications started the business process reengineering (BPR) movement in the United States, which many regarded as a countermeasure to and improvement on the lean concept and the notion of continuous improvement. Perhaps Paul O'Neill, the CEO of ALCOA at the time, stated this attitude best:

> I believe we have made a major mistake in our advocacy of the idea of continuous improvement. Let me explain what I mean: Continuous improvement is exactly the right idea if you are the world leader in everything you do. It is a terrible idea if you are lagging in the world leadership benchmark. It is probably a disastrous idea if you are far behind the world standard....We need a rapid quantum-leap improvement.

The rallying cry of the reengineering movement was to throw out the old, to start over from scratch, and totally redesign the process to achieve quantum leaps in performance improvement, in effect to leap frog the competition. The primary enabler of the reengineering movement was the advances in information technology, which made it possible to not just improve the way we worked, but to work in entirely new ways.

THE CASE FOR RADICAL INNOVATION

The primary motivation for reengineering has always been the promise of major improvements in performance as opposed to small incremental improvements. As Paul O'Neill argued in the previous quotation, sometimes small incremental improvements are not going to do the job, especially when the competition is also making incremental improvements. Something more is required. In addition, some researchers have argued that continuous improvement approaches such as TQM and lean, can result in inflexible organizations that cannot quickly adapt to changing environments (Benner & Tushman, 2003).

However, these radical innovations have been difficult to accomplish and have often not yielded sustainable improvements. As one of the principal architects of the reengineering movement has admitted, hundreds of causalities litter the road to process innovation (Hammer, 2007). One of the reasons is that the required organizational and cultural changes have been much more difficult than originally thought. Another is the inherent resistance of the traditional functional organizational structure with its corresponding reward systems. Nevertheless, the original reasons remain for trying to achieve radical innovation. Indeed, even Toyota, the bastion of continuous improvement, now recognizes this need. The president of Toyota Motor Corporation, Katsuaki Watanabe, recently stated that changes produced by *kaizen* (continuous improvement) also need to be supplemented with *kakushin* (radical change or innovation) when kaizen is not enough (Stewart & Raman, 2007).

Comparison of Continuous and Radical Improvement

There are similarities and differences between the continuous improvement approach and the radical innovation camp. We will first explore some of the similarities and then the differences.

SIMILARITIES AND DIFFERENCES BETWEEN THE APPROACHES

Although we have emphasized the contrasts between the two approaches so far in this chapter, there are many underlying similarities between the two approaches to change. Davenport (1993) outlined the basic similarities between the two. The most important similarity is that both start with a process orientation. For both continuous improvement and process innovation, the basic unit of analysis is the process. Both approaches also emphasize the importance of metrics and rigorous performance measurement. In addition, both approaches also require considerable time investment and both organizational and behavioral change. However, the changes with process innovation tend to be more severe and more threatening to employees of the organization.

There are also many differences between the two. These differences have been summarized in Table 11.1. The first item, level of change, is likely an obvious difference and has been dealt with before in this chapter. The approaches also typically differ in their starting point. Continuous improvement starts with the existing process and asks how it can be improved. Most advocates of process innovation, on the other hand, recommend starting with a clean slate or blank page. The first, and most basic, question is if the process is necessary at all. If so, how would we design the process if we were starting from scratch? The purpose is to avoid repeating mistakes of the past that are embedded in the current process.

Table 11.1   Differences between Continuous Improvement and Process Innovation

	Process Innovation	Continuous Improvement
Level of Change	Radical	Incremental
Starting Point	Blank Page	Existing Process
Participation	Top-down	Bottom-up
Role of Information Technology	Key	Incidental
Scope	Broad, cross-functional	Narrow, within functions
Risk	High	Low to moderate
Type of Change	Cultural and structural	Cultural
Frequency of Change	Infrequent	Continuous

Source: Adapted from Davenport (1993, Fig 1.3, p. 11).

The approaches also tend to differ in terms of employee involvement in the process. Although process innovation does not preclude employee participation, and indeed encourages the participation of those most closely involved in the process, the impetus for the change and the driving force behind the effort tends to come from the top of the organization, with senior management. On the other hand, continuous improvement efforts tend to be originated by those closest to the work, those actively involved in the process. Thus process innovation tends to be forced from top down, while continuous improvement tends to be a bottom-up process. Process innovation also tends to be driven by advances in information technology whereas continuous improvement changes often involve no technology at all.

The scope of continuous improvement efforts has historically tended to be narrower and typically within an organizational function. Process innovation, in contrast, has usually focused on cross-functional, broadly based processes. As a consequence, process innovation tends to be broader in scope and therefore more risky because more of the organization is impacted by the change. Also, because the changes tend to be cross-functional, they must of necessity involve structural change as well as cultural or behavioral change. Because of the large-scale changes, along with the attendant risks, process innovation happens relatively infrequently. On the other hand, as the name implies, continuous improvement activities are ongoing and happen frequently.

THE NEED FOR BOTH TYPES OF CHANGE

The way the question is usually framed implies that an organization has to choose between the two approaches: continuous improvement or radical innovation. More moderate advocates of either approach recognize that both approaches are necessary. Indeed, as the Wantanabe (Stewart & Raman, 2007) interview illustrates, kaizen by itself may not always be sufficient and sometimes kakushin, or radical innovation, is necessary. In fact, periods of continuous improvement may periodically have to give way to more radical innovation, followed by a process of stabilization, including some of the monitoring techniques discussed in Chapter 10. Figure 11.1 illustrates this alternating sequence. However, the figure raises the question of how do we know that it is time for process innovation and that continuous improvement is no longer enough?

Figure 11.1 Alternating Continuous Improvement and Radical Innovation

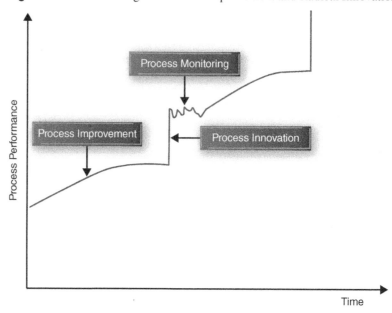

Source: Adapted from Cross, Feather & Lynch (1994, Figure 1.2, p. 32)

Shifting from Continuous Improvement to Radical Innovation

Cross, Feather & Lynch (1994), being advocates of reengineering, logically were more interested in the necessity of process innovation. They presented six reasons for shifting from continuous improvement to process innovation mode.

1. **Your continuous improvement efforts have hit a dead end**: Any process has a theoretical maximum (or minimum) level of performance. When this theoretical level of performance is reached, continuous improvement efforts are not likely to result in much improvement. For example, in Chapter 9 we described the concept of theoretical cycle time. Theoretical cycle time is the time for a flow unit to complete the process when there is no waiting or wasted time in the process. This is a minimum time that cannot be improved upon without changing the process itself. Normally, this will not be possible, at least to any significant degree, without taking a fresh look at the process and performing the work of the process in a very different way, i.e., process innovation.

2. **You have been leapfrogged by your competition**: One of the more compelling reasons for process innovation is when you are seriously trailing your competition. Unfortunately, the track record of this "reactive" process innovation has not been terribly good. In fact, usually companies wait much too long before realizing the competitive threat.

3. **You are approaching the top of the "S" curve:** It is well known that most products, and even entire companies and industries, follow a type of "S" curve, as shown in Figure 11.2. The top of the "S" curve is the point where everything that has made you successful to this point is about to become obsolete. Markets for products become saturated or demographic shifts can wreak havoc with company markets and entire industries. Technological changes or shifts in consumer expectations can also produce such effects. This happened to many U.S. companies in the late 1970s and early 1980s when consumer expectations about product quality changed dramatically. Unfortunately, it is often difficult to abandon the assumptions and methods that yielded the high rates of growth in the past, and many companies wait too long to realize that they are at the top of the curve. This is partly due to

Figure 11.2 The "S" Curve

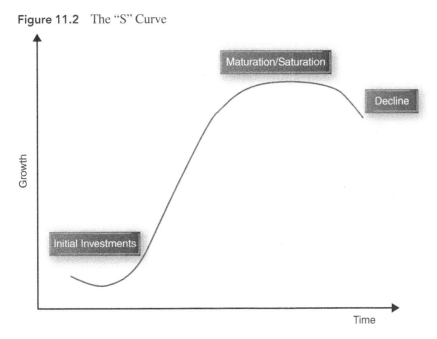

the fact that most traditional metrics, such as market-share, sales, and most financial measures, are backward-looking or "lagging" metrics as we discussed in Chapter 2. Forward looking, or leading, metrics are required to see the top of the "S" curve.

4. **Customer requirements have changed**: Customer requirements and expectations can, and do, change over time. When this happens, old processes may no longer be adequate to meet customer expectations. For example, many consumers' expectations about waiting times for service have changed drastically over the past 10 years. What people were once willing to tolerate in terms of waiting may no longer apply. The Internet, with almost instant access, and the expectations this has created, has meant that many unrelated industries have had to scrap old processes that were simply too slow to meet customer expectations.

5. **Technological advances change what is possible**: Increasingly, technological advances are changing our perceptions of what is possible and thereby are redefining entire industries. Although no one can yet predict what the exact outcome will be, the Human Genome Project will likely have a very significant impact on the pharmaceutical and health care industries. Organizations can no longer afford to be ignorant of the state of technology, and many of them are beginning to actively experiment with new technologies, no matter how farfetched they may seem.

6. **Fundamental shifts in the industry**: Sometimes there are fundamental shifts in an entire industry, often due to technology but sometimes for other reasons. Examples of technology-induced changes are common over the past few decades. Among the hardest hit industries have been traditional publishing and the music industries. Research into new light-weight super-strong materials could revolutionize the auto industry. Political or environmental changes can induce far-reaching changes in some industries. For example, the first oil crisis in the early 1970s created a sudden change in demand for smaller cars, which caught Detroit totally by surprise. The increasing awareness of the potentials of global climate change may have similar far-reaching consequences in a variety of industries.

Although much of our discussion to this point has been about the need for process innovation, there are also arguments as to why continuous improvement cannot be ignored either. In our view, there are two compelling arguments for the continued necessity of continuous improvement efforts.

The Learning Organization

Ever since Peter Senge's (1990) pioneering work, there has been an increased awareness of the importance of organizational learning and a culture of learning and change. Hall (2008) has argued persuasively that lean organizations, with an emphasis on kaizen and continuous change, are particularly suited for becoming learning organizations. Given that a lean organization is one that articulates a culture of problem solving, continuous improvement, and change, they are almost by definition learning organizations.

The Requirements of a Process Organization

The nature of process organizations, with their flat structure and emphasis on flexibility and teamwork, fits well with the culture of continuous improvement and the lean organization. Indeed one could make the argument that lean organizations are uniquely situated to become successful process-driven organizations. Hammer (2007) in his Process and Enterprise Maturity Model (PEMM) framework, which we will discuss in Chapter 13, assessed how ready a company is to become a process organization. Much of this discussion would sound very familiar to lean thinkers. Among the five process enablers discussed by Hammer are metrics. Lean organizations have long used process metrics to track improvements and to monitor processes and are well ahead of the curve in this regard. One of the four enterprise capabilities cited by Hammer is a culture with a customer focus emphasizing teamwork, personal accountability, and a willingness to change. These are also some of the hallmark characteristics of a lean organization with a culture of continuous improvement.

Major Approaches to Process Improvement

In the remainder of this chapter, we will identify some of the leading approaches to process improvement. We have already discussed some of the tools used in process improvement efforts, most specifically in Chapter 7 when we talked about tools for process design and in Chapter 10 when we discussed the use of control charts in monitoring processes. Here we will focus on general approaches to process improvement. Each of these approaches is backed by an extensive literature, and each has something to recommend it. Our goal here is not to provide a comprehensive review of these methods but simply to provide an introduction to the approach and references to further reading.

DEMING'S PLAN-DO-CHECK-ACT (PDCA) CYCLE

In his many writings, W. Edwards Deming discussed his strategy for process learning and improvement, the *PDCA cycle*, which is illustrated in Figure 11.3.[2] This approach would become a key component of the total quality management (TQM) movement.

Plan: An idea for a process improvement leads to a plan for an experiment to test the idea. A good plan is the key to start the process on the right foot.
Do: Carry out the planned experiment or trial according to the plan.
Check: Check the results. Do they agree with our expectations in the plan? If not, why not?
Act: Act on the results. Adopt the change, abandon it, or go through the cycle again with a new plan.

The astute reader will notice the distinct similarity of this cycle to the scientific method. This is not an accident; the work of Deming, and Shewhart before him, had its roots firmly

---

2. You will also see the acronym called DPSA for Plan-Do-Study-Act.

Figure 11.3 Deming's PDCA Cycle

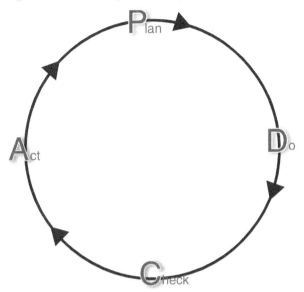

planted in the scientific method.³ As it stands, the PDCA cycle is not so much a method as it is an approach. Deming himself often stressed the importance of the planning stage, indicating that what takes place during this phase determines the likely success or failure of the entire process. He also noted that this is often the most neglected phase of the process.

SIX SIGMA

Six Sigma, like the PDCA cycle, is an overall approach to process improvement. As a process improvement approach, Six Sigma utilizes a variety of tools such as the statistical process control tools described in Chapter 10. Six Sigma is a disciplined, data-driven process improvement approach. The origins of Six Sigma can clearly be traced back to Motorola during the mid-1980s, although the identity of the originator(s) of the approach is a source of considerable debate [See Ramias (2005) for an interesting view of the approach's history]. Since that time, it has spread to other companies such as GE, IBM, and Kodak, among others. Also over this time, it has evolved into a comprehensive approach to process improvement with many adherents, and, of course many consultants to promote its benefits. Six Sigma is often closely associated with the ideas of statistical process control and the concept of the PDCA cycle. It has at its heart, an improvement process called DMAIC, which stands for define, measure, analyze, improve, and control which, while similar in spirit to PDCA, is a much more well-defined and rigorous approach to process improvement. In fact, some research has shown that this systematic approach to improvement, along with a focus on metrics and use of group improvement specialists, is key to the success of Six Sigma efforts in an organization (Zu, Fredendall, and Douglas, 2008). The overall improvement cycle is shown in Figure 11.4.

Define

Before starting an improvement project, it is necessary to define its scope, focus, and desired outcomes. During this phase, the business case for change is made, the process customer is

---

3. In several places, Deming refers to this as the Shewhart cycle for learning and improvement.

Figure 11.4 The DMAIC Improvement Cycle

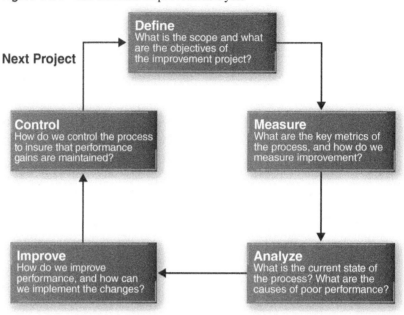

identified, and the tangible benefits and finish date of the project are defined. During this phase the key stakeholders in the process are identified, the most important of which is the customer. Some of the tools used during this phase include a Suppliers, Inputs, Process Steps, Output and Customers (SIPOC) map, stakeholder analysis, and voice of the customer (VOC—similar to quality function deployment in Chapter 2).

Measure

In this phase, the key metrics of the process are identified. These metrics will be used in measuring the results of the improvement efforts. Also, during this phase an analysis of the quality of the metrics is done. Are the measures valid and reliable? Typical tools used are process capability calculations and basic data analysis tools such as histograms and run charts.

Analyze

In this phase, the process is analyzed to discover the root causes of the inefficiencies in the process. This step determines where to focus the improvement efforts.

Improve

Create innovation ideas to improve the way the process is performed to make it more efficient. The goals of the improvement process are to perform the process with lower cost, or faster speed, or to do more with the process than is currently being done. In other words, the goal is to make the process better, faster, or cheaper. Unfortunately, all too often the emphasis is on cost and reducing the number of employees involved in the process. The focus on reducing head count is what has led many people to believe that process improvement is just another name for downsizing. It is unfortunate that more emphasis has not been placed on doing more with the same resources, i.e., performing the process better. In this way the organization may be able to make the process more profitable, not by reducing costs but by increasing revenues.

An important aspect of the improvement stage is the implementation of the proposed changes. This is often where process improvement efforts fail. The change process is such an important part of the process improvement effort that we will discuss it in much more depth in the next chapter of the text.

Control

Once the changes have been made to improve the process, then the process must be controlled to ensure that the improvements are maintained and that the process does not slip back to the old performance (Hall, 2008). The tools described in Chapter 10 are of obvious relevance here.

LEAN

Process improvement was a hallmark of the just-in-time movement of the 1970s and early 1980s (Hall, 1983a, 1983b; Schonberger 1982a, 1982b, 1982c, 1983a, 1986) and has continued under the banner of Lean (Womack, Jones & Roos, 1990; Womack & Jones, 2003). Lean is a large topic, and an extended discussion is beyond the scope of this book. Our concern here is with the emphasis of lean on continuous improvement. The path to continuous improvement in this approach is a quest for the elimination of *waste (muda)*, which is defined as anything that does not add value to the customer. Depending on the source, there are seven or eight sources of waste or muda. Table 11.2 lists eight forms that are commonly considered to be sources of waste, which are applicable to any organization.[4]

Table 11.2 Eight Forms of Waste (Muda)

Transportation	Unnecessary movement of materials or information
Inventory	Work stored waiting for processing
Motion	Unnecessary bending, lifting, walking, etc.
Waiting	People or materials waiting for something to be done
Over-production	Processing too much or before it is needed.
Over-processing	Unnecessary steps in the process or producing higher quality than required by the customer
Defects	Work not done properly and requiring scrap or rework
Skills	Underutilizing the skills of employees and lack of training

Lean uses a variety of methods including such techniques as value-stream mapping and the "5 Ws" to eliminate waste. The 5 Ws have been discussed previously in Chapter 6 in conjunction with the 5w2h framework. The five w questions, who?, what?, when?, where?, and why?, are designed to identify potential non-value-added aspects of the process and where the process could be improved. *Value-stream mapping* visualizes the flow of material and information throughout the value stream from the beginning to the final customer. Value-stream mapping is similar to process mapping, discussed in Chapter 7, but is at a somewhat higher level. The purpose of value-stream mapping is to identify value-adding and non-value-adding aspects of the process. In so doing, it acts as a communication tool and roadmap for improvement efforts. Originally, value-stream mapping, at least as practiced at Toyota, was done with paper and pencil to keep it simple and flexible. As with process mapping, increasingly this technique is being computerized with many organizations selling software for this purpose.

The heart of lean improvement ideas is the notion of kaizen. Recall from the beginning of this chapter that the term kaizen literally means incremental continuous improvement and can

---

4. A useful mnemonic for remembering the forms of waste it to note that the first letters spell *TIM WOODS*.

be viewed as a philosophy of life and of the workplace, as well as a specific technique about process improvement. In the lean movement, kaizen as technique is typically discussed as a kaizen event.[5] The objective of the kaizen event is process improvement. A kaizen event typically gathers workers and managers together in one place to map out the existing process (value-stream or process map) and devise ways of improving the process. The goal is to elicit buy-in from all parties concerning how best to improve the process.[6] Kaizen events are usually highly focused on a particular work area or specific part of the overall process. They are often undertaken in response to specific problems noted in that area in the past.

THEORY OF CONSTRAINTS

The *Theory of Constraints* (TOC) was developed during the 1970s and 1980s by Eli Goldratt and was based on his work on a sophisticated shop floor scheduling system. Eventually TOC became more of a philosophy or approach to business problems and ultimately to a way of thinking about problems. At the heart of TOC is the notion of *constraints*. Constraints restrict the flow of a process and therefore limit how much output can be obtained from the process. The constraint serves as a "bottleneck" to the flow through the process. The analogy to the flow out of a bottle is an apt one: the rate at which liquid can be poured from a bottle is determined by the smallest portion of the bottle, usually the neck, as shown in Figure 11.5(a). Enlarging the rest of the bottle as shown in Figure 11.5(b), will not increase the rate of flow out of the bottle. The only way to increase the rate of flow out of the bottle is to increase the size of the neck of the bottle as shown in Figure 11.5(c).

Figure 11.5 Illustration of Bottlenecks

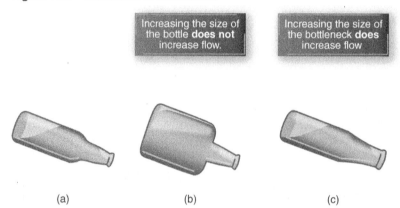

(a)   (b)   (c)

The point is that if you want to improve a process, you must do so at the bottleneck of the process. Improving performance in other parts of the process will not improve the performance of the entire process because the output of the process is determined by the bottleneck. In this way, TOC provides a focus for the improvement process in a way that the other improvement techniques do not. In TOC process improvement is described in terms of the five focusing steps seen in Figure 11.6.

1. **Identify the constraint**: The first step is to identify the constraint or bottleneck of the process. This is usually not too difficult. The bottleneck is the part of the process that is always busy, operating at full capacity. There is usually work piled up in front of the bottleneck, and downstream parts of the process are often idle because of a lack of work.

---

5. A kaizen event is also sometimes referred to a kaizen blitz or kaizen burst.
6. A better Japanese term for a kaizen event is kaikaku, which implies a more radical change and improvement of a process. Kaikaku is sometimes used in a sense more like process reengineering by Japanese executives like Watanabe (Stewart & Raman, 2007).

Figure 11.6 Five Focusing Steps of TOC Improvement

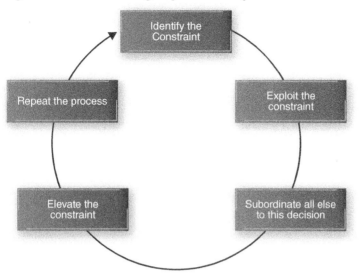

2. **Exploit the constraint**: Using existing resources, decide how to get the most out of the constraint. This may involve things such as removing non-value-adding work, limiting interruptions to this part of the process, and ensuring that there is no idle time at the bottleneck.

3. **Subordinate all else to this decision**: Decisions about all other parts of the process should be made to support the full utilization of the bottleneck constraint. This may mean moving some non-value-adding work from the bottleneck to non-bottleneck resources. Work at other parts of the process should be scheduled so that the bottleneck always has work to do. Lastly, counter to tradition in most organizations, this step involves operating upstream non-bottleneck resources at less-than-full capacity. Managers have traditionally viewed idle resources as an evil to be eliminated, but TOC implies that resources upstream from the bottleneck should be operated at less than full capacity because operating these parts of the process at full capacity is waste. Full utilization of these resources is waste because it uses resources but does not increase the output of the process. Figure 11.7 illustrates the thinking behind this and also illustrates why downstream parts of the process will often be idle because of a lack of work. The figure depicts three parts of a process and their associated capacities in units per hour. You can see that Y is the bottleneck part of the process since it has the lowest capacity. You can also readily see that Z, which is downstream from the bottleneck, will necessarily have idle time because the bottleneck can only provide 5 units per hour. Z therefore has slack capacity of 3 units per hour. You can also readily identify why operating X at full capacity is waste. If X is operated at full capacity, producing 10 units per hour, an additional 5 units of output from X will pile up in front of Y each hour since Y can only process 5 units per hour. Therefore, resources are expended at X without increasing the overall output of the process, which is waste.

Figure 11.7 Process Flow and the Bottleneck

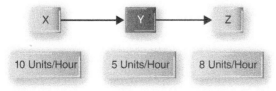

4. **Elevate the constraint**: This involves making investments in terms of additional people, new technology, or other resources to increase the output of the bottleneck. The temptation may be to skip step 2 and begin with this step, but this temptation should be avoided. Step 2 does not require additional investments and should be done first before additional expensive investments are made. When all other options have been exhausted, it then makes sense to make investments to improve the capacity of the bottleneck constraint to increase the output of the process.

5. **Repeat the process**: Once the constraint has been elevated sufficiently, it will have extra capacity. Then another part of the process will become a bottleneck, and the cycle must be repeated. Thus, TOC, like Deming's PDCA cycle and Six Sigma's DMAIC, emphasizes a continual improvement process. By continuing to increase the capacity of the bottlenecks, the output of the overall system continues to increase.

BUSINESS PROCESS REENGINEERING (BPR)

The previous three approaches to process improvement were all based on the assumption of continuous change, which leads to gradual improvement of the process. As discussed earlier in this chapter, business process reengineering (BPR) takes a more radical approach to change. BPR assumes a one-time overhaul of the process, which leads to quantum improvements in the process. Hammer and Champy (1993, p. 32) define reengineering as "the fundamental rethinking and radical redesign of business processes to achieve dramatic improvements in critical, contemporary measures of performance, such as cost, quality, service, and speed." As this definition indicates, reengineering is "radical" rather than incremental and requires a one-time fundamental rethinking of the processes rather than continuous tinkering to improve the process.

Like the theory of constraints with its emphasis on bottlenecks, Hammer and Champy provided criteria for deciding which processes should be redesigned first. As described in Chapter 6, the three criteria are that (1) the process is broken and not meeting expectations; (2) it is an important process, which usually means that it is a customer-facing process or one with a particularly high cost to the organization; and (3) it must be feasible to reengineer the process for dramatic improvement. Chapter 6 discussed these criteria in more detail.

As with other approaches to process improvement, BPR has an established framework for the change effort:

1. State a case for action
2. Identify the process to reengineer
3. Evaluate enablers of reengineering
4. Understand the current process
5. Create the new process design
6. Implement the reengineered process

The case for action makes the business case for the need to change. The case should be brief but very clear and convincing on why the organization has to change. With reengineering, often the case for action stresses that change is a matter of survival. The story about Boeing in Chapter 12 illustrates this point. In conjunction with the case for action, a vision statement should be produced that contains the vision of what the company can, and should, become. The vision statement should contain clear goals in terms of performance metrics that the reengineered organization should attain.

Although it is not necessary that technology be a key ingredient of the reengineered process, often technology will be an important enabler of process redesign. New information technologies are often a key to performing work in innovative and more efficient ways. BPR also stresses beginning the design of the new process from a blank sheet. In other words, discard the old process completely and start the redesign from the point of view of "if this process did not exist, how would we design it?"

The Improvement Paradox

Despite the proven benefits of improvement programs such as Six Sigma, lean, and others, the literature on improvement efforts contains many stories of failures or projects with initial successes that stall out and are abandoned. Indeed, sometimes improvement projects can even lead to worse performance. John Sterman and his colleagues [see for example, Sterman, Repenning & Kofman (1997) and Keating, Oliva, Repenning, Rockart & Sterman (1999)] termed this *the improvement paradox*. They have looked at these failures through the lens of dynamic simulation modeling to attempt to explain this phenomenon. Based on this analysis, their first conclusion was that improvement efforts such as TQM and BPR present organizations with a fundamental trade-off between short-term and long-term effects. Often, the short-term impact is negligible, and even sometimes negative, but the effects of the improvements long term are positive (Sterman, Repenning & Kofman, 1997). Their second conclusion was that this trade-off is because of the inability to manage the improvement process as a dynamic process. Improvement efforts are tightly coupled with other processes and policies of the organization and with external stakeholders, such as suppliers and customers. Failure to account for the feedback from tightly integrated activities may account for the unanticipated effects. The twin lessons from this are that improvement efforts can take time to bear fruit and that these activities are not conducted in isolation but are intertwined with the other activities of the organization and its partners.

BPMS and Process Improvement

Business process management suites can also be very useful tools in process improvement. The most relevant components of the BPMS for our discussion here are highlighted in light blue in Figure 11.8.

Figure 11.8 BPMS Components for Process Improvement

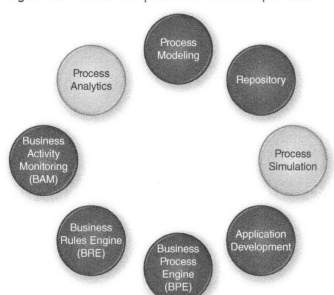

We have extensively discussed the role of process simulation in process design in Chapter 8. By extension, process simulation is also important to process improvement as a tool for trying out different alternative designs before making actual changes to the processes themselves.

Process analytics is a broad term that refers to the use of statistical and other analytical tools on process data to support organizational decision making. The process analytics component makes use of the extensive data collected by the activity monitoring component (BAM). Much has been written about the importance of analytics in general in the business environment (Davenport & Harris, 2007; Davenport, Harris & Morison, 2010). Stephen Baker (2008) has even looked at the social implications of the large amounts of data gathered by modern corporations and the use of this data via analytics.

Davenport, Harris & Morison (2010) have stated that the real advantage of analytics occur when they are embedded in the business processes themselves. zur Muehlen & Shapiro (2010) categorize three different uses of process analytics:

- Historical analysis of completed process instances
- Real-time running process instances
- Predicting the behavior of future process instances

The first use of process analytics is to understand business performance, and it can also provide baseline data for process improvement efforts. The purpose of the second type of analytics is to provide management real-time control over the process. The third type of process analytics is designed to provide the ability to forecast future performance and to predict how different process configurations might perform in the future, i.e., in process redesign. This is probably one of the least-developed components of BPMS and is represented in varying degrees in different product offerings.

It is in this last use of analytics in predicting future performance and how different process configurations might perform that process simulation comes into play. Although not currently well developed, the hope is that the use of simulation utilizing the vast data collected by process analytics will allow rapid process adjustments to adapt to an ever-changing business environment.

Chapter Glossary

Constraint (bottleneck) Anything that restricts the flow through a process.

Continuous improvement Program of regular systematic attempts to improve a process.

DMAIC The define-measure-analyze-improve-control cycle of process improvement associated with Six Sigma.

Improvement paradox The idea that sometimes process improvement efforts do not have lasting effect and can even lead to lower performance.

Kaizen Japanese term for small continuous improvements in quality and efficiency. Also associated with kaizen change events in lean manufacturing.

Kakushin Term used by Katsuaki Watanabi, CEO of Toyota, to refer to radical innovation.

Lean Similar to just-in-time, lean is simply doing more with less along with the notion of continuous improvement.

PDCA cycle W. Edwards Deming's plan-do-check-act cycle for process improvement.

Process analytics The use of statistical and other tools on process data to support organizational decision making.

Radical innovation Radical improvement efforts aimed at achieving quantum leaps in improvement.

Theory of constraints An approach to process improvement and management oriented around constraints or bottlenecks in a process.

Value-stream mapping Depicts the flow of material and information throughout the value stream. Similar to process flowcharting but at a higher level.

Waste (muda) Anything that does not add value to the customer.

Chapter Questions and Problems

1. Read the interview with Katsuaki Watanabe in Harvard Business Review (Stewart and Raman, 2007) and describe the factors at Toyota that led Watanabe to believe that continuous improvement was not sufficient and had to be supplemented by radical innovation at times.

2. Discuss the pros and cons of continuous improvement versus radical innovation. What factors about an organization would lead you to prefer one or the other approach?

3. Kaizen events are highly focused efforts on a particular process or problem area, typically of three to five days in duration. Use the Internet to find at least two examples of Kaizen events. What general procedures were used and what results were achieved during the events? (Hint: You can find many examples just by using Google but the Association for Manufacturing Excellence at www.ame.org has many examples in one location. You may need to register for a free account to access some of the material.)

4. Compare and contrast the Deming cycle and the Six Sigma improvement cycle. In what ways are they similar and in what ways are they different?

5. What is the key factor that differentiates the Theory of Constraints from the other improvement approaches?

6. How does business process reengineering differ from the other approaches to improvement discussed in this chapter?

References

Baker, S. *The Numerati*, 2008, New York: Houghton Mifflin.
Benner, M.J. & Tushman, M.L. Exploitation, Exploration, and Process Management: The Productivity Dilemma Revisited, *Academy of Management Review,* 2003, 28, 2, 238-256.
Cross, K.F., Feather, J.J. & Lynch, R.L. *Corporate Renaissance: The Art of Reengineering*, 1994, Cambridge, MA: Blackwell Business.
Davenport, T.H. *Process Innovation: Reengineering Work through Information Technology*, 1993, Boston MA: Harvard Business School Press.
Davenport T.H. & Harris, J.G. *Competing on Analytics: The New Science of Winning*, 2007, Boston MA: Harvard Business School Press.
Davenport T.H., Harris, J.G. & Morison, R. *Analytics at Work: Smarter Decisions, Better Results*, 2010, Boston MA: Harvard Business School Press.
Davenport, T.H. & Short, J.E. The New Industrial Engineering: Information Technology and Business Process Redesign. *Sloan Management Review*, 1990, 31, 3, 11-27.
Hall, R.W. *Zero Inventories*, 1983a, Homewood Illinois: Dow-Jones Irwin.
Hall, R. W. Zero Inventory Crusade: Much More than Materials Management, *Production & Inventory Management*, 1983b, 3, 1-9.
Hall, R.W. The Vigorous Learning Enterprise, *Target: Innovation at Work*, 2008, 24, 1, 5-14.
Hammer, M. Reengineering work: Don't automate, obliterate. *Harvard Business Review*, 1990, 68, 4, 104-114.
Hammer, M. The Process Audit, *Harvard Business Review*, 2007, 85, 4, 111-123.
Hammer, M. & Champy, J. *Reengineering the Corporation*. 1993, New York: Harper Business.
Hay, E. Japanese Productivity Methods, What Relevance Here? Part II, *Inventories and Production*, 1983, 3, 2, 6-11.

Kidwell, M. Lean Manufacturing and the Environment, *Target: Innovation at Work*, 2006, 22, 6, 13-18.

Kimura, O. & Terada, H. Design and Analysis of Pull System, a Method of Multi-Stage Production Control. *International Journal of Production Research*, 1981, 19, 2, 241-253.

Keating, E.K., Oliva, R., Repenning, N.P., Rockart, S. & Sterman, J.D. Overcoming the Improvement Paradox. *European Management Journal*, 1999, 17(2), 120-134.

Liker, J.K. & Morgan, J.M. The Toyota Way in Services: The Case of Lean Product Development, *Academy of Management Perspectives*, 2006, 20, 2, 5-20.

Rice, J. W. & Yoshikawa, T. A Comparison of Kanban and MRP Concepts for the Control of Repetitive Manufacturing Systems, *Production & Inventory Management*, 1982, 23, 1, 1-14.

Ramias, A. The Mists of Six Sigma, *BPTrends*, October 2005. http://www.bptrends.com/bpt/wp-content/publicationfiles/10-05 WP The Mists of Six Sigma - Ramas1.pdf. Last accessed 5/28/2016.

Ritzman, L.P., King, B.E. & Krajewski, L.J. Manufacturing Performance-Pulling the Right Levers, *Harvard Business Review*, 1984, 62, 2, 143-152.

Schipper, T. & Schmidt, R. Lean Methods for Creative Development, *Target: Innovation at Work*, 2006, 22, 4, 14-27.

Schonberger, R.J. The Transfer of Japanese Manufacturing Management Approaches to U. S. Industry, *Academy of Management Review*, 1982a, 7, 4, 479-487.

Schonberger, R. J. Some Observations on the Advantages and Implementation Issues of Just-in-Time Production Systems, *Journal of Operations Management*, 1982b, 3, 1, 1-12.

Schonberger, R. J. *Japanese Manufacturing Techniques: Nine Hidden Lessons in Simplicity*, 1982c, New York: The Free Press.

Schonberger, R. J. Japanese Manufacturing Techniques: Nine Hidden Lessons in Simplicity, *Operations Management Review*, 1983, 1, 3, 13-18.

Schonberger, R. J. Selecting the Right Manufacturing Inventory System: Western and Japanese Approaches, *Production & Inventory Management*, 1983, 24, 2, 33-44.

Schonberger, R. J. *World Class Manufacturing*, 1986, New York: Free Press.

Senge, P. M. *The Fifth Discipline. The Art and Practice of the Learning Organization*, 1990, London: Random House.

Spear, S.J. Fixing Health Care from the Inside, Today, *Harvard Business Review*, 2005, 83, 9, 78-91.

Sterman, J. D., Repenning, N.P. & Kofman, F. Unanticipated Side Effects of Successful Quality Programs: Exploring a Paradox of Organizational Improvement. *Management Sciences*, 1997, 43, 4, 503-521.

Stewart, T.A. & Raman, A.P. Lessons From Toyota's Long Drive: An Interview with Katsuaki Watanabe, *Harvard Business Review*, 2007, 85, 7, 74-83.

Varian, H.R. Kaizen, That Continuous Improvement Strategy, Finds Its Ideal Environment, *New York Times*, 2007, February 8.

Womack, J.P. & Jones, D.T. *Lean Thinking: Banish Waste and Create Wealth in your Corporation*, 2nd Edition, 2003, New York: Free Press.

Womack, J.P. & Jones, D.T. Lean Consumption, *Harvard Business Review*, 2005, 83, 3, 58-68.

Womack, J.P., Jones, D.T. & Roos, D. *The Machine That Changed the World*, 1990, New York: Rawson Associates.

Zu, X, Fredendall, LD. & Douglas, T.J. The Evolving Theory of Quality Management: The Role of Six Sigma, *Journal of Operations Management*, 2008, 26, 5, 630-650.

zur Muehlen, M. & Shapiro, R. Business Process Analytics. In J. vom Brocke & M. Rosemann (Eds.) *Handbook on Business Process Management, Vol. 2*, 2010, Berlin: Springer-Verlag.

Chapter 12

Managing the Change Process

"It is not necessary to change. Survival is not mandatory."

—W. Edwards Deming

"It is not the strongest or the most intelligent who will survive but those who can best manage change."

—Charles Darwin

Implicit in our discussions throughout the book to this point is the underlying theme of "change." In the final analysis, process design and improvement is about change, which implies that the procedures used to introduce, manage, and implement change are important to the entire system of process improvement. In this chapter, we will review some of the literature on the nature of change and how to manage the change process.

Change in an organizational context can take place on different levels of the organization. We can talk about individual change at the level of the individual employee, group, or team; change at the level of different organizational groups; and lastly, change at the level of the entire organization. The most relevant for our discussion are changes at the organizational level. However there is an oft-repeated maxim in the change-management literature that "organizations don't change, people do." Ultimately we have to discuss change at the individual level as well. Although we will not explicitly discuss change at the team or work-group level, we will touch on aspects of group dynamics and peer influences that are part of the group change literature.

The Nature of Change

Change is an inevitable part of life, and most students of the business scene agree that change is becoming more and more a constant of business life. Despite the obvious importance of change, there is a widely held view, in large part supported by empirical research, that attempts to implement organizational change are predominantly unsuccessful (e.g., Beer, 2000; Elrod & Tippett, 2002; Kotter, 1995; Pettigrew, Woodman, & Cameron, 2001).[1] One reason organizational change is so difficult to get right is because people normally do not like change and tend to resist it if at all possible. The book *Who Moved My Cheese* sold over 26 million copies because people could identify with the psychological discomfort of change (Johnson 1998). Another reason organizational change is difficult is because there is no well-identified road map to planning and managing change. This book does not attempt to offer such a road map either, nor is it intended to provide a complete overview of the vast change management literature. Our purpose here is to provide some food for thought in thinking about change and suggest some additional resources to those further interested in the topic. This is important in its own right because how managers plan and manage change in a business organization is often dictated by their mental models of how individuals behave in response to change, i.e., what they think makes people tick.

Change is also a complex topic because there are different types of change. In other words, not all changes are alike. Bridges and Mitchell (2002) distinguished between planned change and transitions. Planned change is approached from a rational perspective, is a more controlled process, and is the less complex of the two types of change. Transitions, on the other hand, are about letting go of the past and focusing on new beginnings. Transitions are often "imposed" changes from the outside, such as divorce or death of a spouse. There is much more emotional involvement in transitions than in planned change. Of course what is planned change from one person's perspective may be transitional change from another's. The importance of this distinction is to bring out the emotional and psychological aspects of change, which are important to understanding the response of individuals to planned organizational change.

In a business context, we can also distinguish between different types of organizational change. Cameron & Green (2004) distinguish among four different organizational change scenarios: restructuring, or structural change, mergers and acquisitions, cultural change, and finally what they call IT-based process change. The point is that the nature of the change process, individual reactions, and necessary leadership responses depend on the type of change. Here we will focus primarily on the last category, process change.[2]

Organizational Change

The overriding theme of this book is the transition of the organization from a functional point of view to a "process" driven organization. Thus, we are primarily concerned with the way the entire organization thinks about itself, how it organizes its work, and how it manages its day-to-day affairs. The ultimate goal then is organizational change. Here we want to examine ways in which we can view the workings of an organization and manage the change process at the organizational level.

Psychologists have long held that how we as individuals learn about, perceive, and interact with our environment is determined by our mental models of that environment and how it works

---

1. A commonly quoted statistic is that 70% of all organizational change efforts fail to meet the expectations of their designers. However, Hughes (2011), in a review of five published instances of this specific value, found that there was little empirical support for this exact value.
2. Despite the IT-based designation of Cameron and Green (2004), we do not imply by this that the change is IT dominated or even that IT is necessarily involved.

(Johnson-Laird, 1983, 2006). These mental models, or metaphors, allow us to make sense of our world and provide a framework for dealing with it. Managers also have mental models about the organization that they manage, and these mental models influence how they manage and lead. Cameron and Green (2004) selected four such metaphors from the work of Gareth Morgan (1986) that underlie much of the thinking about organizational change. Although in reality how one thinks about an organization is almost always a mix of these models, describing them in some detail allows us to see how our thoughts and actions are often influenced by the mental model that tends to dominate our thinking at the moment.

THE ORGANIZATION AS MACHINE

The metaphor of the organization as a machine is perhaps the most dominant and well-known view. In this view, the organization as a machine can, and should, be rationally designed to achieve certain purposes. It should have a well-defined structure with carefully constructed roles and responsibilities for each individual in the organization, all oriented to achieving the organizational goals. This view of the organization tends to influence how change is approached. From this view, change is initiated and "designed" at the top levels of the organization to achieve certain targets or goals. Changes are rolled out to the employees of the organization with training programs instituted to introduce new skills and modify behaviors as appropriate, and resistance to change is to be managed as it arises.

This way of thinking has heavily influenced the traditional approach taken to strategic planning, especially in the United States. As noted in the strategic planning literature, this approach can work fairly well in a static environment but not in highly dynamic situations. As a model for organizational change, this metaphor tends to lead to viewing change as hard work that will encounter a great deal of resistance. This will then require careful planning and strong management action and control from the top down, accompanied by inspirational vision and leadership. It fact, this viewpoint is prevalent in many writings on organizational change.

THE ORGANIZATION AS A POLITICAL SYSTEM

The view of organization as a political system is also a long-standing metaphor that, like the machine metaphor, is useful precisely because it does yield insights into organizational life. It is useful because it acknowledges that power, competing interests, and conflict do play a role in any organization. In this view, politics is an inherent part of organizational life, and there is an underlying political structure that often has more bearing on what happens within the organization than does the official organizational chart.

This view of the organization also has implications for organizational change. For example, the success of the change effort often depends on the political power of its supporters, which implies that any change initiative needs a politically powerful champion. Since allocation of resources in the organization is a matter of bargaining and negotiation, there are always winners and losers, and it is important to understand who they are in any change situation. Change strategies involve forming coalitions and negotiating issues.

Like the machine metaphor, there are limitations to this view of the organization. For one, it often assumes a zero-sum game with winners and losers, with a goal of being one of the winners. This can lead to complex Machiavellian strategies that can turn an organization into a political battlefield. There is always a hint of Machiavellianism within this metaphor.

THE ORGANIZATION AS BIOLOGICAL ORGANISM

In this metaphor the organization is a living, adaptive system that functions within and interacts with its environment. This "open system" view of the organization implies that it must be open to its environment and the way in which it relates to the environment is the key to its survival. This system view played a role in the writings of several change theorists in the 1990s (e.g., Carr, 1996).

Like all metaphors, this view also has implications for organizational change. It emphasizes information flow within and between different parts of the system, especially between the organization and its environment. Organizational change is in response to changes in the environment, and the goal is to maximize the fit of the organization to its environment. There is no single best way to design an organization because the best way depends on the environment. Strategists often talk about finding the right "niche" for the organization.

This metaphor, like the others, has limitations. The primary limitation is in viewing the organization as simply reacting and adapting to the environment, which ignores the fact that the organization can in fact shape the environment in which it operates. This view can also influence internal processes, such as the hiring and retention of employees, by insisting that employees fit or adapt to the organizational environment. This can promote a lack of diversity in the organization with negative consequences.

THE ORGANIZATION AS A NONLINEAR SYSTEM

Like the biological organism metaphor, the view of the organization as a nonlinear system is an outgrowth of developments in science that have been applied in a variety of other disciplines. However, rather than a single metaphor, this view is a combination of theories that Cameron and Green (2004) and Morgan (1986) have called the flux and transformation metaphor. Since a common, underlying theme is that living systems cannot be understood by conventional linear thinking that decomposes a system into its basic elements and their relationships, we have called this the nonlinear systems metaphor. Like the organism metaphor, the nonlinear systems metaphor has origins in the biological sciences. However, unlike the biological organism metaphor, which deals with an organism and its environment as distinct entities, nonlinear systems deal with entire ecosystems as a whole. Although not a cohesive single view, together these ideas of complex systems challenge many of the traditional theories about how organizations operate.

One aspect of this view is that any dichotomy between an organization and its environment is an artificial one. Humberto Maturana and Francisco Varela, two Chilean biologists, introduced the concept of *autopoiesis* in the 1970s, referring to closed autonomous self-referential systems that are capable of renewing and maintaining themselves (Varela, Maturana & Uribe, 1974). Although originally applied to living cells, the idea of autopoiesis has been generalized to a variety of situations including accounting (Robb, 1991), law (Teubner, 1988), and to human thought and social institutions (Maturana & Varela, 1980, 1987). In effect, Maturana and Varela have argued that living systems are self-referential because a system cannot enter into interactions with other systems in its environment that are not defined in the same pattern of relationships that define the system itself. Thus, how a system interacts with its environment is really a reflection of its own organization; the environment is really part of the system. We can draw an artificial boundary between the system and its environment, but when we do, we fail to understand the totality of relations that define the system. In this view, changes do not arise from external influences but from variations within the overall system that modify the mode of organization. In essence, the whole is more than the sum of its parts and can only be understood as a whole. Organizations and their environments are best viewed as elements of the same interconnected pattern. In biological evolution it is that pattern that evolves.

Morgan (1986) has identified some implications of this view for business organizations. For example, he argued that what he calls egocentric organizations run into problems when they view the environment as "out there" and fight to impose their notion of who they are on this environment at all costs without considering the wider system of relations in which they exist. As an example, Morgan cites the action of the commercial fishing industry which has depleted the resources on which their very businesses rely.

The other aspects of the nonlinear systems metaphor are *complexity theory* and *chaos theory*. Although there are technical distinctions between these two theories, there are overall more similarities than differences. For our purposes, we will consider them together. According to Morgan (1986) the essence of this view is that complex nonlinear systems, such as organizations and their environments, are defined by systems of interactions that are both ordered and chaotic. Because of this, small, random disturbances can produce unpredictable events that are transmitted throughout the system. However, despite the unpredictability, order always emerges out of the chaos. For most people, this theory is identified with the famous but false image of a small change as insignificant as a butterfly flapping its wings in one part of the world influencing the weather in another distant part of the world.

Among the implications of this metaphor are that changes cannot be completely controlled and managed but "emerge" from the complex interactions within the system. It is the job of the manager or leader to interpret these events and play a more enabling rather than controlling role. Plowman et al. (2007) provide an interesting account from this viewpoint of change at one organization.

Models of Organizational Change

There are many models of organizational change that have been proposed over the years. We will not review all of them here. See Cameron and Green (2004) for a more thorough review.

LEWIN'S FORCE FIELD ANALYSIS

Lewin's (1951) ideas about organizations and change are heavily influenced by the biological organism metaphor and by general systems theory in particular. In Lewin's view, organizations, like biological organisms, attempt to maintain equilibrium (*homeostasis*) in response to change (disruptions). In other words, there are forces that naturally oppose change to maintain the status quo. In his force field analysis, Lewin argues that the driving forces for change must be greater than the resisting forces for change to occur. Moreover, these resisting forces will continue to push the organization back toward the previous status quo unless action is taken to prevent it. This leads to Lewin's three-step model of change. The first step involves unfreezing the current state of the organization by specifying why the current state is no longer tenable and proposing a desired future state. This also involves defining the driving and resisting forces and ways to increase the driving forces and reducing the resisting forces. The next step is to move to the new state by involving all members of the organization. However, these two steps by themselves are not enough because of the tendency of the organization to return to its previous state of equilibrium. Therefore a third step, or refreezing, is necessary to cement the new state of equilibrium by establishing policies and standards that reinforce the new state of the system.

Lewin's ideas have had considerable impact on the organizational change literature and management practice. The notion of driving and resisting forces of change is well ingrained in management thought, and his system view has influenced many other theorists on organizational change, such as Peter Senge whom we will discuss in the following sections. However, in practice, Lewin's ideas have been watered down into a three-step process that more reflects the machine metaphor: planning the change, implementing the change, and a post-change review. Without a thorough "refreezing," many organizations find themselves drifting back to the original state that existed before the change. In other words, the changes don't stick.

KOTTER'S EIGHT-STEP MODEL

Probably the best known and widely cited of the change models is the eight-step model formulated by Kotter (1995, 1996) after observing a large number of organizations and their change efforts. For Kotter, successful change efforts must proceed through the eight steps in order, with each step building on the preceding steps.

1. Establish a sense of urgency.
2. Create a guiding coalition.
3. Develop a change vision.
4. Communicate the vision for buy-in.
5. Empower broad-based action.
6. Generate short-term wins.
7. Never let up. Continue to press for change. Hire and promote those working toward the vision.
8. Incorporate changes into the culture. Changes must be institutionalized.

The influence of the machine, political, and organism metaphors can all be seen in Kotter's model. In particular, the influence of Lewin can be seen in that the first four steps can be interpreted as the "unfreezing" step; the fifth and sixth steps can be interpreted as the "move" phase; and the seventh and eighth steps as the "refreeze" stage. The machine metaphor is evident from the general absence of the individuals from the model, and the first step of establishing a sense of urgency is designed to counter the political influences of the organization.

Kotter's model has had a major impact on change-management practices over the last decade and a half. The difficulty in practice, according to Cameron & Green (2004), is the tendency for upper levels of management to be enthusiastic and involved in the first four or five steps and then delegate the later planning and execution steps to lower levels of the organization while withdrawing from the process. This often leads to change efforts not being refrozen in Lewin's terms and the organization drifting back to the status quo. In fact, Kotter (2012) has recently suggested that this model of change may not be sufficient in an era of relentless change.

BECKHARD AND HARRIS CHANGE EQUATION

The views of Beckhard and Harris (1987) are heavily influenced by the biological organism metaphor of the organization. There are slightly different versions of their change equation. Our version here is based on the discussion in Cameron & Green (2004),

$$C = f(A, B, D) > X \qquad (12\text{-}1)$$

where C is change, f means "is a function of," A is the level of dissatisfaction with the status quo, B is the desirability of the proposed change or end state, D is the practicality of the change (how minimal is the risk and disruption), and X is the "cost" of changing (often stated as the resistance to change).

In words, the equation states that the amount of change will be a function of the extent to which the level of dissatisfaction with the status quo, desirability of the proposed future state, and the practicality of the change exceed the perceived cost of changing. The functional form is often written as a multiplicative one.

$$C = A \times B \times D > X \qquad (12\text{-}2)$$

This equation has important implications for change. Principally it means that a high level on one factor cannot compensate for a very low value on another. For example, if the level of dissatisfaction with the status quo is zero, nothing about desirability or practicality can produce change. Similarly if the practicality of change is zero, then no level of dissatisfaction or desirability can produce change.

Although less influential than Kotter's eight-step model, the Beckhard and Harris equation serves to focus discussion on the individuals in the organization and the factors that influence the amount of change that may be possible. Notice that these factors are largely perceptual in nature. The perceived dissatisfaction, desirability, practicality, and "cost" are what will drive the amount of change.

PETER SENGE

In his writings, Peter Senge operates from a distinct systems theory point of view, which is influenced both by the "organization as organism" and "organization as nonlinear system" metaphors. In fact, the fifth discipline in the title of his first book (Senge 1990) refers to *system thinking* which ties the other disciplines together. However, Senge does not really offer a model, in the sense of the Beckhard and Harris change equation, or a how-to-manual, such as the eight step approach of Kotter. Rather both of his major works, Senge (1990) and Senge, et al. (1999), are written to stimulate thought and discussion about the nature of organizations and organizational change rather than to define a recipe for bringing about that change. Perhaps his greatest contributions are in emphasizing systems thinking (i.e., the whole is more than the sum of its parts) and the influence of mental models on how we view the organization and approach change.

Individual Change

Recalling our maxim "Organizations don't change, people do," any discussion of organizational change is incomplete without some discussion of how individuals in the organization respond to change efforts.

Cameron & Green (2004) identify four different approaches to individual change, which have some similarities to the organizational metaphors discussed previously. As with the metaphors, each of the approaches has some important ideas about change, but no one approach has all of the answers.

THE BEHAVIORAL APPROACH

The behavioral approach gets its name from prominent behaviorists in the field of psychology such as B.F. Skinner. This approach focuses on behaviors only and how behaviors can be changed through the use of positive (reward) and negative (punishment) reinforcement. In this approach, the objective is to reward desired behaviors with positive reinforcement and use negative reinforcement with undesirable behaviors. The reinforcements used can be financial or non-financial in nature. Behaviors that receive positive reinforcement should increase in frequency and those that receive negative reinforcement should decrease in frequency.

A pure behavioral approach to managing change is often closely associated with the "machine" metaphor of organizational change mentioned earlier. It tends to assume that individuals dislike work and need to be controlled and directed via reinforcements to get them to perform. This approach in its extreme totally ignores what individuals are thinking about the proposed changes or their emotional responses to change. The behavioral approach is useful, however, in that it focuses attention on the fact that the reward systems of the organization may need to be revised in order to be in sync with the desired behaviors under the proposed organizational change.

THE COGNITIVE APPROACH

As opposed to the behavioral approach, the cognitive approach focuses not on employee behaviors but rather on their values, beliefs, attitudes and feelings and how these influence their behaviors. This approach tends to focus on goals and the setting of appropriate objectives and can be seen quite clearly in Kotter's eight-step model of organizational change. The creation of a sense of urgency and development and communication of a vision are all designed to convince the individuals in the organization that the change is both necessary and beneficial.

A good example of the cognitive approach has been developed by Prosci, a change-management consulting and training company. Although their change model does include a reinforcement component similar to the behavioral approach, the main focus is on attitudes, emotions, and knowledge. Their model of individual change is called ADKAR for the five key building blocks of individual change.

A: Awareness of the need for change
D: Desire to participate in and support the change
K: Knowledge of how to change
A: Ability to adopt required skills and behaviors
R: Reinforcements needed to sustain the change.

Hair (2006) contains a more detailed description of these building blocks, the factors that influence them, and some of the tools that can be used to develop them. Table 12.1 contains a summary of the five blocks and some of the influence factors.

Table 12.1 ADKAR Building Blocks and Influence Factors

Awareness of the need for change	An individual's view of the current state of the organization
	How an individual perceives problems (mental model)
	Credibility of the sender of need to change messages
	Circulation of misinformation and rumors
	Contestability of the reasons for change
Desire to participate in and support the change	What the change is and how it will impact the individual
	Individual's perception of the environmental and organizational context of the change
	The individual's personal situation
	The intrinsic motivators unique to the individual
Knowledge of how to change	Current knowledge base of the individual
	Capability of the individual to gain additional knowledge
	Organizational resources available for education and training
	Existence of and access to the required knowledge
Ability to adopt required skills and behaviors	Psychological blocks
	Physical capabilities
	Intellectual capabilities
	Time available to develop needed skills
	Availability of resources to support the development of new skills

Reinforcement needed to sustain change	The degree to which the reinforcement is meaningful to the individual
	The association of the reinforcement with actual demonstrated progress or accomplishment
	The absence of negative consequences
	An accountability system that creates ongoing reinforcement of the change

Source: Adapted from Prosci website, http://www.prosci.com/adkar-model/overview-3/. Last visited on 1/8/2014.

THE PSYCHODYNAMIC APPROACH

What Cameron and Green (2004) call the psychodynamic approach is a recognition that change can be traumatic for many individuals in the organization and that these individuals can go through different psychological states during the period of change. The origins of this approach lie in the familiar research of Elisabeth Kubler-Ross (1969) on death and dying. In working with terminally ill patients, Kubler-Ross realized that the patients would typically pass through five stages in dealing with this profound change in their lives: denial, anger, bargaining, depression, and acceptance. The argument of the psychodynamic approach is that individuals in organizations undergoing change, although obviously not as traumatic as death and dying, can go through similar stages as they deal with change.

The ideas of Virginia Satir, a family therapist, also fit within this framework (e.g., Satir et al., 1991). In this model, individuals (and families in Satir's work) normally operate in a state of maintaining the status quo (equilibrium). This changes when what Satir calls a foreign element is introduced. In our context this would be some agent of change. After this, a period of chaos occurs in which the individual's world seems turned upside down, efforts to maintain the status quo are increased, and elements of anger can appear. During this period of chaos, an idea or insight occurs that is the beginning of acceptance in Kubler-Ross's model. Satir calls this the transforming idea. This insight allows the individual to begin to integrate the foreign element into a new status quo. The Satir model has been incorporated into Weinberg's (1997) model of change in software organizations.

The main contribution of the psychodynamic approach is to call attention to the range of emotional reactions that individuals may go through during a change process. The Satir model also stresses the importance of a transforming idea which allows the individual to modify his or her old model of the world or integrate the foreign element into a new model of the status quo.

THE HUMANISTIC PSYCHOLOGY APPROACH

Humanistic psychology arose in reaction against two dominant forces in psychology in the last century, namely behaviorism and psychodynamic psychology (Freudian psychoanalysis). Humanistic psychology emphasizes the whole individual and each individual's inherent dignity and stresses the importance of personal growth and self-actualization. Perhaps the best-known representative of this approach in the management literature was Abraham Maslow. Maslow is best known for the Maslow hierarchy of needs, shown in Figure 12.1.

As a theory of motivation, Maslow believed that the lower-level needs, such as physiological needs of hunger and thirst and safety needs, have to be satisfied before the higher-level needs have a motivational impact. As the lower-level needs are satisfied, the

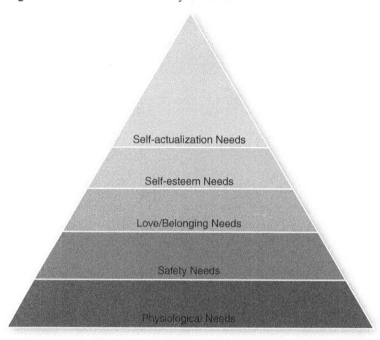

Figure 12.1 Maslow's Hierarchy of Needs

Source: Adapted from Maslow, 1954.

higher-level needs become important motivators. The highest level, and the one humans strive toward, according to Maslow, is self-actualization, which means, in the words of a well-known television commercial, "to be all that you can be." According the humanistic psychology approach, humans are driven to grow and achieve their fullest potential, i.e., self- actualization.

The principal contribution of the humanistic psychology approach is to point out that people are motivated by different things and that the traditional reward in most organizations (money) is not even the most important one.

Leading Change

There is a vast literature on leadership that we will not address here. Rather, we are concerned exclusively with leader behavior in a change situation. This is still a vast literature, and our goal here is to simply highlight some of the salient ideas.

SELLING THE URGENCY OF CHANGE

Most accounts of change management begin with detecting and communicating the need for change, the "vision" thing. This relates to steps 1, 3 and 4 of the Kotter model of change and the A for awareness in the ADKAR model of individual change. In many accounts, the vision is designed to create a sense of urgency, the "burning platform," and is generally viewed as the responsibility of change leadership (See sidebar Boeing and the burning platform). Hurst (1995) talks of creating a crisis to induce organizational change. In his *Harvard Business Review* interview, Katsuaki Watanabe, then CEO of Toyota, talked about similar measures used at Toyota (Stewart and Raman 2007).

> **Boeing and the Burning Platform**
>
> In the 1990s, aerospace giant Boeing initiated large scale changes in how they conducted their business in response to several "learning" trips to Japan and the many perceived threats on the horizon. To create a sense of urgency, they had a local Seattle television station produce a film for them that showed the Boeing Renton plant (at that time the plant most identified with the company as a whole) with a deserted parking lot and the building boarded up with tumble weeds blowing by. This was accompanied by very serious sounding music and a voice narration set in the not-too-distant future. The obvious message of this film to employees was that unless changes were made immediately, Boeing would not exist in a few years. This film, shown at employee meetings, had an immediate and visible impact on the employees of Boeing.

However, the use of "fear" as a motivator for change should be exercised with caution. Eckes (2001) has argued that fear can be an effective motivator in the short term, but will usually fail in the long run.[3] Heath and Heath (2010) have noted that fear is a terrible motivator when new behaviors are desired since it usually leads to tunnel vision and going back to the "tried and true" way of doing things.

An added danger is that if the burning platform approach is used too often it will eventually cease to have its intended impact on the employees of the organization as they become immune to the implied threats. It is common in the change literature to find references to employees simply "tuning out" the urgency messages because they have heard them so many times before.

THE ROLE OF THE LEADER

Although there is wide agreement in the change management literature that the role of a leader or group of leaders is crucial to any change situation, there is much less agreement on what that role should be and how important it is to the success of the change effort.

The dominant view of change leaders is that they reside in the highest levels of the organizational hierarchy and have positions with a great deal of authority. Their role in the change process depends upon one's view of the organization in terms of the four organizational metaphors. In the machine metaphor the change leader is the designer and implementer of change. The leader makes the case for change, designs the changes, and then orders the implementation of the changes. The political system metaphor is similar, with the added notion of the leader as politically powerful in the organization and a visionary speaker and charismatic leader.

Hurst (1995) has called the traditional view of the change leader the "rational manager" view. The rational change manager changes the organization in a rational fashion much like a craftsman using their tools. Change is primarily a technical problem and the change leader is outside and above the change. Hurst argues that this intellectual detachment of the designers and managers of the change from the process itself should be identified as the leading cause of failure of organizational change efforts.

---

3. An example used by Eckes is Billy Martin who was a famous player and later manager in major league baseball. Martin was known for a volatile temper and "fear" played a major part in his management style. His career was highlighted by successful transformations of losing teams into winners in a short time period. However, after a few years those successes disappeared as his temperament and leadership behaviors began to wear on the players and other members of the organization.

In the biological organism metaphor of the organization, the role of the leader acts as coach, counselor, and consultant who guides the organization through change. Thus the change leader is an active participant in the change process, but is not necessarily the chief architect of the change, nor its main advocate.

In the nonlinear systems metaphor, the leader is a facilitator of change, which emerges from outside or from within the organization. As in the biological organism view, the leader is neither the main designer of the proposed change nor its main cheerleader. Rather the change leader uses the resources at their disposal to facilitate and smooth the way for change.

Cameron and Green (2004) have argued that the different stages of the change process require different leadership styles, both in terms of the observable behaviors of the leader, but also in the inner traits required in the leader. Thus inner traits and outer behaviors that might serve the leader well during one stage of the process may not be positive assets at another stage. Therefore, leaders have to be constantly aware of the current stage of the change process and what is required of them at that stage.

Some have argued that the differing requirements imposed on change leaders mean that no single individual can file the role. Rather, multiple leaders need to be involved in any successful change initiative, and that these leaders are not just located at the top levels of management. Senge et al. (1999) argue that little significant change will occur if strictly driven from the top of the organization and that senior executives do not have as much power to create change as they think. Rather, they argue that the organization needs to develop a community of interdependent leaders across the organization. Pascale & Sternin (2005) call these people the company's secret change agents or positive deviants. Hammer (2004) called them catalysts, and Heath and Heath (2010) call them "bright spots." All three sources argue that these change leaders exist in most organizations and are already doing things in a radically better way. The key is to find these bright spots or positive deviants as Pascale and Sternin call them, and use them to achieve organizational change. Pascale and Sternin (2005) call this the positive deviance approach as opposed to the traditional approach to change. An excellent example of this approach is provided by Bevington & Sampson (2012, P. 89-90). In this example, a retail pharmaceutical company had two "rogue" sales people who outperformed all of their counterparts, but were known for their unconventional behavior, and were even targeted for dismissal by some of their superiors. During a review of problems related to product returns, it was discovered that the unconventional activities of these rogue sales people actually reduced wasteful product returns to virtually zero. Adopting their methods across the sales force increased sales penetration by 30 percent over a six-month period and virtually eliminated product returns.

Resistance to Change

One of the most widely cited consequences of organizational change is the inevitable resistance of many individuals in the organization against the proposed changes. The traditional view of resistance to change is that this resistance is an irrational response on the part of employees that must be overcome by management for change to occur. This is one reason for the heavy emphasis in most change models on steps such as establishing a sense of urgency, developing a change vision, and communicating the vision to obtain buy-in. The most common recommendations for countering resistance involve communication, both to reduce fear and increase understanding of the need for change, and employee involvement in the change process. Since resistance to change is viewed as an irrational response, most of the methods to reduce that resistance are rational appeals. However, a different view of resistance to change comes from modern cognitive psychology.

Although psychologists have long discussed emotional responses to events as the opposite to rational responses, this distinction has gained recent attention through the work of people such as the Nobel Prize winner Daniel Kahneman. Kahneman (2011) proposes that the human brain formulates thoughts in two different ways. System 1 is subconscious, intuitive, emotional, and very fast while System 2 is conscious, calculating, logical and slow.[4] System 1 can be equated with the old managerial admonition to "trust your gut" when making decisions, while System 2 is more like the analytical approach to decision making. This notion of two different modes of thought was extended by Jonathan Haidt to concepts such as happiness (Haidt, 2006) and moral reasoning (Haidt, 2012) and by Chip and Dan Heath for change (Heath and Heath, 2010). Heath and Heath (2010) adopt the elephant and rider metaphor first used by Haidt (2006) to explain recent findings in the social sciences about what makes change so difficult. The elephant is the emotional, subconscious, System 1 side of thinking. The elephant has great passion and drive but is short term in its thinking and into instant gratification. The rider is the rational, logical, System 2 side. The rider thinks more logically and has a more long-term viewpoint but the rider can be indecisive and overanalyze things. Heath and Heath (2010) also added the concept of the path that the elephant, ridden by the rider, walks on. The path is the situation or environment. Often change can happen simply by modifying the environment. The rider appears to be in charge of the elephant, but the rider's control is limited. In a test of wills, when the rider and the elephant are in conflict, the elephant usually wins because of its size and physical power.

To achieve change in this metaphor, you must direct the rider, motivate the elephant, and shape the path. Failure to do these things can lead to failure to change. To summarize the basic thesis, Heath and Heath (2010) offer the following guidelines:

- Direct the rider
  - Follow the bright spots (positive deviants). Investigate what is already working in the organization and use it.
  - Script the critical moves. Think in terms of specific behaviors that need to change.
  - Point to the destination. Let the rider know where he or she is going and why the destination is worth it.
- Motivate the elephant
  - Find the feeling. The elephant is motivated by emotions, not logic.
  - Shrink the change. Break down the change into smaller parts so as to not frighten the elephant.
  - Grow your people. People are motivated more by a sense of identity, "who am I," than by the consequences of decisions or change.[5]
- Shape the path
  - Tweak the environment. Change the situation so that behaviors change.
  - Build habits. When behavior is habitual it doesn't tax the rider.
  - Rally the herd. The elephant tends to follow the herd so make sure the herd is going in the right direction.

The Future of Change Management

With the exception of Japan, with its long history of continuous improvement, change management has largely been viewed as one-time projects. The change has a definite beginning and ending point and may even be scheduled like a project. Employees working on the change do so in addition to their regular job duties. Most large organizations have a multitude of change projects going on at any one time but the projects have very little overall coordination and usually involve very different personnel.

---

4. Note that this is not the traditional left brain/right brain distinction that has been largely debunked by modern brain research.
5. Hurst (1995) has made the argument that basic values are very important in times of change and that strong organizational values are the anchor of successful change.

In an increasingly complex and changing business climate, this view of a change project as a unique event is beginning to change. Starting with Peter Senge's notion of a learning organization (Senge, 1990; Senge et. al., 1999), many have argued that the traditional notions of implementing periodic organizational changes in response to events in the business environment are not enough [e.g., Hamel and Zanini (2014)]. Even Kotter (2012) argues that the traditional approach to change is not sufficient anymore. As Fishman (1997) has put it, "Instead of an external program, change today is intrinsic to business, an integral expression of how any successful business operates." There is growing agreement that the traditional hierarchical organizational structure is not up to the task of managing continuous organizational change. What is needed is a new model of the organization that takes into account that change is an ongoing process for any organization. What is needed is what Gossage, Silverstone & Leach (2010) call a change-capable organization. We will return to this discussion in Chapter 13 when we discuss building the process enterprise.

Chapter Glossary

Autopoiesis The property of a system that allows material inflow and outflow while maintaining their structure through self-regulation and self-reference.

Chaos theory A part of complexity theory that attempts to explain complex phenomena with a mathematical framework of nonlinear systems. It predicts that small changes in initial conditions can lead to large differences in outcomes, making such systems inherently unpredictable.

Complexity theory Attempts to explain complex phenomenon without breaking the system down into component parts. Believes that these phenomena consist of interconnected networks of components that interact using simple rules, which produces complex behavior.

Homeostasis The property of a system such that manipulations produce relatively stable and constant conditions, i.e., equilibrium.

System thinking Idea that the components parts of a system can be understood only in relationship with each other and the system as a whole rather than as separate elements. Problems with the system must be viewed holistically.

Chapter Questions and Problems

1. Compare and contrast how the four approaches to individual change would view the problem of resistance to change. How would they compare with the ideas in Heath and Heath (2010)?

2. Recall a successful personal change that you have made in your life. What factors helped the change be successful? Recall an attempted change in your life that was not successful. What factors hindered the change process?

3. Analyze Kotter's eight-step model in terms of the four approaches to individual change. What do these different perspectives have to say about how Kotter's model would work in practice?

4. Discuss the implications of the Beckhard and Harris change equation for managing organizational change. If we adopt the organization as a nonlinear system point of view, how would this impact our perceptions of the Beckhard and Harris model?

5. Describe how the different approaches to individual change (behavioral, cognitive, humanistic psychology, and psychodynamic) are reflected in the change ideas of Heath and Heath (2010). Which approach do you think is most prevalent? Explain your reasoning.

References

Beckhard, R.F., & Harris, R.T. *Organizational Transitions: Managing Complex Change,* 1987, Reading, MA: Addison-Wesley.

Beer, M. Research That Will Break the Code of Change: The Role of Useful Normal Science and Usable Action Science, a Commentary on Van de Ven and Argyris. In M. Beer & N. Nohria (Eds.), *Breaking the Code of Change*. 2000, Boston: Harvard Business Press.

Bevington, T., & Samson, D. *Implementing Strategic Change: Managing Processes and Interfaces to Develop a Highly Productive Organization*, 2012, London: Kogan Page.

Bridges, W., & Mitchell, S. Leading Transition: A New Model for Change. In F. Hesselbein & R. Johnson (Eds), *On Leading Change*. 2002, New York: Jossey-Bass.

Cameron, E., & Green, M. *Making Sense of Change Management*, 2004, London: Kogan Page

Carr, C. *Choice, Chance & Organizational Change: Practical Insights from Evolution for Business Leaders & Thinkers*, 1996, New York: AMACOM.

Eckes, G. *Making Six Sigma Last: Managing the Balance Between Cultural and Technical Change*, 2001, New York: John Wiley & Sons.

Elrod, P. D. II, & Tippett, D.D. The Death Valley of Change. *Journal of Organizational Change Management*, 2002, 15, 273-292.

Fishman, C. Change, *Fast Company*, April-May, 1997. http://www.fastcompany.com/28199/change. Last accessed on 1/17/2015.

Gossage, W.G., Silverstone, Y. & Leach, A. The Change-capable Organization. *Outlook: The Journal of High-Performance Business*, 2010, 3, 1-11. http://www.accenture.com/SiteCollectionDocuments/PDF/Accenture Outlook Change Capable Organization.pdf. Last accessed on 1/17/2015.

Haidt, J. *The Happiness Hypothesis: Finding Modern Truth in Ancient Wisdom*, 2006, New York: Basic Books.

Haidt, J. *The Righteous Mind: Why Good People Are Divided by Politics and Religion*, 2012, New York: Vintage Books.

Hair, J.M. *ADKAR: A Model for Change in Business, Government, and Our Community*, 2006, Loveland, CO: Prosci Learning Center Publications.

Hamel, G., & Zanini, M. Build a Change Platform Not a Change Program. *McKinsey & Company Insights and Publications*, 2014. http://www.mckinsey.com/insights/organization/build a change platform not a change program. Last accessed 1/20/2015.

Hammer, M. Deep Change: How Operational Innovation Can Transform Your Company. *Harvard Business Review*, 2004, 82, 4, 84-93.

Heath, C., & Heath, D. *Switch: How to Change Things When Change is Hard*. 2010, New York: Broadway Books.

Hughes, M. Do 70 Per Cent of All Organizational Change Initiatives Really Fail? *Journal of Change Management*, 2011, 11, 4, 452-464.

Hurst, D.K. *Crisis & Renewal: Meeting the Challenge of Organizational Change*. 1995, Boston, MA: Harvard Business School Press.

Johnson, S. *Who Moved My Cheese?* 1998, New York: G.P. Putnam.

Johnson-Laird, P.N. *Mental Models: Towards a Cognitive Science of Language, Inference, and Consciousness*, 1983, Cambridge: Cambridge University Press.

Johnson-Laird, P.N. *How We Reason*, 2006, Oxford: Oxford University Press.

Kahneman, D. *Thinking, Fast and Slow*, 2011, New York: Farrer, Strauss, and Giroux.

Kotter, J.P. Leading Change: Why Transformation Efforts Fail. *Harvard Business Review*, 1995, 73, 2, 59-67.

Kotter, J. P. *Leading Change*. 1996, Boston, MA: Harvard Business School Press.

Kotter, J.P. Accelerate! *Harvard Business Review*, 2012, 90, 11, 44-58.

Kubler-Ross, E. *On Death and Dying*, 1969, London: Routledge.

Lewin, K. *Field Theory in Social Science,* 1951, New York: Harper & Row.

Maslow, A. H. *Motivation and Personality*, 1954, New York: Harper and Row.

Maturana, H., & Varela, F. Autopoiesis and Cognition: the Realization of the Living. In R. S. Cohen & M. W. Wartofsky (Eds.*), Boston Studies in the Philosophy of Science* 42. 1980, Dordecht: D. Reidel Publishing Co.

Maturana, H. R., & Varela, F. J. *The Tree of Knowledge: The Biological Roots of Human Understanding.* 1987, Boston: Shambhala Publications.

Morgan, G. *Images of Organizations,* 1986, Thousand Oaks, CA: Sage Press.

Pascale, R.T., & Sternin, J. Your Company's Secret Change Agents, *Harvard Business Review,* 2005, 83, 5, 72-81.

Pettigrew, A. M., Woodman, R. W. & Cameron, K. S. Studying Organizational Change and Development: Challenges for Future Research. *Academy of Management Journal,* 2001, 44, 697-713.

Plowman, D.A., Baker, L.T., Beck, T.E., Kulkarni, M., Solansky, S.T. & Travis, D.V. Radical Change Accidentally: The Emergence and Amplification of Small Change. *Academy of Management Journal,* 2007, 50, 3, 515-543.

Robb, F. Accounting – A Virtual Autopoietic System? *Systems Practice,* 1991, 4, 3, 215-235.

Satir, V., Banmen, J., Gerber, H. & Gomori, M. *The Satir Model: Family Therapy and Beyond,* 1991, Palo Alto, CA: Science and Behavior Books.

Senge, P. *The Fifth Discipline: The Art and Practice of the Learning Organization,* 1990, New York: Doubleday.

Senge, P., Kleiner, A., Roberts, C., Ross, R., Roth, G. & Smith, B. *The Dance of Change: The Challenges of Sustaining Momentum in Learning Organizations,* 1999, New York: Doubleday.

Stewart, T.A. & Raman, A.P. Lessons From Toyota's Long Drive: An Interview with Katsuaki Watanabe, *Harvard Business Review,* 2007, 85, 7, 74-83.

Teubner, G. (Ed). *Autopoietic Law: A New Approach to Law and Society,* 1988, Berlin: Walter de Gruyter.

Varela, F.J., Maturana, H.R. & Uribe, R. Autopoiesis: The Organization of Living Systems, Its Characterization and a Model. *Biosystems, 1974, 5,* 187–196.

Weinberg, G. *Quality Software Management: Volume 4, Anticipating Change.* 1997, New York: Dorset House Publishing.

Chapter 13

Building the Process Enterprise

"Business Process Management is primarily an attitude."

—unknown

"... the most important strategic element of a Six Sigma initiative is the creation and maintenance of the Business Process Management System."

—George Eckes

There is general agreement that processes are the only way to create the agile organization needed in times of continuous change in the business climate. Yet despite several decades of work on business processes, the true process enterprise remains a rarity. In fact, there is no widespread agreement on what exactly constitutes a process enterprise. There is widespread agreement, however, that the journey to becoming a process-focused organization is a difficult one with many stumbling blocks along the way. The task of improving key organizational processes as described in earlier chapters is not the problem. Many organizations have been very successful in improving operational efficiency over the last two decades. The difficulty lies in transforming the organization to truly be process focused so that the successes can be sustained. To achieve this, process thinking must become ingrained in the organizational culture and a central element of organizational strategy. In this chapter, we will look at some of the major issues in developing a true process enterprise.

Process Maturity Assessment

Before undertaking any transformation activities, it is a good idea to first assess your organization's current state of process maturity. There are a variety of indexes that purport to measure an organization's process maturity, but most belong to one of two categories. The first type of assessment was developed by Hammer (2007). The second is patterned after the Capability Maturity Model (CMM) developed at Carnegie-Mellon, which was originally aimed at software development rather than general business processes. All of these assessments, of either type, have multiple uses in building a process-based enterprise, including

- Assess the readiness of an organization to undertake a process-based transformation,
- Discover areas of weakness which need development, and
- Assess an organization's progress in developing a process-based enterprise.

PROCESS AND ENTERPRISE MATURITY MODEL (PEMM)

The process and enterprise maturity model (PEMM) was developed by Hammer (2007) as a framework to help organizations plan and execute process-based transformations. The framework consists of five process enablers that determine how well processes will function over time and four enterprise capabilities that are necessary in order for a company to successfully put the process enablers in place.

Process Enablers

- **Design**: How comprehensive is the specification of the process? Includes sub-dimensions of purpose, context, and documentation.
- **Performers**: How capable are those who will execute the process? Includes sub-dimensions of knowledge, skills, and behavior.
- **Owner**: How well specified is the role of the process owner? Includes sub-dimensions of identity, activities, and authority.
- **Infrastructure**: How well developed is the infrastructure to support processes? Includes sub-dimensions of information systems and human resource systems.
- **Metrics**: How well developed are the process metrics? Includes sub-dimensions of definition and uses.

Enterprise Capabilities

- **Leadership**: How strong is the organizational leadership in supporting processes? Includes sub-dimensions of awareness, alignment, behavior, and style.
- **Culture**: How well does the organizational culture support processes? Includes sub-dimensions of teamwork, customer focus, responsibility, and attitude toward change.
- **Expertise**: Is the expertise necessary for the development of processes present in the organization? Includes sub-dimensions of people and methodology.
- **Governance**: Has the necessary governance structure been established? Includes sub-dimensions of process model, accountability, and integration.

Each of these factors is evaluated on a four-part strength scale with each part of the scale accompanied by a statement describing that level of strength of preparedness. The organization is to assess each statement as largely true (coded green for go), somewhat true (coded yellow for caution), or largely untrue (coded red for stop). The pattern of results created by the assessment provides an indication of where the organization is well prepared to transform into a process driven-organization (green), where it is weak and needs strengthening (yellow), and where it needs to do considerable work to prepare for the transformation (red). Obviously this rating

Figure 13.1 A Partial Process Matrix from the PEMM

		P-1	P-2	P-3	P-4	P-1	P-2	P-3	P-4
Design	Purpose	The process has not been designed on an end-to-end basis. Functional managers use design primarily as a context for functional performance improvement.	The process has been redesigned from end-to-end in order to optimize its performance.	The process has been designed to fit with other processes and with the IT systems in order to optimize enterprise performance.	The process has been designed to fit with customer and supplier processes in order to optimize interenterprise performance.	Green	Yellow	Red	
	Context	The process's inputs, outputs, suppliers, and customers have been identified.	The needs of the process's customers are known and agreed upon.	The process owner and the owners of other processes with which the process interfaces have established mutual performance expectations.	The process owner and the owners of customer and supplier processes with which the process interfaces have established mutual performance expectations.				
	Documentation	The documentation of the process is primarily functional but identifies the interconnections among the areas involved in executing the process.	There is end-to-end documentation of the process design.	The process documentation describes the process's interfaces with and expectations of other processes and links the process to the enterprise's system and data architecture.	An electronic representation of the process design supports its performance and management and allows analysis of environmental changes and process reconfigurations.				
Owner	Identity	The process owner is an individual or group informally charged with improving the process's performance.	Enterprise leadership has created an official process owner role and filled the position with a senior manager who has clout and credibility.	The process comes first for the owner in terms of time allocation, mind share, and personal goals.	The process owner is a member of the enterprise's most senior decision-making body.				
	Activities	The process owner identifies and documents the process and sponsors small scale change projects.	The process owner articulates goals and vision of the process; sponsors redesign and improvement efforts; plans and ensures compliance with the design.	The process owner works with other process owners to integrate processes to achieve organizational goals.	The process owner develops a rolling strategic plan for the process, participates in enterprise-level strategic planning, and collaborates with counterparts working with customers and suppliers to sponsor interenterprise process redesign initiatives.				
	Authority	The process owner lobbies for the process but can only encourage functional managers to make changes.	The process owner can convene a process redesign team and implement the new design and has some control over the technology budget.	Process owner controls the IT systems that support the process and any change efforts and has influence over personnel assignments as well as the process budget.	The process owner controls the process budget and exerts strong influence over personnel assignments and evaluations.				
Metrics	Definition	The process has some basic cost and quality metrics.	The process has end-to-end metrics derived from customer requirements.	The process metrics as well as cross-process metrics have been derived from the enterprise's strategic goals.	The process's metrics have been derived from inter-enterprise goals.				
	Uses	Process metrics are used to track performance and drive improvements.	Metrics used to compare process performance to benchmarks, best-in-class performance and customer requirements.	Managers provide metrics to process performers for awareness and motivation. They use dashboards based on the metrics for day-to-day management of the process.	Managers regularly review and refresh the process's metrics and targets and use them in strategic planning.				

Green: Largely True   Yellow: Somewhat True   Red: Largely Untrue

Source: Adapted with slight modifications from Hammer (2007).

system is highly subjective and requires that the organization be completely honest with itself in its self-assessment. Once completed, the matrix provides a detailed roadmap of what needs to be done in transforming the organization and provides a mechanism for tracking progress toward the goal, which is for both process enablers and organizational capabilities to have a rating of largely true. It is highly doubtful that any organization could currently attain this goal. A partial process maturity matrix is shown in Figure 13.1.

BUSINESS PROCESS MATURITY MODEL (BPMM)

The Capability Maturity Model (CMM) was originally developed at Carnegie-Mellon University for the Department of Defense to evaluate the capability of software contractors as part of awarding software contracts. The CMM was first published as a technical paper in 1987 and as a book in 1989 (Humphrey, 1987; 1989). Since that time, the model has become a standard in evaluating the software development process and has been applied to a variety of different areas including such different domains as workforce development. The process version, the Business Process Maturity Model (BPMM), was published by the Object Management Group as a standard in 2008[1]. The model consists of five levels of maturity as shown in Table 13.1.

---

1. The official specification can be accessed at http://www.omg.org/spec/BPMM/.

Table 13.1 Business Process Maturity Model (BPMM)

Level 1: Initial	Business processes are performed in inconsistent and often ad hoc ways with unpredictable results
Level 2: Managed	The work is stabilized within local work units that can be performed in repeatable ways that satisfy the primary requirements of the units. Different work units may perform the processes in different ways.
Level 3: Standardized	Standardized processes are used across work groups with some guidelines that support different business needs. Standard procedures provide economy of scale and provide a foundation for learning based on common measures and experience.
Level 4: Predictable	Process performance is managed throughout the workflow to understand and control variation so that processes become predictable.
Level 5: Innovating	Processes are continuously improved to improve business performance.

Source: Adapted from the Object Management Group (OMG) Released Version 1.0 of BPMM located at http://www.omg.org/spec/BPMM/1.0/. Last accessed on 4/13/2015.

The BPMM provides a framework that is intended to guide organizations from immature, inconsistent processes to mature, disciplined processes. It can be applied to an individual process or the processes of the organization as a whole. There are many variations on this model published by different authors and consultants but most all of them utilize the same five-level framework with different terms sometimes used for each level. For example Level 1 is often described as "chaotic" and level 5 as "optimized." The term innovative is preferred here because the term optimized often implies automation, which should never be the overarching goal of process improvement. Some simple processes may well be automated, but more complex and more important processes will likely never be automated. The term optimized also implies that the process design is now completed and that the process cannot be further improved. In the modern, rapidly changing business environment, such an assumption is very dangerous.

COMPARISON OF THE TWO FRAMEWORKS

There are obvious differences between the PEMM and the BPMM. Perhaps the most dramatic difference is the almost complete absence of any mention of the enterprise or organization factors in the BPMM. There is nothing about organizational culture or about governance issues in the basic outline of the model. The lack of attention to organizational, cultural, and other factors crucial to BPM is a common weakness of maturity models based on the CMM. To be fair, in the full specification of BPMM, some of these aspects are mentioned, but they are not emphasized as much as they are in the PEMM. For example, the term "process owner" is used twice, briefly, in the BPMM specification, and on neither occasion is the role of the process owner addressed in any meaningful way. Yet in the writings of Hammer & Hershman (2010), Jeston & Nelis (2006, 2008), and Jeston (2009), the role of the process owner is considered critical in moving the organization toward being a process-focused enterprise. We will examine some of these aspects of BPM in the later sections of this chapter.

Curtis and Alden (2007), two of the original authors of the BPMM, have criticized the PEMM model of Hammer as being purely descriptive because it has no guidelines on how to move from one level of maturity to another. They claim that the BPMM is better because it contains best practices for moving from one level to the next. However, the OMG version of the maturity model has not achieved widespread acceptance and is rarely used in practice (Harmon 2014).

Power (2007) has also criticized certain aspects of the PEMM, including questioning the need for two different analyses, one for processes and one for the enterprise as a whole. Maybe more telling are his criticisms that the model does not make any connection between the maturity levels and business outcomes, particularly financial results. This criticism can be leveled at all of the maturity models and is an important weakness. Power also criticizes the PEMM model for ignoring strategic alignment, arguing that organizations with different strategies may rightly view process improvement activities in different ways.

THE QUT-BPMM

A recent expansion of the BPMM addresses some of the criticisms of the original model, at least with regard to including more organizational factors. This maturity model was developed at the Queensland University of Technology (QUT) in Australia, and we will refer to the model as QUT-BPMM (de Bruin, 2009; de Bruin & Rosemann, 2005; Rosemann & de Bruin, 2005). Derived using a combination of cross-sectional and longitudinal case studies along with surveys, the QUT-BPMM was designed to provide a more scientific and rigorous framework for measuring process maturity. The model retains the five levels of maturity of the BPMM but adds other components to obtain a multidimensional or holistic model of BPM maturity. The additional components are labeled factors, perspective, organizational scope, and time.

A *factor* is defined as a measurable and independent characteristic of business process management that impacts process performance. The five factors identified in the QUT-BPMM model are information technology, culture, accountability, methodology, and performance. Information technology refers to the commitment and use of technology and information systems to support BPM. Culture relates to the overall awareness, acceptance, and practice of BPM in the organization. Accountability is the extent to which responsibility for BPM practices and performance is assigned and supported for the processes within the organization. Methodology relates to the extent to which well-defined and repeatable techniques for conducting BPM are adopted within the organization. Finally, performance refers to the extent to which the performance of individual processes, and the employees related to the processes, are measured and the resulting metrics utilized by the organization.

A *perspective* is a phase of BPM derived from common BPM life-cycle models in the literature. Perspectives apply to an individual process, or to BPM in general, and are similar to the DMAIC cycle of Six Sigma (see Chapter 11). The five perspectives in the QUT-BPMM model are align, design, execute, control, and improve. The align phase involves aligning the BPM initiatives with the overall strategic plan for the organization. This perspective measures how well this alignment has taken place for an individual process or for all organizational processes as a whole. The remaining four perspectives more directly relate to the life cycle models of designing, executing, monitoring and controlling, and improving processes.

Organizational scope is the unit to which the model is applied, e.g., a department, business unit, subsidiary, or entire corporation. Finally, time refers to the particular point in time at which the model is assessed. The data generated from assessing the same organizational unit at different points in time can be used to measure progress in attaining process maturity.

The five factors combined with the five perspectives yield a total of 25 assessment fields that can be assessed for an organizational unit at a particular point in time. Each of the fields is assessed in terms of both coverage (how extensively the practices are spread throughout the unit) and proficiency (how well they are performed). As it is currently designed, the model does not yield a single overall measure of process maturity for the unit being analyzed, but provides a single numerical value for each of the 25 assessment fields on both coverage and proficiency so that there are two scores for each field. The overall model is shown in Figure 13.2, where the colored rectangles represent numerical ratings on a scale of 1 to 5. Note that the scope factors may be on the basis of time or organizational unit or may not even be used in a given situation.

Figure 13.2 The QUT-BPMM

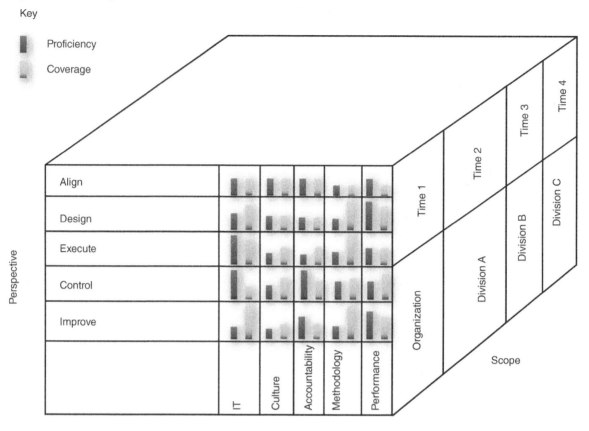

Source: Adapted from Figure 2 in Rosemann, de Bruin & Hueffner (2004).

SUMMARY OF THE MATURITY MODELS

All of the currently available process maturity models have limitations. They are all vulnerable to Power's (2007) criticism that they are not connected to other business outcomes. Failure to connect to financial outcomes is especially a problem in trying to "sell" BPM to senior-level executives in most organizations. Also of concern is the lack of connection to organizational strategy. The QUT-BPMM model is the only one that makes this connection in any meaningful way. Any model that ignores the organizational aspects of maturity in process management is certainly inadequate. The Garvin (1995) interview with CEOs of organizations that were involved with reengineering projects makes it clear that organizational aspects are extremely important.

All of the models also require an individual or group to make the subjective evaluations to use the models. Who these individuals should be is not addressed in the models nor is the issue of how meaningful these evaluations will be. Although there is some evidence with the QUT-BPMM model that measurement issues such as validity and reliability have been addressed in at least a limited way, by and large these issues have been ignored in the literature.

There is much debate in the literature about whether one maturity model is better than another. Van Looy, De Backer, Poels & Snoeck (2013) have even created a procedure for determining which maturity model is the "right" one for a particular organization. However, given the limitations of all of the models and the diversity of needs for different organizations, this question may not be the right one. The right question may well be which elements of the various models are most relevant to a particular organization. For example, some aspects of the models may be most relevant to large businesses with multiple business units in different geographical locations. These aspects may not be relevant to a smaller organization with only one physical location. The "best" maturity model for most organizations may well borrow aspects from more than one different model and be tailored to the specific organization. However, any such model should be attentive to two aspects, connection to organizational strategy and connection to key business outcomes. A maturity model without grounding in organizational strategy and key business performance measures will be of limited utility.

Process Governance

Building a process-focused organization requires adding appropriate organizational structures to support that effort and adopting a governance framework to assign roles and responsibilities and establish controls. Jeston and Nelis (2008) argue that the governance issue is so important that without it BPM is not sustainable in an organization. Similarly, in their seminal book on reengineering, Hammer and Champy (1993) note that one of the major causes of reengineering failures was focusing only on process redesign and ignoring the tremendous organizational changes required. However, that does not mean that an organization begins its transition to a process-based organization by creating a structure for process governance. The need for governance structure arises as an organization increases in process maturity, however modeled. Organizations with low levels of process maturity have little need for formal organizational structures for process governance. Their primary need is for a strong leader with credibility and clout throughout the organization to champion the process transition. The formal process governance structure can grow organically as the organization matures. In fact Jeston (2009) argues that process governance should be kept as simple as possible at the beginning.

The governance structure also needs to be tailored to the specific organization. For example, some of the governance mechanisms that are necessary for large diverse organizations may not be necessary for smaller organizations. Although organizational and governance structures must be tailored to the individual organization and its mission and strategy, there are some common elements that successful process-focused organizations have implemented that we will cover here. The section following this one will examine some of the key organizational changes necessary to build and sustain BPM.

The first question that must be addressed is "What do we mean by governance?" The term governance is used in many different ways by different people and in different contexts. Merriam-Webster Dictionary defines the term as "the way that a city, company, etc., is controlled by the people who run it."[2] The American Heritage Dictionary defines the term with a rather circular definition of "the action, manner, or power of governing."[3] Investopedia defines governance in the business context as "The system of rules, practices, and processes by which a company is directed and controlled."[4] In a BPM context then, governance would mean the system of rules, practices, and processes by which the BPM initiative and all its projects are directed and controlled. Common to all definitions are two central concepts.

- **Responsibility**: Who is to be held accountable for specific duties, tasks, and decisions?
- **Authority**: Who has the power to influence and direct behavior of the members of the organization?

---

2. Merriam-Webster online Dictionary at http://www.merriam-webster.com/dictionary/governance.
3. American Heritage Dictionary at https://ahdictionary.com/word/search.html?q=governance.
4. Investopedia definition of corporate governance at http://www.investopedia.com/terms/c/corporategovernance.asp?ad=dirN&qo=investopediaSiteSearch&qsrc=0&o=40186

GOVERNANCE ROLES

A good starting point in talking about BPM governance then is the specific roles and organizational structures that are often established in the governance of a process-focused enterprise. Unfortunately, there is no standard blueprint for such a structure nor even a common naming convention for the roles involved. Different names used by authors for similar roles are a source of considerable confusion. We will try to simplify the discussion here by focusing on two main sources and attempting to combine their accounts into a single structure. The main sources of material on process governance used here are the two key books related to forming a process-oriented organization: Hammer & Hershman (2010) and Jeston & Nelis (2008). We will also discuss all structures regardless of the maturity state of the organization and clarify how the maturity state relates to that particular role.

Transformation Leader

Becoming process focused is a major undertaking by any organization and requires a strong champion from within the ranks. As noted by Hammer and Hershman (2010) and Jeston (2009), this transformation leader must have sufficient clout to get things done and needs widespread respect throughout the organization. Therefore, in successful organizational transformations, the leader of the effort is usually a top-level executive and in some cases may even be the CEO.

The transformation leader functions as a BPM "cheerleader" in the organization and actively recruits process improvement projects and other process enthusiasts throughout the organization. At the beginning, at least, all of this is normally done in addition to the leader's normal organizational duties.

Process Owner/Process Steward

Outside of a transformation leader, the first role usually identified in process governance is the process owner (Hammer & Hershman, 2010). Jeston & Nelis (2008) use the term process steward for this function. No matter what terminology is used, the process owner or steward is the most important element for any individual process. Finding the right person for this job is critical to the success of the transformation process (Jeston & Nelis, 2008). Indeed, Chang (2006) has argued that a poor process owner of a critical process can do much more damage to an organization than a poor functional manager. Although the exact role of the process owner or steward will vary from one organization to another, and indeed should be tailored to the needs of the organization, there is widespread agreement on certain points. The process owner is responsible for

- the design and documentation of the process,
- the ongoing performance of the process, including its key performance metrics,
- continuous improvements of the process,
- managing the interfaces of the process with other processes and with existing functional roles within the organization, and
- promoting process thinking throughout the organization.

A process owner must have a big-picture view of the organization and how his or her process fits within the overall organizational strategy, and especially how it impacts the ultimate customer. Early on, Hammer (2001) argued that the process owner must be a senior-level executive, but later, Hammer & Hershman (2010) modified this thinking and argued that the process owner does not have to be a senior-level executive but that he or she must have sufficient organizational clout to negotiate with top-level functional managers that are involved in the process. Above all, the process owner must have good communication and negation skills. To a certain extent, the specific requirements for a process owner depend on the type of organizational structure adopted. We will discuss this connection later in this chapter.

Process Executive

Jeston & Nelis (2008) discuss a governance role called a process executive. The p*rocess executive* is basically a supervisor of several process owners or stewards. Therefore, this role is likely only present in larger organizations where there are a large number of process owners. Jeston & Nelis (2008) state that the process executive is likely to be a senior functional executive who is capable of taking a larger organizational viewpoint rather than the more narrow functional view. The key responsibilities of the process executive include

- supporting the work of the process owners or stewards by providing coaching, training, and other resources,
- ensuring that the processes under their jurisdiction are aligned with the organization's strategy and are achieving established performance targets, and
- collaborating across the organizations to resolve problems and issues with other processes or functional areas.

Chief Process Officer (CPO)

Although both Hammer & Hershman (2010) and Jeston & Nelis (2008) discuss a role called the chief process officer (CPO), there is disagreement about the role and timing of its introduction during the process-focused transformation process. The CPO is the point person for the process-based transformation in the organization. Neither Hammer & Hershman (2010) nor Jeston & Nelis (2008) view the CPO as being the "boss" of the process owners. Rather, both regard the position as more of a senior staff position that serves as coach and mentor for all for the process-focused efforts in the organization. However, both have the CPO in charge of the BPM Center for Excellence (see the following section). Jeston and Nelis (2008) do see the process executives reporting to the CPO from a process perspective, but not from a formal reporting point of view.

There is widespread agreement that the CPO role is not one that is established early on the road to becoming a process-focused organization. In other words, the CPO is not the transformation leader. Rather, the role emerges as the organization becomes more process mature. Indeed, Hammer & Hershman (2010) argue that the transformation leader can often morph into the CPO role as the organization matures. Jeston & Nelis (2008) further argue that the role of CPO is transitory and that as an organization becomes fully process mature there will be no need for a CPO because everyone in the organization will be involved with and believe in the power of process. Since there is no known organization that has reached this stage at this point, this is largely speculation.

Many consultants view the role of CPO as a combination of chief operating officer (COO) and chief information officer (CIO). This is not surprising given that the major emphasis of most process improvement projects has been on operational excellence and that information technology is widely regarded as being a major facilitator of process improvement. However, there is not widespread agreement on the role of the CPO, which is not surprising since there are very few good examples of CPOs at this point. Indeed, as Jeston & Nelis (2008) have noted, and several surveys have confirmed, there are currently very few CPO positions in existence anywhere in the world. This paucity of CPOs does not necessarily mean that the role is not important in a process-focused organization. More likely it is simply another indication of the overall level of process maturity in business organizations today. Indeed, there are still predictions for the emergence of this role in the future (Kirchmer, Franz & von Rosing, 2015; Franz & Kirchmer, 2012).

BPM CENTER OF EXCELLENCE (COE)

When a company begins the process-focused journey it typically has sporadic process improvement projects that are disconnected and uncoordinated. Eventually, as the organization begins to reach a more mature stage, it begins to see a need for a central repository for process information and mappings that have been created. If the organization is also serious about becoming a process-focused organization, it makes sense to have a central repository of knowledge and expertise on the technical aspects of BPM such as process modeling and simulation, lean, Six Sigma, and other techniques. The result is a center that begins to serve as the central point for the process activities of the organization. Although these centers go by various names, there is evidence that many organizations are establishing such groups. The most common term used by industry consultants is Center of Excellence (CoE), but Gartner uses the term Business Process Competency Center. Other terms used for the same concept are Center for Business Innovation (Jeston, 2009; Jeston & Nelis, 2008), Process Program Office (Hammer & Hershman, 2010), and Center of Competence (Garimella, 2006). No matter what name is used, such centers provide vital services to an organization undergoing a process transformation. Although the exact structure and roles of the CoE will vary widely from one organization to another, and with organizations at different levels of process maturity, ultimately a CoE should develop four general capabilities (Jesus et al., 2009):[5]

- Diffusion of BPM concepts and benefits
- Creation of convergence of BPM initiatives to increase synergies and consistency
- Alignment of organizational strategies and BPM activities
- Creation of a BPM culture throughout the organization

Diffusion of BPM Concepts

As the center for all that is BPM in the organization, the CoE, along with the CPO if there is one, must take the lead in spreading the word about BPM throughout the organization. It should track and document the successes of early improvement efforts and publicize them widely. It must share its expertise in BPM methodologies and techniques with those in the organization who are trying to implement improvement projects through its process consultants and change experts. The CoE tracks and monitors progress of all improvement projects in the organizations and generally serves as a clearing house for all BPM resources.

Create Convergence of BPM Initiatives

The CoE should gather information on all of the scattered process improvement projects in the organization to incorporate lessons learned in new projects and to develop consistency in approach, tools, and techniques used in improvement projects. From this, the CoE can begin to develop and enforce BPM standards for the organization, which will ensure consistency and improve the likelihood of project success in the future. As the central repository for all process documentation, the CoE is also in the best position to examine the relationships and interconnections between processes and to resolve conflicts between processes when they arise.

Alignment with Organizational Strategy

Process outcomes should be aligned with organizational strategy so that they contribute to the achievement of organizational goals. This means that the improvement outcomes of process design efforts should be directly related to organizational objectives. It also means that the CoE should manage the portfolio of improvement projects so that processes most closely linked with organizational strategy will be implemented before less directly linked projects. In other words, the goal of all improvement projects ultimately should be to achieve the strategic objectives of the organization, not just to improve the performance of a process.

Create a BPM Culture

More than anything else, creating a process-focused organization is about changing the way that employees and managers think about their work, and how what they do relates to the success

---

5. Jesus et. al. combined the last two capabilities into one. However, these two capabilities are sufficiently different that they can stand on their own.

or failure of the organization as a whole. In other words, it is about changing the culture of the organization. As Eckes (2001) noted in the context of Six Sigma, large scale changes are as much or more about changing the culture of the organization than they are about adopting different techniques and methodologies. Following Eckes (2001) symbolically

$$R = BPM \times C \qquad (13\text{-}1)$$

where R stands for the results of the transformation effort, BPM represents all of the methods and techniques of BPM, and C represents the cultural acceptance of BPM. Implicit in this relationship is the implication that if the culture does not change (C=0), the results will be nonexistent as well. We will have more to say about the cultural aspects later in this chapter.

Services Provided by the CoE

Rosemann (2008) developed a list of services that may be provided by a BPM Center of Excellence. A more detailed breakdown of these services, which also includes necessary support and management services required to manage the CoE, are developed in Jesus et al. (2009). In presenting this list of possible services, we do not mean to imply that the CoE must provide all of these services or even that all of them have to exist in an organization at a given moment in time.[6] The structure and services of the CoE must be tailored to each individual organization but the services may include the following:

- **BPM Maturity Assessment**: Ongoing assessment of the process maturity of the organization as a whole, along with that of different parts of the organization, which is important to assessing progress and identifying BPM priorities.
- **Strategic Alignment**: Continual assessment of the alignment of the processes with the mission and strategy of the organization. Processes that are not in alignment need to be changed. This service requires in-depth knowledge of the organization's strategy and mission.
- **Process Modeling**: Maintaining a repository of existing organizational process models, ownership of process modeling tools and methodologies for the organization, and associated training and support services.
- **Library Management**: Maintaining related artifacts such as policies and procedures, business rules, best practices, and other documents and documentation related to organizational processes.
- **Process Improvement**: Providing process analysts with the requisite skills in process analysis, improvement techniques, and change management.
- **Designing Process Aware Information Systems**: Providing IT knowledge and skills necessary to convert process models into any necessary IT components.
- **Process Automation**: Services dedicated to the implementation and execution of business processes including evaluation, selection, and implementation of necessary IT systems and technologies such as Web services and Service-Oriented Architectures (SOA).
- **Process Change Management**: Ensuring consistency of resulting process changes with conceptual process models and support services for organizational change.
- **Management of BPM Projects**: Expertise and skills related to project management methodology.
- **Process Governance**: Services related to setup, maintenance, and training in process governance structures including role descriptions and mediation of cross-process related issues.
- **Process Compliance**: Knowledge about established internal and external requirements for organizational processes. May include monitoring services to ensure compliance with these standards.

---

6. Some of these services, especially those more strategic and companywide in nature, may be located in a Strategic Process Council if it exists.

- **Process Performance Measurement**: Defining appropriate performance metrics for the organization's processes and collection and dissemination of process performance data.
- **Process Forensics**: Knowledge and services related to process-performance failures including root cause analysis and other problem-solving techniques.
- **Process Education and Training:** Continued education and training services related to the philosophy, methods, and techniques of business process management.
- **Process Portfolio Management**: Managing the portfolio of organizational processes including analyses identifying which processes are higher priorities for improvement projects because of changing priorities or business conditions.

Not all of these services need to exist in every organization at every moment in time. Also, some of them may be located in other places in the organizational structure. Typically the needs for some of these services evolve over time as an organization increases in process maturity. Indeed, the need for a CoE may evolve organically as well, rather than being established at the beginning of the journey to becoming a process-focused organization. However, the need for an organizational home for the transformation effort will likely become apparent at an early point in the journey. Panagacos (2012) and Franz & Kirchmer (2012) have more detailed accounts of the types of personnel and skill requirements for a CoE.

STRATEGIC PROCESS COUNCIL

Both Jeston & Nelis (2008) and Hammer & Hershman (2010) hypothesize an additional very senior level governance group called the Strategic Process Council by the former and simply Process Council by the later. This level of governance is primarily for the most process-mature organizations and is largely hypothetical at this point. Such a group would serve as the final authority of all things process and would be composed of very senior-level functional managers, possibly including the CEO, along with the CPO, and other high-level process executives. This group is intended to keep the needs of the organization as a whole in view, serve to mediate disputes between processes, and ensure that the processes are aligned with organizational strategy.

BUILDING A GOVERNANCE STRUCTURE

Governance structures differ widely from one organization to another. There is no one-size-fits-all, and the governance structure needs to be tailored to the organization. However, there are some generalizations that can be made based on the experiences of other companies.

Start Small and Grow Organically

Governance structures should be minimal when an organization first begins the journey to become process focused, and governance structures should be added only when they become necessary. Initially the only structural necessity is the transformational leader. Without a strong champion, the effort will not get off the ground. This is not to say that the movement must come from the top down organizationally. The movement can begin at lower levels of the organization but will very soon need a leader with sufficient organizational clout to make the effort sustainable. To be successful, the right leadership is crucial. Once processes are established, the issue of process ownership will come up naturally. As an organization continues to analyze and model its processes, issues such as what software should be used to model processes, where the process documentation should be maintained, and who will be in charge of that documentation will naturally lead to the possible establishment of some type of central structure to be in charge of things process related. The key is to add the elements when the need for them becomes apparent, not before they are needed.

Select Leaders Carefully

Selecting the right leaders, especially the transformation leader and the owners of key processes, is critical to getting the effort started. The appointment of process owners is perhaps one of the most crucial decisions made in the transformation effort (Jeston, 2009; Hammer & Hershman, 2010). Appointing an owner to a key process who does not have the skills and organizational clout to deal with senior functional managers can doom the transformation efforts from the very beginning.

It is also critical to get senior executives involved as soon as possible. It is difficult to imagine how any type of organizational transformation can proceed very far without the support of the CEO and most senior executives.

Maturity is Important

Many elements of governance make sense only after the organization has progressed a certain distance on the process-focused journey, i.e., when the organization reaches a certain level of process maturity. For example, trying to establish a BPM Center of Excellence when only one or two processes have been documented and only a few employees in the organization are fully onboard, will only add bureaucratic overhead if successful, and likely stifle innovation in process improvement efforts. Add structure only when the organization needs it and is ready for it.

Err on the Side of too Little

When considering how much governance structure is necessary, it is best to err on the side of too little rather than too much. Excessive governance structure can actually lead to reduced efficiency and effectiveness in organizational processes. Make sure that a governance mechanism is actually needed to mitigate business risks or to further the transformation effort before introducing it.

Organizational Structure

Perhaps one of the most contentious issues in developing a process-focused organization is the organizational structure for authority and control. Since most organizations seeking to adopt a process focus are not starting from scratch but rather are working within the confines of an existing organizational structure, there is bound to be a great deal of confusion and tension between required new structural elements and the old existing structure. How to design and manage these conflicting structures is still a difficult issue.

Of course, the traditional structure since at least the time of Alfred P. Sloan at General Motors in the 1920s is the hierarchical structure based around organizational functions, such as marketing, manufacturing, finance, engineering, and so on. Although there are differences in terms of the specific functions represented, the typical structure for most organizations looks something like that depicted in Figure 13.3.[7] Some large companies would also have senior-level executives responsible for particular product lines or geographical locations.

The point of Figure 13.3 is that most organizations have traditionally had a hierarchical structure built around functions that are performed in the organization. Since a "process" is not a function within the organization and most important processes cross organizational boundaries, that leaves the question, "Where do processes fit into the organizational structure?"

There are obviously many different ways of structuring a process-focused organization, but most of the options discussed in the literature are from three general types.

---

7. A bank, for example, would not have a manufacturing or engineering department but may well have an operations function. Also, not all staff functions would report directly to the CEO. However, the reporting relationships will be similar.

Figure 13.3 Traditional Hierarchical Organization by Function

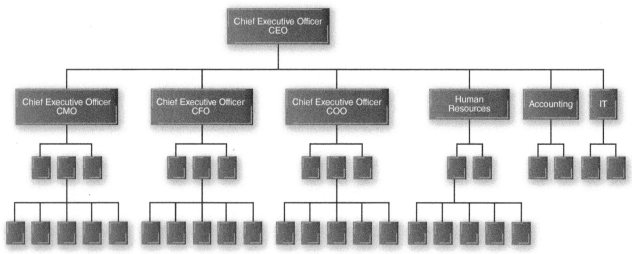

The default option would be for the functional managers to maintain responsibility for the parts of the process that are within their functional area. We will call this the *traditional organization,* which is shown in Figure 13.4. The lack of any color in the process part of the organization indicates that there is no formal hierarchical structure for the process. The blocks lettered A through I represent employees working on parts of a particular process. The arrows in the figure represent reporting relationships. In this case, all employees report to a functional manager. In other words, functional managers directly manage that part of the process that takes place within their functional area.

Although this may seem to be the easiest structure to implement in an organization, in most cases, it is not a very desirable situation. For one thing, this structure maintains the functional silos and the "hand-offs" between functional areas that have historically been so problematic to efficient process performance. In addition, this type of structure creates a difficult reporting relationship for the process owner. If the process owners report to one of the functional managers involved in the process, what is their relationship with the other functional managers involved in the process? How are the inevitable conflicts between different parts of the process involving different functional managers resolved? If one of the functional managers is appointed as a "super manager" in charge of the entire process, charges of favoritism toward their part of the process are inevitable.

Another obvious solution is to replace the functional hierarchy with a process hierarchy where each major process would be a separate branch of the structure under the overall CEO. This is what Chang (2006) calls the *process organization* and is pictured in Figure 13.5. Here the functional units have no formal hierarchical authority, and all process employees report to the process owners. The difficulty with this option is that the traditional functions still need to be performed in the organization. Should these functions be duplicated within each process so that each process has its own human resource function, its own IT function, and so on? While some of these staff functions may be centralized to serve all of the processes, the issue for traditional functions, such as marketing or engineering, are not so clear cut. Some duplication seems inevitable making this a potentially very costly option.

Other potential organizational structures are all derived from what has been traditionally called a *matrix structure.* In matrix structures the organization is organized in two different ways and employees often have two different reporting relationships.[8] In other words, many

---

8. In essence the organization is structured both horizontally and vertically, hence the term "matrix structure."

Figure 13.4 Traditional Organization

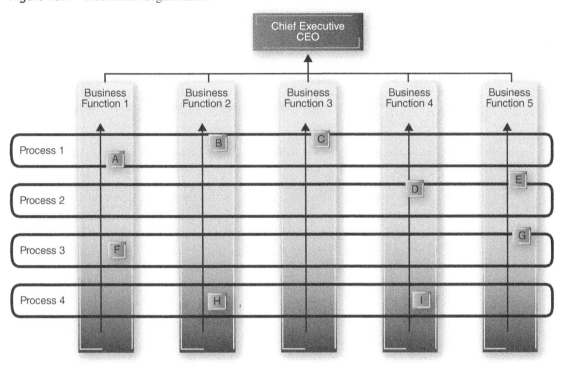

Figure 13.5 Process Organization

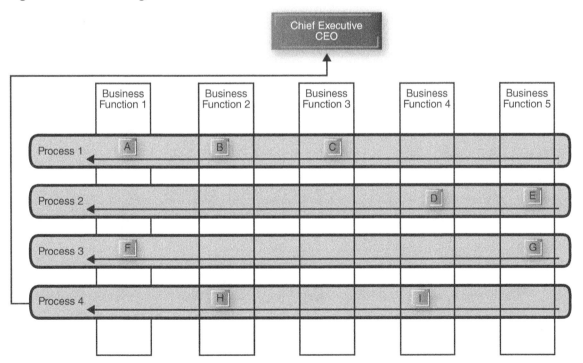

Figure 13.6 Network Organization

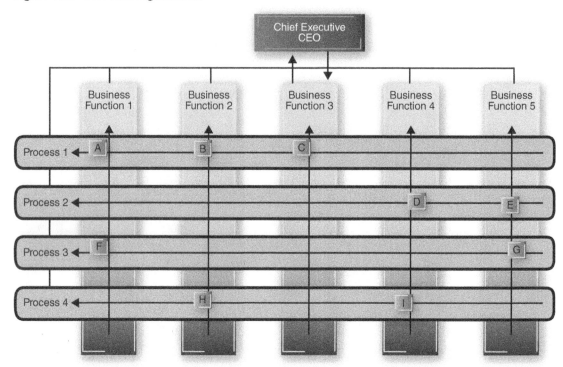

employees have two bosses. In the traditional matrix structure, the organization was usually organized by function and by project and employees would have a reporting relationship with both a functional manager and a project manager for a particular project. In one variant that Harrington & Harrington (1995) call the *case management organization,* employees report to both a functional manager and a case manager who is responsible for providing a particular product or service to a customer.[9] This type of structure has become very popular in industries such as health care, social work, and in the legal profession.

In a process-focused organization, the horizontal dimension would be processes. Following Harrington and Harrington (1995), we will use the term *network organization* to describe such structures. This situation is shown in Figure 13.6.

Borrowing from matrix literature we can distinguish between weak, strong, and balanced structures. The traditional organization depicted in Figure 13.4 is a very strong structure. The process organization shown in Figure 13.5 is at the other end of the spectrum, is a very weak structure. The network organization shown in Figure 13.6 is a more balanced structure located between the two extremes. However, network or matrix organizations are notoriously difficult to manage. The lines of authority can become confused and contentious. Many questions remain to be answered in such structures. For example, where is the formal reporting authority for employees, to the process owner or to the functional manager? What is the nature of the relationship between process owners and functional managers? Although most authors are largely silent on this matter, Jeston & Nelis (2008) argue that the reporting authority should be to the process owner but that the functional structure still performs an important function in the organization and should remain intact. In their view, the relationship between process managers

---

9. The term "case management" comes from the health care industry where employees often report to functional managers but also report to a case manager who is in charge of an individual patient's case from beginning to end.

and functional managers is one of cooperation and collaboration and their authority should be balanced. As you might suspect, this degree of balance can be difficult to attain in an organization where the functional hierarchy has existed for years. Hammer & Hershman (2010) cite two organizational factors that can help in maintaining this balance:

- **Shared goals and metrics**: If process owners and key functional managers are accountable for the same results and evaluated on the same metrics, then they are more likely to find a way to make things work. Competing goals and metrics are likely to be deadly to the needed collaboration.
- **Clear ground rules on authority and decision making**: Clear lines of authority and who is responsible for which decisions are necessary to maintain a balanced working relationship. Unclear lines of authority and a lack of clear decision roles will quickly lead to friction and problems in collaboration.

The difficulty in implementing a workable organizational structure that balances the needs for functionality with the process needs is one of the main stumbling blocks to building a true process-focused organization. Even the most mature process organizations find this transition difficult. As Adler, Heckscher & Prusak (2011) put it, "[M]atrix structures actually offer a huge competitive advantage precisely because they are so hard to sustain."

Necessary Organizational Changes

Building a process-focused organization requires a great deal of organizational change. As Majchzak & Wang (1996) demonstrate, simply changing from a functional organizational structure to a process-oriented structure is not sufficient. In addition to the introduction of governance structures and changes in reporting relationships, there are other organizational changes necessary to become a process focused organization. We will explore some of those issues here.

BUILDING A PROCESS CULTURE

Organizational culture has been defined in many different ways. For our purposes we will define it as the shared set of values, beliefs, and principles that guide the daily behavior and decision making of the members of the organization. There is no doubt that in order for BPM to have a lasting impact on an organization, process thinking must become part of the organizational culture (vom Brocke & Sinnl 2011). As Franz and Kirchner (2012) put it, "If value-driven BPM is going to be more than a one-time project, the different parts of the organization . . . will have to absorb BPM so that it becomes part of the way things get done." Louis Gerstner former CEO of IBM was even more emphatic about the importance of culture when he stated that "I came to see, in my time at IBM, that culture isn't just one aspect of the game—it is the game."

Based on a global Delphi study, Schmiedel, vom Brocke & Recker (2013, 2014) identified four basic components of an organization culture that facilitates BPM, which they label CERT:

- Customer Orientation (C): An attitude of pleasing the customer (both internal and external) of the outputs of a process.
- Excellence (E): An attitude toward continuous improvement and innovation in improving process performance.
- Responsibility (R): A commitment to process objectives and acceptance of responsibility and accountability for process decisions and performance.
- Teamwork (T): A positive attitude toward and identification with cross-functional cooperation

Hammer & Hershman (2010) also identified the factors of customer orientation, excellence, responsibility, and teamwork and offered an additional factor called discipline that they viewed as being part of a BPM culture.[10] A close examination of this additional factor, however, indicates that it is really part of what Schmiedel and colleagues call teamwork. It is the attitude of willingness to work within the team structure rather than valuing individual performance. This is really part of creating what Adler et al. (2011) called collaborative communities. According to Adler et al., (2011) this requires

- creating and communicating a shared purpose,
- cultivating an ethic of contribution,
- developing processes that enable people to work together in flexible but structured ways, and
- creating an infrastructure in which collaboration is valued and rewarded.

So how does one go about building a culture with an attitude of pleasing the customer and seeking continuous improvement and innovation, responsibility, and teamwork? Unfortunately there is no simple roadmap for organizational change. It is a long and difficult process, and the factors that will determine the success of the effort vary from one organization to another. Here we will explore some guidelines suggested by the limited literature on this subject.

Hammer and Hershman (2010) suggest that the starting point should be a clear, honest assessment of the current organizational culture and the organizations past history with regard to change initiatives. Something like the instrument developed by Schmiedel, vom Brocke, and Recker (2014) may help in this regard. Such an assessment should at least provide a background for assessing the difficulty of the change effort, how long it may take, and which cultural components require the most attention.

The process of changing attitudes and values needs to start at the top levels of the organizations. As Hammer and Hershman (2010) state, "If leadership doesn't change, neither will the culture." Employees are not likely to change their attitudes and beliefs if they see their managers acting as if it is business as usual. Therefore, it is vital to obtain buy-in from leadership and all levels of management as soon as possible, and to enlist them in the effort to change the attitudes and beliefs of others in the organization.

At least a rough-cut assessment of the process maturity of your organization should be made. If the maturity level is very low, then changing the organizational culture will require considerable educational efforts concerning what it means to be a process-focused organization and the benefits of moving in that direction. A more mature organization might start working at a higher level on the specific factors related to BPM revealed in the initial assessment of the organization's culture.

Since developing a process-focused organizational culture is a change effort, the material of Chapter 12 relating to change is certainly relevant here. By definition organizational culture is a shared set of beliefs and values, so that changing this culture will not be easy, and there will likely be considerable resistance. Considerable effort will need to be dedicated to mitigating and overcoming this resistance.

Cultural change takes a long time. Eckes (2001) estimated that changing an organization's culture to accept Six Sigma takes from two to three years. Changing the culture to become process-focused will undoubtedly take at least as long, and quite possibly longer. However, changing the organizational culture is critical if the process transformation is to have a lasting impact.

Earlier we defined organizational culture as a shared set of values, beliefs, and principles that guide the daily behavior and decision making of the members of an organization. Ultimately any attempt to change the organizational culture will require changes in the behaviors of

---

10. Hammer & Hershman (2010) use the term "change" when referring to the excellence factor but it is clear from the discussion that this is the same basic concept.

the individual members. The literature in organizational behavior is clear that changes in behavior will not occur without appropriate changes in the reward structures of the organization. It is now time to discuss a critical aspect of the transition to a process-focused organization, namely necessary changes to the organizational employee evaluation and reward structures.

PERFORMANCE EVALUATION AND REWARD STRUCTURES

There is an old adage that says "You can expect what you inspect."[11] In standard management terminology what this quote means is that people will tend to behave in ways consistent with how they are evaluated and rewarded. Therefore, if we want employees to behave in ways consistent with a process culture, we have to evaluate and reward them for the appropriate behaviors. Although this is not the place for a comprehensive review of the vast literature on performance evaluation and rewards, we do want to expand on a few points, most specifically those related to evaluation and reward in process-focused organizations. Most of these observations relate either directly or indirectly to the four basic components of organizational culture in the previous section (CERT).

As much as possible, performance evaluation and rewards should be tied to customer evaluations and metrics. Although not every employee performs process work that directly impacts external customers, all employees have internal customers that use the results of their work.

At least some effort should be made to evaluate and reward process improvement efforts. Although this may be difficult to do on an individual basis, it can be done more easily in terms of group efforts at process improvements.

Evaluate and reward only factors under the employees' control. Traditionally evaluation has been based on individual performance, but not all outcomes are under the control of the individual employee. Deming famously stated that up to 85% of employees performance is due to the system in which they work which is designed by management. Although it is difficult, if not impossible, to separate out the effects of system variables from the individual variables in daily performance, it may be possible for evaluators to have a rough idea of how much of performance is outside the individual employees' control. This is why Kennet & Maisel (1998) recommended that employees be evaluated only on a three-point scale: below system-expected performance, within the system-expected performance range, and above the system-expected performance range. Most of the employee ratings would fall within the system-expected range, with only exceptional cases in the below or above range.

Evaluations and rewards should be focused on process outcomes, not functional ones. It is not uncommon for organizations in the early stages of becoming process-focused to urge employees to be process focused but leave the old functional reward structures in place. The inevitable result will be employees working toward functional goals rather than process goals.

The focus should be on team and group rewards rather than individual rewards. Process work is inherently team work, and the reward structure should reflect this fact. Cooperation and collaboration are the hallmarks of a process-focused organization, and a reward structure should reward that behavior.

DEVELOPING PEOPLE

As Hammer & Champy (1993) made clear, jobs and roles change in a process-focused organization. Jobs are no longer a simple set of tasks to be performed but rather the work is more multidimensional with employees more empowered to make decisions. Also, rather than working

---

11. The source of this quote is in some dispute. Wikipedia attributes this quote to W. Edwards Deming, other sources cite military origins for the quote, and still others attribute the quote to a past president of the American Management Association. http://www.barrypopik.com/index.php/new_york_city/entry/you_can_expect_what_you_inspect_management_adage. Accessed on 7/28/2015.

as individuals, employees are now working in a team environment associated with a particular process or improvement project. Even a cursory reading of the CERT cultural factors described earlier in this chapter makes clear that the type of employees who are comfortable and thrive in a traditional hierarchical command-and-control structure will not prosper in a process-focused organization. This requires changes in the hiring process for new employees and almost always involves some degree of training of existing employees.

In a traditional organization the hiring process typically involves detailing the skills and experiences required to perform a particular job and then finding people with those skills and experiences. Some degree of skill level is obviously still of relevance in hiring in a process-focused organization. However, equally important are such attributes as

- works well with others in a team environment,
- is flexible and able to deal with change,
- accepts personal responsibility and accountable for results, and
- thinks creatively and is focused on outcomes not just on working hard.

Training needs also change in a process-focused organization. In traditional organizations training is primarily in terms of job skills. There is some training in process-focused organizations that is similar in nature, namely training in the use of specific tools related to process design, management, and improvement discussed in sections I, II, and III in this text. However, other training (or, better termed, education) is more general in nature and relates to the philosophical aspects of process-focus and general problem-solving and innovation methods. In general, employee development changes from "training" to "education" with an emphasis on truly developing employees to become more creative and innovative partners in business innovation and improvement, or what Senge (1990) called creating a learning organization. Boeing is a good example of this new emphasis with its Leadership Center near St. Louis and its Learning Together program in which the company has invested more than $1 billion in tuition, books, and fees.

The Future of Process Management

Trying to predict the future is fraught with danger and in general leads to certain failure. However, there is still a need to plan for the future and there are a few trends that have begun to emerge that are likely to continue. We will discuss just a few of them here.

One thing that is relatively easy to predict is that the need for flexibility and responsiveness to change, along with a constant drive for improvement, are not going to go away. The term generally used for this is agility. There is general agreement that efficient well-designed processes that can be quickly redesigned in response to changes in the business environment are the best way to achieve this agility in a rapidly changing world. Agility is more than simply reacting quickly to changes in the environment. As Franz & Kirchmer (2012, p. 188) state, "Agility is the combination of fast reactions and methodical orderly thinking." The focus on processes balances the freedom required to innovate and respond quickly with the need for standardization and order. This implies that the pressure on organizations to become more process focused will only increase in the future.

The tools for designing and improving processes such as lean and Six Sigma are well developed and proven to be capable of producing very efficient processes. The problem is in maintaining the drive for continuous improvement. Brad Power (2010) has talked about the episodic nature of management's emphasis on process improvement which he called "process attention deficit disorder." He compares it to a diet and exercise program where people often start out with great enthusiasm and begin to achieve some results but ultimately lose interest and move on to other matters only to repeat the cycle again later. The point is that continuous improvement and being a process focused organization takes effort. The default is always the status quo, and without management attention the focus on processes and continuous improvement will go away. Toyota has long known this. There are two pillars in the "Toyota Way," namely continuous improvement and respect for people (see Stewart and Raman 2007). Continuous improvement and process focus have to be a "way of life," not a project. This means that management must maintain a focus on processes and, equally important, continue to allocate time and resources to the effort. For this to happen, process will need to become the main focus of senior levels of management. This should lead to rise of the Chief Process Officer (CPO). Although Jeston and Nelis (2008) have predicted that ultimately the role of CPO will fade away as the focus on process spreads throughout the organization, this "visionary state" is still a long way off. This author agrees with Kirchmer, Franz & von Rosing (2015) that the position of CPO will become more common and more visible in the near future.

Discussions of process improvement and design have typically focused on one process at a time. However, processes do not exist in isolation; there are usually connections with other organizational processes. Incorporating interactions with other processes in process planning and design will become an increasingly important focus of research and discussion. Hammer & Hershman (2010) propose that one of the roles of the Strategic Process Council is to ensure that the design of one process to make it more efficient does not negatively impact the performance of another process. However, this presupposes the ability to detect the potential negative interaction between the two processes. Currently there are few tools available even for documenting and visualizing such interactions. The only relevant tools available now are the matrix of change by Brynjolfsson, Austin-Renshaw & van Alstyne (1997), which is based on the house of quality matrix, and the process interaction matrix in Kaganov (1994). With increased emphasis on process automation and the availability of automation components in BPMS software, avoiding the negative effects of suboptimization could become an issue in the future.

BPMS software will continue to evolve and improve. There will be further integration of process modeling and documentation with software development and process automation (Jeson & Nelis, 2008, p. 249-250). Further standards, such as BPMN, will help in this regard. Recent developments in process mining will help in process modeling activities and will likely be gradually incorporated into BPMS software. Process mining occupies the space between data mining and process modeling and involves processing event logs and other event information generated by information systems to extract process-related information (see van der Aalst 2011; Mans, van der Aalst & Vanwersch, 2015). Process mining currently serves three primary purposes:

- Automated discovery of existing processes
- Checking the conformance of executing processes to their design
- Enhancing existing process models

Additional enhancements in the future are likely to make this approach even more useful in BPM.

The drive for process-focused companies is not spread equally in global terms. As they did with other improvement efforts such as just-in-time (lean) and the quality movement, U.S. firms lag behind some other parts of the world in terms of an emphasis on process focus. This is despite the success and widespread adoption in the United States of Six Sigma. Jeston (2009) believes that the most advanced country in the world for BPM is the Netherlands because of their long-term view and logical thinking. In his view countries like the United Kingdom and the United States lag behind because of

- a lack of emphasis on the importance of processes and their improvement in formal education courses,
- the tendency of management to make decisions on the basis of emotion and intuition rather than pure logic,

- the tendency of managers to view process improvement as an overhead or cost rather than a strategic weapon, and
- the lack of courage and boldness to take on a long-term transformation process.

The current author would add two more reasons to this list:

- A culture oriented toward short-term financial results rather than a long-term focus.
- A belief that process improvement is strictly an "operations" issue aimed at costs and is not a strategic concern.

Other factors can certainly be added to this list but the fact remains that process-focused organizations remain rare in these two countries. However, there is hope that the situation will change. Consulting organizations such as Gartner and Accenture are beginning to focus on processes, and the last five or six years have seen publication of more books on process focused improvements. However, Franz & Kirchmer (2012) still predict that emerging market multinationals will lead the way in adopting what they term value-based BPM. Only time will tell.

Chapter Glossary

Factor A measurable and independent element that reflects a fundamental characteristic of business process management and impacts process performance.
Perspective A phase of BPM derived from BPM life-cycle models that applies to an individual process or to BPM in general.
Organizational scope The organizational unit to which the process maturity model is applied.
Process Executive A supervisor of one or more process owners or stewards.
Traditional organization The organizational structure where the functional managers maintain control over the parts of the process that fall within their functional area.
Process organization The organizational structure in which the process owner has control over the entire end-to-end process and there is no formal functional hierarchy.
Matrix structure The organizational structure that is organized around two different factors so that employees have two different reporting relationships.
Case management organization The matrix-type organizational structure in which employees report both to a functional manager and to a case manager who is responsible for providing a particular product or service to a customer.
Network organization The matrix-type organization organized by functional departments and by process.
Organizational culture The shared set of values, beliefs, and principles that guide the daily behavior and decision making of the members of the organization.

Chapter Questions and Problems

1. Which of the three organizational structures (traditional, process, or network) would be the best structure to enable the organization to move toward being a more mature process organization? Provide supporting evidence for your choice.
2. Which of the governance roles do you think would be most important to establish in the beginning of the organization's push to become a process-focused organization? Explain the reasons for your choice.
3. How might the role of the BPM Center of Excellence (CoE) change as an organization goes from a very immature to a process-focused organization?

4. What factors in traditional organizations do you feel cause the greatest difficulty in trying to become process-focused organizations? Explain your reasoning.

5. Outline and explain how the different governance roles might evolve over the different stages from the time an organization first begins its transition with very low process maturity to the time it becomes a fully mature process-focused organization.

6. Comment on the business process maturity model (BPMM) published by the Object Management Group as a model for an organization beginning to undertake the journey to become a process-focused organization. Especially note factors that may be crucial during this journey but are not present in that model.

References

Adler, P., Heckscher, C. & Prusak, L. Building a Collaborative Enterprise, *Harvard Business Review*, 2011, 89, 7/8, 95-101.

Brynjolfsson, E., Austin-Renshaw, A. & van Alstyne, M. The Matrix of Change: A Tool for Business Process Reengineering, *Sloan Management Review*, 1997, 38, 2, 37-54.

Chang, J.F. *Business Process Management Systems: Strategy and Implementation*, 2006, Boca Raton, FL: Auerbach Publications.

Curtis, B. & Alden, J. Maturity Model du Jour: A Recipe for Side Dishes, *BPTrends*, October, 2007. http://www.bptrends.com/bpt/wp-content/publicationfiles/10-07-COL-maturitymodeldujour-CurtisAlden-final.pdf. Last accessed on 4/13/2015.

de Bruin, T. Business Process Management: Theory on Progression and Maturity, 2009, Ph.D. Thesis submitted to Queensland University of Technology. http://eprints.qut.edu.au/46726/1/Tonia_de_Bruin_Thesis.pdf. Last accessed on 5/13/2015

de Bruin, T. & Rosemann, M. Towards a Business Process Management Maturity Model. In Bartmann, D, Rajola, F, Kallinikos, J, Avison, D, Winter, R, Ein-Dor, P, et al. (Eds.) *ECIS 2005 Proceedings of the Thirteenth European Conference on Information Systems*, 2005, Regensburg, Germany.

Eckes, G. *Making Six Sigma Last: Managing the Balance between Cultural and Technical Change*, 2001, New York: John Wiley & Sons.

Franz, P. & Kirchmer, M. *Value-Driven Business Process Management: The Value-Switch for Lasting Competitive Advantage*, 2012, New York: McGraw-Hill.

Garimella, K.K. *The Power of Process: Unleashing the Source of Competitive Advantage*, 2006, Tampa FL: Meghan-Kiffer Press.

Garvin, D.A. Leveraging Processes for Strategic Advantage: A Rountable with Xerox's Allaire, USAA's Herres, Smithkline Beecham's Leschly and Pepsi's Weatherup, *Harvard Business Review*, 1995, 73, 5, 76-90.

Hammer, M. *The Agenda*, 2001, New York: Crown Business.

Hammer, M. The Process Audit, *Harvard Business Review*, 2007, 85, 4, 111-123.

Hammer, M. & Champy, J. *Reengineering the Corporation*, 1993, New York: Harper Business.

Hammer, M. & Hershman, L.W. *Faster Cheaper Better: The 9 Levers for Transforming How Work Gets Done*, 2010, New York: Crown Business.

Harmon, P. Harmon on BPM, *BPTrends*, June, 2014. http://www.bptrends.com/bpt/wp-content/uploads/06-03-2014-COL-Harmon-on-BPM-OMG-BPM-STDS-3.pdf. Last accessed on 5/13/2015.

Harrington, H.J. & Harrington, J.S. *Total Improvement Management*, 1995, New York: McGraw-Hill.

Humphrey, W.S. Characterizing the Software Process: A Maturity Framework, 1987, Technical Report CMU/SEI-87-TR-11, Software Engineering Institute, Carnegie-Mellon University.

Humphrey, W.S. *Managing the Software Process*, 1989, SEI series in software engineering. Reading, MA: Addison-Wesley.

Jeston, J. *Beyond Business Process Improvement, On to Business Transformation: A Managers Guide*, 2009, Tampa FL: Meghan-Kiffer Press.

Jeston, J. & Nelis, J. *Business Process Management: Practical Guidelines to Successful Implementation*, 2006, Burlington MA: Butterworth-Heinemann.

Jeston, J. & Nelis, J. *Management by Process: A Roadmap to Sustainable Business Process Management*, 2008, Burlington MA: Butterworth-Heinemann.

Jesus, L., Macieira, A., Karrer, D. & Rosemann, M. A Framework for a BPM Center of Excellence, *BPTrends*, September 2009. http://www.bptrends.com/bpt/wp-content/publicationfiles/FOUR 2009-09-ART-Framework for BPM Ctr Excellence-Jesus et al.pdf. Last accessed on 6/16/2015.

Kaganov, M. A Process Interaction Matrix, *Quality Progress*, 1994, 27, 10, 104.

Kenett, R.S. & Maisel, M. Process Performance, Appraisal and Employee Development Planning. In Madu, C. (Ed.) *Handbook of Total Quality Management*, 1998, Dordrecht, the Netherlands: Kluwer Academic Publishers.

Kirchmer, M., Franz, P. & von Rosing, M. The Chief Process Officer-An Emerging Top Leadership Role, In M. von Rosing, A. Sheel, & H. von Sheel (Eds). *The Complete Business Process Management Handbook: Body of Knowledge from Process Modeling to BPM, Volume 1*, 2015, Waltham, MA: Elsevier.

Majchzak, A. & Wang, Q. Breaking the Functional Mind-Set in Process Organizations, *Harvard Business Review*, 1996, 74, 5, 92-99.

Mans, R.S., van der Aalst, W. & Vanwersch, J.B. *Process Mining in Health Care: Evaluating and Exploiting Operational Healthcare Processes*, 2015, Berlin: Springer Verlag.

Panagacos, T. *The Ultimate Guide to Business Process Management*, 2012, Middletown, DE: CreateSpace Independent Publishing Platform.

Power, B. Does Your Company Suffer from Process Attention Deficit Disorder? *Harvard Business Review Digital*, September, 2010. https://hbr.org/2010/09/does-your-company-suffer-from. Last Accessed on 10/3/2016.

Power, B. Michael Hammer's Process and Enterprise Maturity Model. *BPTrends*, July 2007. http://www.bptrends.com/publicationfiles/07-07-ART-HammersPEMM-Power-final1.pdf. Last accessed on 5/13/2014.

Rosemann, M. The Service Portfolio of a BPM Center of Excellence, *BPTrends*, September, 2008. http://www.bptrends.com/bpt/wp-content/publicationfiles/09-08-ART-BPM-Service-Rosemann.doc-final.pdf. Last accessed on 9/9/2016.

Rosemann, M. & de Bruin, T. Application of a Holistic Model for Determining BPM Maturity, *BPTrends*, February, 2005. http://www.bptrends.com/bpt/wp-content/publicationfiles/02-05 WP Application of a Holistic Model- Rosemann-Bruin -....pdf. Last accessed on 4/15/2015.

Schmiedel, T., vom Brocke, J., & Recker, J. Which Cultural Values Matter to Business Process Management? *Business Process Management Journal*, 2013, 19, 2, 292-317.

Schmiedel, T., vom Brocke, J., & Recker, J. Development and Validation of an Instrument to Measure Organizational Cultures' Support of Business Process Management, *Information & Management*, 2014, 51, 1, 43-56.

Senge, P. M. *The Fifth Discipline. The Art and Practice of the Learning Organization*, 1990, London: Random House.

Stewart, T.A. & Raman, A.P. Lessons From Toyota's Long Drive: An Interview with Katsuaki Watanabe, *Harvard Business Review*, 2007, 85, 7, 74-83.

van der Aalst, W. *Process Mining: Discovery, Conformance and Enhancement of Business Processes*, 2011, Berlin: Springer Verlag.

Van Looy, A., De Backer, M. Poels, G. & Snoeck, M. Choosing the right business process maturity model. *Information and Management*, 2013, 50, 7, 466-488.

vom Brocke, J. & Sinnl, T. Culture in Business Process Management, A Literature Review. *Business Process Management Journal*, 2011, 17, 2, 357-377.

Index

Note: Page numbers with *f* indicate figures; those with *t* indicate tables.

A

actionable, as SMART guideline for metrics, 29
activities
 business process and, 4–5, 4*f*
 business process management, 8–11
 business-value-adding, 5
 defined, 4
 non-value-adding, 4, 5
 value-adding, 4–5
Activity blocks, XLSim, 100–103, 100*f*, 101*f*, 102*f*
activity times, 66
ADKAR model of individual change, 252, 252–253*t*
Adler, P., 277, 278
agility, 280
Akao, Y., 26
Alden, J., 264
Allen-Cunneen approximation, 77
American Medical Group Association (AMGA), 49
American Productivity and Quality Center (APQC), 6
 benchmarking database, 49
 code of conduct for benchmarking, 47
 organizational processes classification, 6–7, 7*f*
 performance measures (*see* APQC performance measures)
analytical queuing models, 70–77
 G/G/S model, 77, 77*f*
 Kendall notation and, 70–71
 Little's law, 72–73
 M/G/1 model, 76–77, 76*f*, 90
 M/M/1 model, 71–72, 75*f*, 88
 M/M/s model, 73–74, 73*f*, 88
 M/M/s/K model, 74, 75*f*, 88
 overview of, 70
 Queue Solver.xlam and, 73–74, 73*f*, 74*f*, 75*f*, 76*f*, 77*f*
analyze, of DMAIC cycle, 236, 236*f*
Anderson, B., 44
Anupindi, R., 191, 201

A-Plant, 174
APQC performance measures, 32–42
 business capabilities, develop/manage, 41–42
 customer service, manage, 35–36
 enterprise risk compliance/remediation/resiliency, manage, 40–41
 external relationships, manage, 41
 financial resources, manage, 38–40
 human capital, develop/manage, 36–37
 information technology, manage, 37–38
 physical products, deliver, 34–35
 products and services, develop/manage, 32–33
 products and services, market/sell, 33–34
 property, acquire/construct/manage, 40
 services, deliver, 35
 vision/strategy process measures, develop, 32
 see also American Productivity and Quality Center (APQC)
Armstrong, M. J., 47
arrival process, 61, 62–63
Association for Manufacturing Excellence (AME), 2, 228
Association of Business Process Management Professionals (ABPMP), 8
 BPM lifecycle, 9*f*
Attribute blocks, XLSim, 104–105
attributes, defining, 98, 106–107, 106*f*
Austin-Renshaw, A., 281
authority, governance and, 267
autopoiesis, 248
availability measures, of supplier metrics, 29

B

Baba, M. L., 11
Baker, S., 242
balanced scorecard, 49–55
 adopters of, 57–59
 components of, 50–51
 described, 43–44

 examples of, 51, 52*f*, 53–55
 overview of, 49
 performance areas of, 50*f*, 51
 strategy and, 51, 52*f*
Balanced Scorecard Institute, 53, 54
balking, 61
Ball, A., 48
batching flow units, 101
Beckhard, R. F., 250–251
behavioral approach, to individual change, 251
benchmarking, 43–49
 code of conduct, 47–48
 competitive, 44
 competitor, 44, 45*f*
 definitions of, 44
 described, 43–44
 difficulty of performing, 45
 examples/best practices of, 48–49, 49*f*
 global, 44–45, 45*f*
 improvement, 44
 internal, 44, 45*f*, 46
 performance, 45, 45*f*, 46
 process, 45, 45*f*, 46
 product, 45, 45*f*
 strategic, 45, 45*f*, 46
 surveys, 49
 10-step approach to, 46–47
 types of, 44–46
Bevington, T., 140, 256
biological organism, organization as, 247–248
Bitner, M. J., 134
blocking, 61, 188
 probability of, 75
 cost of, 75, 78
bottlenecks, 190, 238, 238*f*
 process flow and, 239*f*
 resource pools and, 187
 see also constraints
Bowerman, M., 48
BPM. *see* business process management (BPM)
BPMM. *see* Business Process Maturity Model (BPMM)
BPMS. *see* business process management suites (BPMS)
Bridges, W., 246

285

broken processes, 119
Brynjolfsson, E., 281
buffers
    business process and, 4–5, 4f
    defined, 4
business activity monitoring (BAM), 12, 218
business process
    activities and, 4–5
    buffers and, 4–5
    classifications, 6–8
    components of, 4f
    defined, 3
    flow units, 4
    information flows and, 4f, 5
    inputs, 3–4, 4f
    outputs, 3–4, 4f
    resources and, 5
    supplies, 4
business process classifications, 6–8, 7f, 8f
Business Process Competency Center, 270
    see also Center of Excellence (CoE)
business process engine (BPE), 12, 217–218
business process management (BPM)
    activities, 8–11
    Center of Excellence, 269–272
    concepts, diffusion of, 270
    culture, creation of, 270–271
    history of, 1–3
    initiatives, conversion of, 270
    introduction to, 1–19
    lifecycle, 8–9, 9f
    metrics in (see metrics)
    process classifications, 6–8
    process defined, 3–5
    process improvement, 11
    technology and, 11–13
business process management suites (BPMS), 11–13
    application development, 217
    business activity monitoring and, 218
    business process engine and, 217–218
    business rules engine and, 218
    components of, 11–12, 12f, 217f
    defined, 11
    for process design, 144–147
    process implementation/monitoring with, 216–218
    process improvement and, 241–242
    software, metrics and, 30
business process management suites (BPMS) for process design, 144–147
    components of, 145f
    reference models, 146–147

simulation component, 147
software applications, 147
tools/repositories, 146, 146f
Business Process Maturity Model (BPMM), 263–264, 264t
    comparison with PEMM, 264–265
    QUT, 265, 266f
Business Process Model and Notation (BPMN), 147
business process reengineering (BPR) movement, 229, 240–241
business rules engine (BRE), 12, 218
business-value-adding (BVA) activity, 5, 100

C

calling population, 61, 61f, 62
Cameron, E., 246, 247, 248, 249, 250, 251, 253, 256
Camp, R. C., 46
Capability Maturity Model (CMM), 262, 263, 264
capacity
    effective, 187–188
    flow rates and, 185–190
    measuring, 185
    process, 188
    resources and, 185–189, 186t
    theoretical, 186–187, 187t
    throughput and, 188
    utilization, 188–189
case management approach, 123
case management organization, 276
c-charts, 205–206
Center for Business Innovation, 270
    see also Center of Excellence (CoE)
Center of Competence, 270
    see also Center of Excellence (CoE)
Center of Excellence (CoE), 269–272
    conversion of initiatives and, 270
    diffusion of concepts and, 270
    organizational culture and, 270–271
    organizational strategy alignment and, 270
    overview of, 269–270
    services provided by, 271–272
    term, use of, 270
CERT, 277
Champy, J., 2, 119, 121–122, 124, 229, 240, 267, 279
Chang, J. F., 199, 268, 274
change, 245–258
    equation, Beckhard and Harris, 250–251
    individual, 251–254
    Kotter's eight-step model of, 250

leader role in, 255–256
leading, 254–256
Lewin's force field analysis of, 249
management, future of, 257–258
models of organizational, 249–251
nature of, 246
organizational, 246–249
overview of, 245
planned, 246
resistance to, 256–257
Senge and system thinking, 251
urgency of, 245–255
chaos theory, 249
check sheets, for monitoring qualitative data, 203, 203f
Chief Process Officer (CPO), 269, 281
Clausing, D., 26
client, benchmarking and, 44
code of conduct, benchmarking, 47–48
coefficient of variation (CV), 77
cognitive approach, to individual change, 252, 252–253t
collaborative communities, 278
common cause variability, 201
comparison, benchmarking and, 44
competitive benchmarking, 44, 45f
complexity theory, 249
confidence intervals, 159–160, 160t
Connector blocks, XLSim, 97, 106
constant distribution, 98
constraints
    defined, 238
    elevate, 239f, 240
    exploit, 239, 239f
    full utilization support of, 239, 239f
    identify, 238, 239f
    repeat cycle and, 239f, 240
continuous attributes, XLSim, 105, 105f
continuous improvement in processes, 228–229, 230–234
    case for, 229
    comparison with radical innovation, 230–234, 231t
    historical origins of, 228
    need for, 231, 232f
    organizational learning and, 234
    process organizations and, 234
    shifting from, to radical innovation, 232–233, 233f
continuous simulation models, 81
control, of DMAIC cycle, 236f, 237
control limits, 203–204
convergent flows, 174
cost measures, of supplier metrics, 28

costs
    can be estimated, decision making and, 78, 78*f*
    cannot be estimated, decision making and, 79, 80*f*
    defined, 27
    as resource-related metric, 29
Cox, J., 2, 177–178
critical activities, 182, 184
Cross, K. F., 134, 232
cross-functional flowcharts, 132–133, 133*f*
cross-functional training, 123
Curtis, B., 264
customer input, quality function deployment and, 140
customer metrics, 25–26
    customer satisfaction as, 25
    house of quality and, 26, 27*f*, 28*f*
    product/service requirements, 25–26
Customer Orientation (C), in CERT, 277
customer product requirements, 25–26
customer satisfaction measures, 25
customer service requirements, 25–26, 27*f*
customer touch points, 132–133
cycle time (CT), 176
    defined, 26
cycle-time efficiency, 183

D

data, process monitoring and types of, 202
data-flow diagrams (DFDs), 137, 137–138*f*
data-oriented diagrams, 137, 138*f*
Davenport, T. H., 2, 11, 122, 229–230, 242
De Backer, M., 266
Decision blocks, XLSim, 104, 104*f*
decision making, queuing theory and, 78–80
    costs can be estimated, 78, 78*f*
    costs cannot be estimated, 79, 80*f*
defects, as form of waste, 237*t*
define, of DMAIC cycle, 235–236, 236*f*
Deming, W. E., 2, 24, 201, 202, 234–235
descriptive models, defined, 78
Desmet, D., 118
deterministic arrivals, 62
deterministic simulation models, 80–81
discrete attributes, XLSim, 105, 105*f*
discrete event simulation, 81, 82*f*
divergent flows, 174

DMAIC Improvement Cycle, 235–237, 236*f*
dynamic simulation models, 80
dysfunctional processes, 119

E

earliest due date (EDD) rule, 65
Eckes, G., 255, 271, 278
effective capacity (EC), 187–188
eight-step model of change, Kotter's, 250
80/20 rule, 203
elimination-of-waste principle, 5
enablers, of process redesign, 121–123
    human resource, 122
    new technologies, 121, 122*f*
    organizational, 122–123
enterprise application integration (EAI), 12
enterprise capabilities, 262
estimation of parameters, 159
European Network for Advanced Performance Studies (ENAPS), 6, 7–8
    organizational processes classification, 8*f*
evaluation/reward structures, 279
event lists, 81
Excel, flowcharting with, 140–142, 141*f*, 142*f*
Excellence (E), in CERT, 277
exponential distribution, 99, 99*f*
extract, transform, and load (ETL) systems, 12

F

factors, defined, 265
Feather, J. J., 232
feedback control principle, 201–202, 202*f*
financial metrics, 24
Fingar, P., 11, 147
"The First Law of Science" (Maister), 67–68
first-come-first-served (FCFS) rule, 65, 66*f*
Fishman, C., 258
5w2h framework, 120, 120–121*f*
flow rates, 174–175, 175*f*
    capacity and, 185–190
    measuring, 185
flow times, 176
    benefits of shorter, 178
    cycle-time efficiency and, 183
    heterogeneous flow units and, 179, 181–182, 181*f*

levers for managing, 183–185
measuring, 178–180
multiple paths and, 181–183
parallel activities and, 182–183, 182*f*
process boundaries and, 180
rework and, 180, 181*f*
flow units, 4, 4*f*, 62
flowchart symbols, 131*f*
flowcharting software tools, 140–144
    Excel, 140–142, 141*f*, 142*f*
    PowerPoint, 140, 141
    Visio, 142–144, 143–144*f*, 145*f*
    Word, 140, 141
flowcharts, 131, 132*f*
    cross-functional, 132–133, 133*f*
    multilevel, 135, 136*f*
flow-oriented diagrams, 128–136
    cross-functional flowcharts, 132–133, 133*f*
    flowcharts, 131, 131*f*, 132*f*
    multilevel flowcharts, 135, 136*f*
    process activity charts, 131, 132*f*
    process-flow diagrams, 129–130, 130*f*
    relationship mapping, 128–129, 129*f*
    service blueprinting, 133–135, 134*f*
    service system mapping, 134–135, 135*f*
force field analysis, Lewin's, 249
Ford, H., 2
Ford Motor Company, 2
Forrester, J. W., 81
Francis, G., 48
Franz, P., 9, 146, 272, 280, 281, 282

G

Gane, C., 137
Gane-Sarson Data-Flow Diagrams, 137–138*f*
Garvin, D. A., 2–3, 266
General Motors, 2
Generator blocks, XLSim, 98–100
    constant distribution and, 98
    dialog for, 98*f*
    exponential distribution and, 99, 99*f*
    normal distribution and, 100, 100*f*
    uniform distribution and, 98–99, 99*f*
Gerstner, L., 277
G/G/S (Allen-Cunneen approximation) analytical queuing model, 77, 77*f*
global benchmarking, 44–45, 45*f*
Goldratt, E., 2, 177–178, 238
goodness of fit tests, 158–159, 158*f*
Gossage, W. G., 258
governance, defined, 267

governance roles, 268–269
  chief process officer, 269
  process executive, 269
  process owner/process steward, 268
  transformation leader, 268
Green, M., 246, 247, 248, 249, 250, 251, 253, 256

H

Haidt, J., 257
Hair, J. M., 252
Hall, R. W., 228, 229, 234
Hammer, M., 2, 3, 119, 121–122, 124, 229, 234, 240, 256, 262, 264, 267, 268, 269, 272, 277, 278, 279, 281
hard metrics, 24
Harrington, H. J., 276
Harrington, J. S., 276
Harris, J. G., 242
Harris, R. T., 250–251
Harvard Business Review, 3, 254
Harvard Business School, 2–3
Hauser, J. R., 26
Heath, C., 255, 256, 257
Heath, D., 255, 256, 257
Heckscher, C., 277, 278
Hershman, L. W., 264, 268, 269, 272, 277, 278, 281
heterogeneous flow units, 62, 179, 181–182, 181f
hierarchical structure, 273, 274f
hierarchy of needs, 253, 254f
histograms
  creating, 156–158, 157f
  for monitoring quantitative data, 206–207, 207f, 207t
homeostasis, 249
homogeneous flow units, 62
Hopp, W. J., 191
house of quality, 26, 27f, 28f
human resource enablers, of process redesign, 122
humanistic psychology approach, to individual change, 253–254
Hurst, D. K., 254, 255

I

Iacobucci, D., 49
important processes, 119
improve, of DMAIC cycle, 236–237, 236f
improvement benchmarking, 44
the improvement paradox, 241

individual change, 251–254
  behavioral approach, 251
  cognitive approach, 252, 252–253t
  humanistic psychology approach, 253–254
  psychodynamic approach, 253
Industrial Revolution, 2
information flows
  business process and, 4f, 5
  metrics and, 10
inputs/outputs of business process, 3–4, 4f
  described, 3
  flow units, 4, 4f
  supplies, 4, 4f
interface activity noise, 140
interface mapping, 140
interfacing activities, 140
internal benchmarking, 44, 45f, 46
interval estimates, 159
inventory, 175–176, 175f
  analysis of, 190–192
  capacity utilization and, 191–192, 192f
  cycle time reduction and, 191
  defined, 26
  as form of waste, 237t
  levers for managing, 191–192
  throughput rate reduction and, 191
  variability reduction and, 191, 192f
inventory turns
  defined, 178
  inventory cycle time, 178
  inventory financial measures, 178
I-Plant, 174

J

Japanese manufacturing techniques, 1–2
Jeston, J., 264, 267, 268, 269, 272, 276–277, 281
Jesus, L., 271
jockeying, 63
joining flow units, 101
Jones, D. T., 228
just-in-time manufacturing, 2, 5, 11, 228, 237

K

Kaganov, M., 281
Kahneman, D., 256–257
kaizen concept, 228, 230, 238
kakushin, 230
Kaplan, R. S., 24, 43, 49, 50
Kendall, D. G., 70–71
Kendall notation, 70–71

Kenett, R. S., 279
key performance indicators (KPIs), 12
  defined, 27
Kirchmer, M., 146, 272, 280, 281, 282
Kock, N., 137
Kotter, J. P., 250
Kotter's eight-step model of change, 250
Kubler-Ross, E., 253

L

lagging metrics, 24–25
Laguna, M., 134
Leach, A., 258
leading metrics, 24–25
lean concept, 228–229, 237–238
  waste (muda) and, 237, 237t
Lean Enterprise Institute, 228
lean manufacturing movement, 2, 5, 11
learning, benchmarking and, 44
Lewin, K., 249
Lewin's force field analysis, 249
lifecycle, business process management, 8–9, 9f
linear flows, 174
Link blocks, XLSim, 98, 105–106, 105f
Little, J. D. C., 72–73
Little's law, 176–177
  analytical queuing model, 72–73
load, in process-flow diagrams, 129
load batch, 187
  throughput and, 190
Lynch, R. L., 232

M

machine, organization as, 247
The Machine that Changed the World (Womack, Jones, and Roos), 228
Maisel, M., 279
Maister, D., 67–68
Majchzak, A., 277
Malcolm Baldridge Quality award, 228
management processes, defined, 6
Marklund, J., 134
Masao, M., 26
Maslow, A., 253–254
mass-production process, 2
Mathias, K., 9
matrix structure, 274, 276
Maturana, H., 248
Mazur, G., 26
measurable, as SMART guideline for metrics, 29
measure, of DMAIC cycle, 236, 236f

Meliones, J., 54
metrics
 BPMS software and, 30
 classifying, 23–25
 components of, 10
 customer, 25–26
 defined, 10
 financial *vs.* nonfinancial, 24
 guidelines for, 29–30
 leading *vs.* lagging, 24–25
 observed *vs.* subjective, 24
 pitfalls in, 30
 process, 26–28
 resource, 29
 supplier, 28–29
M/G/1 (General Service Times) analytical queuing model, 76–77, 76*f*, 90
Mintzberg, H., 118
mission-oriented processes, defined, 6
Mitchell, S., 246
Mizuno, S., 26
M/M/1 model analytical queuing model, 71–72, 75*f*, 88
M/M/s analytical queuing models, 73–74, 73*f*, 88
M/M/s/K (finite queue) analytical queuing model, 74, 75*f*, 89
model validation, simulation and, 156
model verification, simulation and, 155
Morgan, G., 247, 248–249
Morison, R., 242
motion, as form of waste, 237*t*
multilevel flowcharts, 135, 136*f*
multiple paths, in process, 124
multi-vari charts, for monitoring quantitative data, 208, 209*f*

N

Nelis, J., 264, 267, 268, 269, 272, 276–277, 281
net availability of resource units, 187–188
network organization, 276, 276*f*
new technologies, enablers of process redesign, 121, 122*f*
new-product development process, 25
nonfinancial metrics, 24
nonlinear system, organization as, 248–249
nonterminating processes, 108
 simulation and, 154, 155*t*
non-value-adding activities, 4, 5, 100
Nordhielm, C., 49
normal distribution, 100, 100*f*

Norman, D. A., 68–69
Norton, D. P., 24, 43, 49, 50

O

Object Management Group, 263
observed metrics, 24
O'Neill, P., 230
operational processes, defined, 6
order fulfillment, 6
organization
 as biological organism, 247–248
 as machine, 247
 as nonlinear system, 248–249
 as political system, 247
organizational change, 246–249, 277–280
 evaluation and reward structures and, 279
 Lewin's force field analysis of, 249
 models of, 249–251
 organization as biological organism and, 247–248
 organization as machine and, 247
 organization as nonlinear system and, 248–249
 organization as political system and, 247
 organizational culture and, 277–279
 overview of, 246–247, 277
 people development and, 279–280
organizational culture
 building, 277–279
 CERT and, 277
 collaborative communities and, 278
 defined, 277
organizational enablers, of process redesign, 122–123
organizational learning, 44, 46, 234
organizational production structure, 2
organizational scope, defined, 265
organizational strategies/BPM activities, alignment of, 270
organizational structure, process enterprise building and, 273–277
 case management organization, 276
 hierarchical structure, 273, 274*f*
 implementing, 276–277
 matrix structure, 274, 276
 network organization, 276, 276*f*
 process organization, 274, 275*f*
 traditional organization, 274, 275*f*
over-processing, as form of waste, 237*t*
over-production, as form of waste, 237*t*

P

Panagacos, T., 272
parameters, estimation of, 159
Pareto, V., 203
Pareto charts, for monitoring qualitative data, 203, 204*f*
Pascale, R. T., 256
p-charts, 204–205, 206*f*, 214
PDCA cycle. *see* Plan-Do-Check-Act (PDCA) cycle
PEMM. *see* process and enterprise maturity model (PEMM)
people development, 279–280
performance, estimation of, 159–160, 160*t*
performance benchmarking, 45, 45*f*, 46
performance measures, queuing theory and, 66–67
person to person processes, 199
person to system processes, 199–200
perspective, defined, 265
Plan-Do-Check-Act (PDCA) cycle, 202, 234–235, 235*f*
planned change, 246
Plowman, D. A., 249
Poels, G., 266
point estimates, 159
Poisson process, 62, 63
Poka-Yoke, 124, 183
political system, organization as, 247
population size, 62
post-processing approach, 184
Power, B., 264–265, 266, 280
precedence requirements, 184
pre-processing approach, 184
prescriptive models, defined, 78
probabilistic arrivals, 62
probabilistic simulation models, 80–81
process activity charts, 131, 132*f*
process analytics, 242
process and enterprise maturity model (PEMM), 234, 262–263, 263*f*
 comparison with BPMM, 264–265
process benchmarking, 45, 45*f*, 46
 approach to, 46–47
process boundaries, 180
process capability, 212–213
process capability index, 212–213
process capacity (PC), 188
process control charts
 c-charts as, 205–206
 for monitoring qualitative data, 203–206
 for monitoring quantitative data, 208–211

process control charts *(continued)*
  p-charts as, 204–205, 206*f*
  R-charts as, 210–211
  s-charts as, 210–211
  use of, 211–212, 212*f*
  x-bar chart as, 209–210, 211
process design tools, 127–147
  BPMS software, 144–147, 145*f*
  combining methods of, 138, 139*f*
  customer input, 140
  data-oriented diagrams, 137, 138*f*
  flowcharting software tools, 140–144
  flow-oriented diagrams, 128–136
  interface mapping, 140
  process mapping, 127–128
process design/redesign, 117–125
  enablers of, 121–123
  5w2h framework, 120, 120–121*f*
  overview of, 117
  principles of, 123–124, 125*f*
  selection of, 119–120
  simulation and (*see* simulation)
  strategy and, 118–123
  subprocesses of, 120
  understanding, 120–121
process enablers, 262
process enterprise building, 261–282
  future process management, 280–282
  organizational changes, 277–280
  organizational structure, 273–277
  overview of, 261
  process governance, 267–273
  process maturity assessment, 262–267
  see also individual headings
process execution, 200
  with BPMS, 216–218
process executive, 269
process flow, concept of, 174–178
  financial measures and, 177–178
  flow patterns and, 174
  flow rates and, 174–175, 175*f*
  flow times and, 176
  inventory and, 175–176, 175*f*
  Little's law and, 176–177
  manufacturing plant types and, 174
  process measures and, 177–178
process flows, managing, 173–192
  flow concept and, 174–178
  flow rates/capacity analysis and, 185–190
  flow times and, 178–185
  inventory analysis and, 190–192
process governance, 267–273
  Center of Excellence, 269–272
  governance structure building, 272–273

  overview of, 267
  roles/organizational structures in, 268–269
  Strategic Process Council, 272
process governance roles/organizational structures, 268–269
process implementation, 198–200
  with BPMS, 216–218
  determining factors for difficulty of, 198–199
  person to person processes and, 199
  person to system processes and, 199–200
  system to system processes and, 200
process improvement, 227–242
  BPMS and, 241–242
  business process reengineering and, 240–241
  continuous improvement approach to, 228–229, 230–234
  the improvement paradox and, 241
  lean improvement approach to, 237–238
  overview of, 227
  PDCA cycle approach to, 234–235
  radical innovation approach to, 229–234
  Six Sigma approach to, 235–237
  Theory of Constraints and, 238–240
process improvement potential, 120
process instance, 217, 218
process management, future of, 280–282
process mapping, 127–128
process maturity assessment, 262–267
  Business Process Maturity Model, 263–265, 264*t*
  model summary, 266–267
  process and enterprise maturity model, 262–263, 263*f*, 264–265
  QUT-BPMM, 265, 266*f*
process metrics, 26–28
  APQC list of, 32–42
process mining, 281
process monitoring, 200–211
  with BPMS, 216–218
  data types and, 202
  feedback control principle and, 201–202, 202*f*
  overview of, 200
  purpose of, 200–201
  tools, 201
  tools for qualitative data, 202–206
  tools for quantitative data, 206–211
process organization, 274, 275*f*
process owner/process steward, 268

Process Program Office, 270
process redesign, 117
  broken/dysfunctional processes and, 119
  enablers of, 121–123
  important processes and, 119
  improvement potential and, 120
  selection, 119–120
  see also process design/redesign
process simulation, XLSim in, 91–112
process steward, 268
process view of organization
  defined, 3
  importance of, 2
  see also business process
process-flow diagrams, 129–130, 130*f*
process-strategy matrix, 118, 119*f*
product benchmarking, 45, 45*f*
product mix, 179, 184–185
productivity, defined, 27
Pro-Model software, 91
Prusak, L., 277, 278
pseudo random numbers, 82
psychodynamic approach, to individual change, 253

Q

qualitative data, process monitoring tools for, 202–206
  check sheets, 203, 203*f*
  Pareto charts, 203, 204*f*
  process control charts, 203–204
qualitative measures, 24
qualitative metric, defined, 202
quality, defined, 27
quality circles, 228
quality function deployment (QFD), 26, 236
quality measures, of supplier metrics, 29
quantitative data, process monitoring tools for, 206–211
  histograms, 206–207, 207*f*, 207*t*
  multi-vari charts, 208, 209*f*
  process control charts, 208–211
  run charts, 208, 208*f*, 209*f*
quantitative measures, 24
quantitative metric, defined, 202
Queensland University of Technology Business Process Maturity Model (QUT-BPMM), 265, 266*f*
queue configuration, 61, 63–64, 64*f*
queue discipline, 61, 65, 66*f*
Queue Solver.xlam, 73–74, 73*f*, 74*f*, 75*f*, 76*f*, 77*f*
queue-length formula, 191

queues, 4
   termed, 60
queues, economics of, 67–70
   costs curves, 70f
   economic costs of waiting and, 69
   need for models and, 69–70
   psychology of waiting and, 67–69
queuing models, need for, 69–70
queuing system, 61, 61f
queuing theory, 61–80, 61f
   activity times and, 66
   analytical models of (see analytical queuing models)
   arrival process, 61, 62–63
   calling population, 61, 62
   decision making and, 78–80
   economics of, 67–70
   overview of, 61–62, 61f
   performance measures and, 66–67
   queue configuration, 61, 63–64, 64f
   queue discipline, 61, 65, 66f
   terminology of, 61–67
QUT-BPMM. see Queensland University of Technology Business Process Maturity Model (QUT-BPMM)

R

radical innovation approach to process improvement, 229–234
   case for, 230
   comparison with continuous improvement, 230–234, 231t
   historical origins of, 229–230
   need for, 231, 232f
   organizational learning and, 234
   process organizations and, 234
   shifting from, to continuous improvement, 232–233, 233f
random number generators, 81
random number seed, 82
Rank Xerox, 48, 49f
rational manager view, 255
R-charts, 210–211
Recker, J., 277, 278
reengineering movement, 2, 229–230
   defined, 240
   Hammer and definition of, 3
   see also business process reengineering (BPR) movement
reference models, 146–147
relationship mapping, 128–129, 129f
relationship quality measures, of supplier metrics, 29
relevant, as SMART guideline for metrics, 30

reneging, 61
replications, simulation and, 153–155, 155t
Resource blocks, XLSim, 103, 103f
resource metrics, 29
resource pool, 185
   capacity utilization for, 188–189
resource units, 185–186
   net availability of, 187–188
resource well-being, 29
resources
   business process and, 5
   capacity and, 185–189, 186t
   defined, 5, 98, 107, 107f
   scheduled availability of, 186–187
   theoretical capacity of, 187
responsibility, governance and, 267
Responsibility (R), in CERT, 277
rework, 180, 181f, 237t
Roos, D., 228
Rosemann, M., 271
Rouse, W. B., 11
run charts, for monitoring quantitative data, 208, 208f, 209f
run length, simulation and, 153–155, 155t

S

"S" curve, in products, 232–233, 233f
Samson, D., 140, 256
Sarson, T., 137
Satir, V., 253
s-charts, 210–211
scheduled availability of resources, 186–187
Schmiedel, T., 277, 278
Schonberger, R. J., 228
scientific management movement, 228
Senge, P., 46, 229, 234, 249, 251, 256, 258, 280
sequential processing, 124, 184
service blueprinting, 133–135, 134f
service system mapping, 134–135, 135f
service-oriented architecture (SOA), 147, 200
Shapiro, R., 242
Shingo, S., 124
shortest activity time (SAT) rule, 65, 65f, 66f
Shostack, L., 133–134
Silverstone, Y., 258
simulation, 80–84, 151–169
   defined, 80
   deterministic vs. probabilistic models, 80–81

   discrete event, 81, 82f
   discrete vs. continuous models, 81
   framework for business process design using, 152f
   inputs analysis, 156–159
   model validation and, 156
   model verification and, 155
   nonterminating processes and, 154, 155t
   outputs analysis, 159–160
   overview of, 151
   replications and, 153–155, 155t
   role of, in process design, 152–153, 152f
   run length and, 153–155, 155t
   spreadsheet, building, 82–84, 83f, 84f
   static vs. dynamic models, 80
   terminating processes and, 154, 155t
   time units in XLSim and, 153, 153f
simulation clock, 81
simulation executive, 81
simulation inputs analysis, 156–159
   estimation of parameters and, 159
   goodness of fit tests and, 158–159, 158f
   histograms and, 156–158, 157f
   probability distributions and, 156–159
simulation outputs analysis, 159–160
   alternative design comparisons and, 160
   performance estimates and, 159–160, 160t
Six Sigma, 2, 213, 235–237
   DMAIC Improvement Cycle and, 235–237, 236f
skills, as form of waste, 237t
Skinner, B. F., 251
Sloan, A. P., 2, 273
small group improvement activities, 228
SMART guidelines for metrics, 29–30
   actionable, 29–30
   measurable, 29–30
   relevant, 30
   specific, 29
   timely, 30
Smith, A., 2
Smith, H., 11, 147
Snoeck, M., 266
soft metrics, 24
Sower, V. E., 48
SPC templates, using, 214–216
Spearman, M. L., 191
special cause variability, 201
specific, as SMART guideline for metrics, 29
specification limits, 212

spreadsheet simulation, building, 82–84, 83f, 84f
Srikanth, L., 174
stable process, 175
stable system, 72
starvation, 188
state of the system, defined, 70
static simulation models, 80
statistical process control (SPC), 201
statistics/results, simulation, 81
steady-state system, 108
Sterman, J., 241
Sternin, J., 256
Storage blocks, XLSim, 103, 103f
strategic benchmarking, 45, 45f, 46
Strategic Process Council, 272, 281
strategy
  defined, 118
  as pattern of actions over time, 118
  as perspective, 118
  as plan, 118
  as position, 118
  process design and, 118–123
  term, use of, 118
structural variability, 201
subjective metrics, 24
suboptimization, 10, 124
subprocesses, 120
supplier metrics, 28–29
Suppliers, Inputs, Process Steps, Output and Customers (SIPOC) map, 236
supplies, 4, 4f
Supply Chain Reference Model (SCOR), 147
support processes, defined, 6
surveys, benchmarking, 49
swim lanes, 132
system thinking, 251
system to system processes, 200

T

Target, 228
target organization
  benchmarking and, 44–45
  categories based on, 44
Taylor, F., 228
Teamwork (T), in CERT, 277
technology, business process management and, 11–13
terminating processes, 108
  simulation and, 154, 155t
theoretical capacity (TC), 186–187, 187t
  throughput and, 189
theoretical cycle time, 183

Theory of Constraints (TOC), 2, 238–240
  bottlenecks and, 238, 238f
  defined, 238
  focusing steps of, 238–240, 239f
throughput (TH), 175
  capacity and, 188
  defined, 26
  levers for managing, 189–190
time, QUT-BPMM model, 265
timely, as SMART guideline for metrics, 30
Total Quality Management (TQM) movement, 2, 11, 228, 234
touch points, customer, 132–133
Toyota Production System, 2
T-Plant, 174
traditional organization, 274, 275f
transformation leader, 268
transient-state system, 108
transitions, 246
transportation, as form of waste, 237t
turnover ratio, financial measures and, 178

U

Umble, M., 174
uniform distribution, 98–99, 99f
unit load (UL) for resource, 186
  throughput and, 189–190
utilization, 67
  defined, 27
  as resource-related metric, 29

V

value-adding (VA) activity, 4–5, 100
value-driven business process management, 9
value-stream mapping, 237
van Alstyne, M., 281
Van Looy, A., 266
Varela, F., 248
variability
  common cause, 201
  processes and, 200–201
  special cause, 201
  structural, 201
Visio, flowcharting with, 142–144, 143–144f, 145f
Visual Basic for Applications (VBA), 92
voice of the customer, 26, 236
vom Brocke, J., 277, 278
von Rosing, M., 281
V-Plant, 174

W

waiting
  economic costs of, 69, 70f
  as form of waste, 237t
  psychology of, 67–69
Wang, Q., 277
waste (muda)
  defined, 237
  forms of, 237t
Watanabe, K., 230, 254
Weinberg, G., 253
well-being, as resource-related metric, 29
Who Moved My Cheese (Johnson), 246
Wold, A., 121
Womack, J. P., 228
workflow engine, 217–218
work-in-process inventory (WIP), 175

XYZ

x-bar charts, 209–210, 211
XLSim in process simulation, 91–112
  Activity blocks, 100–103, 100f, 101f, 102f
  Attribute blocks, 104–105
  attributes, defining, 98, 106–107, 106f
  Connector blocks, 97, 106
  continuous attributes, 105, 105f
  Decision blocks, 104, 104f
  discrete attributes, 105, 105f
  Generator blocks, 98–100, 98f
  language of, 92
  Link blocks, 98, 105–106, 105f
  macro security settings, 92–93, 92f, 93f
  model building blocks, 97, 98–106
  model building with, 97–106
  model canvas, 97
  output options, 109f, 110
  overview of, 91
  Resource blocks, 103, 103f
  resources, defining, 98, 107, 107f
  ribbon tab, 94–96, 95f
  running software for, 92–94
  sample model, 110–112, 110f, 111f
  simulation, running, 109
  simulation parameters section, 96, 96f
  simulation setup, 107–109, 107f
  Storage blocks, 103, 103f
  time units in, 153, 153f
  trusted location use for, 94
  working environment, 94–97, 95f
zur Muehlen, M., 242

The Soul Tree
Poems and Photographs of the Southern Appalachians

Laura Hope-Gill
John Fletcher, Jr.

Grateful Steps
Asheville, North Carolina

The Soul Tree: A Celebration of the Mystic Appalachia

A poet often looks looks back at his or her freshman effort and views it wistfully through a fog of nostalgia with great fondness, but with jaundiced eyes nonetheless. Poor Whitman never finished his first book, the inimitable *Leaves of Grass*, but wondered to his grave if he ever got it right. Books and poets grow. "The riches of the poet," said Delmore Schwartz, "are equal to his poetry," but a first book is the opening act in a long engagement with the right word in the right place, lending a little light. But this first book, I am happy to report, is different from almost any other you will find.

It is a collaboration and a dance, and the star is not the poet or the photographer; it is the mountains, the oldest in the world, the Southern Appalachians. And as the poet and the photographer engage the mountains, they form a chain, a trio atwirl, and at various moments take turns leading us across the page in full color, with a panoply of subtle movements, and a commitment to the partnership that is deeply felt. Where one ebbs, the other rises. "If I ever emerged," writes Laura Hope-Gill in "The Forest Heart," "it was / to find what part of me was missing." But her search is pure, graceful and meditative, almost Persian is its quiet insistence that all things that grow are connected, and in between the lines of dramatic demarcation, when we are barreling through life pell-mell, the silences are where we find our True Self, the velvet spiritual interiors.

The T'ang Dynasty poet Han-Shan wrote,

> People ask the way to Cold Mountain
> Roads do not go through
>
> When our minds are one
> You will be here too.

There is no way that someone can grow up in these timeless surroundings and not be affected by the rhythms and colors of the Natural World. There is a bond with the mountains, a pull that never leaves you, no matter where you travel or why you left. When I am coming home from a long trip, and I begin that long slow ascent into the landscape and see the four shades of blue mountain mist shifting and morphing against the horizon, my whole body changes its tempo. My eyes and hands and feet relax and listen to the smoky silences falling on both sides of the road. The weather and the animals are intimately part of the mountain experience; and the proximity of the wilderness is impossible to ignore, or you ignore it at your peril. These poems are filled with animals and trees and streams giving voice to a power and instinct that is pure and untainted by the appetites of men. Most poems are begun with a confluence of visceral sensations, out of the body's conduit, at the threshold of the unconscious.

Real wilderness is, like the imagination or the underground river of our future, completely unknown and changing second by second. The photographer, Cartier-Bresson believed that his lens had to be aimed at the decisive moment, when the photograph was willing to surrender, or when the confluence of events was at its apex. John Fletcher's photos here seem not to be leaning in with breathless insistence, but are saturated with confidence and color, powerfully waiting, at one with the mist's movement, the flower's luxurious unraveling. Learning to listen properly may take a thousand years, but it begins at the point of repose, where man stands apart from himself, "a transparent eyeball" as Emerson said, when man stands outside his own creations of the suburb and steel mill and shopping mall boutique. To confront reality, as all writers must, without the context of the forest and the meadow, would be, for me, to confront the facts in total bleakness, because a wilderness of tract homes is a world without imagination, and a world without imagination is a lie.

Though these images take place in the Appalachian Mountains, they, and the poems that seek to define them, are universal, speaking to the experiences and myths of all people, regardless of place. Though we are at the mercy of our memory and experience, these small epistles to these Southern ridges evoke the otherness and ethereal mysticism that winds its way into our colloquialisms and speech patterns. Our medicines and superstitions and tribal nature have been formed in isolation, at odds with the world and resistant to change, because survival, intellectual or otherwise, has depended on the constant repetitions and routines inside the consistency of the seasons. This obstinance creates great characters, self-reliant, colorful and sturdy, keenly aware of their bodies. This exoticism and physicality is attractive to those on the outside of this experience, and like bouquets in chocolate pots, Southern writers have sold the stories of their eccentric families to the publishers in the middle of the idle urban collectives on both coasts. But we are more than noble savages, peddling buckdances and moonshine; the real work of the Southern writer is to capture the musicality of the language and the authenticity of the protagonists, struggling inside legitimate spiritual places.

The rhythms of the poems in The Soul Tree are more sedate than the ecstatic call and response of the gospel choir or the hootenanny; their sympathies lie with the hoot owl and white pine, mouthing the prayers of the hounded and the solitary. "Everything that grows shines," concludes Hope-Gill in "The Secret of Green." This still center in her poetry, their settings and pace already dictated by the images in front of her, become more valuable for the poet in her absence from them, just as Eden was more precious to Adam after the Fall. And in his travels, Adam carried Eden inside him, sharing the memory and perfection of it with any person who would aspire to feel that state of grace.

> I'm a believer
> In the darkness first
> That broke open upon nothing
>
> And spread its
> Story out for all light to fill. ("Faith").

Without a clear value system, it would be easy for the regional to dissolve too obediently into the picturesque, but the best of the Appalachian writers are not limited by place, they are writing poems that are bound to the mountains but with currencies that are universal and everywhere. When Robert Hass writes, in Meditation at Lagunitas, "a word is elegy to what it signifies," he is suggesting that words are as real as the places they represent and, perhaps more importantly, become a place themselves where the mind makes real what the senses can feel. And only through the creative act can the place and its progenitors be made whole, by leaving their record of the sensations behind them as they travel the larger world.

Most Appalachian writers, excepting Thomas Wolfe, are not known for their verbosity, but more for their brevity and precision. My favorite poems in this collection continue this tradition, but with a twist. "The Soul Tree," "The Golden Blue," "Conversation," "The Alphabet of Trees," "The Rock and The Rainbow," "Pour, Silver Light" and "Where You Lose Me" all contain a cloistered dialogue with their nearest object, in repeated attempts to find a curdled understanding at the minimum, or better yet, redemption, transformation or renewal. Just as most writers acquire a language to tell the stories that are already within them, their God or Buddha or Allah only lives in the next sentence, the one unwritten. So these poems and photos are saturated with the colors of vibrant longing, in an Arcadia that still exists, however precariously. "This is the place / where water turns to feather / And flies up." ("The Catalogue of Rushing Water")

Many natives of this region are opposed to outside influences because outsiders have always come to raise the price of the land or take it outright, to ridicule a pace and a way of life uninterested in the onslaught of technology or science. Tradition may be the illusion of permanence, but it secures a unique system and is resistant to change. The challenge of the Appalachian writer in the 21st Century is to walk into the new country with the old one still strapped on her back and create a language that moves our literature forward with the mixture of both. Appalachian writers are keenly aware of their Bible and their bluegrass, but they must also consider the *Bhagavad-Gita* and Borges as well. Laura Hope-Gill has fashioned a first response to these unforgettable images that would make a Rumi or Rilke proud, equal to the challenge that her partner has presented, with a language as indelible and translucent as morning dew.

– Keith Flynn
editor, *Asheville Poetry Review*

Look to this day for it is Life, the very Life of Life.
—*Rig Veda* "The Salutation to the Dawn"

For my grandmothers, Grace and Mollie, my mother, Margaret, and my daughter, Andaluna.

—Laura

Thanks to God for strength and guidance—and to the Blue Ridge Parkway for 469 miles of sanctuary.

For my parents, John and Judy, and my sister, Janet.

—John

CONTENTS

The Soul Tree	1
The Partial View	2
When I Have Vanished	5
I Spoke My Love	6
Weathered	7
The Golden Blue	9
Winter Red	10
What Changes	11
Spring in the Mountains	12
Mountain Sea	13
Conversation	14
The Alphabet of Trees	15
Wild Morning Glory	16
The Secret of Green	17
Beyond This There Is Another	18
What Keeps Me from Looking Away	20
Open and Close	21
Black Ridge	22
The Rock and the Rainbow	23
Come Home	25
The Ghost and the Evergreen	27
Out of Many	28
Ice Is What Rejoices	30
The Forest Heart	31
Abandon	32
Mountain Music	34
Leafless Not Lifeless	35
Panorama	36
Watershed	37
The Cloud Sea	38
The Old Ones	39
Pour	41
Silver Light	42
The Shadowed Light	43
Where the Wind Has Been	45
Ever	46
Mountain Lessons	48
The Mist Has Renamed Everything	51
I Was Without	53
Whisper	54
Tree Dictionary	55
The Catalogue of Rushing Water	56
Numbers	58
Bright as God	59
The Smoothest of Places	60
All That Is Familiar Grows Magnificent	62
Where My Life Has Brought Me	65
Sightread	66
A Theory of Winter	67
The Covering Touch	68
Where You Lose Me	69
Smoke	70
Dreaming	72
Mountain and Moon	73
Sky Dolphin	74
Dusk	75
The Burning Mountain	76
Where We Learn To Fly	77
Sky Prayer	78
Postlude	79
They Will Speak	81
Covenant	82
Geometry	83
Not Egypt	84
Waves of a Vaster Sea	85
Mantra	86
It Will Remain Here as Our Evidence	88
The Lion	89
Where the Light Got Through	90
Rose	91
Faith	92
Paling	93
The Roughness of Life Holds Us to It	95
Wash	96
The Sky at Play	97
Autumn	98
Sudden	99
Fallen	100
Cloud Level	102
Light	103

THE SOUL TREE

I have become the place
I grew into
And out of. Hear what my branches teach.

Hear how the loosest limb whispers
How I will be the first to feed, first fallen.
How I will fall from the inside out
And let what's in me out.

I have become the dry thing.
The mountain air strives to revive me.
Anymore I've no need

For rain or sleep. These have fed me enough.
Or even light. What arises for all things
I now become.

I've climbed my branches out of myself.

THE PARTIAL VIEW

It is as easy to forget
Everything that matters as
It is easy to lose a mountain to the sky.

Things can vanish.
It is a truth in life we hold to.
It makes death more pleasing to the eye.

Walking here,
Remembering the depths
And crests can make us wiser.

The blue ridge is a teacher
Even when we can't hear it.

WHEN I HAVE VANISHED

What you may remember best
Is all you never knew. How I stood
Before you and we were

Beautiful on our edge.
We grew upward as the mountain
Sloped out from under us. We begged the soil

To keep its place.
We knew our place.
Often violently, to keep

From changing as deeply into
The mountain's seeming stillness as we
Could, we pressed our roots.

In strong
Winds, our branches
Sometimes even touched.

I SPOKE MY LOVE

I spoke my love
To the mountain. In my
Heart I felt the echo. And my love

Was the sound
Of the mountain then.
It shifted and it shamed the sun.

I spoke my love
To the mountain. Mountain,
Make me immense enough to hold this.

My love was
The sound of the mountain
Then. I shift and I shame the sun.

WEATHERED

Barkless and bent
In the place where all is woven,
Half-alive in the breaking morning

Living and dead things,
Lichen-encloaked, still visit. Internal
Skin of tuber, root wide, collects

Memory enough
Of life the night covered from us.
From the earth, even in winter I've felt

It warm me into a moss.
I covered myself and hid. My own
Wet branches have concealed me. Listen

When you walk.
Discover how I've grown accustomed
To the skinless life, how I've come to allow

Nothing not to touch me.

THE GOLDEN BLUE

We who live here
Know it. Like the shoulders
Of sleeping friends how

They extend. Lovers

WINTER RED

Silence
Can explode
Like the heart

Extending outward
Beyond the impossible
Language of snow

Or skin.
It shouts of love
Grown patiently, miraculously

Sending itself
High above the skyline
Of the known.

What the snow
Has said
Is loudness hushed

And offers everything to the birds.

WHAT CHANGES

What lasts is
What releases.
What holds is
What we allow.
What questions
Is what extends.
What damages
Is what heals.
What lives on
Is what is dying.
What keeps is
What keeps leaving.
What remains
Is what we remember.

SPRING IN THE MOUNTAINS

Everyone expands when
Looking at it. We become
Giants in our minds and imagine

Ourselves walking ridge
To ridge, such steps
Of legend.

We meet ourselves
In the depths and converse
With friends at the heights.

Even the trees
Welcome us

MOUNTAIN SEA

Some would like
Never to know where we
Come from

But hold a moment
Of ancient mystery between two hands,
Kiss it gently with soft lips

As one would
A wounded bird once
Healed and about to be let go.

Have you stood here long
Watching the clouds collect
What always belonged to them?

CONVERSATION

The tree said to the sunlight:
How is it I do not grow tired?

The sun said to the evergreen:
You are what I turn into

When I want to touch the earth.

THE ALPHABET OF TREES

The first writings
Were branches.
The people heard them

Hum. Written down,
The wood spoke. It told the people
Everything. So on a cloud day

Like today I have returned to these books
Where I sit like a word among the pages.
Lost in them I search for my own meaning.

WILD MORNING GLORY

Sometimes I forget
How things grow wild
Until I have grown wild

And find myself low,
Astounded by a vine of flowers
The mountain has thought

About for a long time
And placed here. Beside
Me and the blossom, the fern is also

Planning something wonderful.

THE SECRET OF GREEN

The forest is the lesson
Of standing under things,
Of lying down amid the
Understory to understand them.
And go from there. From deep
We go to rising. From dark
We go to light. Leaves spread
To catch what they can of the sun
And hold onto it and let it go in dying
Into everything that grows and shines.

BEYOND THIS THERE IS ANOTHER

Full-blown blue counsels me.
Make it five shades bluer in the distance
And I am yours

Beyond any cloud cover.
I never thought the mountains
Could echo each other like this

Against the silence of the sky.
I was taught things grow small
In the distance but know now

How the past expands into glowing,
Being nearer the sun
That has faded

But still shines behind the dark.

WHAT KEEPS ME FROM LOOKING AWAY

All my life
Is the brilliance
All things hold for each other,

That lifts life out of life
And raises it to itself sweetly,
Though painfully. I like to watch

Spring happen through a single
Flower's eye and know that kind
Attention that calls beautiful wings

Toward it and lifts its face
To receive what needs to be taken.
For more of this,

I would sit still here
Like this forever and let
Life take me where I need to be

Without moving, only smiling.

It does not matter to me
That you are slower.

Or that you keep your words
Locked up inside the petals

I flagrantly display. It isn't
Your fault I am so fast to eat

The sun. I will wait fast, too,
And keep my roots to myself.

I know I should ready to close
The moment I know that you

Are right to take things slow.
We can so elegantly argue

Burgeon against suddenly
Emerging, how long we should

Hide our gold or shine it.

BLACK RIDGE

When I lose myself it's as though
I've lost a mountain to the clouds,
Been swallowed like a whistle

So I sing. The amplitude of
Disappearance is communal
Singing out of all lost things that joins me.

I dive deep as a cloud
Into the valley cleaning the leaves
Of trees. I forget the nearest things

Are darkest and always
Seem much steeper than they
Are and are more silent than the air.

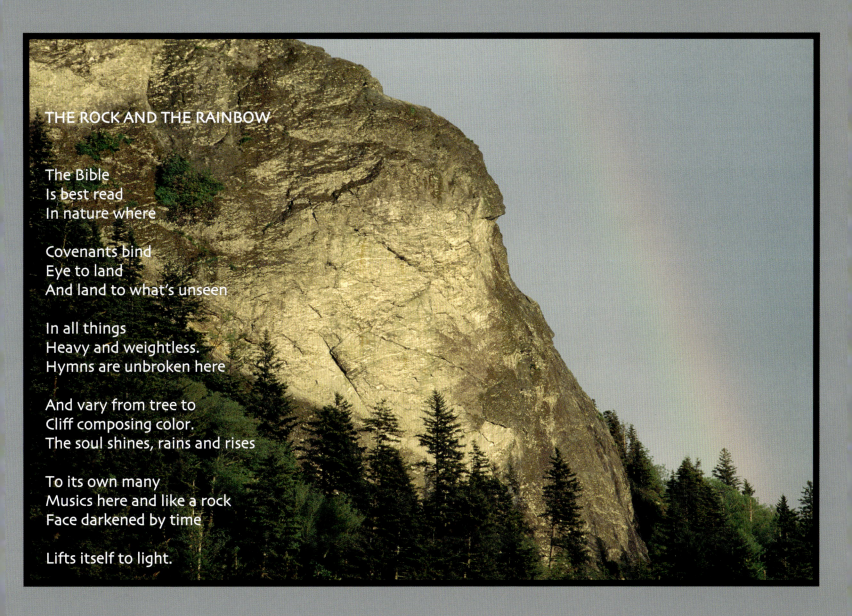

THE ROCK AND THE RAINBOW

The Bible
Is best read
In nature where

Covenants bind
Eye to land
And land to what's unseen

In all things
Heavy and weightless.
Hymns are unbroken here

And vary from tree to
Cliff composing color.
The soul shines, rains and rises

To its own many
Musics here and like a rock
Face darkened by time

Lifts itself to light.

COME HOME

Sometimes only
Cloud is the next step
And we allowing the open

To hold us
In terror move
Upon green grass higher.

Every step grows
The top of the mountain.
And sometimes the next step is

The hole through
The clouds beyond what
We know can hold us. And so we

Willingly
To outside ourselves
Go walking.

THE GHOST AND THE EVERGREEN

In the dead trees
I often see myself
Lingering on the edges of my life.

It is hard knowing
What we have yet to grow into.
I don't want to lose my green

But know the beauty also
Of what lies beyond so much having.
My boughs are heavy

With light sometimes
And I am not so tall as those
Who've gone before me.

From my low place
On the mountain I look up
To find what's waiting, broken open

So it can wholly hold
Onto nothing
But the sky.

OUT OF MANY

It is this. It has always been
This one brief dream of tree
That keeps me writhing

In my branches. It is this.
It has always been this one part of me
That holds everything together

With my light,
My beauty, my simple,
Everyday efforts at being.

It is this, my quiet
Offering to the whole that stills
Me when everything abounds binding

Me within it
Until I feel I disappear
At times and am no longer alone.

It is this.
It has always been this vastness
I'm a part of that speaks of me, my witness.

It is this.
It has always been this one
Brief dream of a tree that whispers me

Into the sky
Like a single seed
Just newly broken open

Inside of the most
Ancient soil giving its life
Always upward.

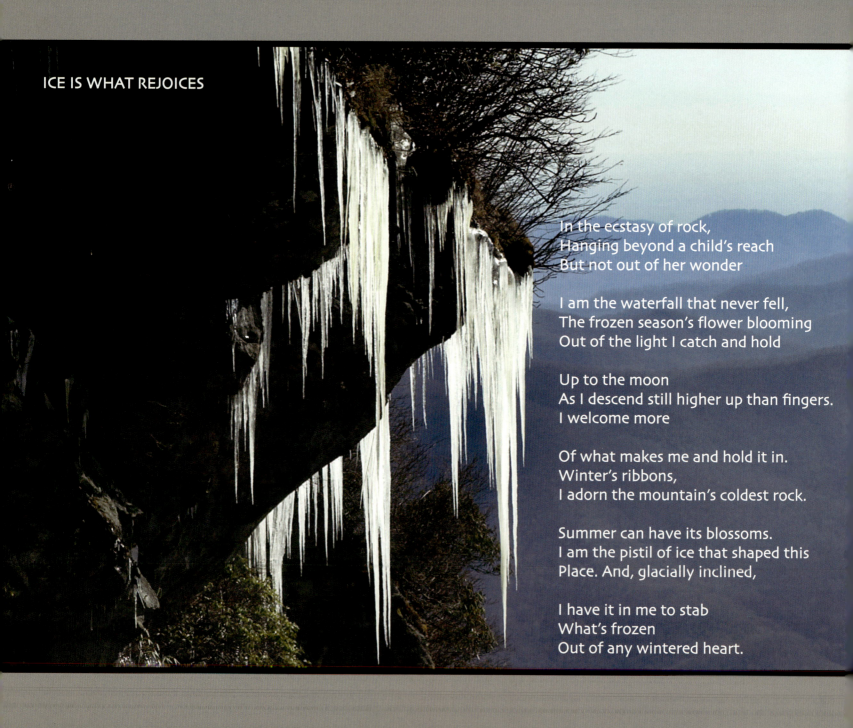

ICE IS WHAT REJOICES

In the ecstasy of rock,
Hanging beyond a child's reach
But not out of her wonder

I am the waterfall that never fell,
The frozen season's flower blooming
Out of the light I catch and hold

Up to the moon
As I descend still higher up than fingers.
I welcome more

Of what makes me and hold it in.
Winter's ribbons,
I adorn the mountain's coldest rock.

Summer can have its blossoms.
I am the pistil of ice that shaped this
Place. And, glacially inclined,

I have it in me to stab
What's frozen
Out of any wintered heart.

THE FOREST HEART

I have never
Been what I seemed to myself.
Always something hid me. It was shielding,

Effective as light.
If I ever emerged it was
To find what part of me was missing.

Then I went back into my hiding.

ABANDON

Who would abandon you
And hold you close at once,
Who watches over you

Pressed invisible into you
As you sleep dayward, like one

Who walking through heavy snow,
Unseen, is compressed by silence so
Deep it becomes aware it is the thing

That covers you so that
In only saying its name at last you
Disappear knows too much to let

You ever entirely go.

MOUNTAIN MUSIC

A dulcimer is curved
Like the places two
Mountains meet

In the distance and release
The sound we see
When looking with our hearts.

Let your music be my
Cloud, it says, and I will be
The rock that sings it.

Forever in my sleep,
Let me rise and fall
In breathing the way

The Smokies do extending
Farther past my sight, and music
Of this landscape shall then

Forever strum me.

LEAFLESS NOT LIFELESS

For what the wind
Has taught me, I give thanks
Each sunset as I lean West

Away from it
To get a better view. So I am
Gnarled and old, my body

Worn as—well, sometimes we are
The metaphor we are trying to make—
The truth is I have become myself.

What the winter knows
About me, I let it spread out
Against the sky in spelling clouds.

My name has become
Too heavy to bear so I am neither
And grow now shaped

By the story
All old things know
Never well enough to tell.

PANORAMA

At the core of the mountain
Grow these trees, stately, particular
In their angles. The earth is filled with them

And we grow from them,
Our own conifer lives, sharp, voluptuous.
The clouds grow there, too, and so we feel

The world trembling each time
We look out and find what's within,
Each time we open our eyes and find ourselves

Blinded by clarity.

WATERSHED

From here,
All that comes down
Will nourish you at the base.

Remember what
This promise was
When you are down there.

You will not see this tree.
It is well-hidden at a distance.
What you take from here is mapless.

Here, you lick the rain
From leaves to sustain yourself.
It is fresh. It is abundant.

To this place in yourself,
Return as many times as you can
Until you never have to leave.

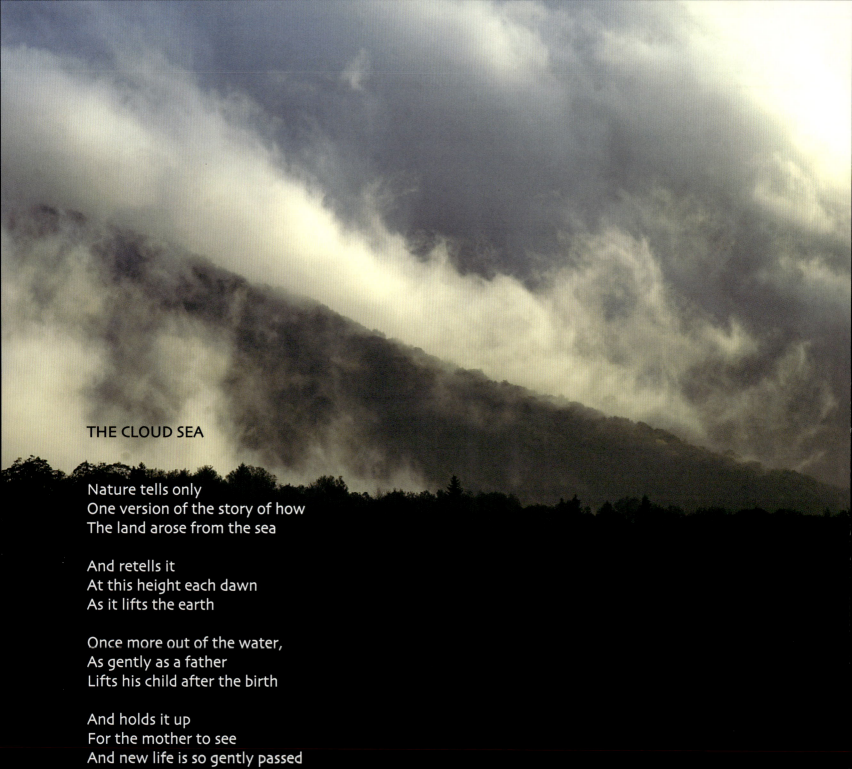

THE CLOUD SEA

Nature tells only
One version of the story of how
The land arose from the sea

And retells it
At this height each dawn
As it lifts the earth

Once more out of the water,
As gently as a father
Lifts his child after the birth

And holds it up
For the mother to see
And new life is so gently passed

Between them that the young cry
Rises like a mountain
The child will climb forever.

THE OLD ONES

Well, they called
Her mother nature
Because her breasts

Were many and held
So much life in them
The people imagined

They were nestled
There safely forever.
This is called civilization's

Infancy.
It is before we were broken.
In the morning each day

My daughter stretches
Her hand across my breast
And tells me I am warm and soft.

She draws closer
And because she is so small
I nestle into her like something

Much smaller.

POUR

Once I said to the mountains
Pour into me what you are so
I can know.

Once I said to the mountains
Let me lie here upon you so
I can not know.

In my grief, I have gone
To the mountains and poured
My sorrow into them.

I have stayed up there for hours.

Once I said to the mountains
All they do down
There is broken. Let me stay with you

Because you are whole.

Once I said to the mountains
I am broken, make me whole.
They have said press your body into me,

Let us pour our spirits
Into one another's so when you
Walk down there you will walk as tall as I.

SILVER LIGHT

I'd cut open the sky
For you, said a man to God,
So you could come behold all.

The clouds parted
And God indeed poured through,
And the man repeated

What he'd said, seeing
No change. In my heart
Sometimes I have waited

For the divine knife
To be lifted, for strange light
To shine. And the rocks and the water

Have lifted me
From so deep inside myself
I shout down sometimes and hear an echo.

THE SHADOWED LIGHT

I trade breaths
With the clouds.
This is how to breathe this high
And this beautifully.

Bright beam
Of my own skin,
The sighted world
Blinds me into the silence

Of natural exchange
'Til I am breathless and all I see
Breathes for me
And I go suddenly dark.

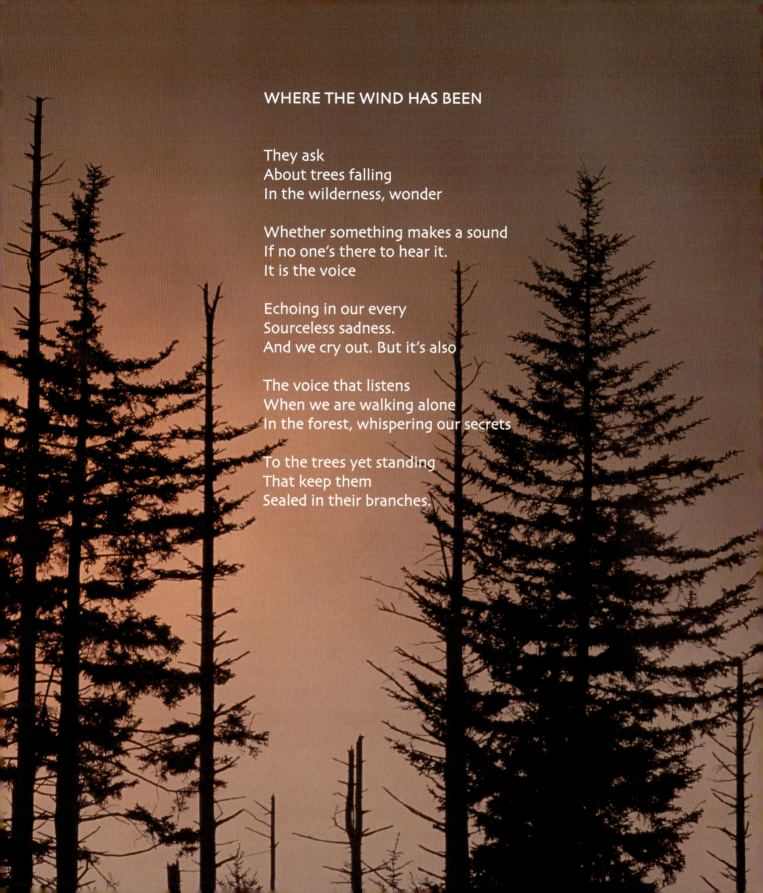

WHERE THE WIND HAS BEEN

They ask
About trees falling
In the wilderness, wonder

Whether something makes a sound
If no one's there to hear it.
It is the voice

Echoing in our every
Sourceless sadness.
And we cry out. But it's also

The voice that listens
When we are walking alone
In the forest, whispering our secrets

To the trees yet standing
That keep them
Sealed in their branches.

EVER

This is the silence
That does not break
And which I give to you

Who stands there
Gazing long enough to hear.

This is the silence
That follows you in your
Blood even after you have left this place

That you have loved enough
To listen to and see.

When you carry me away
I am a shadow cast by thunder,
I am a breaking light within the distance

That will hasten closed
Every time you think of me.

MOUNTAIN LESSONS

The trees too young
To speak hasten to listen
As the un-hearing listen, always

Missing something
Of the conversation as though
Some words were the clouds covering

Their meaning.

THE MIST HAS RENAMED EVERYTHING

At this elevation
Everything is utterance
Our clouds speak in shapes.

Dwellers of beauty,
We learn not to memorize.
We know the language is changing

And let it. When I
Returned to here the fourth time
I understood falling to one's knees

And digging hands
Into dirt that didn't resist.
I understood what it means to haunt.

We learn to wrap
The world around us
Like a cloak woven by strange hands.

This is the one
I choose to move in,
Fog-bound, disciplined

By the hard voice of tree.

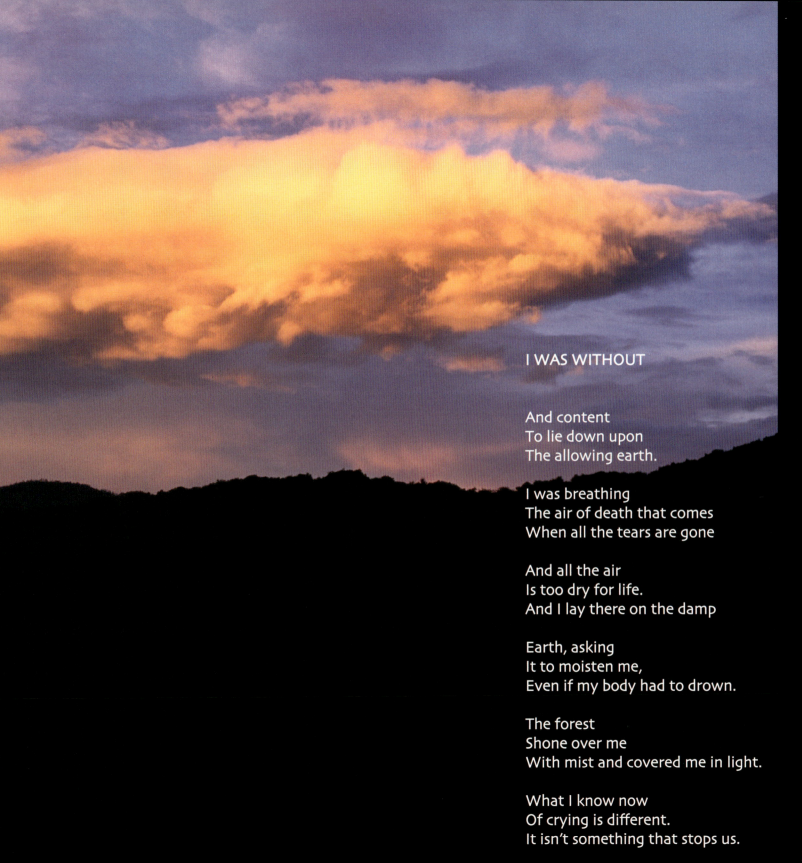

I WAS WITHOUT

And content
To lie down upon
The allowing earth.

I was breathing
The air of death that comes
When all the tears are gone

And all the air
Is too dry for life.
And I lay there on the damp

Earth, asking
It to moisten me,
Even if my body had to drown.

The forest
Shone over me
With mist and covered me in light.

What I know now
Of crying is different.
It isn't something that stops us.

WHISPER

Much is the song
The music plays behind itself.
Much is the light the darkness forms out

Of itself as
Thought follows thought
Follows another, receding, unfolding

Shadow into form
Into memory of form and sadness
Often follows form's return to shade.

But this is a glimpse
Unwieldy and strong. I am ever-
Green as a voice that love never allows

To fall silent.

TREE DICTIONARY

In the trees' own
Language let these
Words mean the danger

Of becoming. Let those
Words you can't say yet
Be spoken as bough and cone

So your voice will
Never die here, only call
Out like a voice with another voice

Behind it that rises
Mountain-like, billowing.
Define all speech as versions

Of mountainside in autumn.
Keep the boughs heavy and deep.
Tether every sound to the hues of changes.

THE CATALOGUE OF RUSHING WATER

There is the place
Where water turns to feather
And flies up.

There is the place
Where rock dips into itself
To let the water in.

There is the place
Where an old tree has fallen
And turns to stone.

There is the place
Where the Sanskrit word for peace
Spells itself in the descent.

There is the place
Where a face appears in the current
And it is always your own face.

There is the place
Where moss and fern drink deeply
Inviting you to drink.

There is the place
Where the only reason to leave it
Is so you can once return and don't.

There is the place
Where the thing you were looking for
Found you and washed you clean.

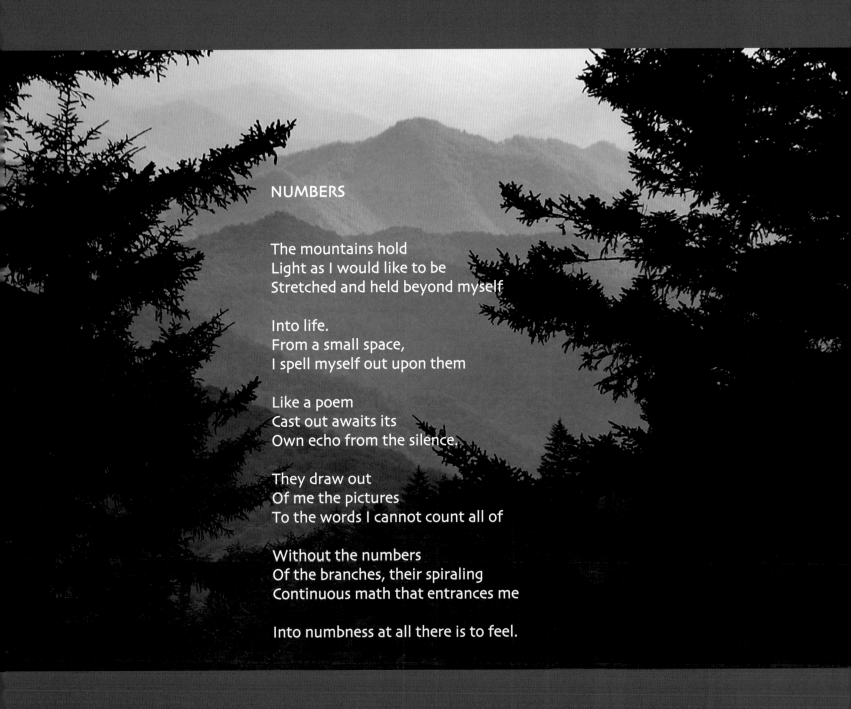

NUMBERS

The mountains hold
Light as I would like to be
Stretched and held beyond myself

Into life.
From a small space,
I spell myself out upon them

Like a poem
Cast out awaits its
Own echo from the silence.

They draw out
Of me the pictures
To the words I cannot count all of

Without the numbers
Of the branches, their spiraling
Continuous math that entrances me

Into numbness at all there is to feel.

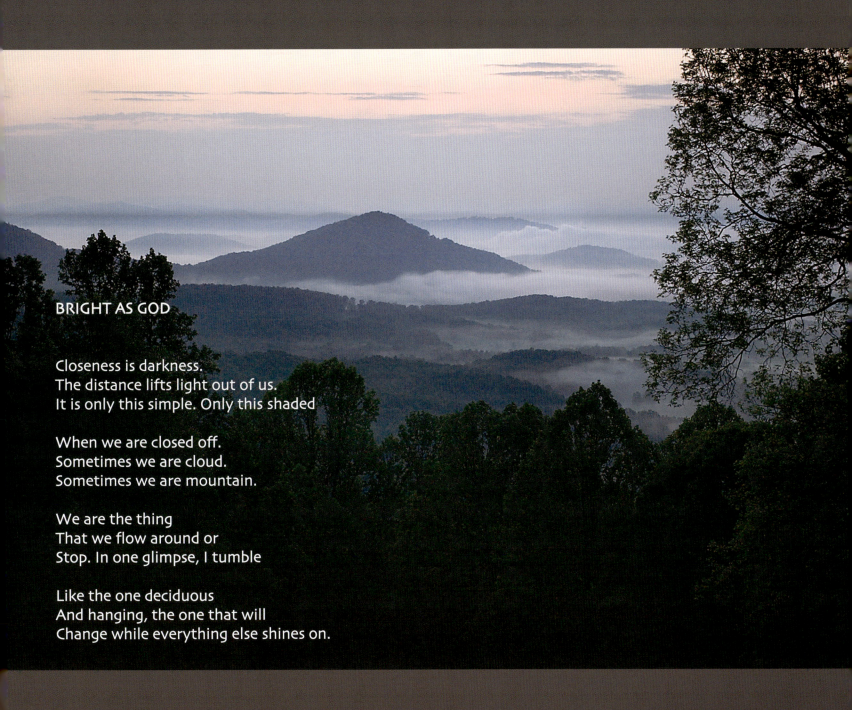

BRIGHT AS GOD

Closeness is darkness.
The distance lifts light out of us.
It is only this simple. Only this shaded

When we are closed off.
Sometimes we are cloud.
Sometimes we are mountain.

We are the thing
That we flow around or
Stop. In one glimpse, I tumble

Like the one deciduous
And hanging, the one that will
Change while everything else shines on.

THE SMOOTHEST OF PLACES

To get here,
Grow old. Lose the edges
Younger mountains have to hold

For fear the sky
Will drop them. Allow
Yourself to drop, to be worn down,

Trodden upon
By clouds' sorrowful feet.
Don't try to hold back the sky

You feel always
Descending. Where you end
It will begin, where you curve, it

Will bow like
A bent branch an archer
Holds, and you the string, your

Beauty in flight, will hum.

ALL THAT IS FAMILIAR GROWS MAGNIFICENT

Your shadows
Are my light. I believe
We have been placed here together—

Your outstretched arms
Over my purpling blooms,
To create from one scene a scenery.

Down low
In the mists you
Drip into me. I forget everything

About the sun.
I am happy to be overcast
By your grandness. Your immensity

Reaches into me,
Teaching me the glare
I hold within.

WHERE MY LIFE HAS BROUGHT ME

I have written entire
Books on how things can disappear,
And won many prizes for them, said the poet,

An expert on loss.
And how to follow a loss through,
He continued, to see how everything returns

In some other form,
That is the lesson only of patience.
We stood together on the mountain that day,

Under the clouds' approach.
I looked at his aging hands and held onto
One of them, wondering how I would recognize

It when he returns.

SIGHTREAD

Often I hear their own
Music included in my thoughts
And with my mind's violins or flutes, I've

Played each song,
Almost perfectly. Suggesting
Rise and fall, congestion of notes,

A THEORY OF WINTER

Some thoughts,
I don't climb out of
But stay withered inside.

They encase what
In me wants limb and life
To come beyond. Some thoughts

Are branches
Waiting to be blown
Off. Some are the wind.

THE COVERING TOUCH

At the clouds'
Covering touch
The mountains draw,

Like a sudden
Breath taken,
Back their trees.

Everything inside
Them loosens as from
Between every branch wind

Rises in response.

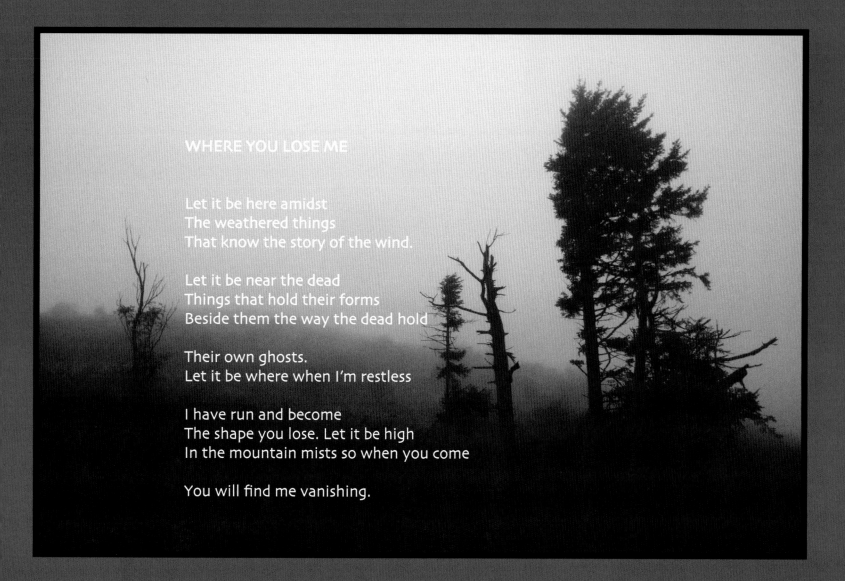

WHERE YOU LOSE ME

Let it be here amidst
The weathered things
That know the story of the wind.

Let it be near the dead
Things that hold their forms
Beside them the way the dead hold

Their own ghosts.
Let it be where when I'm restless

I have run and become
The shape you lose. Let it be high
In the mountain mists so when you come

You will find me vanishing.

SMOKE

The valley is a silent
Creature carried on its
Own back. Fold within fold,

It overlays itself
With light. Thickened
As smoke, the moments

Build upon it.
Fuming up into evening, it
Expands. Earth meets

Sky in the mending
When by night we condense
Back into liquid

And rest in the sudden lake.

DREAMING

I still think it lifts
Me high. Even my soils
Respond to it. I become the wind.

These thoughts
Of air still me when I sleep.
Awake, I breathe, I reminisce

Of things that never happen.

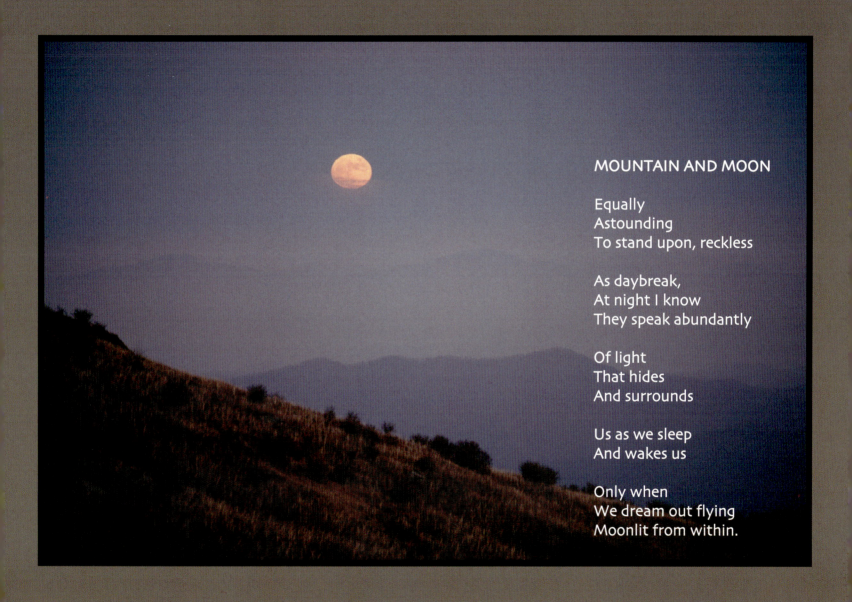

MOUNTAIN AND MOON

Equally
Astounding
To stand upon, reckless

As daybreak,
At night I know
They speak abundantly

Of light
That hides
And surrounds

Us as we sleep
And wakes us

Only when
We dream out flying
Moonlit from within.

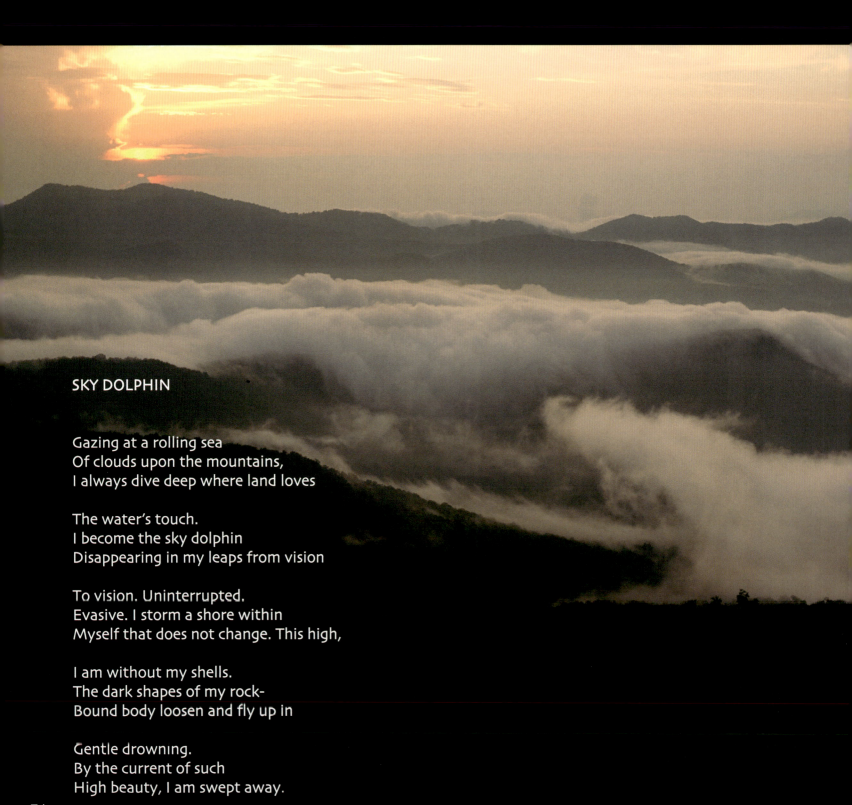

SKY DOLPHIN

Gazing at a rolling sea
Of clouds upon the mountains,
I always dive deep where land loves

The water's touch.
I become the sky dolphin
Disappearing in my leaps from vision

To vision. Uninterrupted.
Evasive. I storm a shore within
Myself that does not change. This high,

I am without my shells.
The dark shapes of my rock-
Bound body loosen and fly up in

Gentle drowning.
By the current of such
High beauty, I am swept away.

DUSK

What I learn to love
Is how I can let go forever,
Opening ever wider like the sky.

For this reason
The evening light is rose,
A bloom of cloud and mountain

Burgeoning from one stem.

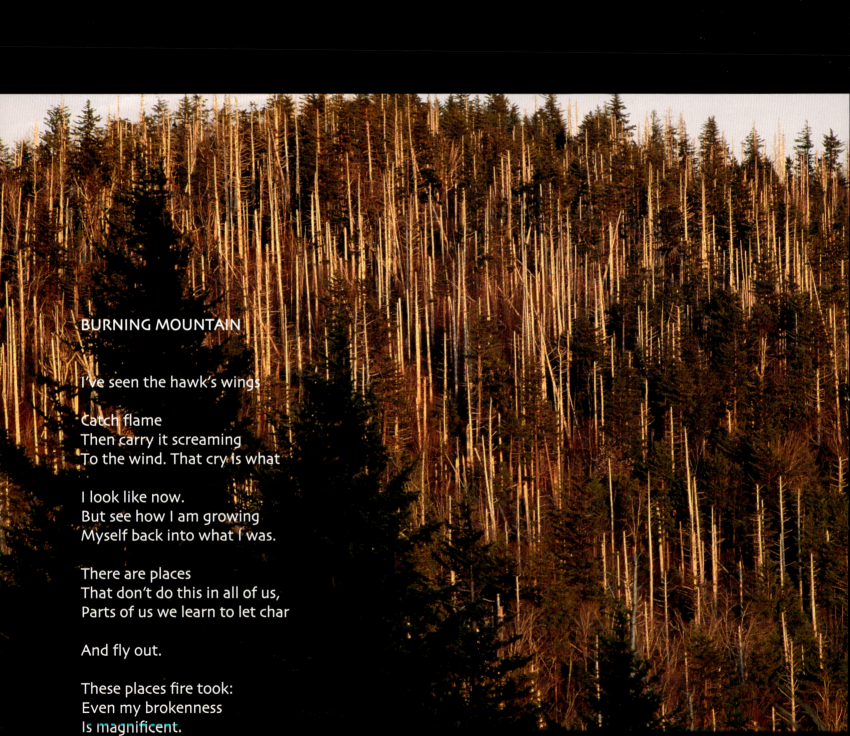

BURNING MOUNTAIN

I've seen the hawk's wings

Catch flame
Then carry it screaming
To the wind. That cry is what

I look like now.
But see how I am growing
Myself back into what I was.

There are places
That don't do this in all of us,
Parts of us we learn to let char

And fly out.

These places fire took:
Even my brokenness
Is magnificent.

WHERE WE LEARN TO FLY

We return to the mountains
For peace
And to remember

That some part of us
Soars above the sun.

We return to the mountains
For strength
To know that the edge of one peak

Flies our sight out
To the farthest one where beyond
All things there is a heaven

Within us
Teaching us our wings.

SKY PRAYER

The beauty stretches upon itself
And merges with a harrowing light.

Let bough and branch
Like children at play with words
Unfold their stories upon us as though

We were the sky
Learning unspoken colors. Open us,
O mountain, up whole enough to hold

You, to be strong enough
To engage you with our small
And speechless bodies. Teach us

How to call to you
When we don't know
What to say.

POSTLUDE

When I have
Surrendered the last
Thing, let go the life I thought

I once had, when tree-
Like I've returned to soil,
Given up my branches, my cones,

Returned what I'd
Understood of form,
Made moss, then I will

Know of my heart
What the moon below
A secret knows and you can be

Its keeper.

THEY WILL SPEAK

They will speak
Of impossible
Things to you,

Break your ears
With their voices
So only from within

Your deafness will you
Hear them. Only
The winter can teach you

That language it binds to
Your bones, the great
And smallest ones,

And restores you
To the parts you
Think of the least.

They are here as you
Feared, to undermine
You, leave you

Root uncut, snowbound.

COVENANT

When Noah saw his
He was like to fall overboard,
Remembering all those he left behind

So he could carry
Forward the stories of the animals.
The lesson was always to see more than

Just one color, one part
Of the story, even if it meant
Reminding the people they aren't

The only ones. Yet how they
Howled to learn God was favoring
The beasts for this one. It was a new world

Run by hoof and paw.
All the finned things carried them.
And Noah stepped ashore gratefully, a steward

On his own ship,
And lowered the gate for the beasts
Who clamored down and past him, leaving

Him awash in their dust.

GEOMETRY

Remind me, longing,
Of how God longs for us.
In my desire, show me God's desire

To be held.
Teach me, sky, to behold,
Without touching all things beyond

My hands, all things
My mind fails to encircle
But with faint light illumines

With awareness of their presence.

NOT EGYPT

These are not the tombs
Of Egypt. At day's end no pharaohs
Rise from spiced sleep to loosen prayers

From hieroglyph walls.
The sun emblazons none of their
Sleep and holds no fires for any

But the living. Still,
I'd give my life to know the power
Of the mountain and hold it to me like gold.

I'd embalm myself
In the oils of this my home-earth
And descend to where descending ends.

I'd wait a million
Years for my finding
And live by the darkness of the lamp

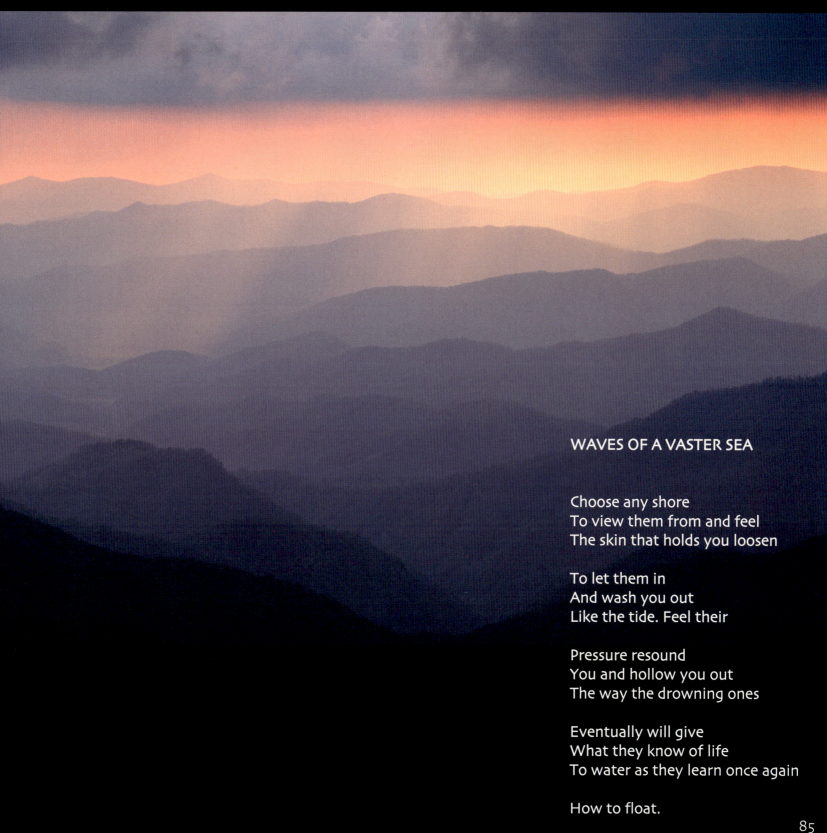

WAVES OF A VASTER SEA

Choose any shore
To view them from and feel
The skin that holds you loosen

To let them in
And wash you out
Like the tide. Feel their

Pressure resound
You and hollow you out
The way the drowning ones

Eventually will give
What they know of life
To water as they learn once again

How to float.

MANTRA

Water,
wash me.

Earth,
support me.

Fire,
change me.

Wind, carry me
through.

IT WILL REMAIN HERE AS OUR EVIDENCE

As sound decays
And the movements slow,
As the prolonged wind nestles

Within the path
Of the moving water,
All I have touched of this

Place reshapes
Me from within. All I taste
Of rain becomes my speech.

The roughness
Of the grasses draws
Once more my fingerprints

To include the faces in the rock.

THE LION

At the sea
I have found elephants
In the driftwood and marveled

How the sea remembers
Stories the land has told it,
And how the earth translates

Beast into soil and brush
To tell the stories of the savannah
Where a lion walks his golden path

And feels somehow
He is born higher and more
Free than all the rest of them he hunts,

More ancient even
than those he feels chasing
him in his many mountained sleep.

WHERE THE LIGHT GOT THROUGH

There was once
Too much to see so
We blinded ourselves.

It was a way out
Of explaining ourselves
Out of ourselves, of not having.

We devoted the
Following years to forgetting
All of it. It was like erasing footprints

First, and then our
Own feet which ached
With each step we took away

From ourselves
Regardless of how
Fast we tried to run and fell

So we could rest.

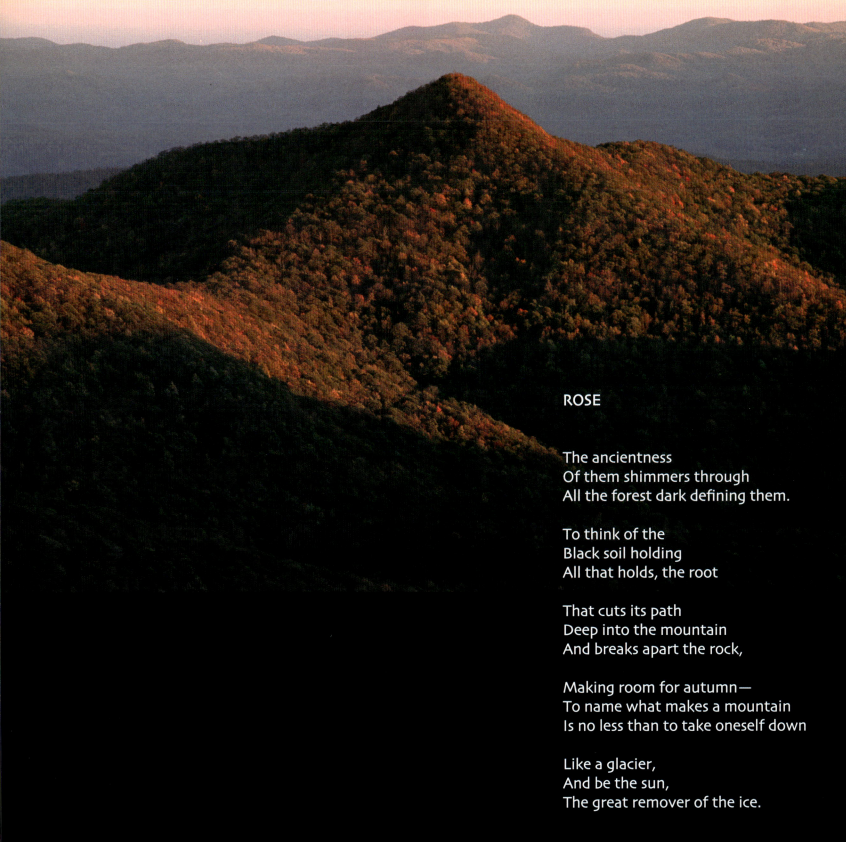

ROSE

The ancientness
Of them shimmers through
All the forest dark defining them.

To think of the
Black soil holding
All that holds, the root

That cuts its path
Deep into the mountain
And breaks apart the rock,

Making room for autumn—
To name what makes a mountain
Is no less than to take oneself down

Like a glacier,
And be the sun,
The great remover of the ice.

FAITH

I'm a believer
In the darkness first
That broke open upon nothing

And spread its
Story out for all light
To fill. I'm a knower of the immediate

Agony I've learned
Not to run from but to climb
Like something small out of something

Far and immense
I have to find. When others
Speak of light, I want to close my eyes

And remember
How what came first
Is still what must come first if I am to see.

PALING

How long you
Must sit before
Any of this will speak

To you. Sometimes
All night it takes just to
Hear a single word and the word

Is never loud,
Never intense or worth
The wait. It is only in the afterspeech

That the meaning
Comes, breaking forth gently
As moonlight sharing its secondary glow

Of sun with the whole earth.

THE ROUGHNESS OF LIFE
HOLDS US TO IT

The washing over
Of light smoothing
Each branch and rock ledge

Has led us here
To live amongst ourselves
As strangers. I feel the last trust

Break like a shadow.
It challenges me to stay
Subdued, patient as a sunset

With so much
Day ceaselessly ending
But I can say nothing about it.

The folds of peaks
And vanishings are the language
Of the sky I have had to borrow from

The smallest of words.

WASH

I'm not the smallest
Part of you. Not
The hiding leaf. I never intend

To remain here
Long. Travel stills me.
The current of life thrills too much.

Still, here, aware
Of all that's waiting,
I chose to stop a while

This close to all I want to have move me.

THE SKY AT PLAY

I once saw two
Crows in full romp
Between two mountain peaks.

The wind there was
So severe, the birds found
Paths of its absence and flew them.

I see it in
All things, the play of life,
The childhood in all things from

Which even children
At times of a fearful ecstasy
Will ask to take a little break.

AUTUMN

What greened now goldens,
Russets its way back
Into the earth. So

Glowing we go,
Our gloved hands woven
Finger by finger like a year.

Of seasons
Holding us together.
By now, the mountains

Have coldened
And yet they are aflame
With every changing color.

SUDDEN

The high ridge
Bridges earth to sky
And sends the trees on first

So we will know
On the other side where
We came from, all we had to love.

The young trees
Study the roots of their dead.
They interpret the lessons of ages

So the bridge will never fall.

FALLEN

I've fallen silent
Under the weight of snow.
It has absorbed all of my words.

The calls of birds are nothing.
Sound is suffocated now, at rest.
Boughs reach out to the sun in sign

Not even the clouds can speak.

CLOUD LEVEL

Unheld, I rise.
Being held, I illuminate.
My whisper is simple wind.

My heart
Is often a cloud
Fastened to the pine's branches

Wanting no more
To drift and dissipate, undoing
itself into rain. It lives to lift and begin.

In my flight,
The sun washes itself
Over the earth through me.

Up here,
I dream my way between
The sharpness of life and its

Inutterable, ungathered softnesses.

LIGHT

Erupt within
Or pour down upon
Me, mountain wisdom.

Speak through
Or let me listen deeply
Enough not to hear a word.

Reach me beyond
Touch, into heaven's earthly
Light which on this night is beaming

And I am watching
Gravity throw its definition
Up into the air where something else

Will catch it.

Poems of The Soul Tree

The Soul Tree poems came to me in a beautiful rush. A few days prior, I had met John when he photographed me for Asheville Wordfest Poetry Festival. On his website, I found his photographs of the Southern Appalachians and felt the impulse to write about them. To write each of these, I right-clicked on a photo on his website, pasted it into a word document and wrote the poem. It was as though the poems were already written, and I devoted the whole day to writing as many as I could, for fear I would lose their music if I stopped. After I had written thirty-six and exhausted the online collection, I contacted John for more.

These poems are musically driven, not rational at all in their invention. Behind me, as I wrote, were years of submersion in sacred texts—the *Baghavad-Gita*, *Tao-te-Ching*, *The Holy Bible*, *Qur'an* and more. From these, I found myself drawing on the idea of "prima materia" and seeing the sky, sun, moon, trees and clouds as eternal reflections of our experiences in life. As mirrors of our rawest emotional states they are instruments, when we write of them, of transformation. Ten years before writing these poems, I lived alone in a cabin on the Olympic Peninsula. During that year, I discovered a shape of a sentence which allowed me to write about the nature I saw in a more participatory, not merely descriptive, way, one that allows me to change while I write about the changes. This sentence shape worked as a sort of algorithm in drafting this collection. I have moved to Asheville four times, but I had only written one poem about the mountains before, back in 1991. At that time, I was living in Melbourne, Australia. A busker played a dulcimer; the sound stopped my heart. One line from that poem lives on in this collection. I have had a tumultuous relationship with the mountains, leaving at times because I did not feel at home here. These poems are my surrendering to them and their gift to me.

John and I thank Sundara Fawn for her hours spent with us designing the layout, and Micki Cabaniss Eutsler, Lindy Gibson and Stephanie DeLoach at Grateful Steps. I give my deep gratitude to my dear friends Megan Haas, Stephanie Winters, Audrey Sprenger and my poetry sister Glenis Redmond; the poets who have encouraged this collection Kathryn Stripling Byer, Richard Chess, Galway Kinnell, Keith Flynn, Li-Young Lee, Katherine Soniat, Fatemeh Keshavarz and Eleanor Wilner; and the men and women who take care of and protect the Blue Ridge Parkway and the surrounding Pisgah and Great Smokies National Forests. Ultimately these poems would not exist without my family's encouragement to dream a life of poetry—my everlasting love to Poppee, Nanny, Mom, Dick and Andaluna.

– Laura Hope-Gill

Laura Hope-Gill holds an MFA in Poetry from the Warren Wilson MFA Program and is the Director of Asheville WordFest Poetry Festival (AshevilleWordFest.org). She was named a 2008 NC Arts Fellow for her writings on going deaf. Through her company, The Healing Seed (TheHealingSeed.com), she helps people and groups use inner alchemy and creative writing to loosen rigid thinking at times of change.

Photographs of The Soul Tree

These photographs represent several projects that I collectively call Appalachian Light. They are my attempt at capturing the essence of light, weather, and atmosphere as they define the Blue Ridge and characterize the mountains of Southern Appalachia.

I also hope to share, through this collection of images, some of the remarkable experiences I have had while mingling with the elements in our Southern Highlands. Interactions between the elements are often dramatic and inspiring during stormy weather, dense fog and those amazing twilight hours. I thank God for these experiences, and for constantly reminding me that I am just a visitor.

Most of these images were created in the mid-1990s, as I discovered the joys of using slow speed transparency film (ISO 50) with a 35mm camera—an abrupt departure from my roots as a black-and-white photographer with a passion for creative printing techniques. While working with color, I liked to "push" or underexpose the film two stops (to ISO 200) to help enhance the contrast and graininess of the final image. This would also allow me to use fast shutter speeds so that I could hand-hold the camera, thus saving me from having to haul my tripod with me on the trail.

More often, however, I would shoot the film at ISO 50 while using small apertures and long exposures with my Nikon FM-2 anchored to a tripod . . . a more classical approach that values increased depth-of-field while taking advantage of this film's inherent fine grain. No effects filters were used during the creation of any of the images.

Also included in *The Soul Tree* are images that I have made recently using a 35mm digital camera. For those interested, these images are marked on the list of photographs on the following pages. Virtually no digital effects beyond the range of darkroom printing techniques were implemented during the creation of any of the images. The digital medium has changed much about the way we make images, even though the fundamentals of image-making remain quite the same. For more information about my technique and philosophy, please visit our website at www.TheSoulTree.org.

– John Fletcher, Jr.

John Fletcher, Jr. is a photojournalist and fine-art photographer based in Asheville, North Carolina. He maintains a national following of clients while working as a staff photographer for The *Asheville Citizen-Times* and as a wedding photojournalist throughout the Southeast. When not on assignment, John can often be found along the Blue Ridge Parkway or at his studio in Asheville's River Arts District. He maintains an online gallery on his website at www.FletchPix.com.

List of Photographs

iv	Mount Pisgah trailhead, Blue Ridge Parkway, NC*
viii	Billowing Fog, Red Spruce from the Blue Ridge Parkway, Transylvania County, NC*
1	Red Spruce Snag, Haywood County, NC
3	Mt. Mitchell and the Black Mountain Range from Grandfather Mountain, NC
5	Spruce/Fir Forest along the Blue Ridge Parkway, Transylvania County, NC*
6	Cold Mountain, Haywood County, NC
7	Fog and Trees at Craggy Gardens, Blue Ridge Parkway, NC
8	Sunset from the Blue Ridge Parkway, Jackson County, NC
10	Rime Ice, Mountain Ash at Craggy Gardens, Blue Ridge Parkway **
11	Fraser Fir, Transylvania County, NC
12	Valley in springtime near Asheville, NC
13	Dawn from Black Balsam Knob, NC
14	Red Spruce, Sun, Blue Ridge Parkway, near Mt. Pisgah, NC* **
15	Nature Trail at Mt. Mitchell State Park, NC* **
16	Morning Glory near Asheville, NC* **
17	Umbrella Magnolia at Looking Glass Rock, NC
18	Dawn, Little Pisgah Mountain, Henderson County, NC
20	Wildflowers along the Blue Ridge Parkway Near Asheville, NC
21	Lotus at Jarvis Gardens, Madison County, NC* **
22	Dawn from Black Balsam Knob, NC
23	Rainbow, Sun Reflection at Devil's Courthouse, Blue Ridge Parkway.
24	Clouds at Max Patch, Madison County, NC*
26	Fog, Mt. Mitchell State Park, NC* **
29	Fraser Fir along the Blue Ridge Parkway, Transylvania County, NC **
30	Icicles at Craggy Gardens, Blue Ridge Parkway, NC* **
31	Fog and Trees near Asheville, NC* **
33	Winter at Roan Mountain along the Appalachian Trail, NC/TN*
34	Dawn, Blue Ridge Parkway, Transylvania County, NC*
35	Tree at Mt. Pisgah, NC*
36	Sunset, Great Smoky Mountains National Park*
37	North Fork Reservoir/Asheville Watershed, Buncombe County, NC
38	Rising Fog near Mt. Pisgah, NC*
39	Dawn, Blue Ridge Parkway near Asheville, NC*
40	Fontana Lake, NC
42	Clearing Storm at Graveyard Fields along the Blue Ridge Parkway, NC*
43	Sunrise near Mt. Pisgah, NC
44	Sunset, Spruce/Fir Forest, Jackson County, NC
46	Black Balsam Knob and Tennet Mountain, NC*
48	Dusk along the Cherohala Skyway, near Robbinsville, NC*
50	Fog, Shining Rock Wilderness, NC
52	Clearing Storm and the Black Mountain Range, NC
54	Dusk, Jackson County, NC
55	Fog and Trees along the Blue Ridge Parkway, NC

57	Roaring Fork Falls, Yancey County, NC
58	Blue Ridge Parkway Vista, Jackson County, NC*
59	Dawn, Ball Mountain, Buncombe County, NC*
61	Spring at Sunset, Blue Ridge Parkway, Jackson County, NC
63	Mountain Laurel near summit of Mt. Pisgah, NC*
64	Clearing Storm, Sunset, Black Balsam Knob, NC*
66	Spring, Spruce/Fir Forest, Jackson County, NC
67	Trees near Craggy Gardens along the Blue Ridge Parkway, NC
68	Clearing Storm, Sunset, and the Black Mountain Range, NC
69	Fog, Black Balsam Knob, NC
71	Lake Logan and the Canton valley, Haywood County, NC
72	Clearing Storm, Jackson County, NC
73	Moonrise, Shining Rock Wilderness Area, NC
74	Sunset from the Blue Ridge Parkway near Asheville, NC
75	Sunset from the Blue Ridge Parkway near Asheville, NC
76	Spruce/Fir Forest, Jackson County, NC
77	Sunrise from Black Balsam Knob, NC*
78	Clearing Storm, Red Spruce, Transylvania County, NC*
79	Fog, Sun, Fraser Fir, Transylvania County, NC*
80	Snowfall at Lake Logan, Haywood County, NC*
82	Rainbow near Mt. Pisgah, NC
83	Rainbow over the Shining Rock Wilderness Area, NC
84	Sunrise, Fog, Ball Mountain, Buncombe County, NC
85	Sunset from Waterrock Knob, Blue Ridge Parkway, NC
87	Clearing Storm, Jackson County, NC*
88	Art Loeb Trail, Shining Rock Wilderness Area, NC
89	Art Loeb Trail, Shining Rock Wilderness Area, NC
90	Clearing Storm near Mt. Mitchell, NC
91	Pilot Mountain, Transylvania County, NC
92	Sunset from Richland Balsam, Blue Ridge Parkway, NC
93	Moonrise from Graveyard Fields, Blue Ridge Parkway, NC
94	Clearing Storm at Craggy Gardens, Blue Ridge Parkway, NC
96	Rock, Water, and Leaf along the Blue Ridge Parkway, NC
97	Dawn, Looking Glass Rock, Transylvania County, NC
98	Fall, Graveyard Fields, Blue Ridge Parkway, NC*
99	Fraser Fir Forest on summit of Mt. Mitchell, NC
100	Winter at Roan Mountain, NC*
102	Rising Fog, Jackson County, NC
103	Clearing Storm, Jackson County, NC
108	Clearing Storm, Mount Pisgah, Blue Ridge Parkway, NC

*Images made using a 35mm digital camera.
** A special thanks to the Asheville Citizen-Times for allowing the reproduction of these images.